Iceland

WORLD BIBLIOGRAPHICAL SERIES

General Editors:
Robert L. Collison (Editor-in-chief)
Sheila R. Herstein
Louis J. Reith
Hans H. Wellisch

VOLUMES IN THE SERIES

1 *Yugoslavia*, John J. Horton
2 *Lebanon*, Shereen Khairallah
3 *Lesotho*, Shelagh M. Willet and David Ambrose
4 *Rhodesia/Zimbabwe*, Oliver B. Pollack and Karen Pollack
5 *Saudi Arabia*, Frank A. Clements
6 *USSR*, Anthony Thompson
7 *South Africa*, Reuben Musiker
8 *Malawi*, Robert B. Boeder
9 *Guatemala*, Woodman B. Franklin
11 *Uganda*, Robert L. Collison
12 *Malaysia*, Lim Huck Tee and Wong Sook Jean
13 *France*, Frances Chambers
14 *Panama*, Eleanor DeSelms Langstaff
15 *Hungary*, Thomas Kabdebo
16 *USA*, Sheila R. Herstein and Naomi Robbins
17 *Greece*, Richard Clogg and Mary Jo Clogg
18 *New Zealand*, R. F. Grover
19 *Algeria*, Richard I. Lawless
21 *Belize*, Ralph Lee Woodward, Jr.
23 *Luxembourg*, Carlo Hury and Jul Christophory
24 *Swaziland*, Balam Nyeko
25 *Kenya*, Robert L. Collison
26 *India*, Brijen Gupta and Datta Kharbas
27 *Turkey*, Meral Güçlü
28 *Cyprus*, P. M. Kitromilides and M. L. Evriviades
29 *Oman*, Frank A. Clements
30 *Italy*, Emiliana P. Noether
31 *Finland*, J. E. O. Screen
32 *Poland*, Richard C. Lewanski
33 *Tunisia*, Allan M. Findlay, Anne M. Findlay and Richard I. Lawless
34 *Scotland*, Eric G. Grant
35 *China*, Peter Cheng
36 *Qatar*, P. T. H. Unwin
37 *Iceland*, John J. Horton
38 *Nepal*, Dina Nath Wadhwa
39 *Haiti*, Frances Chambers
40 *Sudan*, M. W. Daly
41 *Vatican City State*, Michael J. Walsh
42 *Iraq*, Abdul Jabbar Abdulrahman
43 *United Arab Emirates*, Frank A. Clements
44 *Nicaragua*, Ralph Lee Woodward, Jr.

VOLUME 37

Iceland

John J. Horton
Compiler

CLIO PRESS
OXFORD, ENGLAND · SANTA BARBARA, CALIFORNIA

© Copyright 1983 by Clio Press Ltd.

All rights reserved. No part of this publication may be reproduced, stored in any retrieval system, or transmitted in any form or by any means, electronic, mechanical, photocopying or otherwise, without the prior permission in writing of the publishers.

British Library Cataloguing in Publication Data
Horton, John J.
Iceland. – (World bibliographical series; 37)
1. Iceland – Bibliography
I. Title II. Series
016.9491'2 Z2590.A3

ISBN 0-903450-78-X

Clio Press Ltd.,
55 St. Thomas' Street,
Oxford OX1 1JG, England.
Providing the services of the European
Bibliographical Centre and the American
Bibliographical Center

American Bibliographical Center-Clio Press,
Riviera Campus, 2040 Alameda Padre Serra,
Santa Barbara, Ca. 93103, U.S.A.

Designed by Bernard Crossland
Computer typeset by Peter Peregrinus Ltd.
Printed in Great Britain
by the Camelot Press, Southampton

THE WORLD BIBLIOGRAPHICAL SERIES

This series will eventually cover every country in the world, each in a separate volume comprising annotated entries on works dealing with its history, geography, economy and politics; and with its people, their culture, customs, religion and social organization. Attention will also be paid to current living conditions — housing, education, newspapers, clothing, etc. — that are all too often ignored in standard bibliographies; and to those particular aspects relevant to individual countries. Each volume seeks to achieve, by use of careful selectivity and critical assessment of the literature, an expression of the country and an appreciation of its nature and national aspirations, to guide the reader towards an understanding of its importance. The keynote of the series is to provide, in a uniform format, an interpretation of each country that will express its culture, its place in the world, and the qualities and background that make it unique.

SERIES EDITORS

Robert L. Collison (Editor-in-chief) is Professor Emeritus, Library and Information Studies, University of California, Los Angeles, and is currently the President of the Society of Indexers. Following the war, he served as Reference Librarian for the City of Westminster and later became Librarian to the BBC. During his fifty years as a professional librarian in England and the USA, he has written more than twenty works on bibliography, librarianship, indexing and related subjects.

Sheila R. Herstein is Reference Librarian and Library Instruction Coordinator at the City College of the City University of New York. She has extensive bibliographic experience and recently described her innovations in the field of bibliographic instruction in 'Team teaching and bibliographic instruction', *The Bookmark*, Autumn 1979. In addition, Doctor Herstein co-authored a basic annotated bibliography in history for Funk & Wagnalls *New encyclopedia*, and for several years reviewed books for *Library Journal*.

Louis J. Reith is librarian with the Franciscan Institute, St. Bonaventure University, New York. He received his PhD from Stanford University, California, and later studied at Eberhard-Karls-Universität, Tübingen. In addition to his activities as a librarian, Dr. Reith is a specialist on 16th century German history and the Reformation and has published many articles and papers in both German and English. He was also editor of the *American Society for Reformation Research Newsletter*.

Hans H. Wellisch is Associate Professor at the College of Library and Information Services, University of Maryland, and a member of the American Society of Indexers and the International Federation for Documentation. He is the author of numerous articles and several books on indexing and abstracting, and has most recently published *Indexing and abstracting: an international bibliography*. He also contributes frequently to *Journal of the American Society for Information Science, Library Quarterly*, and *The Indexer*.

For my daughter
FREYA
(*Jónsdóttir!*)

Contents

INTRODUCTION xiii

THE COUNTRY AND ITS PEOPLE 1
    Shorter accounts 1   Photographic presentations 10
    Longer accounts 5   Local accounts 12
    Handbooks 9   Icelanders abroad 14

EXPLORATION AND TRAVEL 15
    Early discoveries 15   20th century 30
    18th-19th centuries 17   Ocean-faring accounts 34

TRAVEL GUIDES 36

MAPS 40
    Modern 40   Cartographic history 43

REGIONAL GEOGRAPHY 44
    General 44   Fieldtrips 47

PHYSICAL GEOGRAPHY, GEOLOGY, CLIMATOLOGY 50
    Evolutionary structure 50   Geothermal and volcanic areas 53
    Descriptive geology 51   Glaciology and climatology 59

NATURAL HISTORY, ECOLOGY, FLORA AND FAUNA 63
    General and ecological 63   Ornithology 69
    Botany 66   Land animals 73
    Zoology 67

PHYSICAL ANTHROPOLOGY 75

ARCHAEOLOGY 78

GENEALOGY AND HERALDRY 83

Contents

HISTORY 85
   Scandinavian and   16th-19th centuries 95
     Viking 85   20th century 100
   Icelandic history,
     general 88
   Settlement and
     Commonwealth 89

RELIGION 105
   Pre-Christian 105   Christianity and church
                                history 108

CUSTOMS, FOLKLORE AND BELIEFS 112

FAMILY LIFE AND ORGANIZATION 115
   General 115   Women and children 117

POPULATION AND SOCIAL CHANGE 119
   Demography 119   Social change 121

HEALTH 124

EDUCATION AND RESEARCH 129

STATISTICS 133

CONSTITUTION, PARLIAMENT AND THE LAW 135
   The old laws 135   Parliament 137
   Constitutionalism 136   Modern justice 138

POLITICS 140
   General 140   Prime ministers and
                               presidents 143

FOREIGN POLICY 145
   Co-operation and   Territorial waters and
     security 145   fishing disputes 148

ECONOMICS 152
   General 152   Economic monitors 155

CO-OPERATIVE MOVEMENT 158

AGRICULTURE 159

Contents

FISHERIES 164
    General reviews   164   Local communities   167
    Stocks, the fleet and   Whaling   168
      processing   165
    Safety   167

NATURAL RESOURCES AND ENERGY 169
    Historical surveys   169   Modern applications   170

FOREIGN TRADE AND TOURISM 173

TRANSPORT AND POSTS 176
    Transport   176   Stamps   178
    Posts   177   Coins   179

ENVIRONMENT 180
    General   180   Nature protection   182
    Housing and planning   181

SPORT AND RECREATION 184

LANGUAGE 188
    Norse and Old   Modern Icelandic   195
      Icelandic   188
    Dictionaries (Old and
      modern Icelandic)   191

LITERATURE, OLD ICELANDIC 202
    Texts and translations   202   History and criticism   221

LITERATURE, MODERN ICELANDIC 242
    Historical aspects   242   The novel   254
    Poetry   244   Short stories   262
    Drama   251

FOREIGN LITERATURE ON ICELANDIC THEMES   265
    Medieval settings   265   Modern settings   267

CHILDREN'S PRESENTATIONS 270
    Ancient themes   270   Modern themes   272

FINE ART 274

MUSIC 280

Contents

THEATRE AND CINEMA 282

TELEVISION 284

PERIODICALS 286
    Newspapers and   Specialist periodicals   290
    Magazines   286

DIRECTORIES 294

MUSEUM AND LIBRARY SERVICES 296

CATALOGUES AND BIBLIOGRAPHIES 298

INDEX OF AUTHORS, TITLES AND SUBJECTS 303

MAP OF ICELAND 348

Introduction

This bibliography is the first analytical guide to English-language materials on Iceland. It contains around 1500 items, made up of 960 main entries and half as many subsidiary items. It is a systematic attempt to provide a rounded survey of the sources available to the English-speaking reader with general or specific interests in Iceland, its culture and society from the time of the original settlement to the present day.

Foreign misconceptions about Iceland abound. The general hazy picture is of a barren and icy landscape, an ancient form of literature known as the 'saga', and a recent involvement in 'cod wars'.

Indeed, it is to these three categories that foreign study and comment has likewise been mainly directed, in the form of investigations into the country's natural phenomena, criticism of the literature of the Eddas and sagas, and reports on the disputes concerning fishing limits. Much of this work has been of great value, but too often, these facets of Iceland and its people have been studied in isolation: the geographical field-worker has only occasionally paused to consider how this elemental landscape has bred and moulded the character and activity of those who live upon it; the literary student rarely follows through from the old to the modern period of Icelandic literature; and those who have had their attention drawn towards Iceland for the first time by the international implications of its fisheries or security policy have reacted or reported with a frustratingly frequent lack of awareness of those traditions, cultural, social, political and economic, which so clearly help towards explaining Icelandic attitudes. It is difficult to think of another country in the world where geography, culture and contemporary affairs are so closely interrelated, and where the key to an understanding of the country requires a triple engagement of the old, the new and the constant.

That Iceland should exist at all as a modern independent nation state is remarkable in itself. Inhospitably located on the north-western outpost of Europe, it has sustained for over 1100 years an alternately

Introduction

resolute and vibrant society against all the odds. Today it exhibits in microcosm most of the features of a developed European country, except for its own army and a railway network (neither of which does it need), and yet the development of its elemental resources is still to be fully exploited — to categorize Iceland as either developed or underdeveloped is more than usually meaningless. Internationally it has created an impact out of all proportion to its size, its total population of around 235,000 (December 1982) being no more than that of an average English city, on a landmass roughly equivalent in area to that of Ireland; on several fronts its conduct and achievement have been a model for small-state diplomacy.

It is not the primary aim of this introduction to present a potted history of Iceland; nevertheless, it may be helpful to identify for the newcomer some of the main points of Icelandic history to put into perspective the character of the Icelandic nation today.

The permanent settlement of Iceland began in 874, although there is clear evidence of a Celtic presence pre-dating the Viking settlement by perhaps three quarters of a century; these Christian Celts appear to have left when faced with the arrival of the heathen Norsemen, but further Celts came to Iceland along with the Norse settlers, evidence of which can be confirmed by observations of aspects of the physical anthropology and national character of today's Icelanders when compared with continental Scandinavians. The settlement of Iceland was a process which took nearly sixty years; both the exact provenance and the total number of the settlers are matters of some debate, but a figure of over 25,000 with a significant proportion from Norway could be reasonably suggested from approximately contemporary evidence. There are two features of significance for the subsequent development of the Icelanders which stem from the nature of this original settlement. The first is that, although the settlement took place at a time when Viking expansion was at its height, it was events in Norway and the class of people affected which gave the settlement its initial impetus and particular character: for, those who took the option of emigrating from Norway rather than enduring subjugation by King Harald Finehair were themselves of aristocratic status — this was an exodus not of refugees belonging to a politically downtrodden class, but of noblemen with their retinues and followers, fired by a fierce spirit of independence rather than resigned to an inevitable exile; a significant degree of sophistication, both political and artistic, was therefore inherent from the start of the Icelandic settlement. The second important factor concerning the nature of the settlement of Iceland is that the land contained no indigenous population; there was, therefore, none of the problems,

Introduction

then or since, associated with relationships between colonists and colonized. These two factors have been underestimated in their relevance to the remarkable degree of cultural awareness and social cohesion which characterizes contemporary Iceland.

By the year 930 the Old Icelandic Commonwealth became fully established with the foundation of the Alþing, or national parliament. Iceland was the last country in Europe to be settled, but the first to adopt a representative parliamentary system. Although it acted more as a safety valve than as a political regulator, the system was a fundamental element in both the rise of the Commonwealth and its eventual fall. Uniquely, it managed to solve by political means a religious question of the greatest magnitude – that of the adoption of Christianity in the year 1000. (Shortly before this, the Viking spirit of adventure had been rekindled and between 982 and 1000 resulted in an Icelandic colonization of Greenland and the discovery of the North American continent).

It was the conversion to Christianity which laid the foundations for the greatest achievement of the Commonwealth period. The 11th century was a time of relative peace and stability, in which the Icelandic bishops exerted great influence upon the intellectual development of the new nation: religious writings from abroad were translated, and the seeds of an Icelandic vernacular literature were thus sown, which were to produce the remarkable flowering of Icelandic writing in the 12th and 13th centuries – an isolated beacon of cultural achievement at a time of comparative darkness in continental Europe – in forms such as the vernacular history by the meticulous Ari, the literary genius and historical acumen of Snorri, and the splendid 'sagas of Icelanders'; these sagas, although they cannot be said to have affected the European literary tradition (hardly surprising in view of their isolation), themselves owed, conversely, virtually nothing to external influences, which serves only to emphasize their unique character. Their own influence upon many Icelandic writers of the modern period, however, has been both subtle and profound. Poetry, too, flourished during the early centuries, in two major forms: the mythical-heroic poems of the Edda owe more to the continental tradition, but their themes are magnificently enhanced by the poets; and whereas the personal and commemorative expression of the skaldic poets can never reach a foreign audience as directly as can the sagas because of their intensely intricate structure and word-play, it is these very qualities which imply much about the intellectual facility of this class of people and their audience.

In several ways the Old Icelandic Commonwealth contained the seeds of its own destruction. The Age of the Sturlungs (1230-64),

Introduction

named after the most powerful of the Icelandic families at that time, saw the Commonwealth complete a fateful transition from a form of democracy to an outright oligarchy, which in turn bred civil strife as the local chieftains sought to extend their power and influence beyond their own localities, and to flout violently the traditional relationships between themselves and their farming freeholders. Assistance was sought and readily forthcoming from Norway, whose king had already won support from the Church in Iceland. The Golden Age of Iceland and its Commonwealth ended in 1262-64, when Iceland was brought under the Norwegian crown.

In the following century, during which the authority of the Norwegian manipulated Church increased, Iceland was violently struck by a series of volcanic disasters followed by famine and disease, and the outbreak of the Black Death in Norway resulted in a decimation of Icelandic trade. In 1380 Iceland along with Norway came under Danish rule (formalized by the Kalmar Union, including Sweden, in 1397) where it was to remain over the next 500 years, for the most part of which the Icelandic people battled almost unconsciously against overwhelming odds imposed by natural disasters and foreign oppression. The effect of the Black Death, which reached Iceland in the first years of the 15th century and obliterated a third of the population, was longlasting, and an already shattered economy was subjected to trading wrangles between Denmark, England and the German Hanse.

The 16th century was dominated by the politics of religion. The Lutheran cause at first infiltrated and later overtly imposed itself on Iceland amidst increasing bitterness and eventual violence, culminating in the murder of the last Catholic bishop of Iceland in 1550. The Reformation thus began, and with it a period of the two darkest centuries in Icelandic history, during which the country was subjected to further climatic deterioration, volcanic activity and epidemic outbreaks, to foreign piracy, and to total domination by Denmark on two fronts: economic, through the imposition of a foreign trade monopoly in 1602, and political, through the declaration of absolute monarchy over Iceland by Frederick III in 1662. Yet, in spite of all this, the 16th and 17th centuries in Iceland were notable for a spiritual, intellectual and literary creativity which seemed to grow out of adversity and unrelieved poverty; the influence of the religious poet Hallgrímur Petursson (1614-74) is profoundly felt to this day.

During the 18th century there was some improvement on the economic front, chiefly as a result of the efforts of Skúli Magnússon, the first Icelander to hold the office of tax collector, who chipped away at the practices of the Danish Trading Company to such effect that in

Introduction

1787 the Danish trade monopoly was removed. But once again natural and political factors intervened to retard any more broadly based progress: a massive eruption of the Laki volcano in 1783-84 devastated most of the country with its notorious 'mist'; shortly afterwards the continuity of the country's religious and political institutions was severed by a reorganization of the bishoprics and by the abolition of the Alþing.

It was not until the 19th century that Iceland, for the first time, became significantly affected by events on the European continent. The economic disintegration of Denmark as a result of the Napoleonic wars was inevitably reflected in Iceland. (The bizarre case of Jorgen Jorgensen's revolution in 1809, q.v., was perhaps no more than an episode in Icelandic history, but it did serve to underline Iceland's vulnerability). However, it was the rise of European movements which was most deeply to affect the development of the Icelandic nation in the 19th century. Iceland had been only superficially affected by the earlier ideas of the Enlightenment; but the romantic and nationalist movements were to dominate the course of Icelandic history, the former reawakening the passion of the Icelanders for their literary heritage, the latter firing the thrust towards a national autonomy. A parallel movement for the preservation and purification of the Icelandic language added another strand to the patriotic and nationalist cause. The literary renaissance was personified by a number of Icelandic writers of the 19th century, but the political advances were due chiefly to the efforts of one man, Iceland's national hero Jón Sigurðsson. Three major advances were achieved during the middle of the 19th century: in 1843 the Alþing was reconstituted; in 1854 trade restrictions with the rest of the world were lifted; and in 1874 (the millennium of the original settlement) a constitution was granted which bestowed legislative, though not executive, powers upon the Alþing, and gave Iceland control over her own finances.

Although these developments represented a major and, in retrospect, uncheckable advance towards long-term independence, a general dissatisfaction with the slow pace of political change and economic progress, coupled with continuing climatic problems, led to large-scale emigration of Icelanders to the North American continent during the last thirty years of the century.

But the momentum towards independence was being maintained: the birth of the co-operative movement in 1882, the establishment of the National Bank in 1885, the inauguration of the University of Iceland in 1911, and the gaining of female suffrage in 1915, were all factors which helped to underpin the advance of Iceland towards home rule

Introduction

(granted in 1904) and to the penultimate stage whereby, amist the hastening repercussions of the Great War, Iceland became in 1918, by public referendum and by the mutual agreement of both countries, an independent sovereign state in personal union with Denmark, by which Iceland was to share the Danish king, and entrust to Denmark only matters of national security and foreign relations. This Act of Union was to be reviewed at the end of 1940, at which time either party could seek a revision; if no agreement were possible within a further three years, either country could unilaterally abrogate the union.

With a new Constitution and a Supreme Court, Iceland duly sailed forth under her own steam into the bright waters of the 1920s, before encountering the darker seas of the Great Depression in the 1930s. In between, Iceland played out to the full the millennial celebrations of her national parliament, a festive yet purposeful re-affirmation of her independent status.

On 9th April 1940 Germany occupied Denmark. From that moment Denmark was in no position to conduct the foreign affairs of Iceland, and on the following day the Alþing resolved to exercise the powers thitherto assigned to the Danish King by the Constitution. In the following year the Alþing gave notice of its intention to sever the Union, and in May 1944 the issue was put to a referendum: the turnout was 98.61%, of which 97.35% voted for abolition of the Act of Union, and 95.04% for the new Republican Constitution. The Republic of Iceland was born at Þingvellir (the site of the original Alþing) on 17th June 1944 (the birthday of the national hero Jón Sigurðsson).

If the war years brought Iceland's political development to its climax, they also transformed her economic situation. Iceland was catapulted into the 20th century and onto the international arena. The British and, one year later, the American occupying presence on Icelandic soil during the war resulted in the construction of two airfields which were to revolutionize Iceland's communications with the outside world. Likewise, the amount of money brought into Iceland with the American base, although not huge in absolute terms, nonetheless acted as a catalyst on the employment opportunities and standard of living in a small-scale economy, and provided the springboard for the post-war development of Iceland.

However, this sudden meeting with the world outside brought to Iceland the problems as well as the benefits of supranational politics and economics: the wartime military base became a NATO base, and internal argument between commitment and neutrality has seldom been beneath the surface; a small-scale economy is vulnerable not only to global inflation, from which Iceland, in European terms, has suffered

Introduction

badly, but also to specific sectoral trends. Attempts to diversify the economy have been partly successful, particularly in the field of geothermal and hydroelectric energy, but Iceland's economy remains overwhelmingly dependent upon fish, and for the foreseeable future it is with the fish that Iceland's prosperity or otherwise will lie — it is against this background that her stance in successive disputes concerning fishing rights and territorial waters has to be understood. What is remarkable is the way in which Iceland in so short a time, and without any period of transition, has adapted itself to a successful international profile. The deeper reasons for this are to be explained only by reference to the many strands which have historically shaped the Icelandic national character.

Iceland is small, and beautiful. But there are many indicators which point to Schumacher's renowned equation of these two terms: Iceland has the highest life expectancy in the world; she has one of the highest standards of living in Europe (including the highest per capita car ownership) and the most widely distributed; politically she has remained stable in spite of, or because of, coalition politics; social class differences are observably narrower than in other western societies; and her population is 100% literate.

Yet for more than a millennium the very survival of the Icelandic nation was threatened by either natural or economic disasters. The basic art of survival has in Iceland become a fine art, in which sophistication has been added to fortitude. Today it is not the nation, but rather the national identity which is seen by some to be under threat. Of all the international pressures to which Iceland has been exposed since the Second World War the most subtle has been that of 'cultural' intrusion. But the Icelanders' perception of their own cultural tradition remains firmly rooted throughout a changing but still homogeneous society which in spite of urbanizing factors will continue to be dominated by its natural environment.

Perhaps the most cohesive defence of its culture lies in the Icelandic language. The equation of language and race is a concept often challenged by anthropologists and historians, but in the case of Iceland it is undeniable. The Icelandic language has changed comparatively little from the Norse standard of Viking times. Linguistically, as well as in literature, there remains a strong bond between the modern era and the Golden Age. The language, by geographical accident and latterly by conscious design, has remained relatively free from foreign influences. It is spoken only by the Icelandic nation; within Iceland its character is uniform; it is what most obviously distinguishes the Icelanders from other peoples; and it is the constant living reminder of their origin,

Introduction

culture and national identity. It is hardly unexpected that Iceland's most eminent literary figure of this century, Halldór Laxness, should have offered the most eloquent expression of this feeling: 'However limited it is, his home base will in the long run be a writer's mainstay. Make the place where you belong your stronghold is my advice to small and large alike — at least until we know for sure what is large and what small in this world. You might have some success in faraway places where they make you king for a day, but the only group that matters finally is the one, however, small, which stands behind you through thick and thin in your own bastion'.

Because this bibliography appears in a series intended mainly for the English speaker there is a danger of promoting an approach to the study of Iceland through foreign eyes alone. Fortunately the Icelanders have done much to present their own views upon and studies of their country through a variety of publications from Iceland in the English language. The inclusion in this bibliography of such material and of contributions by Icelanders to foreign books and periodicals should help to restore the balance. The bibliography is not, of course, comprehensive, but it is hoped that most of the publications of importance or interest to the general reader or student have been included, as well as more specialized items of an original or influential nature. An attempt has been made to identify material for the study of all major aspects of Iceland; however, certain topics are better represented than others either because of their particular relevance in an Icelandic context, or because of the relative availability of materials in the English language. It must be mentioned that in two major areas, natural history and Old Icelandic literature, this bibliography is particularly selective: the physiographic nature of Iceland has attracted copious research activity resulting in numerous papers of a highly technical character, which for reasons of balance and space have been generally excluded from the bibliography, although the advanced specialist will find many references to such material listed within several of the works which are included; likewise, in the botanical and zoological study of Iceland there is a corpus of specialist papers on the smaller organisms — these, too, have been excluded, but many examples will be found amongst the references in the two serial collections *The botany of Iceland* and *The zoology of Iceland* (q.v.). In the humanities, Old Icelandic literature has long been the subject of much scholarly research and criticism, and material additional to that presented in this bibliography can be identified through several of the bibliographical works mentioned in the final section of this volume.

All the items described in this bibliography have at some stage been either read, consulted or examined by the compiler; but inevitably a

Introduction

work such as this must reflect some of the compiler's personal views and preferences. I am acutely aware that as a non-Icelander I have been at a distinct disadvantage. In defence I can offer only an early and, to some extent, maintained specialization in Icelandic studies; the techniques of the professional librarian; and, above all, an unquenchable enthusiasm for all things Icelandic.

This bibliography would undoubtedly have benefited from greater consultation than has been possible, and any omissions, errors or misinterpretations are entirely my own responsibility. There are, however, several people to whom at different times and in different ways I am indebted: to Douglas Gray, Emeritus Fellow of Pembroke College, Oxford (latterly Tolkien Professor at Lady Margaret Hall) for awakening my initial interest in this field; to the late Gabriel Turville-Petre, Professor and Vigfússon Reader in Ancient Icelandic at the University of Oxford, the awesomeness of whose knowledge of Icelandic studies was tempered by his ability to generate the enthusiasm of his students; to Rory McTurk, Supervisor of Icelandic studies at the University of Leeds, for some welcome encouragement in the awkward final stages of this compilation; to Ann Farr, Librarian responsible for the valuable Icelandic Collection in the Brotherton Library of the University of Leeds, and to counter staff in the Parkinson wing for their help and efficiency; to the National Library of Iceland in Reykjavík for entrusting me with many items via the international library loan service; to staff at the Icelandic Embassy in London who have dealt with a string of what must have seemed to them totally unrelated points of detail; to Dick Phillips of Alston, both for his own bibliographical work in the field and for some helpful conversations; finally, and especially, to my wife Jennifer, who was so beguiled by the Icelandic atmosphere that she accepted my proposal of marriage there, and to my daughter Freya, who will probably get tired of having to explain why she has a Norse name — both of them have shown considerable patience at my absence from the family circle which the writing of this bibliography has often caused.

Iceland leaves a lasting impression upon nearly all those who encounter it in whatever context. It has much to teach others in a variety of ways, and it is my hope that this guide to publications about an extraordinary country may go some way towards enhancing the study which Iceland both deserves and unfailingly repays.

Shipley, Yorkshire
December 1982

Note on the Icelandic alphabet

During the thousand or so years of its separate existence the Icelandic language has changed less than that of any other European nation.

The Icelandic alphabet has retained two characters outside the Roman tradition: Þ, taken from the runic alphabet, is the symbol used for the sound of unvoiced *TH* (as in English THORN) and occurs chiefly in an initial position in words, its lower case form being þ; the voiced equivalent of the sound *th* (as in English 'this') is represented by the symbol ð, which never occurs initially, but whose upper case form is Ð. These symbols have been used throughout the text of this bibliography, except in the case of names of expatriate Icelanders who have chosen to transliterate them to *TH* and *d* respectively.

Also to be noted in the Icelandic alphabet is the frequent occurrence of the diphthong symbol *æ* (the vowel sound in English 'sky'), and the umlaut *ö* (the vowel sound in English 'earth'). The diacritical mark ´ over Icelandic vocalic characters affects the quantity and/or quality of the base vowel. The official regulation of 1974, according to which *z* was to be written as *s*, has not been retrospectively applied in this text.

The Country and Its People

Shorter accounts

1 **Iceland first seen.**
William Morris. In: *William Morris: stories in prose, stories in verse, shorter poems...* Edited by G. D. H. Cole. London: Nonesuch Press; New York: Random House, 1974. 671p.
'Lo from our loitering ship/a new land to be seen;/toothed rocks down the side of the firth/on the east guard a weary wide lea,/and black slope the hillsides above/striped adown with their desolate green:/and a peak rises up in the west, from the meeting of cloud and sea,/foursquare from base unto point/like the building of Gods that have been.' The first sighting of Iceland is an experience which affects every visitor. This extract is taken from the first of the six stanzas (p. 467-69) which form Morris' short poem about the experience. He first visited Iceland in 1871.

2 **Modern Iceland.**
Guðmundur Kamban. *Geographical Review* (US), vol. 5 (1918), p. 195-207.
An imaginary tour for the foreigner around Iceland in the early part of this century, of interest as the personal view of the eminent Icelandic novelist and playwright Guðmundur Kamban, who was thirty years old at the time and living in Denmark.

3 **Iceland: some impressions.**
Alan E. Boucher. Reykjavík: Prentfell, [1948?], 48p.
Not so much a travel guide as a series of observations and personal impressions which the intending traveller is invited to share. Perhaps too old to appear on a recommended reading list for today's visitor, as it is long out of print, but if the reader should stumble on a copy, it is worth a good look. Written by an English-

1

The Country and Its People. Shorter accounts

man turned Icelander. A rather less successful booklet of British impressions of Iceland from the same decade is *Iceland as we know it* by the publisher Stanley Unwin, the geologist John Mitchell and the philologist William A. Craigie (London: Bodley Head; Edinburgh: White, 1942. 30p.).

4 Iceland tapestry.
Deena Clark. *National Geographic Magazine*, vol. 100, no. 5 (Nov. 1951), p. 599-630. illus.

A nice piece of reportage offering a vivid, if superficial, view of various aspects of the Icelandic life-style during the years immediately after the Second World War. Accompanied by the imaginative photography usual in this magazine.

5 Iceland: country of sagas and volcanoes.
Clifford Embleton. *Geographical Magazine*, vol. 42, no. 5 (Feb. 1970), p. 333-42. illus.

A clear and short survey of the Icelandic landscape, its climate, geological formations, geothermal energy, glaciers, waterfalls, etc. An article for the general reader. Illustrated.

6 Out of the wilderness.
Peter Ackroyd. *Spectator* (UK), (6 Sept. 1980), p. 10-12.

Iceland has not been alone in suffering from the instant generalisations of short profiles written by foreign reporters. Occasionally, however, one comes across a piece which, although in this mode, is particularly well written and emits some flashes of what it is like to be an Icelander today. Recording an episode of an Icelandic boy's delight at seeing the lights of London from the air, the writer elevates it with considerable insight: 'It tells us of what the Icelanders never had, what history and what possibilities have been denied them. And yet what have they raised in its place - what intensity of longing, what affirmation of themselves, what willing embrace of the land and its spirits. Who could say where the advantage lies?'.

7 Iceland; a special report.
The Times (UK), (17 Feb. 1982), suppl. p. i-iv.

A special supplement issued to coincide with the state visit of the Icelandic president, Vigdís Finnbogadóttir to Britain. Magnús Magnússon, Dick Phillips and Denis Taylor contribute articles illustrating the national character, the legacies of earlier times, and the modern state with its new president. A previous special report by *The Times* was published in the issue of 1 December 1970

8 The Icelanders.
Guðmundur Finnbogason. Reykjavík: Anglia/Anglo-Icelandic Society, 1943. 24p.

Written by the then director of the National Library of Iceland, this paper retains a considerable interest as a concise evaluation of the forces which have helped to shape the Icelanders' culture and their national character.

The Country and Its People. Shorter accounts

9 The thousand years struggle against ice and fire.
Sigurður Þórarinsson. Reykjavík: Bókaútgáfa Menningarsjóds, 1956. 52p.

Text of a lecture delivered at Bedford College, London, in 1952. The description of Iceland as a land of ice and fire has long been a cliché, and many photographic volumes have been published illustrating the truth of this description. This lecture, however, is one of the few sources to offer an historical survey of the effects of these extremes upon the population and their sustenance. Particular attention is paid to the Arctic drift ice, the cultivation of cereal crops, and to the demographic cycles. 'The past of Iceland can be less unravelled by the historian alone than that of other peoples. He needs the co-operation of the scientist for tracing the story of volcanic action and earthquakes, the story of climate and the drift ice, the story of the interplay of soil erosion and formation'. This publication also includes the text of a second lecture entitled *The kingdom of Vatnajökull*. See Sigurður Þórarinsson's 'Population changes in Iceland' (q.v.).

10 Iceland 1918-1968.
Gylfi Þ. Gíslason. London: University College, 1968. 16p.

Text of a lecture delivered by the Icelandic Minister of Culture and Education, which encapsulates for the uninitiated the spirit of the country in its endeavour to strike a balance between the richness of its heritage and the problems of the modern world, after half a century of independence. See the same writer's article 'Problems of Icelandic culture' in *American-Scandinavian Review*, vol. 54 (1966), p. 241-48.

11 The problem of being an Icelander: past, present and future.
Gylfi Þ. Gíslason, translated by Pétur Kidson Karlsson. Reykjavík: Almenna Bókafélagið, 1973. 92p. photos.

A well laid out volume, which by means of short chapters and accompanying photographs by Gunnar Hannesson, introduces the reader to the historical background of Iceland, and to its contemporary social, economic and political organisation. The author concludes with an eloquent essay on the need to safeguard and strengthen both the political and the cultural independence of Iceland and its people.

12 To become an Icelander.
Árni Þórarinsson. *Atlantica and Iceland Review*, vol. 15, no. 1 (1977), p. 33-38; no. 2, p. 16-21.

A feature in two parts, in which a series of six profiles throws a revealing light on life in Iceland as seen through the eyes of foreigners who decided to make Iceland their permanent home. Three of the subjects have gained a considerable reputation in the arts: Alan E. Boucher, Professor of English at the University of Iceland, and a writer and translator; the Catalonian-born painter Baltasar Samper; and the Norwegian-born photographer Mats Wibe Lund. The other three, an American, a German and a Dane, work as teacher, horsebreaker and gardener respectively. Their reasons for living in Iceland are sometimes individual, sometimes shared.

The Country and Its People. Shorter accounts

13 **Perspectives in culture: a round-table discussion.**
Atlantica and Iceland Review, vol. 11, no. 2 (1973), p. 24-36.
The question of Icelandic cultural identity is one which is discussed in many sectors of the community. Presented here is an interchange of views between an editor, a publisher, a journalist, a lecturer, a critic and a theatre director. Two of the topics discussed are translations and the purity of the language, but it is the general interplay of themes that helps the foreign reader to appreciate the problems of retaining the cultural identity of a small nation. 'Perhaps', says one participant, 'our cultural heritage is this: the art of surviving, come hell or high water'.

14 **Iceland's unique history and culture.**
Hannes Jónsson. Reykjavík: Leiftur, 1964. 3rd ed. 24p. illus.
A well-written booklet designed as an introduction to the country for the first-time visitor to Iceland. Basically a potted history, briefly describing the major milestones and some features of modern living in independent Iceland. Photographic illustrations. Compare this volume with the booklet *Iceland: a nation of ancient culture, a country of contrasts*, text by Bjarni Guðmundsson, photographs by Þorsteinn Jósepsson (Reykjavík: Ministry for Foreign Affairs, 1962 and reprintings, 16p.).

15 **Iceland past and present.**
Björn Þórðarson, translated by Sir William A. Craigie. Reykjavík: Hlaðbúð, 1953. 3rd ed. 56p.
Another brief history of Iceland and its culture, with a survey of the political and economic situation of the new nation state. Written by the former Prime Minister of Iceland, this illustrated booklet, originally published to meet the new interest in Iceland from abroad as a result of the Second World War, was well used for two decades. The first two editions were published by Oxford University Press in 1941 and 1945.

16 **Iceland and the Icelanders.**
Helgi P. Briem, colour photographs by Vigfús Sigurgeirsson. Maplewood, New Jersey: McKenna, 1945. 96p.
A clear and entertaining description of the country and its people. Frequently cited as one of the most helpful introductions to pre-republican Iceland. In spite of being produced under wartime conditions it is a particularly attractive book to read. The photography is appealing, and the larger type face makes it suitable for the poorly-sighted reader. The younger reader, too, will be helped by the simple style. The author was formerly the Icelandic Ambassador to the United States.

17 **Iceland: the island in the limelight.**
Amadeo Astraudo, adapted from the French by Gaston Benedict. Los Angeles: American Herald, 1941. 47p.
A publication motivated by the decision to send US forces to Iceland in 1941. Its author was a European diplomat who wrote several books about the small states of Europe and their problems. His aim was simply to include in a short space as many facts as possible about the organisation of life in Iceland.

The Country and Its People. Longer accounts

The land and people of Iceland.
See item no. 870.

Smoky bay: the story of a small boy in Iceland.
See item no. 872.

Longer accounts

18 **When I was a girl in Iceland.**
Hólmfríður Árnadóttir. Boston, Massachusetts: Lothrop, 1919. 209p.

A little gem of a book, written by an Icelandic woman who had emigrated to the United States in 1917. It has no pretensions other than to recount the daily life of a child in Iceland during the last quarter of the 19th century. The memories are recalled with disarming simplicity, and yet they seem to reveal more about what home life in Iceland was like at that time than any historian's or foreign traveller's approach. She takes the reader through the four seasons and their various festivals from a child's viewpoint, and the impressions which she leaves are vivid. Further recollections (by an Icelandic emigrant to Denmark) of childhood in Vík on the south coast of Iceland from the early part of this century are recorded in 'Rural life in Iceland' by Ólafur Gunnarsson in *Norseman* (Norway), vol. 15 (1957), p. 314-18.

19 **Iceland: a land of contrasts.**
Hjalmar Lindroth, translated from the Swedish by Adolph B. Benson. Princeton, New Jersey: Princeton University Press for the American-Scandinavian Foundation, 1937. 234p. bibliog.

This is a sound, well-written and entertaining account of the Icelandic nation. The author has dug deeper beneath the surface of the Icelandic way of life than many other foreign writers (Iceland has been well served by Swedish observers). The section on material civilisation includes a chapter on national dress, and an illuminating essay about life on the farms. The section on intellectual life includes a chapter on sports, games and dances, and an extended survey of the Icelandic language (the author was a professor of Scandinavian languages).

20 **Iceland: the first American republic.**
Vilhjalmur Stefansson. New York: Doubleday, 1939. 274p. bibliog. Reprinted Westport, Connecticut: Greenwood Press, 1971.

The subtitle of this book implies no political claims towards Iceland by the United States. It is meant to imply, not altogether convincingly, an Icelandic link with the American continent in terms of geography and the history of exploration (rather than political adventurism). The clue is to be found in the author's autobiography *Discovery* (New York: McGraw-Hill, 1964, p. 334-35), where he records that he was asked by the Icelandic government to write a book about Iceland which could be sold on the Icelandic site at the New York World's Fair of 1939; it was duly published with the help of, and with a preface by, Theodore

The Country and Its People. Longer accounts

Roosevelt. 'Stef' (1879-1962) was born in the United States of recently-immigrated Icelandic parents, and is renowned as an Arctic explorer. His book on Iceland, deservedly reprinted thirty years on, is a sector by sector account of Iceland's social and economic condition during the 1930s. It is still valuable both as a record of the times, and as a point of reference from which to compare the dramatic development of Iceland in the post-war period.

21 Iceland: new world outpost.
Agnes M. Rothery. New York: Viking Press; Toronto: MacMillan, 1948. 214p. bibliog. Reprinted London: Melrose, 1952. 192p.

Also appearing under the title *Iceland: bastion of the north*, this book was an enterprising publication at the time, and one which was quite well received by the Icelanders. Unusually accurate, rather than particularly profound, but it is remarkable how Iceland's nature, people and culture can elicit casual yet, at the same time, revealing observations. The book is both easily read and worth reading in the context of Iceland's newly found independence, although its style is rather jolly at times, and it is not altogether free from the patronising attitude often found in pre-republican accounts by foreigners, e.g. 'Despite the insinuations of the Communists, the United States has no ambition to annex Iceland. This small country has proved that it can manage its own affairs in a highly enlightened fashion. The less interference from alien powers, the better the Icelanders get along'. The book also contains some interesting photographs. Agnes Rothery's other book on Iceland *Iceland roundabout* was published in the same year (New York: Dodd Mead. 200p.). It introduces the traditional tales of Iceland to the younger reader.

22 Iceland yesterday and today.
Horace Leaf. London: Allen & Unwin, 1949. 205p.

A lively account of Iceland by a geographer, in which several chapters on the country's social and political past are followed by a descriptive tour of the country. One chapter is a rare description of the small island of Viðey in the bay north-east of Reykjavík, on which was once the Danish governor's residence and before that a monastery.

23 Iceland, old-new republic: a study of its history, life and physical aspects.
Amy Elizabeth Jensen. New York: Exposition Press, 1954. 362p.

A comparatively unheralded and infrequently-cited book. Why this should be so is difficult to explain, since it is certainly one of the more helpful books of its kind on Iceland. It is long, and perhaps takes on too much too sketchily, but it was justifiably designed to introduce Iceland topic by topic in a series of twenty-seven short essays covering history, ecology, flora and fauna, culture, religion, education, agriculture and fisheries, co-operative organisations, health and diet, sport, music and theatre, painting, domestic power supply, town planning, trade, international relations, and emigration. On the historical side the book is not strong, but the grasp is much firmer in the more numerous chapters on living in the new republic. The book occasionally reads rather like a crowded notebook, but in a sense this is its value, for it is packed with facts, mostly correct, which throw considerable light on the framework of Icelandic society.

The Country and Its People. Longer accounts

24 Ripples from Iceland.
Amalia Líndal. New York: Norton, 1962. 239p.

'There is an attitude midway between that of the tourist and that of the native Icelander which has been publicized very little so far, and which should be included in the picture of modern Iceland... This book does not attempt to repeat the material already available on Iceland, but to supplement it. To quiet the murmurs of protest from Icelandic readers I stress emphatically that this book represents only my viewpoint - that of an American woman resident; I write from a housewife's point of view. This, then, is Iceland as it has seemed to me from 1949 through July 1961'. Thus in her preface the author describes the motive and character of her book. Frú Líndal met her Icelandic husband-to-be when they were both students in the United States and went to Iceland to live. Her book is an entertaining, not altogether uncritical, but affectionate record of her initial experiences in Iceland and her daily life. It is the only book of its kind which allows the foreign visitor to read between the lines to get an impression of the Icelander's typical reactions. Amalia Líndal later became editor of the extremely enterprising quarterly magazine (now unfortunately defunct) on Icelandic life for English readers, *Sixty-five Degrees* (q.v.).

25 Modern Iceland.
John C. Griffiths. London: Pall Mall Press; New York: Praeger, 1969. 226p.

This book was the first systematic treatment in English of the structure of Icelandic society for three decades, and as a serious 'area-study' it has still not been entirely superseded. It is written by a journalist with an empathy with Iceland, rather than a specialist. It is well written, objective, and, although its primary purpose is descriptive, it contains many points of fresh insight. The book is particularly successful in relating the social, political and economic problems faced, and in many cases, resolved by the Icelandic state to the nation's historical and cultural context. The fisheries question is examined in some detail, and an appendix gives the English text of the eighty-one articles of the Icelandic constitution of 1944. The essential framework and character of Iceland emerges from this book rather more clearly than from many other accounts, and for this reason it is still to be strongly recommended as a most helpful introduction to modern Iceland, although, unfortunately now out of print.

26 The Icelanders and their island.
Mary McCririck. Bangor, Wales: 1976. 169p. bibliog.

An enterprising publication both in content and in production. Although published privately by the author, it has found its way into the hands of many individuals and libraries. The market is not exactly flooded with recent books introducing Iceland to the reader in a substantial but digestible way, and this book, while not pretending to be original, conveys a freshness and a balance of the various aspects of Iceland that makes it perhaps the one to be recommended first to the general reader. It is a book which will prepare travellers beforehand, inform them while they are there, and make things fall into place on their return.

27 Daughter of fire: a portrait of Iceland.
Katherine Scherman. Boston, Massachusetts: Little, Brown; London: Gollancz, 1976. 354p.

This volume also appears under the title *Iceland: daughter of fire*. In the course of reading this book the reader may feel somewhat disoriented - it is not primarily a travel book, nor a history, nor a natural history, but an amalgam of all

The Country and Its People. Longer accounts

of these. When one has finished reading it, however, there is a feeling that one has grasped most of the essential qualities that give Iceland its remarkable cohesion. The author's intention was that the book should 'arrange itself around the compelling blend of past and present'. This is one of the most absorbing books on Iceland, and its success lies in its depiction of the interaction of environments, social and cultural history, and present-day society.

28 Northern sphinx: Iceland and the Icelanders from the settlement to the present.
Sigurđur A. Magnússon. London: Hurst; Montreal: McGill/Queens University Press, 1977. 261p. bibliog.

An extremely welcome publication. The author, chairman of the Writer's Union of Iceland, is one of his country's most respected commentators on cultural and political affairs. His book is divided into three parts: the first covers the period of the Old Icelandic Commonwealth, its organisation, personalities, cultural tradition and literary achievement, and contains many fresh observations; the second depicts the six centuries of Iceland's 'dark age'; the third introduces the framework of the modern nation state, and though the last section would have benefitted from more expansive descriptions of the country's institutions and their activities, these short accounts of government, religion, broadcasting, education, health, infrastructure etc. form a useful basis for further reading. There is also a perceptive chapter on the national characteristics of the Icelanders, a very useful survey of the modern artistic scene, and a final description of the Icelandic landscape. The author appends a substantial bibliographical list of English-language books on Iceland. A sound and stimulating introduction to the country and its people.

29 Iceland: the first new society.
Richard F. Tomasson. Minneapolis, Minnesota: University of Minnesota Press, 1980. 247p. bibliog.

In examining Iceland as 'the first new society' the author states his deliberate intention to echo the title of Lipset's work *The first new nation: the United States in comparative and historical perspective*. Tomasson calls Iceland 'the first new society founded *prior* to the modern period'. He has produced a coherent survey in English of Icelandic society, examining in detail its demographic structure, family life, literacy and cultural levels, language, religion, alcoholism etc., and has a particularly interesting chapter on the values of Icelanders. The findings in some of these areas are based on a cross-sectional survey of one hundred Icelanders, named, with date of birth, residence and occupation. Questions asked in the survey are given in an appendix. What emerges is an indication of Icelanders' contemporary attitudes to their own society. This was always likely to be a provocative book, and, for this reason, the reader may wish to be referred to two reviews by Icelanders: one favourable, by the literary critic and author Sigurđur A. Magnússon in *Atlantica and Iceland Review*, vol. 19, no. 1 (1981), p. 10-11; the other, somewhat harsh, by a sociologist, Katrín Friđjonsdóttir, entitled 'The egalitarian and permissive Vikings, or, sociology for the tourist trade' in *Acta Sociologica*, vol. 24, no. 3 (1981), p. 199-208. Some of the themes in this book are introduced by the author in his article 'Iceland: the first new nation' in *Scandinavian Political Studies*, vol. 10 (1975), p. 33-51.

Handbooks

30 Scandinavia past and present.
Edited by Jørgen Bukdahl. Odense, Denmark: Arnkrone, 1959. 3 vols.

Compilers of Scandinavian compendia frequently display an irritating reluctance to include Iceland in their treatment. This set is an exception, as short contributions on a wide variety of social, political, economic, geographical, historical and cultural aspects of Iceland are to be found throughout its pages. Its main value lies in the comparative approach which it affords to the study of the institutions of the Scandinavian countries. The individual titles of the three illustrated volumes are: *From the Viking age to absolute monarchy*; *Through revolution to liberty*; and *Five modern democracies*.

31 Iceland 874-1974.
Edited by Jóhannes Nordal, Valdimar Kristinsson. Reykjavík: Central Bank of Iceland, 1975. 416p. maps. bibliog.

This handbook, published on the occasion of the eleventh centenary of the settlement of Iceland, offers the student a compendious survey of the development and state of the nation. Specialists in the various fields have contributed substantial sections under the following headings: country and population, history and cultural heritage, government and administration, foreign relations, industries and energy, economic policy and finance, foreign trade and payments, social conditions, religion and education, science and the arts, recreational activities. The volume is illustrated and includes two maps, a detailed index, and a bibliography of non-Icelandic materials for further reading. Previously issued as *Iceland 1966* (1967. 390p.). Prior to these, similar handbooks had been published by the National Bank of Iceland. *Iceland 1946*, edited by Þorsteinn Þorsteinsson, was issued on the 60th anniversary of the bank (previous editions having appeared in 1926, 1930, 1936). These retain some value for the study of pre-republican conditions, containing many useful statistics.

32 Facts about Iceland.
Ólafur Hansson. Reykjavík: Bókaútgáfamenningarsjóds. various eds. c. 72p.

A useful booklet for the visitor to Iceland, providing a basic introduction to the nation's institutions and activities, with a section on 'who runs what', and appending the score and text of the national anthem, 'O, Guð vors lands' (score by Sveinbjörn Sveinbjörnsson, words by Matthías Jochumsson).

33 Iceland: country and people.
Sigurður A. Magnússon. Reykjavík: Iceland Review, 1979, 64p.

An illustrated introduction to Iceland past and present. Fits neatly into the pocket as a handy reference guide. The earlier version appeared as *Handy facts on Iceland*.

The Country and Its People. Photographic presentations

34 Iceland..
 Reykjavík: Icelandair. various eds.

The national airline has issued many informative pamphlets on Iceland over the years. One set deserves particular mention: each pamphlet deals with a specific topic (bird life, climbing and skiing, flora and vegetation, geography, the Iceland horse, salmon and trout fishing, weather, etc.), and consists of ten pages of illustrated text by experts in each field. A second set is devoted to specific regions of the country. They should be read on the plane there, and be kept among the documents carried by any alert traveller around Iceland - their format is designed for this purpose.

Photographic presentations

35 Iceland: nature and nation in photographs.
 Reykjavík: Ísafoldarprentsmiðja, 1938.

Photographic volumes on Iceland are numerous and spectacular. This volume, published in co-operation with the Tourist Association of Iceland, possesses a particular appeal as an early example: its 264 plates are in black-and-white, and, in spite of the unchanging nature of most of the country's landscape, they convey a distinct feeling of the character of Iceland before its post-war rush into the developed world. The volume includes an introductory essay in Icelandic and English by Pálmi Hannesson. The photographs are also provided with English captions.

36 Iceland.
 Kurt Drost, introduced by Björn Þ. Björnsson, translated by Peter Kidson. Munich: Andermann, 1963. 61p.

A photographic introduction to Iceland. Photographic presentations of similar size and period include *Iceland*, with photographs by Helga Fietz, and introduction and picture captions by Sigurður Þórarinsson (Munich: Reich, 1961. 74p). Also *Iceland: land in creation*; photography and picture texts by William A. Keith and introduction by Kristján Eldjárn (Reykjavík: Keith Films, 1967. 66p.).

37 Golden Iceland.
 Samivel, translated and adapted by Magnús Magnússon. Reykjavík: Almennabókafélagið; New York: Evans, 1967. 307p.

Originally published in Paris in 1963 under the title *L'or de l'Islande* this volume by the notable French film-maker and writer Paul Gayet-Tancrède (pseudonym, Samivel) is a copiously illustrated description of Iceland, with the emphasis on landscape, history and culture. A book designed to whet the appetite of the intending traveller, or as a substantial souvenir upon return. Iceland emerges resplendent.

The Country and Its People. Photographic presentations

38 Iceland.
Photographs by Franz-Karl von Linden, Helfried Weyer. Bern, Switzerland: Kümmerly & Frey; London: Hale; New York: McKay; Reykjavík: Almennabókafélagið, 1974. 224p.

An attractively-presented volume of excellent photographs, accompanied by a series of essays covering Iceland's landscape, geology, bird life, the volcanic creation of Surtsey, and the Icelandic economy. There are two contributions by Icelanders: Gylfi Þ. Gíslason, on the Icelandic people and their contemporary problems; and by Kristján Eldjárn on the history and customs of ancient Iceland. The book was published to commemorate the 1,100th anniversary of the settlement of Iceland in 874. Kümmerly also published *Iceland: impressions of a heroic landscape* by travel photographer Alfred Nawrath, with essays by Halldór Laxness and Magnús Magnússon, translated by B. M. Charleston. Simultaneously published (Chicago: Rand McNally; Berlin: Kümmerly, 1959).

39 Iceland in pictures.
John B. Burks. New York: Sterling; London; Oak Tree Press, 1975. 3rd ed. 64p. (Visual Geography Series).

A broad, albeit superficial, description of the land, history, culture, and the social, political and economic character of Iceland, illustrated with many of the standard photographs in black-and-white. Contains a few errors, otherwise an undemanding introduction for the first-time visitor or school student.

40 Iceland: the surprising island of the Atlantic.
Haraldur J. Hamar. Reykjavík: Iceland Review, 1977. 96p.

A neatly-produced book of colour photographs, accompanied by an informative text, depicting the natural landscape and how the Icelanders have adapted to it. An earlier similar version was published in 1972 under the title *Iceland: the unspoiled land*.

41 Iceland.
Photographs by John Chang McCurdy. Reykjavík: Almennabókafélagið, 1979. 140p. 74 plates.

A volume of spectacular photography containing seventy-four colour plates of the Icelandic landscape, which, it is only fair to say, gives any photographer an immediate advantage. Halldór Laxness lends his name to the introduction, and Magnús Magnússon contributes the text.

42 Ice and fire: contrasts of Icelandic nature.
Hjálmar R. Bárðarson, translated by Sölvi Eysteinsson. Reykjavík: 1980. 3rd ed. 171p.

A very popular volume, published privately by the author, which, perhaps more than any other, captures and clarifies the constant interplay of elements that is Iceland's foremost natural characteristic. The author has successfully blended technical explanations of the natural phenomena with a readily understandable account of the forces at work, and has enhanced his presentation with some breathtaking photography. The latter is the main feature of another privately published volume *Ísland* (1965, 208p). High quality photography of landscape and life, with multilingual captions.

The Country and Its People. Local accounts

Local accounts

43 Thingvellir: birthplace of a nation.
Björn Þorsteinsson, Þorsteinn Jósepsson. Reykjavík: Heimskringla, 1961. 50p. 55 plates.

A description of the locality of the ancient home of Iceland's parliament and of the features which made the site so suitable, followed by an account of the origins, formation and function of the Alþing during the Old Icelandic Commonwealth, with further notes on the modern parliament. Text accompanied by fine photography in black-and-white, including an especially interesting aerial shot with all the main features of the old site indicated.

44 Reykjavík: the capital of Iceland.
Björn Þ. Björnsson, photography by Leifur Þorsteinsson. Reykjavík: Heimskringla, 1969. 134p.

An informative text on the history and development of Reykjavík as home of the first settler, as farm and church, as royal manor and dependency, as Danish market town, and as the capital of Iceland. Many of the unusual photographs illustrating past and present are of places 'off the beaten track'. Another respected Icelandic photographer, Gunnar Hannesson, also shows Reykjavík in a different light in his collection *Reykjavík: a panorama in four seasons* (Reykjavík: Iceland Review, 1974. 96p). Most tourists know the capital only by summer; at other times it takes on a different character, and, indeed, has more to offer. Introduced by the playwright Jökull Jakobsson.

45 Vestmannaeyjar.
Páll Steingrímsson. Reykjavík: Kassagerð, [1971?] 64p. 59 plates.

A brief introduction to life past and present on the Westmann Islands (text in English, German and Icelandic), followed by a collection of fifty-nine photographic plates which appealingly convey the spirit of these islands, of which there are fifteen in all, but only one inhabited by humans.

46 The Westmann Islands.
R. M. Lockley. *Geographical Magazine*, vol. 4, no. 5 (March 1937), p. 349-56. photos.

A sketch, with photographs, of life on the Westmann Islands before the last war, in which the reporter emphasises the isolation of the islands, not only from the wider world, but also from mainland Iceland itself. It is interesting to compare his impressions of the Faroe Islands, which he conveyed at about the same time in the same magazine, vol. 6, no. 3 (Jan. 1938), p. 215-24.

47 Vestmannaeyjar.
Páll Magnússon, Alan Rettedal. *News from Iceland* no. 73 (Feb. 1982), suppl. 16p.

The events surrounding the volcanic eruption which occurred on Heimaey on 26 January 1973 should not obscure the fact that the Westmann Islands were, and are again, a thriving community (Iceland's third largest after the capital conurbation and Akureyri). This special supplement on the life of Heimaey includes an

The Country and Its People. Local accounts

historical sketch, aspects of the fishing industry, energy potential of the new lava, sporting activities, etc.

48 Akureyri.
Gísli Sigurgeirsson, Alan Rettedal. *News from Iceland*, no. 68 (Sept. 1981), suppl. 20p.

Another special supplement to the monthly newspaper in English from Iceland, offering an informative and contemporary sketch of the social, economic and cultural situation in the northern Icelandic town of Akureyri. A further supplement of twelve pages on Akureyri appeared in issue no. 75 (April 1982).

49 Akureyri and the picturesque north.
Reykjavík: Iceland Review, 1975. 96p.

A portrait in pictures and words of Iceland's second largest town, and of the many compelling sights to be seen in this region of north Iceland. Introductory text by the poet Kristján frá Djúpalæk.

50 Arctic living: the story of Grímsey.
Robert Jack, foreward by Vilhjalmur Stefansson. Toronto: Ryerson Press, 1955. London: Hodder, 1957. 181p.

Grímsey, and one other even smaller island Kolbeinsey, are the only parts of Iceland to lie within the Arctic Circle. Robert Jack, a Scot, first came to Iceland when, as an English league footballer, he was invited to become the coach to the Valur club of Reykjavík in 1936. Unable to leave Iceland at the start of the war, he attended the theological seminary at the University of Iceland, entered the Lutheran ministry, and spent most of the first decade of that ministry on the island of Grímsey. This utterly captivating book is an evocative depiction of all aspects of life and community spirit on a climatically inhospitable Arctic island. See also Robert Jack's short article 'A sporting parson' in the series on adopted Icelanders featured in the Icelandic magazine *Sixty-five Degrees*, no. 8 (Nov. 1969), p. 25-27.

51 An Englishman visits Grímsey.
Alan Moray Williams. *Norseman* (Norway), vol. 6, no. 5 (1948), p. 333-43.

Extracts from a diary kept during a fortnight's visit to Grímsey in early summer 1936. Superficial compared with the account of resident Robert Jack (q.v.) who was there to meet him, but almost any piece about this island reveals something of its character. Published in the same year is another chronicle of Grímsey by Evelyn Stefansson, wife of Arctic explorer Vilhjalmur Stefansson. Her book *Within the Circle: portrait of the Arctic* (New York: Scribner, 1948, p. 38-51) includes a chapter entitled 'Grímsey: an Arctic chess paradise'.

Volcano: ordeal by fire in Iceland's Westmann Islands.
See item no. 191.

Icelanders abroad

52 Modern sagas: the story of the Icelanders in North America.
Thorstina Walters. Fargo, North Dakota: North Dakota Institute for Regional Studies, 1953. 229p.

Between 1870 and 1900 there occurred a mass emigration from Iceland to the North American continent - probably a quarter to a third of the country's total population uprooted itself from the background of delayed economic and political independence. Today, Canada is the home of the majority of the descendants of these original emigrants, but over a third is in the United States, especially in Utah, Minnesota and North Dakota. It is to the history and social organisation of the Icelandic settlers in North Dakota that the author, herself a member of this community, introduces the reader in this book, which is particularly successful in portraying the pioneering spirit and consolidating efforts of the settlers and their descendants. Their economic, religious, educational, cultural and domestic life is described. An appendix records the events surrounding the attempted 'colonisation' of Alaska by Icelanders in 1874. Under her former name of Thorstina Jackson the writer also published two earlier articles in the course of her research, which appeared in the periodical *Social Forces*: 'Icelandic communities in America: cultural backgrounds and early settlements', vol. 3, no. 4 (1925), p. 680-86; and, 'The Icelandic community in North Dakota: economic and social development period 1878-1925', vol. 4, no. 2 (1925), p. 357-60.

53 The Icelanders in Canada.
Walter J. Lindal. Winnipeg, Manitoba: National Publishers, 1967. 502p. (Canada Ethnica, vol. 2).

A substantial insight into the history and development of the Icelandic settlement in Canada, and the balance achieved between integration into the fabric of Canadian society and the retention of an Icelandic community spirit. 'If one can speak of the "Icelandic mind", this study will have been an attempt to show to what extent the Icelandic mind has continued and carried into the Canadian national stream'. See the same author's earlier work *The Saskatchewan Icelanders: a strand of the Canadian fabric* (Winnipeg, Manitoba: Columbia Press, 1955. 363p.).

54 The Icelandic people in Manitoba: a Manitoba saga.
Wilhelm Kristjanson. Winnipeg, Manitoba: Wallingford Press, 1965. 557p.

A comprehensive historical survey of the Manitoban Icelanders. Of all European countries which saw emigration to North America in the 19th and early 20th centuries, only Iceland sent more of its people to Canada than to the United States. In 1875 Winnipeg, Manitoba, became the key city and cultural centre for New World Icelanders - today there are an estimated 25,000 people of Icelandic stock around the city, and an Icelandic Department at the University. A volume which evokes memories of the early settlement of Manitoba is *The Icelanders*, edited by David Arnason and Michael Otito (Winnipeg, Manitoba: Turnstone Press, 1981). This book is a miscellany of personal histories, reminiscences and especially photographs.

Exploration and Travel

Early discoveries

55 Ultima Thule: further mysteries of the Arctic.
Vilhjalmur Stefansson. New York: MacMillan, 1940.
London: Harrap, 1942. 256p. bibliog.
The question of the land of Thule, and whether it was meant to refer to Iceland, is the basis of this book. The author devotes his attention to two explorers and the possibilities or otherwise of their having reached Iceland: the Greek geographer of the 4th century B.C., Pytheas (whose reports were refuted three centuries later by his compatriot Strabo); and Christopher Columbus. The evidence for and against is presented in a thorough and entertaining way, and the affinity between the author (a renowned explorer of the northern world) and his subject is apparent throughout.

56 In northern mists: Arctic exploration in early times.
Fridtjof Nansen, translated by Arthur G. Chater. London: Heinemann; New York: Stokes, 1911. 2 vols. illus.
The Norwegian explorer Nansen is, of course, likewise renowned for his own ventures in the Arctic, particularly for his partly accomplished scheme of freezing his ship Fram into the Siberian ice for the drift to take it towards the North Pole in 1893-95, and for his crossing of Greenland (via the north-west of Iceland in 1888). In the preparations for his journeys he undertook research into the history of Arctic exploration, and in these volumes he describes some of the earliest explorations, which centre largely on the discovery of Iceland, and, from Iceland, of Greenland, etc. The volumes include over 150 illustrations.

Exploration and Travel. Early discoveries

57 **Land under the pole star: a voyage to the Norse settlements of Greenland, and the saga of the people that vanished.**
Helge Ingstad, translated from the Norwegian by Naomi Walford. London: Cape; New York: St. Martin's Press, 1966. 381p. maps. illus.

The results of an expedition by the Norwegian explorer and his wife in 1953 to investigate the history of the Icelandic voyages to and settlement of Greenland, the last of the westward thrusts of the Vikings, inspired by the outlawed Eirík the Red in 982-83, the millennary of which was recently celebrated. Ingstad's account of the settlement, which appears to have lasted for four centuries before vanishing in mystery (see Poul Nørlund's *Viking Settlers in Greenland and their descendants during five hundred years* (q.v.), is a mixture of serious investigation and travel writing). It contains many maps and illustrations. The author's sequel *Westward to Vinland* was issued three years later by the same two publishers. In this book he defended his theories concerning Newfoundland as the headquarters of the Norse discovery of North America, and fuelled fresh controversy.

58 **The Norse Atlantic saga: being the Norse voyages of discovery and settlement to Iceland, Greenland and America.**
Gwyn Jones. London: Oxford University Press, 1964. 246p.

The prolific and respected writer on Norse studies here presents a volume in two parts: the first is a re-telling of the story of Norse discovery on the Atlantic in a synthesis of past and new findings; the second comprises translations of the major literary documents, including the *Book of the Icelanders*, *Book of the Settlements*, the *Greenlanders' saga*, *Eirík the Red's saga*, Karlsefni's voyage to Vinland, and the story of Einar Sokkason (*Grœnlendinga þáttr*). A full and readable presentation with photographs and a map. See also Magnús Magnússon and Hermann Pálsson *The Vinland sagas: the Norse discovery of America* (q.v.). Three earlier works on this topic were also published by Oxford University Press: *Leif Ericksen, discoverer of America A.D. 1003* by Edward F. Gray, (1930); *The Norse discoveries of America: the Wineland sagas*; translated and discussed by G. M. Gathorne-Hardy, (1921, re-issued with new introduction by Gwyn Jones, 1970); *The finding of Wineland the Good: the history of the Icelandic discovery of America*, edited and translated from the earliest records by Arthur Middleton Reeves (1980).

59 **America not discovered by Columbus: a historical sketch of the discovery of America by the Norsemen in the tenth century.**
Rasmus B. Anderson. Chicago: Griggs; London: Trübner, 1874. 104p.

Considering the importance of this topic for the early history of their country, American-based scholars were nearly a century slower than their counterparts in Scandinavia to investigate the evidence of the Norse discovery of America. This somewhat shallow (by later standards) account is nonetheless interesting as one of the earliest attempts to arouse interest in the subject among the American people. The book also includes an appendix on the historical, literary and scientific value of the Scandinavian languages in the view of various scholars. It was to be a further forty years before the first substantial investigation by an American of the discovery of the continent by the Norsemen. William Hovgaard, noted for his many writings in the area of marine engineering, turned his attention to this topic in his *The voyages of the Norsemen to America* (New York: American-Scandinavian Foundation, 1914. 304p. Reprinted by Kraus, 1970).

Exploration and Travel. 18th-19th centuries

60 The Vinland voyages.
Matthías Þórðarson, translated from the Icelandic by Thorstina Jackson Walters, with an introduction by Vilhjalmur Stefansson. New York: American Geographical Society, 1930. 76p. Reprinted New York: Arno Press, 1971. (A.G.S. Research Series, no. 18).

Although not a major study of the Norse voyages to Vinland, this account is noteworthy firstly for its lucid presentation, and secondly as the only book available in the English language by an Icelander on the ventures of Leif Eiríksson and Þorfinn Karlsefni. The book is introduced by Vilhjalmur Stefansson. See J. R. L. Anderson, *Vinland voyage* (q.v.).

61 The life of the Icelander Jón Ólafsson, traveller to India.
Jón Ólafsson, translated from the Icelandic by Bertha S. Phillpotts. London: Hakluyt Society, 1923-32. 2 vols.

Jón Ólafsson (1596-1679) was born at Álftafjörður in north-western Iceland. He travelled widely around his own country, and to England, Denmark, Faroe and Spitsbergen, Norway. In 1622 he travelled as far as India with a Danish garrison. This lengthy autobiographical account of his travels (translated from the Icelandic edition of Sigfús Blöndal) is hardly a work to command the respect of the serious historian - indeed, his style has been called garrulous, and he displays a certain gullibility coupled with a generous imagination, to the extent that his motive seems to have been merely to impress his Icelandic compatriots with tales of adventure in faraway lands. But it is an unusual and richly entertaining story, especially in the second volume with its informative editorial commentary by Sir Richard Temple on the Indian part of Jón's travels. He wrote this autobiography around 1661, but the period after his permanent return to Iceland in 1625, his marriage and later life are anonymously recorded in an appendix from the account of his son Ólaf Jónsson.

The Vinland map and the Tartar relation.
See item no. 156.

18th-19th centuries

62 French travellers in Iceland.
Louis Tissot. *Norseman* (Norway), vol. 10, no. 3 (1952), p. 149-56.

Although travellers to Iceland during the 18th and 19th centuries came mainly, as one would expect, from Britain and northern Europe, the lure of Iceland brought travellers from further afield. The French initiated several scientific and cultural expeditions, and their activities are sketched in this article. Particular mention is made of Xavier Marmier, the famous explorer who published his *Lettres sur l'Islande* in 1837, and Eugène de Groote from Flanders whose *Voyage en Islande* was published in 1891. Surprisingly, there is little mention of the scientist Paul Gaimard, whose expedition in 1835-36, reported in nine volumes, produced copious information on the natural history of Iceland and Greenland, as well as some superb engravings. Although the article mentions one of the earliest French travellers to Iceland, Martin de la Martinière, who was there as an

Exploration and Travel. 18th-19th centuries

unofficial ship's surgeon in 1653 and recorded his experiences in *Voyage des pays septentrionaux* published in 1677, there is no acknowledgment of the earliest French traveller, Isaac de la Peyrère, who visited Iceland in 1644. His diary was translated into English and appears in A. & J. Churchill's *Collection of voyages and travels* (London: Churchill, 1732, vol. 2.).

63 Ultima Thule: some English travellers to Iceland.
Beatrice White. *Essays and studies*, n.s., vol. 14 (1961), p. 81-101.

A comparative sketch of the motivations, marvellings and misgivings of many of the British travellers to Iceland over the century from Joseph Banks in 1772 to Anthony Trollope in 1878, in which the variety of their writings is emphasised; the earlier visits having a scientific or political purpose, the later involving aesthetic or purely adventurous considerations. An overall pattern emerges from this paper which sheds quite as much light upon British attitudes of the time as it does on Iceland itself.

64 Iceland on the brain.
Richard F. Tomasson. *American-Scandinavian Review*, vol. 60, no. 4 (1972), p. 380-91.

Burton's (q.v.) diagnosis of the condition 'Iceland on the brain', which he applied to the large band of foreign explorers and travellers in Iceland during the 18th and 19th centuries, is here used as a starting point for a brief survey of how this affliction manifested itself in the writings of the more important of these and later travellers: Richard Burton himself, Ebenezer Henderson, William Morris, Samuel Kneeland, Joseph Banks, Uno von Troil, William Jackson Hooker, George Steuart Mackenzie, Paul Gaimard, Ida Pfeiffer, Pliny Miles, John Ross Browne, Lord Frederick Dufferin, Frederick Metcalfe, James Bryce, Bayard Taylor, Anthony Trollope, Hjalmar Lindroth, W. H. Auden, Louis McNeice. This article originally appeared in *Atlantica and Iceland Review*, vol. 10, no. 1 (1972), p. 41-49.

65 Eighteenth century Iceland.
Frank Ponzi. Reykjavík: Almennabókafélagið, 1980. 123p. illus.

Two of the expeditions to Iceland during the late 18th century - those led by Joseph Banks and John Thomas Stanley (q.v.) were notable not only for the diaries produced, but also for the pictorial representations; most of the sketches and paintings have been preserved. This finely-produced volume in large format contains colour reproductions of the paintings, accompanied by an introduction and annotations in both Icelandic and English.

66 The journals of Sir Joseph Banks' Voyage.
Roy A. Rauschenberg. *Proceedings of the American Philosophical Society*, vol. 117, no. 3 (1973), p. 186-226.

Sir Joseph Banks (1744-1820) the English botanist who had previously accompanied Captain Cook on his voyage round the world, paid a visit to Iceland via the Hebrides and Orkney in 1772, the first by an Englishman. Banks' own record was not published (but see Uno von Troil, *Letters on Iceland* (q.v.)). This paper is therefore valuable in reproducing his journal of the tour from July to September, which covers the first fortnight of the stay in Iceland. The article also contains a biographical sketch of Banks, and states the reasons for his trip, which created

Exploration and Travel. 18th-19th centuries

considerable interest amongst the English political establishment. See Haldór Hermansson, *Sir Joseph Banks and Iceland* (q.v.). A sidelight on the Banks expedition appears as an article 'The Hekla lava myth' by Christopher Pulvercroft and Guy Mennell in *Geographical Magazine*, vol. 53, no. 7 (April 1981), p. 433-36. This refers to the provenance of the blocks of lava collected on the trip and given to Kew Gardens with which Banks was connected.

67 Letters on Iceland.
Uno von Troil. London: Richardson; Dublin: Price, 1780. 400p.

'Containing observations on the civil, literary, ecclesiastical and natural history, antiquities, volcanoes, basaltes, hot springs; customs, dress, manners of the inhabitants, &c. &c.' Von Troil, a young historian, who later became Archbishop of Sweden, accompanied Sir Joseph Banks to Iceland in 1772. His account is the chief source of information on this expedition, and it set standards which the majority of travellers to Iceland during the following century failed to match in terms of presentation and objectivity. Von Troil's volume comprises the text of twenty-five letters (twenty-two in his own hand) each on a different topic of investigation; in addition to those features listed in his subtitle above there are reports on housing, food, employment, diseases (particularly elephantiasis), fishing and farming, and printing. The work is preceded by a catalogue of 120 items about Iceland written between 1561 and 1779, arranged chronologically, and reproduces Ericssen and Schooning's map of Iceland in 1770. Translated via the German edition of J. G. P. Möller from the original Swedish edition of 1777, this is one of the outstanding records in the history of European travel.

68 The journals of the Stanley expedition to the Faroe Islands and Iceland in 1789. Volume 1: Introduction and diary of James Wright.
Edited and annotated by John F. West. Tórshavn, Faroe Islands: Føroya Fróðskaparfelag, 1970. 216p.

John Thomas Stanley, member of an eminent family (he was the great-grandfather of Bertrand Russell) organised this expedition to the North Atlantic islands at the remarkably early age of twenty-two, probably stimulated by reports of Banks' voyage seventeen years earlier. The expedition is notable for the clear and systematic diary kept by James Wright, who was only nineteen at the time, and was killed in a riding accident five years later. Stanley himself annotated and illustrated Wright's diary and the other two diaries of the expedition kept by Isaac Benners (published as the second volume of this set in 1975) and by John Baine (vol. 3, 1976). This present edition is finely produced and contains extensive and valuable notes by the editor which illuminate many parts of the diary, and on the expedition, which returned to Edinburgh after seven months. An interesting critique of Stanley's expedition entitled 'John Thomas Stanley and Iceland: sense and sensibility of an eighteenth century explorer' was contributed by Andrew Wawn to *Scandinavian Studies*, vol. 53, no. 1 (winter, 1981), p. 52-76, in which he analyses the reasons for Stanley's increasing enthusiasm for Iceland, which was becoming reflected in the outlook of other travellers.

69 Journal of a tour in Iceland in the summer of 1809.
Sir William Jackson Hooker. London: Longman, 1813. 2nd ed. 2 vols.

Hooker, a protégé of Joseph Banks, was primarily a botanist, and, stimulated by the account of von Troil, accepted an invitation to board the *Margaret and Anne*,

Exploration and Travel. 18th-19th centuries

which was sailing to Iceland for commercial purposes. As things turned out, his journal of the trip, as well as being the first full-length account of Iceland and its natural history written by an Englishman, is also a work of historical importance, as Hooker records in some detail his unwitting involvement in the extraordinary events in Iceland in 1809 concerning the 'coup' by Jorgen Jorgensson (Alan E. Boucher 'An Icelandic revolution' (q.v.)) about which he is the chief English source. Despite this distraction, Hooker did manage to reach the Hekla and Laki volcanoes, and also toured the Borgarfjörður district in the west, recording and collecting specimens; these, and his original diary were lost in the confusion of the return trip. The first edition of his journals he had privately printed at Yarmouth in 1811.

70 Travels in the island of Iceland during the summer of the year MDCCCX.
Sir George Steuart MacKenzie.   Edinburgh: Constable, 1810. 491p. map. illus.

MacKenzie (1784-1848) planned his visit to Iceland primarily as a mineralogist (he was President of the Physical Class of the Royal Society of Edinburgh), and this volume contains a lengthy chapter on the mineralogy of Iceland, in addition to the account of his travels. One of his travelling companions was Henry Holland of Edinburgh University, whose contributions to the volume are scarcely less significant than those of MacKenzie himself: Holland wrote a substantial preliminary dissertation on the history and literature of Iceland, chapters on government and education, and an appendix on the diseases of Icelanders. His second companion, like Holland barely of age, was Richard Bright, whose interest was in biology. MacKenzie's journal throws much light on the geographical, social and economic conditions in Iceland at the start of the 19th century. The volume is enhanced with a variety of sketchings, some in colour, and includes a folding map drawn by MacKenzie showing the course of his journey around south-western Iceland. The second edition of this work, published one year later, contains an appended chapter on the so-called revolution of 1809 (see Alan E. Boucher 'An Icelandic revolution' (q.v.)); this incident had been omitted from the first edition through 'motives of delicacy'.

71 Iceland: or, the journal of a residence in that island during the years 1814 and 1815.
Ebenezer Henderson.   Edinburgh: Waugh & Innes, 1818. 2 vols.

The subtitle continues 'containing observations on the natural phenomena, history, literature and antiquities of the island; and the religion, character, manners and customs of the inhabitants; with an introduction and appendix'. Henderson's journal is substantial and detailed, resulting from a longer period spent in Iceland than that of other travellers in the 19th century. He made three journeys during these two years; the first a round trip of the northern, eastern and southern coasts - foreigners travelling to the east were exceptional in the 19th century; the second and third trips covered the north, the west and (again unusually) the northwestern peninsula. He composed an illuminating introduction to his journal, and appended a long essay on Icelandic poetry. The volumes also include a folding map of his routes, and several fine engravings. Henderson, a Scottish Presbyterian, was in Iceland primarily as a missionary, having spent the previous two years in Copenhagen supervising a translation of the Bible into Icelandic. His efforts to distribute this Bible widely in Iceland explain the extent of his travel and his sojourn there out of season over the winter months. The result is a somewhat sprawling account, but packed with unusual detail, and one which,

Exploration and Travel. 18th-19th centuries

amidst the critical flak often hurled at other accounts by subsequent travellers, emerges, if not unscathed, at least still significant.

72 Visit to Iceland, by way of Tronyem in the 'Flower of Yarrow' yacht in the summer of 1834.
John Barrow. London: Murray, 1835. 320p.

John Barrow was the son of the famous explorer and founder of the Geographical Society. This account of his travels in Iceland is full and carefully recorded. His visit centred on Reykjavík and its environs, including the geysers, which are afforded two observant chapters. A particularly valuable chapter records a variety of statistical data on the social structure of Iceland in the 1830s. There is also an interesting and rare glimpse of the Danish overlordship in the form of Prince Frederick, who was on a visit to Iceland at the time.

73 A winter in Iceland and Lapland.
Arthur Dillon. London: Colbourn, 1840. 2 vols.

The first volume of Dillon's account is devoted to Iceland. It is one of the most readable of the Icelandic diaries, being straightforward, clearly presented and relatively unpatronising. After four chapters of historical synthesis he proceeds to a variety of observations on the natural features of the country and the social organisation of its inhabitants. A fresher dimension is present in view of the season in which Dillon unusually chose to make his visit.

74 An historical and descriptive account of Iceland, Greenland and the Faroe Islands, with illustrations of their natural history.
James Nicol. Edinburgh: Oliver & Boyd, 1840, 416p.; New York: Harper, [1841] 360p.

Perhaps because of its span of three countries, this volume by the Scottish mineralogist Nicol has received less attention than many other accounts of Iceland in the 19th century, although it ran to five editions within a decade. And yet his account is unusual in that, unlike the others, he presents his findings not in the form of a travel diary with comments, but as a thematic exposition of the geography, topography, history, literature, national character and social organisation of Iceland (p. 1-221). He thus edited the notes of his travels into a general study of the land, the people and their culture.

75 Visit to Iceland and the Scandinavian north.
Ida Pfeiffer. London: Ingram; London: Bentley; New York: Putnam, 1852. 354p.

This book was also published under the title *Journey to Iceland and travels in Sweden and Norway*. Notable as the account of the first woman to venture to Iceland (her preface is an eloquent apologia for the travels of a woman alone). Madame Pfeiffer was Austrian, and her visit was made in 1845. Her account is a collection of random and often arrestingly hostile impressions - Pliny Miles (q.v.) refers to her 'snarling, ill-tempered journal' ten years later - which nonetheless offer some insight into ways of life in mid-19th century Iceland. She includes diverse appendices: the salaries of Danish officials; lists of invertebrates and plants collected; an essay on Icelandic poetry from the French of M. Bergman, with an English translation of the Eddic poem *Völuspá*. This edition has eight tinted engravings, and is a translation of the original German edition published in Vienna in 1846.

Exploration and Travel. 18th-19th centuries

76 Bunsen's trip to Iceland.
Ralph E. Oesper, Karl Freudenberg. *Journal of Chemical Education*, vol. 18 (June 1941), p. 253-60.

Robert Wilhelm Bunsen (1811-99), the German chemist of Bunsen burner fame, visited Iceland on an expedition led by von Walterhausen during the summer of 1846 to study the effects of the Hekla eruption of the previous year. He produced a number of scientific papers on his findings in Iceland which appeared in German journals, but this article is a general record of his visit as recounted in the letters sent home to his mother.

77 Norðurfari: or, rambles in Iceland.
Pliny Miles. New York: Norton, 1854. 334p. London: Longman, 252p.

As far as the compiler can ascertain, this is the first account of travel in Iceland by an American (indeed, only a half dozen of his countrymen followed him during the rest of the century). It may, therefore, be more than coincidental that this is one of only a handful of 19th-century foreign accounts of Iceland to display a genuine affection for the country, and is almost unique in its willingness to accept Iceland on its own terms. Miles' journey was around the south-west of the country: Reykjavík - Þingvellir - Geysir - Hekla - Krísuvík. Along the way he writes as he feels about the scenery, natural history especially bird life, the people as a whole and as individuals, and about their cultural history. Not the weightiest of the older accounts of Iceland, but one which should be read as a counterbalance to the loftier toned accounts of the period. It also displays an engaging and off-beat sense of humour.

78 Letters from high latitudes... 1856.
Lord Frederick Dufferin. London: Murray, 1857. 428p.

Lord Dufferin (alias Frederick Temple Hamilton Temple Blackwood, Marquis of Dufferin and Ava!) shared many of the characteristics shown by Victorian travellers in their records of Iceland: the self assurance, the occasional patronising, the strange mixture of superficial comment and unusual observation. One characteristic, however, which distinguishes Dufferin's account is the sense of humour shown in this series of lengthy letters, which anticipate the mood of W. H. Auden's letters (q.v.) - Auden, in fact, asterisks Dufferin in his bibliography as especially recommended reading. The tone of this volume is set by Dufferin's listing of the dramatis personae, a cast who accompanied him around southern and western Iceland, and on the more adventurous escapades in his schooner yacht to Jan Mayen Island and Spitsbergen. The volume is illustrated, and includes a map of the routes, and a chronological list of climatological observations. It was published in various editions subsequently.

79 Tracings of Iceland and the Faroe Islands.
Robert Chambers. Edinburgh: Chambers, 1856. 85p.

Robert Chambers was a publisher and journal editor who went to Iceland with little more motive than to fill the pages of his renowned *Chambers' Journal* with something out of the ordinary. His account is brief and contains few surprises, but in attempting to convey to his subscribers the feeling of seeing for the first time a country physically so near to Scotland, yet in other ways so remote, he is appealingly successful. Six years later another notable Scot, the medical scientist Alexander Bryson, turned reporter by serialising his 'Notes of a trip to Iceland in 1862' in the *Scottish Guardian*. He later had them published as a collection (Edinburgh: Grant, 1864. 56p.).

Exploration and Travel. 18th-19th centuries

80 Iceland: its volcanoes, geysers and glaciers.
Charles S. Forbes. London: Murray, 1860. 356p. map. illus.

An energetic account of a journey in 1859, in which the author, a naval commander, displays a nice mixture of reflection and joviality in his observations of the natural phenomena of south-western Iceland, and in his description of intervening encounters. Folding map and many fine drawings.

81 The Oxonian in Iceland.
Frederick Metcalfe. London: Longman, 1861. 424p. map.
Reprinted New York: AMS Press, 1977.

Metcalfe's tour of Iceland in the summer of 1860 was one of the longer of the Victorian tours. His observations on the southern part cover no new ground, but in the north he seems to have stopped at and recorded impressions of an unusual number of places; and as an Oxford don with a keen interest in Old Icelandic literature he visited several locations with saga connections. His tone is somewhat elevated and uncompromising in parts, but the volume is a substantial record, and deserves its recent reprinting. Includes folding map.

82 The north-west peninsula of Iceland: being the journal of a tour in Iceland in the spring and summer of 1862.
C. W. Shepherd. London: Longman, Green, 1867. 162p. map.

Shepherd visited Iceland twice, having been there also in 1861; but then this was boom time for British travel in Iceland -no fewer than nine separate accounts exist over a six year period. Shepherd's belief that his exploration of the northwest was the first foreign attempt is not fully true, as Henderson (q.v.) had been there nearly half a century earlier. However, this is the first diary specifically devoted to the north-western peninsula (he also sailed round to Skagafjörður and Eyjafjörður) and as such offers fresh interest. Shepherd was an ornithologist, and his account contains several observations on the bird life of the region. Folding map (after Olsen) shows author's route: Reykjavík - Steingrímsfjörður - Ísafjörður - Mývatn. The events of his previous trip, which likewise included the peninsula, but also Vatnajökull and an attempted ascent of Öræfajökull, are recorded by his companion E. T. Holland in *A tour to Iceland in the summer of 1861* which appeared in the first volume of the second series of *Peaks, passes and glaciers* (London: Longman for the Alpine Club, 1862).

83 Iceland: its scenes and sagas.
Sabine Baring-Gould. London: Smith, Elder, 1863. 447p.

An extensive account of a journey made in 1862 up the western side and along the north of Iceland as far as the Dettifoss waterfall. Random and very entertaining observations are offered concerning the natural history en route, and there is an important appendix by Alfred Newton on the ornithology, p. 399-421. Baring-Gould's main motives, however were to visit the scenes made famous by the sagas, and 'to fill a sketchbook'.

84 Travels by 'Umbra'.
C. C. Clifford. Edinburgh: Edmonston & Douglas, 1865, 278p.

Pages 1-164 of this book are taken up with a curious account of a trip to Iceland. The party is described by the author, who, as 'Umbra', reveals his identity neither

Exploration and Travel. 18th-19th centuries

on the title page nor in the course of his account, in an introduction which is self-effacingly witty, and which sets the tone of the expedition: his companions include a Scot who was a born leader; an Irish eccentric; a member of parliament, 'Mr X'; a Norse antiquarian and a geologist. One assumes that this trip did take place, although the report of it is presented largely in the form of an off-beat dialogue between the characters on topics which often have little to do with the matter in hand. However, the presence of Iceland is occasionally acknowledged as the party travels to Snæfellsness via Surtshellir, Reykholt, Laxádalur, Hítardalur and Ólafsvík. 'Umbra' was in fact Sir Charles Hugh Cavendish Clifford, 8th Baron Clifford of Chudleigh, Devon (1819-80).

85 The land of Thor.
John Ross Browne. New York: Harper; London: Sampson Low, 1867. 542p.

Iceland was the last port of call on a long journey made by the American Browne across northern Europe from Russia westwards. The last hundred pages of his book are devoted to Iceland. Impressionistic and anecdotal in style, it is rather more mellow than other accounts of the period. One chapter is a homage to his Icelandic guide Geir Zoëga, a family name later to become respected in lexicographical circles. The Icelandic part of the journey Browne also recorded in the first three issues of *Harper's Magazine* for 1863.

86 A summer in Iceland.
Carl W. Pajkull, translated by M. R. Barnard. London; Chapman & Hall, 1868. 364p.

Translated from the Swedish edition of the previous year this work is one of the trio of really fine accounts in Iceland written by Swedes, one from each of the last three centuries. Pajkull, a professor of geology at the University of Uppsala, continues the standard set by von Troil in the 18th century and anticipates that of Lindroth in the 20th century. There is a quality common to each of these three accounts, which can be attributed only to a Scandinavian affinity with Iceland. Pajkull visited Iceland in 1865, south and north, and his account is both pleasant to read and wideranging in its observations. There is a blend of authority and humility in his presentation which displays both a keen mind and a genuine affection. The translated version appends a list of the flora and fauna of Iceland after the French scientist Paul Gaimard.

87 Journals of travels in Iceland.
William Morris. In: *The collected works of William Morris*. Edited by May Morris, London: Longman, 1911. vol. 8.

William Morris made two journeys to Iceland, in 1871 and 1873. He composed a substantial journal, subsequently edited by his daughter. It has been studied mainly for the light which it sheds on Morris himself rather than on Iceland; this is unfortunate, for Morris' account has a flavour quite different from that of other Victorian accounts, being neither effusive nor dismissive (passages have been described by John Purkis as anti-travel writing). He is most akin in spirit to his contemporary in Icelandic travel, James B. Bryce (q.v.), underplaying his genuine respect and fondness for the country before choosing the important occasion to prove it. Morris travelled from south-west to north by two varying routes, and included a long look at Njála territory, motivated by his friend Eiríkur Magnússon, and by his ideas for the magnum opus *Earthly Paradise*. There has been a welcome reprint of Morris' account under the title *Icelandic journals*, with an introduction by James Morris (Fontwell, England: Centaur Press, 1969. 251p.). These travels are discussed and viewed as a crucial stage in Morris'

Exploration and Travel. 18th-19th centuries

development by John Purkis in his admirable booklet *The Icelandic jaunt: a study of the expeditions made by Morris to Iceland in 1871 and 1873* (Kew, England: William Morris Society, 1962. 28p.).

88 Memories of travel.
James B. Bryce. London: MacMillan, 1923. 2 vols.

'Impressions of Iceland' (p. 1-43) is but one chapter of several devoted to travels in different parts of the world by the eminent British statesman Viscount Bryce (see James B. Bryce, *Primitive Iceland* (q.v.)), it has earned a remarkably consistent citation in later works on Iceland. A clue to the chord which it has struck for many readers lies in Bryce's first paragraph: 'all I desire to do here is to give some sort of notion of the kind of impression which the scenery and the people make upon a passing traveller - a thing which is what one chiefly wishes to know about strange countries, though it is often that which is hardest to convey'. Over a century after it was written in autumn 1872 (these memoirs were collated by his family and published posthumously) this essay still stirs, and one can perhaps forgive the author's lack of prescience when he writes 'Iceland had a glorious dawn and has been in twilight ever since; it is hardly possible that she should again be called on to play a part in European history'. This misjudgment is compounded by J. H. Reynolds in an article comparing Bryce's impressions with his own, formed fifty years later 'Iceland in 1872 and 1926', *Geographical Journal*, vol. 70, no. 1 (July 1927), p. 44-49, when he proclaims Iceland as 'destined to remain a backwater of civilisation'.

89 Ultima Thule: or, a summer in Iceland.
Richard F. Burton. London: Nimmo, 1875. 2 vols.

Sir Richard Francis Burton visited Iceland in 1872 and this is his scholarly, provocative and extremely entertaining account, full of acute observations, not all uncritical of life in Iceland. He discusses the classical historiography of the word Thule and the physical and political geography of Iceland, its social anthropology, education and the professions, and taxation. There follows a critical bibliography of the writings of previous travellers to Iceland, and advice on preparations for travelling thither. His travels took him to Reykjavík and environs, Stykkishólmur, Hekla and Geysir, Mývatn, Djúpivogur etc. He appends a substantial essay on sulphur in Iceland. The volumes contain some unusual illustrations and a detailed map upon which are superimposed the routes of Burton's three separate journeys. Also of interest is the author's preface in which he rejects what he sees as the credulous and sensational accounts of some earlier travellers. Sir George Dasent reviews Burton's accounts of Iceland in 'Iceland and its explorers' which appeared in *Edinburgh Review*, vol. 143 (Jan. 1876), p. 222-50. He claims 'Burton would have succeeded much better in his discoveries had he not evidently despised the natural obstacles of the island and the character of the people'. Burton was defended against this charge by C. G. W. Lock (q.v.).

90 To Iceland in a yacht.
R. Angus Smith. Edinburgh: Edmonston & Douglas, 1873. 153p.

Robert Angus Smith, a notable research chemist specialising in atmospherics, visited Iceland in autumn 1872 at the age of fifty-five in the yacht of his fellow Scot, the chemist James Young. His account was privately printed, but his observations also resulted in a paper on fogs in Iceland, presented in *Memoirs of the Literary & Philosophical Society of Manchester*, 3rd series, vol. 5 (1876), p. 150-64.

Exploration and Travel. 18th-19th centuries

91 Off to the geysers: or, the young yachters in Iceland.
C. A. Stephens. Philadelphia: Winston, 1873. 238p. (Camping Out Series).

A remarkable record as the earliest example of a youth party fieldtrip to Iceland (a form of expedition to become popular a century later). These youthful New Englanders set off with their tents and saw what they had planned to see, mainly the geysers, which they observed at greater length than some travellers, and the Mývatn/Námaskard́ area. The account is a lively mixture of description and dialogue, with considerable evidence of preliminary 'homework'.

92 Egypt and Iceland in the year 1874.
Bayard Taylor. New York: Putnam; London: Sampson Low, 1874. 282p.

It is indeed rare to receive two accounts of the same visit to Iceland. Bayard Taylor, the noted American traveller and translator, also recorded the millennial events described in Samuel Kneeland's book (q.v.). His impressions are more immediate and less substantial - he had sampled sub-tropic and sub-Arctic conditions, and published this account of both experiences (Iceland forms the second half of this book) all within the space of a few months, but the book proved very popular and was re-issued several times between 1874 and 1902. Taylor was also accorded an honour in Iceland when his poem *America to Iceland*, included in the text, was translated into Icelandic by the national poet Matthías Jochumsson.

93 An American in Iceland: an account of its scenery, people and history.
Samuel Kneeland. New York: Burt, 1875. Boston, Massachusetts: Lockwood Brooks, 1876. 326p.

Kneeland was Professor of Zoology at the Massachusetts Institute of Technology, and was one of a party of five Americans of note - including Bayard Taylor (q.v.) - who made an official visit to Iceland via Orkney, Shetland and Faroe in connection with Iceland's millennial celebrations in August 1874. He describes the royal reception and the festivities, but his main concern is describing the people, drawing comparisons between the character of Iceland and America. He also concentrates on the country's natural phenomena, particularly its volcanic history, including the eruptions in the Vatnajökull region during 1874 and 1875 (which he missed). Richard Tomasson has justifiably described Kneeland as 'the last of the scholarly generalists to come to Iceland'.

94 Six weeks in the saddle: a painter's journal in Iceland.
S. E. Waller. London: MacMillan, 1874. 177p. illus.

A gentle rather than eventful diary of a summer journey across southern Iceland, inspired by a reading of *Njáls saga*, the settings of which were to be the painter's destination. The feature of this trip which was unusual for the 19th century was that it was made alone, without companions, and this seems to give the diary a rather mellower and more intimate flavour. Includes fifteen sketches.

95 By fell and fjord: or, summer scenes in Iceland.
Elizabeth Jane Oswald. Edinburgh: Blackwood, 1882. 282p. maps.

Although not one of the profounder descriptions of travel in Iceland, this record covers more territory and offers a greater range of impressions of life than do

Exploration and Travel. 18th-19th centuries

many others. The reason for this is that the authoress made three trips to Iceland within the space of five years, in 1875, 1878 and 1879. This implies an enthusiasm for the country, which indeed emerges from many of the pages. Her original motive was to relate the sagas to their settings, although she is less than aware in suggesting that her account is the first to do so. Her trips did in fact take her to most of the major saga scenes, and she was ready to be sidetracked on the way. Includes folding maps of sagasteads visited.

96 Home of the Eddas.
Charles G. Warnford Lock. London: Sampson Low, 1879. 348p. map.

Although on the surface this volume is yet another of the rather disjointed and superficial diaries which Iceland attracted in quantity during the 19th century, it is worth perusal on two counts: firstly, its author, being a Fellow of the Icelandic Literary Society, was fortified in his travels by an academic knowledge of Iceland's heritage, rather than inspired by curiosity alone; secondly, he spent a full year (1875-76) in Iceland, which is somewhat longer than many diarists, and thus was not confined to the summer months, nor to the better known locations (there is an emphasis on the north-eastern region). Characteristically in the case of diaries of Icelandic travel, the appendices are randomly interesting: they include an account of the traverse of Sprengisandur by C. Le Neve Foster; a review of a review of Burton's *Ultima Thule* (q.v.) which had appeared in the *Edinburgh Review* in 1876 - an exchange not without ill-feeling; an explanation of Icelandic topographical names used in the volume; and a compendium of practical information for tourists. Index to local names, and a Royal Geographical Society map are included. This Lock is not to be confused with the W. G. Lock, his contemporary (q.v.), the latter being highly critical of the former in his introduction.

97 Across the Vatnajökull: or, scenes in Iceland.
William Lord Watts. London: Longman, 1876. 202p.

The extension of Watts' title 'being a description of hitherto unknown regions' was no false claim, at least as far as foreign expeditionaries were concerned. His journey was the first serious attempt at exploring the Vatnajökull (others had explored the perimeter) as Watts made a crossing of the western section from Núpsstaður to Kistufell, before proceeding to Mývatn and the north. This part of his trip was fortuitously interrupted by the Askja eruptions of 1875, which he was thus able to witness and report upon in some detail. Further notes are presented on his sojourn in Mývatns öræfi. He concludes with a retrospective essay on the physical characteristics of Iceland. The book includes one general and one local map delineating the author's routes. The previous year Watts had written a volume entitled *Snioland: or, Iceland, its jokulls and fjalls* (London: Longman, 1875, 183p.). This is a report of a preliminary trip to Iceland, taking in Geysir, Hekla, Mýrdalsjökull, and, importantly, an ascent of Vatnajökull in 1874, marginally to the east of his subsequent traverse.

98 How the 'Mastiffs' went to Iceland.
Anthony Trollope, with illustrations by Mrs Hugh Blackburn. London: Virtue, 1878. 46p.

The record of a trip to Iceland in the summer of 1878, comprising a variety of personages, among them the English novelist Trollope. The voyage by a steamer named *Mastiff* in the service of the Scottish and Irish Royal Mail, was not particularly adventurous, but the account is enlivened by Trollope's style. The route took the party to St. Kilda and the Faroes on the way to Reykjavík, whence it ventured inland only as far as the Geysir and Þingvellir areas by pony. Trol-

Exploration and Travel. 18th-19th centuries

lope's impressions of scenes and people illuminate both life in the North Atlantic and the attitudes of Victorian travellers abroad.

99 A narrative of the voyage of the Argonauts in 1880.
William Mitchell Banks. Edinburgh: Argonauts, 1881. 134p. photographs.

Another limited voyage to Iceland via the Faroes, recorded by the eminent Victorian surgeon Mitchell Banks. His party, like Trollope's, confined itself to the Reykjavík - Þingvellir, Geysir axis. An entertaining account with photographs by Richard Caton.

100 Five weeks in Iceland.
C. A. de Fonblanque. London: Bentley, 1880. 180p.

It is not unfair to say that by the end of the 1870s the century of major travels and accounts concerning Iceland was, with a handful of exceptions, coming to an end. From then on there appeared a series of books by visitors who, profiting from the better knowledge of conditions in Iceland supplied by previous travellers, visited the country in a spirit of recreation rather than to impress the cognoscenti. This detracts from their value, but not from their capacity to entertain. One of the early examples of this category is this account by de Fonblanque who writes, with a mixture of good spirits and poor patience, of his party's month long stay in the south-west. Of similarly mild impact is an account of a stay in the same region for the same duration, one year earlier by N. L. van Gruisen, called *A holiday in Iceland* (London: Elliot Stock, 1879. 98p.).

101 Summer travelling in Iceland.
John Coles. London: Murray, 1882. 269p.

Coles was a professional geographer, but his book is directed more towards the tourist and his expectations. The two journeys which he describes take him around the south-west, and through Sprengisandur to Mývatn and the north. There is a separate chapter by E. Delmar Morgan on Askja. An appendix gives advice on equipment and expenses, and Coles also includes translations of three shorter sagas: *Þorðr*, *Bandamanna* and *Hrafnkel*. There is, unusually for this period a good general index. Coles' book is a pleasure to read - we are now passing from the physically cramped editions and small typefaces of earlier accounts. There is also a marked difference in approach, as Coles displays a clear sympathy with the terrain and its inhabitants, thus evoking a warmer and more attractive impression than many of his predecessors saw fit to convey.

102 From England to Iceland: a summer trip to the Arctic Circle.
George Charles Sim. Bradford, England: Gaskarth, 1886. 120p. illus.

This book is a reprinting of a series of pieces which originally appeared in the columns of the *Bradford Illustrated Weekly Telegraph* in 1885, recording a trip from Bradford to Akureyri via the Westmann Islands, Reykjavík, Geysir, Þingvellir, and by boat to the Arctic Circle, a voyage which included an encounter with the Icelandic luminary Jón A. Hjaltalín. The author's account gains much from its use throughout of the historic present. Although this is one of the lesser known accounts of British travel to Iceland, it is commendably digestible, and is a finely-produced little volume which contains eight highly unusual plates, each being a pastiche from several photographs of places visited.

Exploration and Travel. 18th-19th centuries

103 A girl's ride in Iceland.
Ethel B. Harley. London: Griffith Fraser, 1889. 166p.

Mrs A. Tweedie, as she was otherwise known, was the second woman and the first British woman to explore Iceland. Her tour, entertainingly recorded, was unusual in two other ways: firstly, her land route started in Akureyri and finished in Reykjavík (the reverse direction had been the norm); secondly, her pony was fitted with a man's saddle so that she rode astride (the reverse of Victorian custom for women). A rather more conventional trip on horseback made shortly afterwards by a reverend gentleman was recorded in *A ride across Iceland in the summer of 1891* by William T. McCormick (London: Digby Long, 1892. 103p.).

104 Icelandic pictures drawn with pen and pencil.
Frederick W. W. Howell. London: Religious Tract Society, 1893. 176p. illus.

It is indeed the drawings which form the chief interest of this volume, which is a fine example of late Victorian book production. The drawings, many of them unusual, are to be found on most of its pages, illustrating the scenes observed by Howell, a descriptive geographer, during two trips which he made in 1890 and 1891. Although he kept mainly to the beaten track, his journeys were extensive, via the Faroes to the eastern fjords, the southern ice-caps, Hekla and Njála territory, Þingvellir and Geysir, Reykir and Surtshellir, the north-western peninsula, and northern Iceland - virtually a full circle. An earlier volume of line drawings was A. J. Symington's *Pen and pencil sketches of Faroe and Iceland* with an appendix of Icelandic folk-tales translated by Olaf Pálsson, and fifty-one illustrations engraved in wood by W. J. Linton (London: Longman, 1862. 315p.).

105 Three visits to Iceland.
Mary Charlotte Julia Leith. London: Masters, 1897. 218p.

Another book (by Mrs Disney Leith) put together from pieces in a weekly serial 'for home consumption'. The three visits were made in the summers of 1894, 1895, 1896, the destinations being Skálholt, Geysir and Njála territory. Notes 'as much on man, manners and language as on the natural features'. Appendices include translations of Jónas Hallgrímsson's poem *Gunnar's holm*, and Páll Sigurðsson's tale *Aðalsteinn*. Also a postscript on the earthquake in south-west Iceland in 1896. A rare item. From these travels the authoress also wrote a short book for the younger reader, called *Iceland* (London: Black, 1908, 70p. (Peeps at many lands).).

106 A pilgrimage to the saga steads of Iceland.
W. G. Collingwood, Jón Stefánsson. Ulverston, England: Holmes, 1899. 187p.

Not the first trip motivated by the saga settings, but the most purposeful, and a precursor of the sort of trip which has become popular of late. A large format volume, notable for some fine sketches, describing the scenic backgrounds of individual sagas, including Njála territory, Borg *(Egils saga)*, Snæfellsness *(Eyrbyggja saga)*, Hvammsfjörður *(Laxdaela)*, Hrútafjörður *(Kormák)*, Eyjafjörður *(Víga-Glúm)*, and several others. Contains map, plus index of landmarks and characters.

Exploration and Travel. 20th century

107 **Notes on the geography, geology, agriculture and economics of Iceland.**
H. J. Johnston-Lavis. *Scottish Geographical Magazine*, vol. 11 (1895), p. 441-66.
Report of a journey across southern Iceland, with observations on the Reykjanes peninsula, Þingvellir, Geysir, Hekla, Mýrdalsjökull, Skaftárdalur and Laki. The author, a volcanologist, makes comparisons between the Icelandic landscape and the volcanic regions of continental Europe, seeing Icelandic volcanism as continual rather than phased.

Explorations in Iceland during the years 1881-1898.
See item no. 178.

Travels in Iceland (1752-1757).
See item no. 218.

The Faroes and Iceland: studies in island life.
See item no. 220.

Ruins of the saga time: being an account of travels and explorations in Iceland in the summer of 1895.
See item no. 270.

20th century

108 **Across Iceland.**
William Bisiker. London: Arnold, 1902. 236p. maps.
Landfall for this trip in 1900 was made from the Faroes at Seyðisfjörður on the east coast of Iceland - an unusual starting point, thence around the northern coast to Eyjafjörður, down through Kjölur to the south-west, up the western side via Reykholt and Surtshellir caves, across Snæfellsness and Breiðafjörður, and back round the north coast. Compared with many previous itineraries this one was commendably ambitious. The account is a mixture of anecdotes and scientific observation. Appendix by A. W. Hill on plants collected. Maps, including itinerary.

109 **Iceland: horseback tours in saga land.**
Waterman S. C. Russell. Boston, Massachusetts: Badger; Toronto: Copp Clark, 1914. 314p. illus.
Russell, like Oswald (q.v.) for whose account he expresses admiration, is to be noted for the fact that he visited Iceland repeatedly. He made four trips in all between 1909 and 1913, and travelled both widely and off the beaten track. His approach was to dwell at each place of interest and to compose a chapter evoking the essential characteristics of each location. Apart from the more frequented areas, Russell has long chapters on Krísuvík, Seyðisfjörður, Krafla, Vatnsdalur and Reykholt. He seems to have taken care to establish contact with Icelandic advisers. His book includes many of his own photographs, and an indication of his itineraries drawn on the map of Þorvaldur Þoroddsen. It deserves to be reprinted. See Russell's description of the volcano Askja in *Geographical Review*, vol. 3 (1917), p. 212-21.

Exploration and Travel. 20th century

110 **Across Iceland: the land of frost and fire.**
Olive Murray Chapman. London: Bodley Head; New York: Dodd Mead, 1930. 193p.

A straightforward and particularly readable account of the authoress' journeys in south-western and northern Iceland in 1929. She takes a geographer's view from her vantage point on the back of an Icelandic pony. A keenly observed description.

111 **A walking tour across Iceland.**
Isobel Wylie Hutchinson. *National Geographic Magazine*, vol. 53, no. 4 (Aug. 1928), p. 467-98.

Another combination of woman and pony along the coastal route from Reykjavík to Akureyri, a journey vividly described in this article by an American lady, who returned to Iceland several years later to travel the inland route from south to north, a journey which she described in an article that she may be forgiven for calling 'It's a long way to Akureyri: across Iceland by foot and pony', *American-Scandinavian Review*, vol. 22, no. 2 (June 1934), p. 142-52.

112 **Tramping through Iceland.**
D. M. Ramsden. Liverpool, England: Young, 1931. 128p.

A lively account of a not particularly ambitious trip by boat from south to north, returning overland. Ice floes off the north coast, a round trip from Akureyri to Dettifoss waterfall, and the standard triangle of Gullfoss, Geysir and Þingvellir.

113 **Icelandic journal.**
Alice Selby. *Saga-book* (UK), vol. 19 (1974-77), p. 1-97.

Alice Selby was head of the English Department at the University of Nottingham during the 1940s, and taught Old Icelandic studies. She had travelled to Iceland in the summer of 1931, and her impressions of the journey from Reykjavík to Akureyri and Skagafjörður form the content of this diary. The route was well worn by now, but her observations make unusually appealing reading, and offer an interesting comparison with other less sensitive diaries.

114 **Letters from Iceland.**
W. H. Auden, Louis MacNeice. London: Faber; New York: Random House; Toronto: Ryerson Press, 1937. 253p.

Auden and MacNeice made their celebrated visit to Iceland in 1936, although Auden revisited it in 1965, which provided the occasion for a paperback reprinting with a retrospective foreword by the author. In this collection of the experiences and impressions of their visit, composed in both prose and verse, the mood is sometimes objective, sometimes reflective, and occasionally humorous. Quite apart from the authors' standing as eminent figures in western literature, readers who have themselves travelled widely in Iceland will find that their anthology evokes uncanny memories. MacNeice's *Eclogue from Iceland* is a particularly fine piece, and Auden's letter 'Hetty to Nancy' recounting the experiences of a party of women and schoolgirls on a trip around Langjökull is hilariously composed. Also diverting is the chapter 'Sheaves from sagaland', an anthology of paragraphs quoted from the writings of earlier travellers whose intensely patronising approach (an approach not shared by Auden and MacNeice) is made to show through. Indeed, Auden wrote in 1964 that to him Iceland was 'sacred soil', and that its memory was a constant background to what he was doing. Auden's

Exploration and Travel. 20th century

splendid work as a translator of Old Icelandic poetry is indicated elsewhere in this bibliography.

115 Three acres and a mill.
Robert Gathorne-Hardy. London: Dent, 1939. 361p.

The author of this book was a botanist of considerable repute, although his modest description of himself is as a foreign traveller in search of flowers for his own garden (named in the title) in the Thames valley. The last quarter of this entertaining book is an account of his trip to southern Iceland in 1938 (p. 263-345).

116 Climbing higher: an Iceland adventure.
Elizabeth Yates. London: Black, 1939. 216p. New York: Knopf, 1940. Also published under the title *Quest in the northland.*

An easy and unpretentious, if rather trivial, account of a journey centred on Reykholt and Hekla. A later edition, directed at the younger reader, was published in 1955 by Partridge of London. Elizabeth Yates also compiled a book entitled *Around the year in Iceland* (Boston: Hall, 1942. 64p.).

117 They sent me to Iceland.
Jane Goodell. New York: Washburn, 1943. 248p.

In December 1941 a party of eleven women from the American Red Cross group was despatched to Iceland in the wake of the American occupation. Their brief was to supply 'recreation' for the armed forces in Iceland. One of their number saw fit to write an account of their experiences, mainly at the Reykjavík centre, and later in Akureyri (by which time eight centres of the Red Cross were functioning in Iceland). The style is romping, only occasionally reflective, and although the book has no pretensions to serious reportage, it is still of more than nostalgic interest for its view from a different angle of aspects of wartime Iceland and of the behaviour of the visiting forces. It should perhaps be added that the commanding officers come out of this account rather less favourably than the ordinary soldiers.

118 Icelandic spring.
Dorothy Una Ratcliffe, with decorations by Barbara Arnason. London: Bodley Head, 1950. 128p.

A delightful little volume comprising twelve letters (originally sent by the author Mrs Una McGrigor Phillips to the *Cumberland and Westmorland Herald*) recounting the impressions of two trips to Iceland in the spring of 1948 and the summer of 1949; the summer trip involved the circumnavigation of the country by the steamship *Esja* (a service which was sadly suspended in the early 1970s). The letters are interspersed with poems and drawings.

119 Summer saga: a journey in Iceland.
Robin Bryans. London: Faber, 1960. 189p.

A book by a professional travel writer rather than a specialist on Iceland, though nonetheless entertaining for that. The style is excessively jaunty and in places frivolous, but the author travelled more widely through Iceland than many other recent raconteurs, and his description contains variety and occasional insight. It is

Exploration and Travel. 20th century

easy to read, and its portraits of Icelandic scenes and characters will entice the first-time visitor.

120 Home is a tent.
Myrtle Simpson. London: Travel Book Club, 1964. 192p.

Part two of this book (sandwiched between accounts of Spitsbergen and Surinam) is entitled 'Iceland holiday'. Nothing special, except for the motive: realise that Iceland is an unusual place to make for; lay a map of Iceland on the floor; pick out without too much thought what seems to be a remote area; make for it singlemindedly with a tent. The spot in question is Hesteyri on Hornstrandir, the most extreme north-western peninsula of Iceland. The author takes it as she finds it, as do her two small children and one baby. Iceland as it should be visited.

121 The Viking Circle.
Colin Simpson. Sydney: Angus & Robertson, 1966. London: Hodder, 1967. 366p.

A book in which the Australian travel writer records impressions of the six 'Viking' countries. Iceland, as is usual in books on Scandinavia as a whole receives relatively fleeting treatment in a chapter entitled: 'Iceland: the strange crucible', p. 259-92. The style is beckoning rather than authoritative, as the author ventures in some comfort from Reykjavík to the sites of Iceland's natural phenomena. A diverting book for the traveller to compare first impressions, and, of course, the idea of taking in all the Scandinavian countries on a round trip is attractive, if expensive.

122 May in Iceland: a painter's journal.
Keith Grant. *London Magazine*, n.s. vol. 10, no. 2 (May 1970), p. 5-18.

Impressions of travel in southern and northern Iceland during May (in many ways the most rewarding month for seeing Iceland) by a British painter who had won a scholarship from the Icelandic government. He writes about Iceland and its landscape through the painter's eyes, and because of this, his essay, though short, is remarkably fresh, sympathetic and, above all, evocative: 'the continuous light, the resonant colour, the sudden green, the space, birds... I wonder how many more journeys to the north before I am cured'.

Iceland: routes over the highlands..
See item no. 131.

Iceland adventure: the double traverse of the Vatnajökull by the Cambridge expedition.
See item no. 206.

Land of ice and fire.
See item no. 207.

Iceland summer: adventures of a bird painter.
See item no. 241.

Exploration and Travel. Ocean-faring accounts

Ocean-faring accounts

123 **North Cape.**
F. D. Ommanney. London: Longman, 1939. 252p.

A book which conveys a vivid impression of the life of the trawlerman, in this case on board a vessel from Grimsby bound for the North Cape, the most northerly point of the forbidding north-western corner of Iceland. The account is now over forty years old but the characters depicted and their reactions to the inhospitable Icelandic waters are probably timeless.

124 **Dreamers of the day: an Arctic adventure.**
David Lewis. London: Gollancz, 1964. 191p.

Strictly speaking this was not an Arctic adventure, although it might have been. The original intention was to sail by catamaran from Britain to Greenland, but, because of an unforeseeable fault in the design of the mast, the north-eastern coast of Iceland at Langanes was the furthest mark reached - a feat in itself. The trip, made in summer 1963, was monitored by the *Guardian* newspaper, and the record of the journey, now in book form will engage any yachtsman. Landfall was made at Seyðisfjörður, where the crew's stay, which included climbs of the nearby Dyrfjöll and Gullþúfa, is briefly described. But the book is really about the waters off eastern Iceland. One of Lewis' crew members, the cook, Merton Naydler gives his own views of the same voyage in *Cook on a cool cat* (London: Temple Press, 1965.).

125 **Vinland voyage.**
J. R. L. Anderson. London: Eyre & Spottiswoode, 1966. 278p.

The discovery of the Vinland Map, which subsequently coloured the study of the Norse colonising voyages to North America, provided the stimulus for another expedition monitored by the *Guardian* newspaper, and equipped by it. This expedition was designed to reproduce, as far as possible, the voyage of Leif Eiríksson in the year 1001. In May and June of 1966 the party, led by the author, sailed in a cutter from Scarborough in Yorkshire, via the Faroe Islands to Reykjavík, and thence to Frederikshaab in Greenland for the crucial voyage to the Massachusetts island of Martha's Vineyard. For a remarkable reconstruction of a voyage claimed for an earlier period, Ireland to Newfoundland via Iceland, see *The Brendan voyage* by Tim Severin (London: Hutchinson, 1978, 292p.).

126 **Sailing Iceland's rugged coasts.**
Wright Britton, photographs by James A. Sugar. *National Geographic*, vol. 136, no. 2 (Aug. 1969), p. 228-65.

A lively account of a voyage right round Iceland in a forty foot yawl. An anti-clockwise trip punctuated by various landings, with associated impressions on the coastal areas of the country.

Exploration and Travel. Ocean-faring accounts

127 Ocean-crossing Wayfarer: to Iceland and Norway in an open boat.
Frank Dye, Margaret Dye. Newton Abbot, England: David & Charles, 1977. 144p. map. photos. diagrs.

Nearly everyone who visits Iceland from the British Isles nowadays does so by international airliner, since the regular direct steamship service was suspended in the 1970s. It seems almost like cheating, or at least missing out, to set foot on Iceland without having experienced a sea crossing. The heightened feeling of adventure, of what it must be like to achieve this on one's own is captured in the first half of this book, which describes the voyage of the authors, experienced seafarers, in their dinghy from the north-western coast of Scotland up across the North Atlantic to landfall in the Westmann Islands after eleven days. Includes photographs, map, diagrams, and appendices on equipment, techniques and the design of the craft. Also described is a second voyage from Scotland to Norway via the Faroe Islands. Another book which dramatically illustrates the theme of man against the sea in an open boat is H. W. Tilman's *Ice with everything* (Lymington, England: Nautical Publishing Company, 1974, 142p.). It describes three voyages to Greenland via Iceland.

Travel Guides

128 **Sailing directions for the fjords, ports and anchorages of Iceland.**
H. D. Jenkins.   London: Imray, 1896. 111p.
This guide, translated from the work of a French frigate captain, was issued in 1862 and supplemented by later information from Danish and American official sources. It is now of interest mainly to the nautical historian, although, of course, much of the information on coastal currents, approaches and landmarks is still relevant for the modern navigator. The guide comprises, in some detail, a circular clockwise description of the coastal hazards and havens of Iceland, the longest section being concerned with the particularly difficult eastern coast. There is a supplementary section on Faroe. Later editions to 1908.

129 **Arctic pilot. Volume II, Iceland, Jan Mayen, Bjørnøya, Svalbard and the east coast of Greenland, together with adjacent areas.**
Taunton, England: Hydrographer of the Navy, 1975. 7th ed. 303p.
A modern development of the type of compendium exemplified by Jenkins (q.v.). First published in 1901, it has been consistently revised for up-to-date navigational requirements. It is arranged in three main sections: Navigation and regulations; Ports; and natural conditions (tides, currents, climate and meteorological tables). These are followed by a detailed description of the features of the coastal waters of Iceland from Ingólfshöfði to Horn (western and eastern semi-circles), p. 47-139. Also includes ninety panoramic sectional views and photographs of Icelandic coastal features, a glossary of Icelandic topographical terms, and an index chart. Supplements are issued between editions, e.g. no. 2, 1978.

130 **Guide to Iceland: a useful handbook for travellers and sportsmen.**
W. G. Lock.   Charlton, England: 1882. 184p. map.
Published privately by the author, this a very early example of the systematic travel guide. The unchanging nature of many of Iceland's natural features makes this guide interesting even today, if not of practical use. Lock describes routes

Travel Guides

and excursions around the country, with notes on angling and shooting, and an orientating chapter on the country and people. Folding map related to the detail of the text. This handbook is extensively drawn upon by Douglas H. Scott in his *Sportsmen's and tourists' handbook to Iceland*, (Leith, Scotland: Turnbull, 1906. rev. ed.).

131 Iceland: routes over the highlands..
Daniel Bruun. Copenhagen; Reykjavík: Gyldendalske Boghandel, 1907. 119p.

This guide, originally sponsored by the Icelandic government, remains three quarters of a century later a worthwhile reference for the traveller who forsakes the well-worn coastal routes for the tracks through central Iceland. The author presents a detailed description of two routes from north to south-west: the first starts from Sauđárkrókur, over Kjölur, between the Langjökull and Hofsjökull glaciers, and on to Reykjavík; the second more easterly route starts from Akureyri or Húsavík; over Sprengisandur, between Hofsjökull and Vatnajökull, down the Þjórsárdalur valley, and thence to the capital. The book includes a folding map detailing the main part of the Kjalvegur and Sprengisandur routes, and a selection of photographs along the way. Summary in Icelandic.

132 Iceland: a handbook.
Compiled and written by Stefán Stefánsson (an Icelandic guide of Reykjavík). Reykjavík: Gutenberg, 1911. 181p.

The third of the main guides written about pre-independent Iceland. The practical value has diminished with time, but there are things to be learnt in compilations such as this about social and economic conditions at the time. The author is better known for his studies of Icelandic flora. Another well known Icelander to have introduced his country to the early tourist was Snæbjörn Jónsson, whose publication 'Where the sun shines at midnight' appeared as a substitute issue of the *Icelandic yearbook* (Reykjavík: Zoëga, 1928. 60p.).

133 Nagel's encyclopaedia guide: Iceland.
Geneva: Nagel, 1982. rev. ed. 191p. maps.

A very well arranged travel guide to Iceland in this publisher's long-established series. It first appeared in 1963 and has run to several updated editions. A general introduction to the geography, history and commerce of the country is followed by a description of Reykjavík, with map, and by details of twenty-five suggested routes for excursions from the capital and from Akureyri, again with maps. Various practical information is appended, including a short vocabulary of traveller's phrases. Not the most comprehensive guide, but it covers the major features adequately and clearly, and appears in a handy small format.

134 Iceland in a nutshell.
Peter Kidson (Karlsson). Reykjavík: Iceland Travel Books, 1974. 4th ed. 240p. maps.

Quite the best travel guide to Iceland - indeed the one that can be recommended without reservation. It contains all the essential details for those visiting the country: background information about Iceland, practical information for day-to-day purposes, how to make the best use of one's time wherever one may be, in Reykjavík, Akureyri or any other of the towns and villages throughout the country. Indispensable to even the most seasoned visitor to Iceland, and enabling the

Travel Guides

traveller to be independent. Maps, plans, etc. Recommended by the Iceland Tourist Board. First edition (1966) entitled *Iceland: a traveller's guide*.

135 Destination Iceland.
Twickenham, England: Twickenham Travel, 1979. 30p.

The best produced and most informative of the various travel brochures directed at those planning organised or semi-organised visits to Iceland. Practically all tours within Iceland are run by Icelandic operators or agencies; what this brochure does is to present a full range of options available as packages. Perusal of this annual brochure will also give some idea of the effort that has been expended in developing tourism in Iceland in a spirit of conservation rather than desecration. A supplementary brochure *Iceland: land of challenge* offers equally informative details of educational visits and expeditions arranged through the same company.

136 On foot in Iceland 1983.
Dick Phillips. Alston, Cumbria, England: Dick Phillips, 1982. 23rd ed. 12p.

Dick Phillips is synonymous with British travel on foot in Iceland. His quarter century of experience of independent travel in Iceland, and of organising tours for walkers, climbers and cyclists is the foundation of his travel service enterprise. He founded, and also manages, the youth hostel at Fljótsdalur in south-west Iceland, and from north-west England runs his travel service and book/map supply agency, specialising in Iceland and Faroe. His annual booklet is a very useful introductory guide for the walker, with information on hostels, tours, etc. for independent travellers, and practical hints.

137 Youth hosteller's guide to Denmark and Iceland.
St. Albans, England: Youth Hostels Association, [n.d.]. 8th rev. ed.

One of the series of guides issued separately from the *Youth hosteller's guide to Europe*. Facilities for youth hostellers in Iceland are not extensive, but at present there are eight proper hostels dotted around the circumference of the country, making a circular trip with this type of accommodation more feasible than was the case in the 1960s. This booklet is only infrequently updated, so further checks should be made for current information.

138 Iceland road guide.
Edited by Örlygur Hálfdánarson, descriptive notes by Steindór Steindórsson frá Hlöðum, English version by Einar Guðjohnsen, Pétur Kidson Karlsson. Reykjavík: Örn og Örlygur, 1981. 3rd ed. 440p. maps.

An invaluable guide to the complete network of roads in Iceland. Based on the original Icelandic edition of 1973, the guide has been published with the co-operation of the Icelandic Survey and the Ministry of Transport. Nine major routes are described with their minor offshoots (including mountain tracks), route one being the road ringing the country. It includes two general maps, east and west, nine area road maps, and road sketches in the margins of the descriptive text; Also twenty-six town plans. Additional information includes road numbers, road signs, tables of distances, altitude of mountain roads, a list of thirty-three viewdials, and addresses of advertisers of enterprises en route. The text concisely

Travel Guides

describes landmarks and sights. A comprehensive publication, indispensable for anyone using the road system.

139 By the roadside: descriptive notes on the route Reykjavík-Akureyri.
Björn Þorsteinsson, translated by Peter Kidson. Reykjavík: Iceland Tourist Bureau, 1962. 50p. maps.

For those who find the *Iceland road guide* (q.v.) rather expensive, and whose journey is confined to the route between the two main centres, this booklet, although elusive, is well worth trying to get hold of. It is a guide to the traditional westerly route from the capital to the north, with historical notes on places of interest, and descriptions of natural features, accompanied by folding side maps of all sections of this journey of 230 miles.

140 Reykjavík within your reach: the city past and present: a walking guide.
Vigdís Finnbogadóttir, Magnús Magnússon. Reykjavík: Bókabúð Máls og Menningar, 1975. 36+16p. plan.

A nicely-produced booklet describing the points of interest on eight short itineraries for the casual walker around the capital, with marginal drawings for identification of buildings, etc. Folding plan of streets in central Reykjavík, one side showing places of interest, the other showing locations of enterprises advertising in the booklet. Text by two Icelanders of renown. Fine for newcomers.

141 Leiðabók: áætlanir sérleyfisbifreiða. (Scheduled bus timetables.)
Reykjavík: Umferðarmáladeild Fólksflutninga. annual. 80p.

The annual timetable (running from May to May) of omnibus services for the whole of Iceland. Full details of the thirty-five routes (excluding local town services) are shown, each with a sketch map, and, surprisingly in these inflationary times, the fares to each destination. Also details of post bus services, hiring of buses, and full tables of distances.

Maps

Modern

142 **Vegakort Ísland.** (Road map of Iceland.)
Reykjavík: Shell Oil Company; Stuttgart, GFR: Mair, updated.

A touring map issued as an oil company promotion. This double-sided folding map on a scale of 1:600,000 (ten miles to the inch) is particularly clear in its delineation of major physical features, towns, villages, settlements, farms, churches, tourist huts, etc. Principal and secondary roads are numbered and well differentiated from the tracks, and also shown (important to the traveller in Iceland) are overall and intermediate distances on the roads in kilometres, plus a mileage chart and key to traffic signs. Shell service stations are marked. Legend in English and Icelandic. Suitable for conventional touring rather than exploring. Also issued as a BP map. 71 x 46 centimetres.

143 **Ísland.** (Tourist roadmap of Iceland.)
Reykjavík: Ferðafélag Íslands, 1979. rev. ed.

A single sheet map issued by the Tourist Association of Iceland, on a scale of 1:750,000 (twelve miles to the inch). Physical features appear on the recto, while roads and tracks, distances, filling stations, tourist huts, etc. are shown on the verso. English legend. 79 x 57 centimetres. A cheaper alternative on a slightly smaller scale of 1:1,000,000 (sixteen miles to the inch) is the topographical general map of Iceland: *Ísland: staðfræðilegt yfirlitskort* published by the Iceland Survey, Landmælingar Íslands. As above, showing towns graded by population, and with road map on reverse. English legend. 53 x 38 centimetres.

144 **Aðalkort yfir Ísland.** (General map of Iceland.)
Reykjavík: Landmælingar Íslands, 1969-71. rev. eds.

One of the official series of topographical maps of Iceland, of which there are nine sheets in all, 70 x 48 centimetres, on a scale of 1:250,000 (four miles to the inch) showing contours at twenty metre intervals, watercourses, roads, tracks, farms, etc. Also available as a set of detailed maps for the tourist *Turistkort*, combined into four double-sided sheets: 1 and 2 cover western Iceland, 3 and 6

Maps. Modern

southern Iceland, 4 and 7 northern Iceland and 8 and 9 eastern Iceland. The same sheetline and scale is used for the geological maps of Iceland *Jarðfrædikort*, again in nine sheets. Coloured series showing lithological, volcanic and glacial features. English legend, plus ten pages of supplementary notes by Guðmundur Kjartansson. Published in Reykjavík by the Cultural Fund.

145 **Atlas blöðin.** (Atlas map.)
Reykjavík: Landmælingar Íslands.

Published in 87 sheets, this is the largest scale general topographical map which covers the whole of Iceland - 1:100,000, or approximately one-and-a-half miles to the inch. Each sheet measures 44 x 60 centimetres and covers 1,760 square kilometres or 680 square miles. Available flat, or folded in stiff cover. The dates of issue of individual sheets vary greatly, with a span of nearly 50 years, although many are recent. Essential for all detailed or specialist trips and expeditions.

146 **Fjórðungsblöðin.** (Quarter sheet.)
Reykjavík: Landmælingar Íslands. new ed.

In this series each sheet covers one quarter of the corresponding sheet of the *Atlas map* (q.v.), on a scale of 1:50,000, i.e. 170 square miles. The series is restricted to western Iceland and to the southern coastal areas, plus the Mývatn region in the north. It comprises 117 sheets in its original issue. The new edition is in progress, and commenced with the Reykjanes peninsula. Also in progress, on a similar scale, 1:40,000, is the *Gróðurkort*, or vegetation map of Iceland, eventually to comprise 430 sheets, showing in colour over 60 types of vegetation, and indicating the nature of the land surface according to vegetation cover and drainage. Some southern and central sheets are so far available. Published by the Agricultural Research Institute and the Cultural Fund of Iceland. See Björn Jóhannesson, *The soils of Iceland* (q.v.).

147 **Sérkort af..** (Special sheet of..)
Reykjavík: Landmælingar Íslands.

A series of special maps of areas of particular interest, including the following: *Surtsey*, 1964. Scale 1:10,000. Contours of the new island by October 1964, with comments in English on the eruptions. *Vestmannaeyjar*, 1973. Scale 1:50,000. Special edition of the *Quarter sheet* no. 49 NW (q.v.), plus town plan inset and aerial photograph of the eruption of 1973. Þingvellir, 1969. Scale 1:25,000. Covers the National Park, its environs and amenities. Reverse shows aerial colour plan, on a scale of 1:3,500, of the site of the Parliament, with key and historical notes in English. *Skaftafell*, 1974. Scale 1:25,000. Published on reverse of sheets 87 and 88 of the *Atlas map* (q.v.), showing the National Park area. *Mývatn*, 1973. Scale 1:50,000. Map of the lake and its environs, showing roads and tracks. Forms an extra issue of the quarter sheet series.

148 **Jarðfrædikort af Reykjavík og nágrenni.** (Geological map of Reykjavík and vicinity.)
Reykjavík: City Council, 1958.

A coloured map of the landforms of the capital's territory on a scale of 1:40,000, measuring 72 x 48 centimetres.

Maps. Modern

149 Reykjavík.
Águst Böðvarsson. Reykjavík: Landmælingar Íslands, 1971.

A double-sided plan of the capital city, its environs and outliers, including Hafnafjöður, Kópavogur, Seltjarnanes, Garðahreppur and Bessastaðahreppur, on a scale 1:15,000 (four inches to the mile), 86 x 56 centimetres. Street names shown with index, also named buildings. Inset of town centre on enlarged scale. Reverse shows southern vicinity, including Hafnarfjörður. Available flat, or folded in card cover.

150 Akureyri.
Reykjavík: Landmælingar Íslands, 1957.

A coloured plan of Iceland's second town and its surroundings on a scale of 1:7,500 (32 x 54 cm.). Reverse contains index of streets, public buildings, farms etc.

151 Ísland: landlagskort. (Iceland: landscape map.)
Reykjavík: Landmælingar Íslands.

Two wall maps of the physical features of Iceland are available under this title: one on a scale of 1:500,000 (111 x 77 centimetres); the other in four sheets on a scale of 1:350,000 (160 x 110 centimetres) pasted together on canvas and mounted with rollers. They display basically the same features as the *General map of Iceland* (q.v.). Another form of map suitable for wall or table display is the attractively produced plastic relief map of Iceland, with relief in eight colours. Scale 1:1,000,000 (24 x 20 centimetres). Best if framed. Likewise published by Landmælingar Íslands.

152 Iceland.
Washington, DC: CIA, 1973.

A handy, though not particularly detailed single sheet map on a scale of 1:1,510,000, delineating basic communications, population distribution, administrative divisions, land utilisation and economic activity. A rather more detailed political/economic map *Islandiya* was published in the same year in Moscow by GUGK (Glavnoe Upravlenie Geodesii i Kartografii).

153 Iceland: official standard names approved by the United States Board on Geographic Names.
Washington, DC: US Government Printing Office, 1961. 231p.

This gazetteer contains around 16,500 entries for places and geographical features in Iceland, listing names approved by the Board, as well as unapproved variants, and appearing on the Geodetic Institute of Copenhagen's maps of Iceland *Uppdráttur Íslands* on scales 1:100,000 and 1:250,000. The arrangement is alphabetical by name of place or feature; each entry is followed by a descriptor, longitude/latitude, and a code number for the *sýsla* (administrative district) or for the independently administered towns in which the place is located. There is also an Icelandic-English glossary of geographical feature elements occurring in Icelandic placenames.

Cartographic history

154 The cartography of Iceland.
Halldór Hermannsson. Ithaca, New York: Cornell University Library, 1931. 81p. (Islandica, vol. XXI).

An extended essay, which remains the only substantial account in English of the history of maps of Iceland and of their makers. The essay is divided into two parts: the maps of the mediaeval period; maps of the 18th and 19th centuries. Photographic plates of twenty-three historical maps are appended. Series reprinted by Kraus. Volume XVII of the same series (1926) contains the same author's essay 'Two cartographers: Gudbrandur Thorláksson and Thórdur Thorláksson'. Bishop Gudbrandur's map of Iceland first appeared in 1585, on the basis of which his great-grandson Þórdur drew a new map around 1670.

155 The changing face of Iceland in a thousand years of maps.
Haraldur Sigurdsson. *Atlantica and Iceland Review*, vol. 9, no. 2 (1971), p. 24-33.

Haraldur Sigurdsson's major work is *Kortasaga Íslands*, published in Reykjavík by the Cultural Fund in 1971; unfortunately, this comprehensive survey of the history of maps of Iceland is available only in Icelandic, with a summary in English, p. 257-66. The English-speaking reader can also be introduced to this work by the article cited, in which the author points out that it is only during the last 150 years that there has been a generally accurate knowledge of the country's configuration by its inhabitants, and introduces many of the attempts to draw maps of Iceland by cartographers from mediaeval times to the 19th century. The article includes a double-page reproduction of Bishop Gudbrandur Þorláksson's map of Iceland (after Ortelius) dated 1590.

156 The Vinland map and the Tartar relation.
R. A. Skelton, Thomas E. Merton, George D. Painter. New Haven, Connecticut: Yale University Press, 1965. 291p.

The discovery of the 'Vinland map' in 1957, a document throwing light on the Norse voyages of discovery to North America, evoked both enthusiastic anticipation and some scepticism. This volume was the starting point for the wide-ranging scholarly discussions of the map's authenticity and its relevance to Norse studies. The map was the first to delineate, albeit notionally, a part of North America.

Regional Geography

General

157 **Offshore geography of northwestern Europe: the political and economic problems of delimitation and control.**
Lewis M. Alexander. Chicago: Rand McNally for the Association of American Geographers, 1963. 162p. bibliog.
Although there have been many national and international developments concerning territorial waters and the law of the sea since this monograph was published, it is still relevant for its broader considerations of the geographical, political and economic aspects of offshore claims (problems which are unlikely to disappear completely whatever the legislation), and for the way in which it sets Iceland in the wider geographical context of the north-west European seaboard rather than for its presentation of Iceland's dispute with Britain in 1958, with which it also deals.

158 **A geography of Norden.**
Edited by Axel Sømme. London: Heinemann; New York: International Publications Service, 1968. rev. ed. 343p. maps. bibliog. graphs. tables.
First published in Norway in 1960, this volume is a standard work on the geography of Denmark, Finland, Iceland, Norway and Sweden: 'the various authors have been in close contact since 1960 in order to maintain the book as a standard work for advanced geography studies abroad'. The first seven chapters are a thematic treatment of Scandinavia as a whole; the last five are geographical surveys of each individual country. The Icelandic section is contributed by Sigurður Þórarinsson, and covers physical goegraphy, agriculture, fisheries, energy, industry, trade, communications, and population. This excellent volume affords the student an opportunity of a comparative approach to Nordic geography. Maps, graphs and tables enhance the text.

Regional Geography. General

159 **An economic geography of the Scandinavian states and Finland.**
W. R. Mead. London: University of London Press, 1958. 302p. maps.

Still a highly-respected work on Scandinavian geography by a proven authority in the field. The treatment is thematic rather than country by country, which is perhaps to Iceland's disadvantage, but there are continual references to Iceland throughout the text which enable the reader to place Iceland in the more general Nordic context of man and the environment in the northern world. Although an updated edition would be welcome, no serious study of the economic geography of Iceland can omit reference to this work. The lucid text is accompanied by many maps and other illustrative materials. For chapters by Mead (Professor of Geography in the University of London) specifically on Iceland, see chapter seven of his book with Wendy Hall, *Scandinavia* (London: Thames & Hudson, 1972), also his contribution to the multi-author volume *Advanced geography of northern and western Europe*, (Amersham, England: Hulton Educational, 1973. 2nd ed. p. 115-32).

160 **Iceland and Greenland.**
Austin H. Clark. Washington, DC: Smithsonian Institution, 1943. 103p. photos.

Published as one of the Smithsonian's War Background Studies, this contribution is notable for its convenience in contrasting the geography, natural history and culture of Iceland and Greenland rather than for anything fresh that it has to say. Includes photographs. Compare the post-war account for the American Geographical Society by Charles M. Boland also entitled *Iceland and Greenland* (New York: Doubleday, 1959, 64p.). The two countries are described together for little reason other than their geographical proximity in a book again called *Iceland and Greenland*, well written for the younger reader by Helen Peck (New York: Abelard Schuman, 1967, 125p.).

161 **Iceland.**
Edited by Brian B. Roberts. London: Admiralty, Naval Intelligence Division, 1942. 498p. map. bibliog. (Geographical Handbook Series).

Originally produced for official purposes during the Second World War as material for Allied discussion of naval, military and political problems, this volume (one of a valuable series on various countries) was eventually and fortunately released for general reference. Although compiled forty years ago, much of its content remains relevant today, and it contains a mine of factual information on the geographical framework of Iceland, its population growth and distribution, and its social and economic administration. There is a particularly informative background bibliography, a useful series of statistical appendices, a thorough index, and in an end pocket a folding map on a scale of 1:1,000,000. A unique and indispensable historical source.

Regional Geography. General

162 A regional geography of Iceland.
Vincent H. Malmström. Washington, DC: National Academy of Sciences, National Research Council, Division of Earth Sciences, 1958. 255p.

A substantial report of field research conducted in 1956, which, surprisingly, remains the most recent systematic treatment in the English language concerning the general geography of Iceland (publishers please note). Aspects covered include physiography, climate, hydrography, flora and fauna, historical geography, population, agriculture, fisheries, energy, industry, transport, trade, social conditions, and political geography. The sections are unevenly treated, and much material needs updating from other sources, but overall this is a very useful survey of Icelandic geography as a coherent environment, and includes many well chosen maps, figures and tables. The reader will emerge aware of all the major indicators, influences and interactions of the country in relation to its development.

163 The rise of Reykjavík: a study in historico-economic geography.
Vincent H. Malmström. *Proceedings of the Minnesota Academy of Science*, vol. 35-36 (1957-58), p. 360-71. maps.

A short study, accompanied by maps, of the site, growth and functional areas of Iceland's capital city. In under two centuries Reykjavík has developed from an insignificant hamlet into a bustling centre which almost completely dominates the economic, political and cultural life of the nation. 'It is perhaps safe to say that the national life of no other nation in the world is so closely bound up with a single city as Iceland's is with Reykjavík'.

164 Isolations and retreat of settlement in Iceland.
Kirk H. Stone. *Scottish Geographical Magazine*, vol. 87, no. 1 (1971), p. 3-13.

A rather complicated method of examining a straightforwardly observable and explicable phenomenon: the geographical isolation of Iceland on national, regional, local, neighbourhood, and individual farming levels, and the patterns of population drift from smaller to larger settlements. It is, however, one of numerous examples in various fields of how Iceland is used as a case-study to test a model, and makes several points of interest on population movements.

Spatial diffusion: an historical geography of epidemics in an island community.
See item no. 413.

Fieldtrips

165 **Icelandic expedition 1965: report.**
Edited by B. H. Rodwell. London: King's College and London School of Economics Geographical Association, 1966. 52p.

Iceland has been the destination for numerous localised fieldtrips conducted by foreign educational institutions, principally British, since the 1950s, and the resulting reports are recommended reading for those planning similar ventures. The usual pattern has been for a team of specialists or enthusiasts in various fields to carry out multi-faceted observation and research on the geography, geology and natural history of a selected area of Iceland, and to produce a synthesised report of the findings. This report is a good example of a 'one-off' expedition, which was based in the Eyjafjörður district of northern Iceland. Another expedition to the same region, also emanating from London, was that of the Chelsea College Biological and Geological Societies, which produced a fifty-two page report on their visit to Bægisárdalur in 1961.

166 **Durham University Vestfirðir project: fieldwork report and research notes.**
B. S. John, M. J. Alexander. Durham, England: Durham University, Department of Geography, 1975. 82p. maps. photos.

This project on the north-western peninsula of Iceland was a continuing exercise, having started in 1973 (previous reports were published for 1973 and 1974). The team of British, American and Icelandic researchers was concerned mainly with glacial response to climatic fluctuations, but several of the earth sciences are represented in the texts of the nine research notes written up in the report. The report includes an introduction to the development and organisation of the project, and notes on the practicalities, along with maps, photographs and further references. Durham's tradition in this field goes back to 1948 when a team was based on Sólheimajökull.

167 **Report of the expedition to Iceland, 1973.**
Newcastle, England: University of Newcastle upon Tyne Exploration Society, 1973. 82p. maps. tables. diagrs.

A three-pronged expedition which established camp on three different forms of terrain: moorland at Arnavatnsheiði and Jónsvatn, west of Eiríksjökull; volcanic desert at Hveravellir; and coastal marshland at Víkingavatn in Axarfjörður in the north - this last location supplied the bulk of the special studies collected in this report. It contains twenty short papers dealing with aspects of the geology, freshwater ecology, and especially the ornithology of the regions. Many tables, diagrams and maps. Typescript, but well presented.

Regional Geography. Fieldtrips

168 **Vestfirðir studies: Farming, fishing and settlement in Iceland.**
P. T. Wheeler. Nottingham, England: Geographical Field Group, 1983. 112p. maps. diagrs. sketches. (Geographical Field Group Regional Studies, no. 23).

Report of a fieldtrip made in the summer of 1979 by the long-established Geographical Field Group to the western fjords of Iceland and to Fljótshlíð in the south. The report of the field-work is presented under four headings: Physical background; agriculture in Vestfirðir and Fljótshlíð; fishing industry of Vestfirðir; settlement in Vestfirðir. Field-work was concentrated on Bolungarvík, Ísafjörður, Suðureyri, Súðavík, Flateyri and Þingeyri, and was conducted with reference to the historical background and present conditions. Contains over fifty maps, diagrams and sketches. (n.b. this note has been prepared from the pre-publication draft; the bibliographical details are therefore provisional).

169 **The valley of Thorvaldsdalur: report of the 1977 U.C.W. expedition.**
Edited by W. J. Higgs. Aberystwyth, Wales: University College of Wales. 1978. 110p.

Þorvaldsdalur is a small valley running to the western shore of Eyjafjörður. This report covers aspects of the geology, zoology, and especially the botany of the valley. Detailed, with a useful appendix on equipment.

170 **British Schools Exploring Society report 1975-1976: 1975 central Iceland expedition.**
Edited by I. Y. Ashwell. London: British Schools Exploring Society, 1976. 131p. map.

Schools, both collectively and individually, have been no less active in field-work around Iceland than universities. The British Schools Exploring Society has long concentrated its expeditions on the Arctic and sub-Arctic regions. Since 1932 (with the exception of the war years) expeditions have been conducted annually; previous expeditions to Iceland were made and reported in 1951, 1952, 1956, 1960, 1964, 1970-71 and 1972. See Ian Ashwell: *Dust storms in an ice desert* (q.v.). The 1975 expedition of sixty-three boys and thirteen leaders was an exploration to the west of Vatnajökull and the western part of the ice-cap itself. The meticulously presented report covers both the technical organisation and the field-work, including glacial geomorphology, climatology, and a study of the Hamarinn area; there are also observations on the vegetation of the Sylgjujökull moraines, with a folding map of Sylgjujökull (1:10,000) in the end pocket. Further reports appeared in 1978, 1981 and 1982 (Breiðamerkurjökull).

171 **Shirebrook School Icelandic expedition.**
Mansfield, England: Shirebrook School, 1967. 57p.

An example of a report from an individual school fieldtrip to Iceland. This secondary school party stayed for one month on the edge of the Langjökull glacier in west-central Iceland.

172 **Young explorers.**
Richard Gilbert. Easingwold, England: Smith, 1979. 236p.

Ampleforth College in North Yorkshire has established during the last fifteen years a reputation for exploration and field-work in mountainous regions abroad.

Regional Geography. Fieldtrips

Five of their trips are described here by their leader. Two of them were to Iceland: to Mýrdalsjökull in the south; and to the Tröllaskagi mountains in the north. The accounts are entertainingly written as well as informative.

North Iceland Glacier Inventory: manual for field survey parties.
See item no. 214.

Physical Geography, Geology, Climatology

Evolutionary structure

173 More than a drop in the ocean.
John Gribbin. *The Guardian* (UK), (26 March 1981), p. 17.

A comment on the implications of the idea floated by Fred Whipple of the Smithsonian Astrophysical Observatory that the impact of the giant meteor thought to have struck the earth sixty-five million years ago, eliminating most of the species living at that time, is still to be seen in the form of the landmass now known as Iceland. Iceland is a unique example of a mass astride an ocean-spreading ridge, and none of the volcanic rock, of which it is almost totally composed, is more than sixty-five million years old. Speculative to the specialist, astounding to the amateur.

174 Iceland and mid-ocean ridges: report of a symposium.
Edited by Sveinbjörn Björnsson. Reykjavík: Prentsmiðjan Leiftur, 1967. 209p. (Vísindafélag Íslendinga XXXVIII).

The Icelandic landmass is the most spectacular supramarine feature of the mid-Atlantic ocean ridge. This symposium of the Geoscience Society of Iceland comprises a valuable collection of papers on the 'state of the art' in the geology and geophysiology of Iceland, with particular reference to the context of the ridge-rift system and its indications for future research. The report includes eighteen papers by specialists from various research institutions in Iceland. All the contributions are in English. For the general reader Sveinbjörn Björnsson contributed an article on the mid-ocean ridge, entitled 'Serpent of middle earth: scars of continental drift at the old site of Alþing' in *Atlantica and Iceland Review*, vol. 19, no. 1 (1980), p. 17-23.

Physical Geography, Geology, Climatology. Descriptive geology

175 **Geodynamics of Iceland and the north Atlantic area: proceedings of the NATO Advanced Study Institute Symposium held in Reykjavík, Iceland, 1-7 July 1974.**
Edited by L. Kristjánsson. Dordrecht, Netherlands: Reidel, 1974. 323p.

A collection of twenty-one specialised articles covering topics such as transverse ridges, petrochemistry, seismicity and geothermal activity. The papers are contributed by both Icelandic and non-Icelandic researchers in the geosciences.

176 **Iceland: evolution, active tectonics, and structure.**
Edited by W. Jacoby, A. Björnsson, D. Möller. Journal of Geophysics/Zeitschrift für Geophysik, vol. 47, no. 1-3 (1980). 276p. (Inter-Union Commission on Geodynamics. Scientific report no. 59).

A combined issue of this international journal, in which the Geodynamics Project is focussed on Iceland. It contains thirty-four research articles by an international panel of scientists (including several Icelanders) covering the evolution, seismicity and crustal structure of the Icelandic landmass. All the papers are in English, and provide further references.

177 **Contributions to the physiography of Iceland, with particular reference to the highlands west of Vatnajökull.**
Niels Nielsen. Copenhagen: Levin & Munskgaard, 1933. 100p. maps. plates.

A scientific report resulting from the second Danish-Icelandic expedition of 1937. The area investigated lies between the Tungnaá and Þjórsá rivers. The report covers volcanism, tectonics, erosion and hydrography, the first two with particular reference to the displacement theories of Alfred Wegener. Includes thirty-two plates and nine maps. Issued as part of the memoirs of the Danish Royal Academy.

Descriptive geology

178 **Explorations in Iceland during the years 1881-1898.**
Þorvaldur Þoroddsen, translated by J. T. Bealby. *Geographical Journal*, vol. 13, nos. 3+5 (March + May 1899) p. 251-73 + 480-512. map. tables. photos.

Þorvaldur Þoroddsen (1855-1921) was a pioneer of Icelandic geology, as well as a considerable cartographer. He spent the prime years of his life travelling extensively around his native country researching geological phenomena, and constantly adding detail to the mapping of Iceland. This extended essay, in two parts, constitutes a cursive summary of his findings, which he published in greater detail in a variety of sources. Still a valuable introduction to the general geology of Iceland. It is accompanied by various tables, photographs and a folding map (scale 1:1,000,000) which incorporates his own additions. Five years earlier in the

Physical Geography, Geology, Climatology. Descriptive geology

same journal, vol. 3, no. 4 (April 1894), another geologist, Karl Grossman reported his findings from Iceland.

179 **On the geology and geomorphology of Iceland.**
Sigurður Þórarinsson, Trausti Einarsson, Guðmundur Kjartansson. *Geografiska Annaler*, vol. 41, no. 2-3 (1959), p. 135-69.

The 19th International Geographical Congress of 1960 was held in Scandinavia, and this article takes the form of a guide to the Iceland excursion from the geomorphological viewpoint. There are ten chapters, covering plateau basalt areas, the Móberg formation, postglacial volcanism, natural heat, tephra layers in Þjórsárdalur, postglacial history of Mývatn, the Jökulsá canyon and Ásbyrgi, landslides, sandar (alluvial outwash plains), and wind erosion. To each chapter is appended a list of relevant literature. Most of these papers, along with others by Jóhannes Askelsson on Pliocene and Pleistocene deposits, and by G. Böðvarsson on hot-springs were included in the Congress' own guide *On the geology and geophysics of Iceland* (Reykjavík: 1960, 74p). Another of Sigurður Þórarinsson's contributions to *Geografiska Annaler* entitled 'The main geological and topographical features of Iceland' appeared in vol. 19 (1937), p. 161-75.

180 **The landscapes of Iceland: types and regions.**
Hubertus Preusser. The Hague: Junk, 1976. 364p. maps. bibliog.

An original study in which the author attempts, with considerable clarity, to classify Iceland by divisions of natural or landscape regions. After a general survey of the landscape structures, he proceeds to identify and describe nine types of landscape: vegetated lowland, outwash plains (sandar), fjords, tundra plateaux, desert plateaux, highlands, young volcanic landscape, glaciers, and islands. Part three is devoted to a description of the thirty landscape regions into which the author divides the country. The volume includes clearly delineated maps.

181 **The formation and landscapes of deserts in Iceland.**
G. Clarke. *Journal of the Durham University Geographical Society*, vol. 12 (1970), p. 52-64.

An investigation into the 'desert' areas of Iceland, and the extent to which man and animals have accelerated the processes of nature in denuding the landscape. The contrasts among the desert land-forms are surveyed in relation to the geomorphological processes and the differences in the source and lithology of the parent materials. The conclusion is drawn that desert areas are likely to increase 'unless the part played by an ecological breakdown is more widely understood, and action to aid and restore a stable vegetation cover is taken'.

The soils of Iceland.
See item no. 520.

Geothermal and volcanic areas

General

182 Volcanic geology, hotsprings and geysers of Iceland.
Tom F. W. Barth. Washington, DC: Carnegie Institution, 1950. 174p. maps. photos.

An important and substantial survey of the geothermal activity which is so pervasive a feature of the Icelandic landmass. Based on field-work conducted during 1934 and 1937, and supported by subsequent analyses at the Geophysical Laboratory in Washington, this volume is a technical survey of geothermal phenomena, divided into four main sections: the three features mentioned in the title, plus a section describing thirty-two areas of hot spring activity around Iceland. Includes photographs, maps, a glossary of roots appearing in Icelandic place-names, and a geographical index. The same author contributed a shorter and less technical article entitled 'Craters and fissure eruptions at Mývatn in Iceland' to *Norsk Geografisk Tidsskrift*, vol. 9, 1942-43, p. 48-81. This includes a geological sketch-map of the area east and north of Mývatn.

183 The hot springs of Iceland.
Þorkell Þorkelsson. Copenhagen: Høst, 1910, 86p. 13 plates.

Issued by the Danish Royal Academy of Sciences, this research report was compiled from investigations conducted during the summers of 1904 and 1906, and is concerned with the emanations of radioactivity from the hot spring areas. The areas investigated were at Mývatn, Reykir, Hveravellir, Kerlingarfjöll, Grafarbakkahverir, Langarás, Reykjafoss and Henglahverir. Temperatures, boiling points, composition of the gases and radioactivity were all measured. The detailed conclusions drawn upon the nature of hot springs and their emissions have since been widely applied in the study of Iceland's geothermal activity. Contains thirteen plates. A later specialist report by this author, entitled *On thermal activity in Iceland and geyser action* was issued as volume XXV of the publications of Vísindafélag Íslands (1940, 139p.).

The hot springs of Iceland: their animal communities and their zoogeographical significance.
See item no. 232.

South and west

184 The Great Geysir and the hot-spring area of Haukadalur, Iceland.
Trausti Einarsson. Reykjavík: Geysir Committee, 1967. 24p.

It was the Great Geysir which gave its name to all other intermittent hot springs of the world, geysir being Icelandic for 'it spouts'. This paper is a general description of the Geysir basin and the nearby Strokkur etc., and their boiling eruptions, with comments on the theories of MacKenzie (1810), and notes on recent research. It concludes with remarks on the blue water of the springs, caused by

Physical Geography, Geology, Climatology. Geothermal and volcanic areas. South and West

dissolved silica, and on the crust formation known as geyserite. Soap has long been used to trigger a 'performance' by Geysir itself, but there occurred a recent controversy over an apparently unauthorised repair of crust on the rim, which many, including the author of this paper, Professor at the University of Iceland, deemed necessary to improve performance, by removing the build-up of deposit.

185 The Öræfajökull eruption of 1362.
Sigurður Þórarinsson. *Acta Naturalia Islandica*, vol. 2, no. 2 (1958), 100p.

The volcano beneath Öræfajökull, the southernmost arm of the Vatnajökull, which is pierced by Iceland's highest peak Hvannadalshnúkur (2,119 metres), produced its first known eruption in 1362, one of the biggest in the recorded history of Icelandic eruptions. It is believed that the subsequent *jökulhlaup*, or glacier burst, destroyed forty farms, their inhabitants, livestock and arable land. This substantial paper is an analysis of that eruption, based on what is known from contemporary sources and subsequent evidence. The chief geological consequence of this eruption and the eruption of 1727 is there for all to see on the coastal plains of Skeiðarársandur and Breiðamerkursandur.

186 The Lakagígar eruption of 1783.
Sigurður Þórarinsson. *Bulletin Volcanologique*, vol. 33, no. 3 (1970), p. 910-29. maps. tables. photos.

Two centuries ago there occurred in southern Iceland a volcanic eruption which, in terms of volume of lava emitted, has not been surpassed on earth in recorded time. Jón Steingrímsson's remarkable eye-witness account of the eruption furnished many of the contemporary details, but there is so much environmental evidence remaining today for even the casual observer that a still clearer picture of the events can be formed. This paper by Iceland's foremost geologist is the clearest exposition of the eruption of this shield volcano, and of its catastrophic (though not in terms of human life) effects, with particular reference to the eradication of farmland and the action of the volcanic gases on grass growth. Text includes tables, maps and photographs. For other aspects of the Laki eruption see: Vilhjálmur Bjarnar's 'The Laki eruption and the famine of the mist' (q.v.) and Jón Steffensen's 'Smallpox in Iceland' (q.v.).

187 The eruption of Hekla, 1947-1948.
Edited by Trausti Einarsson, Guðmundur Kjartansson, Sigurður Þórarinsson. Reykjavík: Leiftur/Vísindafélag Íslendinga, 1949-74. 5 vols. 16 pts. in 11. map. plates.

In March 1947, Hekla produced a year-long eruption, major in terms of volume, though causing comparatively little damage. It provided the opportunity for full-scale research of the volcanic activity, its emissions and effects. The results have been published over a period of a quarter of a century in this series issued by the Scientific Society of Iceland. The first volume, Sigurður Þórarinsson's *The eruptions of Hekla in historical times: a tephrochronological study* (1957, 183p.), with twelve plates and a folding map of the Hekla region, is an invaluable comparative analysis of the eruptions from 1104-1845, and serves as a basis for the subsequent specialist volumes. *The eruption of Hekla 1947-1948* is also the title of a more general eye-witness account recorded by Guðmundur Einarsson frá Miðdal (Reykjavík: Guðjón O. Guðjónsson, 1948. 184p.). This volume is in Icelandic, but contains an English summary on p. 135-52, with sixty-four plates. An earlier edition had appeared the previous year.

Physical Geography, Geology, Climatology. Geothermal and volcanic areas. South and West

188 Hekla: a notorious volcano.
Sigurður Þórarinsson, translated by Jóhann Hannesson, Pétur Karlsson. Reykjavík: Almenna Bókafélagið, 1970. 116p. photos.

The fifteenth eruption of Hekla occurred over a period of two months during 1970. This lucid account, accompanied by fine photography, is a general description and analysis of this and the earlier eruptions, in a presentation suitable for the specialist or the general reader. (Hekla erupted again in 1980). The author wrote an earlier booklet *Hekla on fire* (Munich: Reich, 1956. 30+52p). See *The Hekla eruption of 1970* by Árni Böðvarsson, (Reykjavík: Litbrá, 1970. 30p.), with Icelandic/English text and illustrations in colour.

189 Surtsey: the new island in the north Atlantic.
Sigurður Þórarinsson. New York: Viking Press, 1967. London: Cassell, 1969. 47p. 50 photos.

On 14 November 1963, when the new island of Surtsey (named after the mythical giant Surtur, thought to have been a god of fire) was created from a submarine volcanic eruption, there began the unique opportunity for the Icelanders to see and understand how their country was originally formed. The eruption and gradual establishment of Surtsey are clearly described and explained by this eminent Icelandic geologist. The text is enhanced by fifty photographs which dramatically convey the natural forces at work. The author presented some earlier thoughts on Surtsey in an article in *National Geographic* vol. 127, no. 5 (May 1965), p. 713-26. See Þorleifur Einarsson's *The Surtsey eruption in words and pictures*, translated by Peter Kidson (Reykjavík: Heimskringla, 1965, 32p.).

190 Surtsey research progress reports.
Reykjavík: Surtsey Research Society, 1964- . maps. graphs.

The Surtsey Research Society was founded in 1964 immediately after the eruption of the island. Its membership comprises Icelandic scientists, with foreign scientists as associates. The creation and development of the new island as a natural laboratory offered so many possibilities for research that a regular outlet for findings was launched in the form of these progress reports, which appeared annually for the first five issues, less frequently thereafter. Each report contains a collection of papers on the geological and biological aspects of Surtsey, with many maps, graphs and further references. The present chairman is Steingrímur Hermannson.

191 Volcano: ordeal by fire in Iceland's Westmann Islands.
Árni Gunnarsson, translated by May Hallmundsson, Hallberg Hallmundsson. Reykjavík: Iceland Review, 1973. 96p. photos.

Less than a decade after the creation of Surtsey the Icelanders were forcibly reminded that all was not quiet on the south-western front, when, less than ten miles from Surtsey, the island of Heimaey and the peace of its 5,500 inhabitants was shattered by a volcanic eruption. The purpose of this volume is threefold: to provide a non-technical account of the eruption and its aftermath; to convey the spirit with which the Westmann Islanders reacted to the event, which obliterated their property but, astonishingly, none of their lives; and to provide a photographic record of the event and its aftermath. The balance between spectacle and disaster can be a fine one, and the book should be looked at with this in mind.

Physical Geography, Geology, Climatology. Geothermal and volcanic areas. South and West

See, as with Surtsey, Þorleifur Einarsson's account *The eruption on Heimaey* (Reykjavík, 1974, 56p.).

192 Eruption on Helgafell.
Chalmers M. Clapperton. *Geographical Magazine*, vol. 45, no. 7-9 (April-June 1973); vol. 46, no. 2 (Nov. 1973).

Foreign magazine editors were quick to react to the volcanic eruption on the Westmann Islands. This reporter contributed four short articles, submitted with each new turn of events, and the swiftness of the action and reaction is thereby clearly conveyed. 'A village fights for its life' is the title of the vivid piece of reportage submitted by Noel Grove to *National Geographic*, vol. 146, no. 1 (July 1973), p. 40-67, accompanied by excellent photography of the aptly named Eldfell (Firehill) eruption and its effects. See Eiður Guðnason's article for *American-Scandinavian Review*, vol. 61, no. 4 (1973), p. 328-39.

193 Intraglacial volcanoes of the Laugarvatn region, south-west Iceland.
J. G. Jones. *Quarterly Journal of the Geological Society of London*, vol. 124, no. 3 (1968), p. 197-211.

An investigation into the individual shape and structure of a group of basaltic volcanoes, in which the formation of steep-sided piles of pillow lava and their vitreous covering is seen as evidence of the volcanic growth having occurred within the melting ice-sheets. Comparisons are made between the formations of basaltic volcanoes within and outside glacial environments. The report of this research is continued and expanded in the second part of this paper, which was published in *Journal of Geology*, vol, 78, no. 2 (March 1970), p. 127-40.

194 Surtshellir.
J. R. Reich. *Atlantica and Iceland Review*, vol. 12, no. 3-4 (1974), p. 56-63. plan.

Surtshellir is the largest and best known system of underground caves formed by volcanic activity to be found in Iceland. It is mentioned as far back as the *Book of the Settlements*. The caves are located east of Reykholt at the foot of the small glacier, Eiríksjökull. A scientific expedition during three summers in the early 1970s, led by the author of this article, resulted in a comprehensive mapping of the cave system. A longitudinal plan of the corridors is included to illustrate the course and the features of the passage through these extraordinary lava tunnels.

195 Geology of the Setberg area.
Haraldur Sigurðsson. *Greinar*, vol. 4, no. 2 (1966), p. 1-52. map.

An issue of the series of occasional papers from the Scientific Society of Iceland, in which the author studies the environs of the Setberg volcano on the northern side of the Snæfellsness peninsula. Includes a detailed map of the district.

Surtsey: evolution of life on a volcanic island.
See item no. 223.

Physical Geography, Geology, Climatology. Geothermal and volcanic
areas. East and North

East and north

196 The Geology of the Fáskrúðsfjörður area.
I. L. Gibson, D. J. J. Kinsman, G. P. L. Walker. *Greinar*,
vol. 4, no. 2 (1966). p. 53-122. map.

A stratigraphical survey of a typical eastern fjord (an area of study given little attention by geologists hitherto). A folding map of the district is included.

197 Geology of the Álftafjörður volcano: a tertiary volcanic centre..
D. H. Blake. *Science in Iceland*, vol. 2 (1970), p. 43-63. photos.

A study of one of the lesser known volcanic areas of Iceland, around Álftafjörður on the east-south-east coast. An introduction to the geology of the area is followed by a descriptive analysis of the caldera, flanks, envelopes, intrusions, and other features. Photographs accompany the text. An article from the enterprising but now defunct journal of the Scientific Society.

198 Table mountains of northern Iceland.
R. W. Bemmelen, M. G. Rutten. Leiden, Netherlands:
Brill, 1955. 217p. maps. drawings. plates.

A thorough examination of the genesis of table mountains in the areas around Mývatn and the Ódáðahraun, particularly Blafjall and Herðubreið. There are also miscellaneous observations on eruptions around Mývatn, and a detailed description of the Dyngjufjöll. Fifty-two pages of plates and several sectional drawings and maps. On a different point, this volume is to be commended for its production - typeface and typesize, page layout, print and paper, and stitching are all of an unusually high standard for a technical publication, and make it a pleasure to consult.

199 Askja: Iceland's largest volcano.
W. G. Lock. Charlton, England: 1881. 106p. map.

The author claimed his book, published privately, to be the first serious analysis of Askja, dismissing previous descriptions as trivial. This lack of serious attention he attributed to the fact that Askja, in spite of its crater's circumference of almost eighteen miles, lies well away from the inhabited coastal districts to the north; he also claimed, with less reason, that it was unknown to the Icelanders themselves until the major eruption in 1875. Lock offers an account of the lava flood in the desert east of Mývatn and his path across the Ódáðahraun to Askja, with his theory of the genesis of Askja, which he then relates to the genesis of Iceland as a whole. Although 20th-century geological techniques have unearthed much greater detail concerning volcanic activity in Iceland, this work remains a valid and original contribution to the study of this elemental area of the north central highlands. He includes a folding map of the country, showing every site of recorded volcanic eruption from the 9th to the 19th century.

Physical Geography, Geology, Climatology. Geothermal and volcanic areas. East and North

200 Askja on fire.
Sigurður Þórarinsson. Reykjavík: Almenna Bókafélagið, 1963. 72p. illus.

Askja erupted again during the winter of 1961. This book comprises a description, with illustrations, of the nature and configuration of this new breach of the caldera, not as fierce as the eruption of 1875, but resulting in a spectacularly formed stream of lava.

201 Neil Armstrong via Iceland to the moon.
Haraldur J. Hamar. *Atlantica and Iceland Review*, vol. 7, no. 4 (1969), p. 16-23. illus.

A brief illustrated feature article on how Neil Armstrong, the first man on the moon, came to Iceland in 1967 as part of the pre-mission training programme, to the area of the Askja volcano, where it was considered that the Icelandic basalt lava, distinguished by its barrenness, would be that part of the earth's surface most likely to resemble the moonscape.

202 Current rifting episode in north Iceland.
Axel Björnsson, Kristján Sæmundsson, Páll Einarsson, Eysteinn Tryggvason. *Nature* vol. 266 (24 March 1977), p. 318-23. maps.

The Krafla area in northern Iceland lies on the belt of volcanic activity that runs through Iceland from the south-west to north-east. Inside the Krafla caldera there is a diatomite plant and a geothermal power station, the continuity of the latter being under continuing threat from the subterranean movements. At the end of 1975 there began a major rifting episode. In this article a team of authors describe the geology of the environs of Krafla and the history of its volcanic activity, before recording and analysing these recent manifestations. They conclude that these rifting episodes occur in the region every 100-150 years as the boundary between the American and European plates widens. Contains two maps.

203 Unpredictable Krafla takes volcano watchers by surprise.
Tony Escritt. *Geographical Magazine*, vol. 53, no. 1 (Oct. 1980), p. 1-12.

On 10 July 1980 the Krafla volcano produced its fourth eruption in five years. The author of this article had been following this succession of events, and reported regularly to the same magazine; his two earlier articles 'An infernal bore' and 'Power station on a volcano' appeared in vol. 48, no. 7 (April 1976), p. 392-93, and in vol. 52, no. 8 (May 1980), p. 521-22. In this article he indicates some of the forecasting methods being applied. His latest report 'Krafla's wintry awakening' can be found in vol. 54, no. 1 (Jan. 1982), p. 2-3.

Physical Geography, Geology, Climatology. Glaciology, Climatology

Glaciology and climatology

204 Glacier: adventure on Vatnajökull, Europe's largest ice-cap.
Photographs by Gunnar Hannesson, text by Sigurður Þórarinsson, translated by May Hallmundsson, Hallberg Hallmundsson. Reykjavík: Iceland Review, 1975. 96p.

Breathtaking photography by the late renowned Icelandic photographer, accompanied by an expert commentary, results in a book of spectacle and authority. Although Vatnajökull is away from the main centres of population it dominates the map and character of Iceland. This book is a tribute. See Jón Eyþórsson's *Vatnajökull* (Reykjavík: Almenna Bókafélagið, 1960, 118p.).

205 Vatnajökull, Iceland: the history of its exploration.
Brian Roberts. *Scottish Geographical Magazine*, vol. 50, no. 2 (March 1934), p. 65-76. map. bibliog.

The leader of the Cambridge expedition to Vatnajökull in 1932 (see J. Angus Beckett: *Iceland adventure: the double traverse of the Vatnajökull by the Cambridge expedition* q.v.) here presents a useful summary of the records of its explorers from the early investigations of the ice margin dating from the early 17th century to the first serious attempts at crossing the ice-cap in the latter part of the 19th century and the subsequent expeditions. He includes a map charting the routes taken by the various expeditionaries, and a short bibliography of writings related to them.

206 Iceland adventure: the double traverse of the Vatnajökull by the Cambridge expedition.
J. Angus Beckett. London: Witherby, 1934. 197p. map. photos.

The Vatnajökull is by far the largest icecap in Iceland - indeed, the largest in Europe, covering an area of 3,400 square miles. Prior to this expedition from Cambridge in 1932 it has been crossed on only five occasions, originally by an Englishman in 1875 (see William Lord Watts: *Across the Vatnajökull: or, scenes in Iceland* q.v.) The aim of the expedition was to cover as much of the unexplored parts of the ice-cap as possible, with particular attention to be paid to the fauna of this desert region compared with the fertile coastal district to the south. The account is mainly a description of the country and conditions through which the expedition passed: 'It is particularly intended to illustrate the lighter side of expedition life, with incidents which could never be recorded in the official reports, but which really leave the most lasting impression'. Includes photographs and map. The technical side of the expedition is reported by Brian Roberts, with contributions from other members of the expedition on their specialisms, in a collective paper read to the Royal Geographical Society and published in *Geographical Journal*, vol. 81, no. 4 (April 1933), p. 289-313.

207 Land of ice and fire.
Hans Wilhelmsson Ahlmann. London: Routledge & Kegan Paul, 1938. 271p. map. photos.

The joint leader of the Swedish-Icelandic expedition to Vatnajökull in 1936 here describes both the preparations for the trip and the expedition itself. The story is simply told, with an entertaining mixture of major and minor events - the techni-

Physical Geography, Geology, Climatology. Glaciology, Climatology

cal aspects are recorded in an appendix. The latter part of the book contains an account of a more informal trip through the Skaftafell district to the south-west of the ice-cap. Includes photographs and a map of Vatnajökull showing the campsites. The research findings of the expedition are recorded by Ahlmann himself, and the Icelandic geologist Sigurður Þórarinsson in a series of reports under the collective title 'Vatnajökull: scientific results of the Swedish-Icelandic investigations, 1936-7-8' in *Geografiska Annaler* between 1937 and 1940.

208 Scientific results of the Polish geographical expedition to Iceland (Vatnajökull), 1968.
Edited by Rajmund Galon. *Geographica Polonica*, vol. 26 (1973), 312p.

A collection of ten reports by the research groups of the Polish expedition. The emphasis of the research is upon glacial land-forms in the marginal zones of Vatnajökull, with particular reference to the Skeiðarárjökull on the south-western margin. All the articles are in English.

209 Under ice volcanoes.
Keith Miller. *Geographical Journal*, vol. 145, no. 1 (March 1979), p. 36-55.

Report of another Cambridge-organised expedition to Vatnajökull, this time with the more specific purpose of studying the phenomenon of *jökulhlaup*, or glacier burst, by means of a new system of radar. Technical information in this field is of practical importance at a time when the Icelanders have finally succeeded in bridging the remaining gap in the coastal road around the country in a form designed to withstand the pressures of glacial outwash from whatever cause. This expedition of 1976 and 1977 concentrated its research on the Grímsvötn lake area on the western part of Vatnajökull. This lake is a major glaciological feature of the region and is centred in a highly active geothermal zone. For another article on this phenomenon in the Grímsvötn lake area see 'Waterflow in glaciers: jökulhlaup, tunnels and veins' by J. F. Nye in *Journal of Glaciology*, vol. 17 (1976), p. 181-207.

210 Scourge of surging glaciers.
D. G. Groot, E. A. Escritt. *Geographical Magazine*, vol. 48, no. 6 (March 1976), p. 328-34.

A more general account of the process whereby normally slow-moving ice suddenly changes its pace to a rapid flow. The reporters survey some of the evidence of the manifestations of this process, including *jökulhlaup*, and indicate current research projects on the behaviour of ice-caps and glaciers in Iceland.

211 Kalfafellsdalur, south-east Iceland: a study of landform and depositional assemblages associated with the wastage of a valley glacier.
A. B. Fishwick. Ambleside, England: Brathay Hall Trust, 1974. 28p. maps. photos. figs.

A report by the Brathay Exploration Group, who have considerable experience of field-work in Iceland. These investigations were conducted in 1969 and 1972 in Kalfafellsdalur, a glacial trough valley on the coastal side of Vatnajökull east of Breiðamerkur; the study is centred on the preglacial moraines and channels associated with the Brokarjökull (an arm of Vatnajökull forming the head of Kal-

Physical Geography, Geology, Climatology. Glaciology, Climatology

fafellsdalur), and on mapping the fluctuations in the glacier's ice margin. The text is supplied with several photographs of the study area, maps of the landforms, ice margins, etc., and other figures.

212 The coast of south-east Iceland near Ingólfshöfði.
Cuchlaine A. M. King. *Geographical Journal*, vol. 122, no, 2 (June 1966), p. 241-46.

Ingólfshöfði is the striking rocky headland, virtually an island, (historically the first landfall of the first settler Ingólfr Árnason) which forms a dominant feature of the south-eastern coastline of Iceland. This article comprises an analysis of the way in which this headland acts as a coastal bar to sands, waves and winds, and thus influences the formation and climatic conditions of this glacier-dominated coast, which contrasts sharply with the fjord coast round to the east. The article elicits a reply by W. V. Lewis in issue no. 4 (Dec. 1966), p. 536-38, to which King appends her own rejoinder.

213 Dust storms in an ice desert.
Ian Y. Ashwell. *Geographical Magazine*, vol. 44, no. 5 (Feb. 1972), p. 322-27.

Summary of investigations by the British Schools Exploring Society (q.v.) into the contrast between dust and snow in Iceland. Their studies of dust storms in the area of the Langjökull ice-cap began in 1956, and have been followed up by subsequent expeditions: the 1970 and 1971 expeditions investigated the climate of the nearby Eiríksjökull and the Flosaskarð pass, producing further information on the exchange of air between the ice and the desert. Reports on the earlier meteorological investigations around Langjökull were written up by Ian Y. Ashwell (with F. G. Hannell) in the periodicals *Weather*, vol. 12 (1957), p. 365-72, and *Meteorological Magazine*, vol. 87 (1958), p. 353ff., vol. 89 (1960), p. 17ff.

214 North Iceland Glacier Inventory: manual for field survey parties.
E. A. Escritt. London: Young Explorers' Trust, 1974. 63p.

The North Iceland Glacier Inventory project (formerly entitled 'Adopt a Glacier') is a voluntary scheme supported by several institutions, and officially recognised by the Icelandic National Research Council. Reports of its field-work are published in *Jökull* (Journal of the Icelandic Glaciological Society, q.v.). The Iceland Unit of the Young Explorers' Trust produced this manual for the use of field-groups working in the Tröllaskagi district north-west of Akureyri, but it is designed to be applicable to glaciological studies in other areas. Coverage includes general aims of the inventory, physiographical and climatic data for Tröllaskagi, procedures and instructions for reconnaissance parties, and appendices on mapping, measurement, etc., with suggestions for further field-work, and references. For details of the Iceland Unit's own bulletin see *Ísland: bulletin of the Iceland Unit* (q.v.).

215 Oscillations of Icelandic glaciers in the last 250 years.
Sigurður Þórarinsson. *Geografiska Annaler*, vol. 25 (1934), p. 1-54.

Glacial variation is a topic which has attracted many researchers both Icelandic and foreign, and which has relevance for the past and the future of the Icelandic climate and landscape. This paper is a substantial and valuable contribution to the field, and has been frequently cited by subsequent field-workers. In the same

Physical Geography, Geology, Climatology. Glaciology, Climatology

journal, vol. 17 (1935), p. 121-37, see Jón Eyþórsson's article on glacial variation with particular reference to Drangajökull on the north-western peninsula of Iceland.

216 **The ice off Iceland and the climates during the last 1200 years.**
I. I. Schell. *Geografiska Annaler*, vol. 43, no. 3-4 (1961), p. 354-62.

An attempt to relate the amount of ice off Iceland to the climatological features and measurements not only of Iceland itself, but also of Greenland, Europe and the Americas. The available evidence tends to show a correlation between the sea ice off Iceland and the climate of these areas over three periods of several centuries since the year 900

217 **The climate and weather of Iceland.**
Jón Eyþórsson, Hlynur Sigtryggson. Copenhagen; Reykjavík: Munskgaard, 1971. 62p. (Zoology of Iceland, vol. 1, pt. 3).

There are surprisingly few sources of information in English specifically on the climatic conditions of Iceland. And yet the effects of the alternating forces of polar air from the north and the warmer south-westerly streams from the Atlantic make Iceland a particularly interesting part of the world for such studies. This survey, which appeared in the long-standing serial publication on the zoology of Iceland, is concerned with those climatic features most likely to influence animal life. But it is also of value to the general meteorologist for its discussions and measurements of temperatures, precipitation, wind, sea and inland ice, etc. It includes many charts and weather tables (by districts) especially for the period 1930-70. An admirably clear introduction to and survey of this topic. Jón Eyþórsson, the notable Icelandic volcanologist and glaciologist, died before this publication was completed, and the work was continued by the co-author.

Jökull. (Glacier.)
See item no. 935.

Natural History, Ecology, Flora and Fauna

General and ecological

218 Travels in Iceland (1752-1757).
Eggert Ólafsson, Bjarni Pálsson. Reykjavík: Örn og Örlygur, 1975. Rev. English ed. 186p. illus.
The descriptive details on the original title page continue: 'performed 1752-1757 by order of his Danish Majesty, containing observations on the manners and customs of the inhabitants, a description of the lakes, rivers, glaciers, hotsprings and volcanoes; of the various kinds of earths, stones, fossils and petrifactions, as well as the animals, insects, fishes, &c.' The product of an awakening Danish interest in its subject territory, this remarkable volume, as Steindór Steindórsson emphasises in his introduction, marks the beginning of a scientific knowledge of Iceland. Eggert Ólafsson was a scientist and poet; Bjarni Pálsson was Iceland's first Director of Health. The book was published in Danish in 1772, but its English translation did not appear until 1805 (London: Richard Phillips) and then only in an abridged form, lacking many of the splendid colour engravings and sketches which adorn the full text of the present revised edition. The authors arranged their materials by the Quarters of Iceland. For an account of the life and work of Eggert Ólafsson, see *Eggert Ólafsson: a biographical sketch* by Halldór Hermannsson (Ithaca, New York: Cornell University Library, 1925. Islandica vol. XVI. Still available in reprint by Kraus.). Compare in same series, volume XXIV 1924 'Jón Guðmundsson and his natural history of Iceland'.

219 The natural history of Iceland.
Niels Horrebow. London: Linde, 1758, 207p. map.
'Containing a particular and accurate account of the different soils, burning mountains, minerals, vegetables, metals, stones, beasts, birds and fishes; together with the disposition, customs and manner of living of the inhabitants'. This trans-

Natural History, Ecology, Flora and Fauna, General

lation is an abridgment of the Danish original of 1752. The author seems to have been motivated by a genuine desire to present Iceland objectively to foreign readers, and at the same time counter the German account of John Anderson, Mayor of Hamburg, published in 1746, which had been compiled without his visiting Iceland, from a variety of secondary sources - Anderson's account is liberally quoted and rectified throughout Horrebow's footnotes. Horrebow's account comprises 115 short essays or notes on all aspects of Icelandic life, and is of considerable significance. He appends detailed records of meteorological observations made at Bessastadir, 1749-51, and includes a folding map of Iceland copied from that of the Danish Royal Corps of Engineers (1734). This volume was overshadowed when the contemporary account of Eggert Olafsson and Bjarni Pálsson (q.v.) appeared in English.

220 The Faroes and Iceland: studies in island life.
Nelson Annandale. Oxford, England: Clarendon Press, 1905. 238p. illus. photos.

This is the sort of book which could hardly appear nowadays; it belongs to a genre which owes its quality to the appealingly random nature of its contents, where the reader is invited to share a miscellany of impressions in a manner and arrangement which is typical of the last century. The author's main interest appears to be in the fauna, but the book contains a variety of observations made on a series of holidays in Faroe and Iceland between 1896 and 1903. Two chapters on life in the Faroes are followed by five on Iceland: impressions of Icelandic life at the turn of the century; the strange affair of the Algerian raids on Iceland in 1627; the bird cliffs of the Westmann Islands; domestic animals, including the Iceland dog; agriculture, with notes on insect life. To complete the miscellany there is an appendix on the Celtic/Icelandic pony by F. H. A. Marshall. The book contains many unusual photographs and illustrations and is a pleasure to read or browse through. The comparison between the Faroes and Iceland is an additional point of interest. Annandale also contributed some notes on the folklore of the Westmann Islands to the anthropological journal *Man*, vol. 3 (1903), p. 107-09.

221 New bottles for new wine.
Julian Huxley. London: Chatto & Windus, 1957. 318p.

The eminent biologist Julian Huxley, accompanied by the similarly respected ornithologist James Fisher, visited Iceland in the summer of 1949. Huxley's essay 'Natural history in Iceland' on p. 155-67 is an examination of 'some of the ways in which Iceland's natural history illustrates or illuminates general evolutionary biology'. The majority of his observations are on the birdlife of Iceland and its relation to the geographical position and climate of the country.

222 Bellamy's Europe.
David Bellamy. London: BBC, 1976. 143p.

Bellamy's successful blend of authority and popularising in his field of natural history is now well known to viewers of British television. Chapter eight of his book entitled 'Some like it hot', p. 115-25 is a more permanent record of his programme on Iceland, in which he casts a penetrating eye on aspects of the country's vegetation.

Natural History, Ecology, Flora and Fauna. General

223 **Surtsey: evolution of life on a volcanic island.**
Sturla Friðriksson. London: Butterworth; New York: Halsted Press, 1975. 198p. maps. photos. tables.

The volcanic birth of the new island of Surtsey off the south-western coast of Iceland on 14 November 1963 was a hey-day for geologists and natural historians. Once it became clear that the new island would, after all, survive the elements, a unique opportunity presented itself to establish a natural laboratory to monitor the process of the genesis and development of life forms under natural conditions. This volume is both a scientific progress report (see the Surtsey research progress reports q.v.), and a general description of the first decade of ecological advance on Surtsey. 'The displays of these natural phenomena were so magnificent, the powers of the elements both in constructing and demolishing land so apparent, and the continuous struggle for the existence of life so fundamental, that they are bound to direct one's thoughts towards the creative forces of the universe and to the origin and destiny of life'. The text includes photographs, maps, tables and references.

224 **Ecology of eutrophic, subarctic Lake Mývatn and the river Laxá.**
Edited by Pétur M. Jónasson. Copenhagen: Íslensk Fræðafélag, 1979. 308p. map. charts. diagrs. tables.

The most substantial synthesis of research on the Mývatn area available in English. An excellently-produced volume, financially supported by several Nordic institutions, it also forms a special issue of the Danish environmental journal *Oikos*. A general introduction by the editor is followed by eighteen varied articles in English, mainly by Icelandic specialists, each engaged in a particular study relating to the ecology of this paradise for naturalists: aspects of climate, physical geography, hydrography, chemistry, flora and fauna, etc. are represented, to form a wide-ranging scientific appraisal of the ecosystem of Mývatn and the Laxá river, which drains into the Arctic ocean. There is a tradition as old as the settlement of Iceland itself of treating the Mývatn area as one for the conservation of nature, a tradition which has resulted in rich rewards in terms of ecological research. Charts, diagrams and tables are liberally used throughout the text, and there is a detailed full-page map of the area. Each article carries a substantial list of references. For any scientifically-orientated visitor to Mývatn this volume is a prerequisite. The editor of this volume briefly describes an ecological project on another of Iceland's lakes in a communication 'Lake Þingvallavatn: a Nordic project in Iceland', *Nordic Ecological Newsletter*, no. 5 (1978), p. 5-7. This project, involving the Universities of Iceland and Copenhagen, was concerned with the dynamics of the ecosystem in Iceland's largest lake.

Acta Naturalia Islandica.
See item no. 933.

Botany

225 The botany of Iceland.
Edited by J. L. A. Kolderup-Rosenvinge, J. E. B. Warming. Copenhagen: Frimodt; London: Wheldon, 1912-

A collection of monographs issued over the years in serial form (volumes and parts) which together form a specialised encyclopaedia of the botany of Iceland. Latterly edited by Johannes Gröntved and published by Munskgaard. The most frequently cited of these monographs include: *Physical geography* by Þorvaldur Þoroddsen (1914. No. 1 = vol. 1, pt. 1.); *Studies on the vegetation of Iceland* by H. M. Hansen (1930. No. 10 = vol. 3, pt. 2); *Studies in the vegetation of the central highlands of Iceland* by Steindór Steindórsson (1940. No. 12 = vol. 3, pt. 4.); and *Pteridophyta and spermatophyta of Iceland* by Johannes Gröntved (1942. No. 13 = vol. 4, pt. 1.).

226 On the age and immigration of Icelandic flora.
Steindór Steindórsson. Reykjavík: Leiftur, 1962. 157p. bibliog. (Vísindafélag Íslendinga, vol. XXXV).

An investigation into 300 species, two-thirds of which are considered to be survivors from the Ice age, and one third introduced since the time of the human settlement of Iceland. The survival of certain groups in specific areas is taken as an indication that those areas had not been entirely glaciated. An important and frequently-cited study of the origins of Icelandic flora. The text is interspersed with 86 figures showing distributions. See Steindór Steindórsson's earlier *Contributions to the plant geography and flora of Iceland*, published as three pamphlets, again by the Scientific Society of Iceland (1935, 1937, 1942) which comprise observations on the vegetation in two areas of Skaftártunga in southern Iceland, and on the island of Æðey in Ísafjarðardjúp. A fourth contribution, also on the vegetation of Ísafjörður appeared as an issue of *Acta Naturalia Islandica* (q.v.), vol. 1, no. 3 (1970).

227 Immigration and naturalisation of flowering plants in Iceland since 1900.
Ingólfur Davíðsson. *Greinar* (Vísindafélag Íslendinga), vol. 4, no. 3 (1967), 32p.

An interesting study which can act as a supplement to Steindór Steindórsson's *On the age and immigration of Icelandic flora* (q.v.). The majority of the flowering plants which have immigrated to Iceland this century have appeared since the last war, owing to the increase in non-natural communications: 186 such species have been noted, most of them being intermittent, but with 26 having established themselves permanently. The immigrant plants are nearly all to be found in towns or on farms, whereas in the uninhabited areas the native or earlier plants hold complete sway. Although there has been occasional deliberate importation, most of the immigration has been accidental. A full descriptive list of the plants is included, with 8 species treated in detail, in respect of location, distribution, etc.

Natural History, Ecology, Flora and Fauna. Zoology

228 **The flora of Iceland and the Faroes.**
C. H. Ostenfeld, Johannes Gröntved. Copenhagen: Levin & Munskgaard; London: Williams & Norgate, 1934. 195p. map.

The first substantial flora of Iceland to be published in English, being a descriptive catalogue with glossary, index of families and genera by Latin nomenclature, and a list of popular plant names used in Iceland. Includes map.

229 **A field key to the flowering plants of Iceland.**
Pat Wolseley. Sandwich, Shetland: Thule Press, 1979. 64p. map. illus.

The short flowering period of many indigenous plants in Iceland presents problems of identification to the travelling botanist; this guide is invaluable in this respect, as, by using leaf shape and habit as a basis for its sectional arrangement, it enables the naturalist to identify plants at any stage of their flowering or fruiting. The 400 line drawings are particularly clear and helpful. Two main floras have been published in Icelandic, but this handy reference book is the obvious choice for the English-speaking student. There is an index which includes, in one sequence, the Latin, English and Icelandic names (also synonyms) of all species of Icelandic flora, which is mainly of European and circumpolar, occasionally of North American, origin. Contains biogeographical map.

230 **The vegetation and flora of Iceland.**
Hörður Kristinsson. *American Rock Garden Society Bulletin*, vol. 33, no. 3 (July 1975), p. 105-11.

A brief article outlining some of the features of vegetational history in Iceland, including the problem of the survival of woodland, and the dispersal of plants. For an earlier similar article see 'The gardens of the Faeroes, Iceland and Greenland' by John W. Harshberger in *Geographical Review*, vol. 14 (1924), p. 404-15.

Three acres and a mill.
See item no. 115.

Acta Botanica Islandica: a journal of Icelandic botany.
See item no. 934.

Zoology

231 **The zoology of Iceland.**
Copenhagen; Reykjavík: Munskgaard, 1937- .

A longstanding series, still appearing in the 1970s, and comprising 76 issues numbered in 4 volumes. The issues in the first volume are devoted to introductory monographs on the geomorphology, climatology and hydrography of Iceland. The three further volumes are devoted to studies on individual species. A fifth volume was projected to synthesise the zoological findings. Contributors are international specialists, and their papers are all presented in English. Sponsored by Ríkissjóður Íslands and the Carlsberg Foundation.

Natural History, Ecology, Flora and Fauna. Zoology

232 **The hot springs of Iceland: their animal communities and their zoogeographical significance.**
S. L. Tuxen. Copenhagen: Munskgaard, 1944, 216p. (Zoology of Iceland, vol. 1, pt. ii).
A research monograph in the series *Zoology of Iceland* (q.v.), divided into four main sections: an analysis of the physical and chemical properties of the hot springs; a definition of the zoological species in the springs; the macro- and micro-fauna living near the springs; and a survey of the evidence for hot springs and their animal communities during the Ice Age. Each section has its own bibliography appended.

233 **Some Icelandic spiders.**
W. Rae Sherriffs. *Annals and Magazine of Natural History*, series 10, vol. xiv (Oct. 1934), p. 435-42.
A short study of the ecology of spiders in Iceland, with notes on thirteen species and their environmental preferences - dry and wet moss, rock, pasture and hot spring areas. Reprinted in *Iceland Papers. Volume 1, Scientific results of Cambridge expeditions to Iceland, 1932-38*, edited by Brian B. Roberts (q.v.).

234 **Synopsis of the fishes of Iceland.**
Bjarni Sæmundsson. Reykjavík: Prentsmiðjan Gutenberg, 1927, 68p. (Vísindafélag Íslendinga II).
A specialist monograph in the form of a classified list of the fishes to be found in Icelandic coastal waters, with an introduction on their environments. Contains detailed records of specimens caught within each genus. Latin and Icelandic nomenclature only.

235 **Salmon and trout in Iceland.**
Íslenzkar landbúnaðarrannsóknir/ Journal of Agricultural Research in Iceland vol. 10, no. 2 (1978), 174p.
A whole issue of the journal published by the Agricultural Research Institute in Reykjavík, devoted to the Icelandic salmon. Eleven of the twelve articles, all of which are presented in English, are of a specialist nature. A more generally-oriented article is the introductory paper (p. 11-39) by Þór Guðjónsson from the Institute of Freshwater Fisheries, dealing with the distribution, life history and culture of the Atlantic salmon in Iceland. Þór Guðjónsson is also the author, with Derek Mills of a booklet *Salmon in Iceland* (Farnham, England: Atlantic Salmon Trust, 1982, 22p.). This covers fishing and culture.

Rivers of Iceland.
See item no. 589.

Ornithology

236 Manual of the birds of Iceland.
Henry H. Slater. Edinburgh: Douglas, 1901. 150p.

In spite of its age, the ornithologist will still find this volume worth tracking down. Its author had been a long-standing observer of Icelandic birdlife, and his book is a directory of residents, summer visitors and birds of passage. One hundred and fifteen birds are listed under Linnaean, Icelandic and English names, followed by a variety of descriptive observations under each heading. Special attention is paid to nesting habits.

237 A handbook of the birds of Iceland.
Masa U. Hachisuka. London: Taylor & Francis, 1927. 128p. bibliog. illus.

This book by a Japanese ornithologist serves to update Slater's manual (q.v.), and is likewise a systematic list of the birds of Iceland. It has the advantage of a cursive introduction summarising the main factors in the study of Icelandic birdlife, and includes a series of photographic illustrations, plus a folding diagram of the egg sizes of ducks, geese, etc. Combined index of Latin and English names. The physical descriptions of the birds are presented in detail.

238 Iceland papers. Volume 1, Scientific results of Cambridge expeditions to Iceland, 1932-1938.
Edited by Brian B. Roberts. Oxford, England: Oxford University Press, 1939. 244p.

The Cambridge University expeditions to Iceland in the 1930s produced many important papers which were published in a variety of learned journals concerned with aspects of natural history. Seventeen of these articles were conveniently collected and reprinted in this volume. A few are noted elsewhere in this bibliography, but over a third are devoted to the ornithology of Iceland, and together constitute a valuable dossier as follows: Brian Roberts' 'Notes on the birds of central and south-east Iceland' (reprinted from *Ibis*, April 1934); Brian Roberts' 'The gannet colonies of Iceland' (reprinted from *British Birds*, Sept. 1934); David Lack's 'Habitat distribution in certain Icelandic birds' (reprinted from *Journal of Animal Ecology*, 1934); David Lack and Brian Roberts' 'Notes on Icelandic birds including a visit to Grímsey' (reprinted from *Ibis*, Oct. 1934); P. F. Holmes and D. B. Keith's 'Observations on the birds of Grímsey and north Iceland' (reprinted from *Ibis*, April 1936); and Alastair Morrison's 'Notes on the birds of north-east Iceland' (reprinted from *Ibis*, Jan. 1938).

239 Icelandic birds.
Michael Bratby. Reykjavík: Víkingsprent, 1941. 32p.

The texts of six talks broadcast from Reykjavík studio in the summer of 1941, originally for the benefit of British servicemen in Iceland. An easy-going and chatty introduction to the more commonly-seen birds of Iceland, including two talks on waders. Also on ducks, geese, gulls, terns, phalaropes, etc. Still helpful for the newcomer.

Natural History, Ecology, Flora and Fauna. Ornithology

240 In search of northern birds.
Seton Gordon. London: Eyre & Spottiswoode for the Royal Society for the Protection of Birds, 1941. 224p.

It is a fair bet that any birdwatcher from the British Isles destined for Iceland will already be familiar with the bird life of northern Britain, and be eager to compare notes. This entertaining diary offers just such an approach, in its observations of the birds of Scotland's highlands and islands, preceded by a first chapter (p. 11-39) on birds in Iceland, which the author encountered mainly in the Mývatn and Þingvellir districts. For another chapter in a comparative work see Arni Waag's contribution on the birds of Iceland and Faroe in *A guide to birdwatching in Europe*, edited by James Ferguson-Lees (Amsterdam: Scientific Pub. Co., 1972; London: Bodley Head, 1975, p. 37-50.).

241 Iceland summer: adventures of a bird painter.
George Miksch Sutton. Norman, Oklahoma: University of Oklahoma Press, 1961. 253p. illus.

A book of appealing presentation, written by an ornithologist with a sympathetic eye for the Icelandic environment - it has found a ready audience amongst similarly motivated visitors to Iceland. Sutton visited Iceland in 1958. Several of his paintings are reproduced in colour in his book, which is a delight to read. He mentions almost a hundred different birds in the text, and these are indexed at the end under their common, scientific and Icelandic names. The book has been reprinted twice, the first time with new plates, the second time (1981) in paperback format, which will further commend it as a companion for the bird lover travelling in Iceland.

242 Wings over Iceland.
Hermann Schlenker, text by Broddi Jóhannesson, translated by Peter Kidson. Reykjavík: Cultural Fund, 1965. 64p. map. 50 photos.

A volume of photographs of Icelandic birds and their surroundings. Includes some fifty plates, in colour or black-and-white, accompanied by an introduction and text in romantic rather than documentary style, plus map on the end papers. A souvenir item.

243 Bird life in Iceland.
Finnur Guðmundsson. *65°/ Sixty-five Degrees*, no. 6 (May 1969), p. 24-27.

Iceland's leading ornithologist here contributes a brief but helpful article for the amateur birdwatcher, identifying the major species which one can expect to see in Iceland without too much difficulty.

244 Review of ornithological studies in south-east Iceland, 1973-75.
R. V. Collier, M. Stott. Ambleside, England: Brathay Hall Trust, 1976. 27p. maps. plates.

The Brathay Exploration Group has been particularly active on the natural history front in Iceland and other northern regions for many years. This review is one of several such publications of its field study reports from Iceland, and is concentrated on the Öræfi area and the Skaftafell National Park. Particular

Natural History, Ecology, Flora and Fauna. Ornithology

attention is paid to the study of the great skua. Maps and plates accompany this valuable research.

245 Abstract of Mr J. Wolley's researches in Iceland respecting the gare-fowl or great auk.
Alfred Newton. *Ibis*, vol. 3 (1861), p. 374-99.

Although the Icelanders were by no means the only members of the human race to threaten the extinction of the great auk, as it happened it was they who finally accomplished this act of natural vandalism when the last known flock, which had been nesting on the volcanic island of Eldey ten miles off the south-western coast of Iceland, and was down to the last pair, was reached by a party of fourteen sailors, who proceeded to skin the two birds and to smash the last egg. This happened in 1844. John Wolley, an eminent Victorian naturalist, subsequently conducted an investigation into the natural history of this posthumously revered bird, and his notebooks of observations from the writings of previous naturalists are abstracted in this paper by one who himself continued the research on the great auk.

246 The great auk, or gare-fowl (Alca impennis Linni): its history, archaeology and remains.
Symington Grieve. London: Jack, 1885. 141+58p. map.

The aim in this volume was to synthesise the state of knowledge concerning the great auk. The paradox of the situation was that it required the extinction of the bird to stimulate its study, which resulted in numerous papers in natural history journals of the mid-19th century. Iceland occupies a north central position within the area which seems to have formed the limits of the auk's North Atlantic habitat. This volume affords the opportunity for a comparative historical study of the great auk, and includes a folding map showing its supposed distribution.

247 The gyr falcon adventure.
Stanley Cerely. London: Collins, 1955. 255p. map. photos.

Since the Middle Ages the gyr falcon has been the most prized and renowned of Icelandic and Arctic birds. Its association with Iceland is reflected in the country's major award of merit - the Order of the Icelandic Falcon. This superb predator is never completely safe from extinction, and is now heavily protected in Iceland, even to the extent of severe penalties for photographing the bird on the nest. This book is an entertaining account of a search for a sight of the falcon in Ísafjarðardjúp on the north-western peninsula. Other birds are also reported on. A map of the area appears inside the boards. Photographs. For an account of an earlier venture see Ernest Lewis' (i.e. Ernest Vesey) *In search of the gyr falcon* (London: Constable; Toronto: MacMillan, 1938. 234p.).

248 The land of the loon.
G. K. Yeates. London: Country Life, 1951. 156p.

Impressions of a birdwatcher and photographer on two trips to Iceland in 1948 and 1949. The author set himself up in two areas: Staður in Hrútafjörður, and at Þingvellir. He studies the bird life in a variety of habitats - hills, valleys, bogs, lakes and scrubland. His main search was for the great northern diver (Icelandic *himbrimi*). Appendix of scientific names.

Natural History, Ecology, Flora and Fauna. Ornithology

249 **A thousand geese.**
Peter Scott, James Fisher. London: Collins, 1953. 240p. maps. bibliog. illus.

One of the very best books on Icelandic bird life - a blend of expertise and entertainment. It is the record of an expedition by the Severn Wildfowl Trust to the Þjórsárver tract near Hofsjökull in 1951 to make a particular study of the pink-footed goose. The trip was remarkably successful. The text is accompanied by illustrations and several informative maps of the area.

250 **The eider farms of Iceland.**
David A. Munro. *Canadian Geographical Journal*, vol. 63 (Aug. 1961), p. 59-63.

Eider ducks inhabit the colder waters of the Northern hemisphere, and Iceland has long been known as one of their frequent breeding grounds; eiderdown was exported from Iceland to Britain as early as the 14th century. Although eiders seldom move far from their breeding grounds during the rest of the year, the systematic farming of them is confined to the breeding season from May to July. Governmental legislation relating to the protection of eiders is strict in Iceland. This article describes the habits and habitats of the birds, and the planning of production of eiderdown by the individual farmers, on whose private islands most of the eider farming is carried out. Eider duck colonies in Iceland are also described by the popular writer on animal life in north-western quarters, Gavin Maxwell, in his book *Raven seek thy brother* (London: Longman, 1968. chpts. 9 and 10.).

251 **Eldey: daring ascent of world's greatest gannet colony.**
Árni Johnsen. *Atlantica and Iceland Review*, vol. 10, no. 2 (1972), p. 23-31.

The protected island of Eldey (of great auk fame) off the south-western tip of Iceland contains the largest colony of gannets in the world. Its sides rise sheer from the sea, and the challenge which it poses to any climber is immense. This feature article is a short account, accompanied by startling photography, by the leader of an expedition of six Westmann Islanders who ventured to observe this colony of around 40,000 gannets on one rock. It had been thirty years since the last visit by humans, and it was not without controversy. See the same writers brief description of the multitudinous puffins on the cliffs of the Westmann Islands in the same magazine, vol. 14, no. 1 (1976), p. 24-26. For another short feature on the gannet see the piece by Arnþór Garðarsson, Professor of Ornithology at the University of Iceland, in the same magazine vol. 17, no. 1 (1979), p. 21-27.

252 **Selection of food by Icelandic ptarmigan..**
Arnþór Garðarsson, Robert Moss. In: *Animal populations in relation to their food resources.* Edited by Adam Watson. Oxford, England: Blackwell, 1970. p. 47-71. (British Ecological Society Symposium, no. 10).

The Icelandic ptarmigan, which is a common sight on the heathlands of Iceland, is shown by this research to be a highly-selective feeder on vegetation. Its feeding habits are shown to vary according to seasonal availability, and to the nutritive value of the food.

Land animals

253 Origins of Iceland and Shetland cattle.
Marshall Watson. *Ark* (UK), vol. 9, no. 8 (Aug. 1982), p. 290-93.

A symposium paper presented in the magazine of the Rare Breeds Survival Trust, in which the contributor discusses the strains of Icelandic cattle from the Viking period to the present, and the characteristics which it shares with the Shetland breed. There has been no significant importation of cattle to Iceland since the Vikings. Today there are 33,500 dairy cows in the country, all of the Icelandic breed; their characteristics and the methods of breeding are briefly described.

254 Pride of the mountains; in the tracks of the reindeer.
Birgir Kjaran, Helgi Valtýsson. *Atlantica and Iceland Review*, vol. 8, no. 4 (1970), p. 37-41.

Reindeer were first imported to Iceland in 1771 from Norway. Today they number over 3,500 and are to be found in the mountains of eastern Iceland. They are virtually the only wild reindeer in Europe; reindeer hunting is strictly controlled in Iceland, and limited to one month in a year. Very little has been written about Icelandic reindeer, and these two brief portraits serve simply to acquaint the foreign reader with the reindeer's survival.

255 Stallion of the north.
Sigurður A. Magnússon, photographs by Guðmundur Ingólfsson (and others). Reykjavík: Iceland Review; Hove, England: Wayland; Nantucket, Massachusetts: Longship Press, 1978. 96p. photos.

Horses came to Iceland along with the first settlers. No horses have been imported since those early years, and it therefore follows that the Icelandic breed is both pure and endowed with unique characteristics. Harsh winters have induced a hardiness, and the terrain has made them remarkably surefooted, as the visitor to Iceland will have opportunities to discover. The breed is small, docile, and has five distinct gaits. Nowadays there are some 50,000 of these ponies throughout Iceland, and although the plane and the car have usurped many of their traditional functions, they are still indispensable at sheep-rounding time, and are popular for leisure activity; they are also starting to contribute to the national balance of payments, as they are being bred for export to North America - not for the sordid purposes which have disgraced European trade, but purely for their traditional abilities and qualities. This book, published in its English and American editions under the title *The Iceland horse*, both in its text and photography, captures the admirable spirit of the animal, its legend, history, breeding, character and activity. An earlier publication was *The Iceland horse*, photographs by Helga Fietz, text by Broddi Jóhannesson (Munich: Mandruck, 1958, 30p).

256 The fox: still fighting for survival.
Páll Hersteinsson. *Atlantica and Iceland Review*, vol. 20 (summer 1982), p. 48-54.

The Arctic fox has maintained a habitat in Iceland since the end of the last Ice Age. From the time of human settlement it has been subjected to constant attempts at extermination, mainly because of its predatory attacks on the sheep

Natural History, Ecology, Flora and Fauna. Land animals

which have always been vital to the Icelanders. Today perhaps one fox in every four can expect to survive such attempts. This article is an illustrated sketch of the family life of the fox in Iceland, and of its sophisticated struggle for survival. The Icelandic fox is either brown or white, the former to be seen around the coastal areas, the latter in the highlands.

257 A research on the Iceland dog (also known as the Icelandic sheepdog).
Mark Watson. Nicasio, California: Wensum Kennels, 1956. 80p. illus. chart.

The only treatise in English on the Iceland dog. The breed has the general appearance of a collie/husky cross, and in its purer form is found mainly in eastern Iceland (the fact that the keeping of dogs in Reykjavík is, uniquely for a capital city, banned by law has no bearing on this!). This book is a remarkably researched collection of primary materials arranged chronologically, describing the breed, mostly from the 19th and 20th centuries. But dogs are mentioned in several sagas; the Icelandic breed was known by export to England in Shakespeare's time (see *Henry V*, Act II, scene 1 'Pish for thee, Iceland dog, thou prick-ear'd cur of Iceland!'); also, three species of Iceland dog are noted by Eggert Ólafsson and Bjarni Pálsson in their natural history, *Travels in Iceland* (q.v.). The author includes several drawings and photographs, a revised standard of points to describe the breed, and a folding chart showing the place of the Iceland dog as a Spitz type within the genealogy of 114 breeds. If the reader experiences difficulties in obtaining this item there is a useful article by this author entitled 'A short history of the Iceland dog' in *Atlantica and Iceland Review*, vol. 10, no. 1 (1972), p. 55-59.

Sheep: providing basic necessities since the settlement.
See item no. 525.

Physical Anthropology

258 The character of races.
Ellsworth Huntington. New York: Scribner, 1927. 393p. Reprinted New York: Arno Press, 1977.
Chapters seventeen to nineteen of this comparative work are frequently cited in relation to Icelandic studies. (The book as a whole has also been often quoted for more controversial purposes). Entitled respectively 'The dispersal of the Northmen', 'Warlike Normans and peaceful Icelanders', and 'The persistence of a selected inheritance', they cover the historical character of the Icelanders 'as influenced by physical environment, natural selection and historical development'. In the last of these chapters the author is particularly original and perceptive: 'According to the hypothesis of this book, the original cause of Iceland's greatness was the repeated selection to which its people were subjected. When the last selection had brought to the island a homogeneous, sober-minded and competent group of people, there ensued within a century or two a wonderful outburst of genius... In our own day, a thousand years later, Iceland still has the right to boast of her people's character and achievement. A selected inheritance, when isolated, protected and kept up to the mark by further selection, seems able to persist indefinitely'. Huntington's views are drawn on by Laurence A. Kratz in his article 'The cultural progress of Iceland', *Journal of Geography*, vol. 45 (Oct. 1946), p. 285-91, in which he evaluates the factors under the headings of natural resources, climate, geographical isolation and natural selection.

259 The physical anthropology of the Vikings.
Jón Steffensen. *Journal of the Royal Anthropological Institute of Great Britain and Ireland*, vol. 83, no. 1 (Jan. 1953), p. 86-97.
'The Viking expeditions constitute the last of those migrations of peoples within Europe which reached any considerable magnitude, and which might be expected to have had a significant effect on the present racial composition of many European countries. The Vikings, furthermore, settled in Iceland, a country until then uninhabited. Because it is of some importance for the study of anthropology to know as much as possible about the physical characteristics of the Vikings, I

Physical Anthropology

have tried to gather all available information'. In this context the Icelandic author of this paper specialises in the measurement of skulls from Viking graves, and concludes that the Vikings represent anthropologically two groups, eastern and western, and that the latter is exhibited in many characteristics of modern Icelanders, with reference to skulls, pigmentation and blood groups. See the same author's paper at the Third Viking Congress (q.v.).

260 The settlement of Iceland.
L. F. Saugstad. *Norwegian Archaeological Review*, vol. 10 (1977), p. 60-83.

Evidence for the racial origin of the Icelanders has been based on archaeological, historical, cultural and linguistic factors, but more recently genetic factors have been adduced. This article is an example of such research: the incidence of the inherited disease phenylketonuria is compared in Iceland, Ireland and Norway, to show a high level of Celtic admixture in Icelandic stock, and a consequently reduced proportion of Norwegian strain amongst the early settlers of Iceland. The article is followed by comments from five specialists on these findings, with a reply.

261 The blood groups of Icelanders.
Joyce A. Donegani, N. Dungal, E. W. Ikin, A. E. Mourant. *Annals of Eugenics* (UK), vol. 15 (1950), p. 147-52.

The authors of this paper relate their findings that the Icelanders have a high frequency of blood group O, similar to that found in Scotland and Ireland but considerably lower than that in Norway, to the debate on the origin of the Icelanders as a racial group. Two more recent and technically presented accounts of similarly motivated research appear in this journal's successor *Annals of Human Genetics*: Ólafur Bjarnason and others report at length in vol. 36, no. 4 (April 1978), p. 425-55; E. A. Thompson applies a stochastic model to the admixture problem in vol. 37 (1973), p. 69-80.

262 Körpermasse und Körperproportionen der Isländer: ein Beitrag zur Anthropologie Islands. (Physical size and physical proportions of Icelanders: a contribution to the anthropology of Iceland.)
Guðmundur Hannesson, translated by W. Humbolt. Reykjavík: Háskóli Íslands, 1925. 254p. illus.

Guðmundur Hannesson was exceptionally active not only as a surgeon (q.v.), but also as a researcher and writer on medical and allied topics. This valuable piece of research, published as a supplement to the yearbook of the University of Iceland, is an ethnological and anthropometric study of the Icelandic population. The text is accompanied by many illustrations and statistical data. This work remains the only full-length survey of the physical anthropology of the modern Icelander available in translation.

Physical Anthropology

263 **Some anthropological characteristics of Icelanders analysed with regard to the problem of ethnogenesis.**
Jens Pálsson. *Journal of Human Evolution*, vol. 7, no. 8 (Dec. 1978), p. 695-702.
A paper reporting results of statistical research into the ethnic origin of the Icelanders, with particular attention to the further factor of pigmentation of hair and eyes, and to the combinations of these characteristics. The findings indicate a closer biological relationship between Icelanders and Scandinavians than Irish and British.

The origin of the Icelanders.
See item no. 300.

Archaeology

264 **Romans in Iceland.**
Kristján Eldjárn. *American-Scandinavian Review*, vol. 39, no. 2 (June 1951), p. 123-26.
The discovery by a farmer on the south-eastern coast of Iceland of two Roman coins from the third century A.D. potentially extended the history of Iceland backwards for a further half millennium. In this brief article, this distinguished Icelandic archaeologist refutes the cynical interpretation that these coins had been brought to Iceland by later Viking settlers - 'Vikings placed no value upon ancient things' - and argues for a Roman presence, however transitory, on Icelandic soil.

265 **Herdsmen and hermits: Celtic seafarers in the northern seas.**
T. C. Lethbridge. Cambridge, England: Bowes, 1950. 146p.
The Norsemen were the first permanent settlers of Iceland, but there has never been any serious doubt that the Celts had been there the best part of a century before, and maybe much earlier - a fact acknowledged, but rarely dwelt on in most accounts of Iceland. Chapter six of this book is a discussion of the Celtic presence there, but its real interest lies in the light which it casts on the North Atlantic traffic of the Celtic seafarers, and on the communication between Ireland, the Scottish islands, Iceland, and even Greenland. The book is not so much an archaeological textbook as a series of entertaining and stimulating deductions.

266 **The Vikings.**
Holger Arbman, translated and edited with an introduction by Alan L. Binns. London: Thames & Hudson, 1961. 212p. (Ancient Peoples and Places, vol. 21).
A readable presentation in this respected archaeological series, in which the Professor of Archaeology at the University of Lund in Sweden describes the expanding world of the Vikings, with particular emphasis upon the economic reasons for their expansion. Supplementary chapter on Viking art. Well illustrated. For a Danish professorial study compare the excellent book by Johannes Brøndsted, Professor of Nordic Archaeology at the University of Copenhagen, translated by Kalle Skov, and likewise entitled *The Vikings* (Harmondsworth, England: Penguin; Santa Fé, New Mexico: Gannon, 1965).

Archaeology

267 Viking expansion westwards.
Magnús Magnússon, drawings by Rosemonde Nairac. London: Bodley Head, 1973. 152p. illus. (Bodley Head Archaeologies).

Chapter six of this volume is devoted specifically to Iceland, and for the newcomer forms an ideal introduction to the four centuries of the Old Icelandic Commonwealth in the light of archaeology. The author presents an objective and clear account, with well-chosen illustrations, of the settlement, living conditions, religion (pagan and Christian), administration, and the sagas. When, in 1979, the BBC embarked on their television serial documentary about the Vikings, Magnús Magnússon, as a native Icelander, Knight of the Order of the Icelandic Falcon, archaeologist and professional communicator, was the obvious candidate to conduct the venture. His superbly illustrated book *Vikings!* (London: Bodley Head for the BBC; New York: Dutton, 1980. 320p.), is based on this series, and draws on fresh archaeological evidence to portray the Vikings in a creative rather than a destructive light. Chapter seven is specifically about Iceland.

268 Þriðji Víkingafundur. (Third Viking Congress, *Reykjavík, 1956.*)
Edited by Kristján Eldjárn. Reykjavík: Ísafoldarprentsmiðja, 1958. 165p. (Yearbook of the Icelandic Archaeological Society, suppl.).

Since 1950 the Viking Congress has assembled eight times at different locations in the northern countries. Iceland has usually been well represented on the agenda. The third congress was held in Reykjavík itself, and included the following contributions by Icelandic participants: 'Iceland in the saga period: some geographical aspects' by Sigurður Þórarinsson, p. 13-24; 'Viking archaeology in Iceland' by Kristján Eldjárn, p. 25-38 (q.v.); 'Stature as a criterion of the nutritional level of Viking age Icelanders', by Jón Steffensen, p. 39-51; 'Þingvellir: the place and its history', by Einar Ól. Sveinsson, p. 74-76; 'On Grágás: the oldest Icelandic code of law', by Ólafur Lárusson, p. 77-89; and 'The Icelandic glíma', by Þorsteinn Einarsson, p. 138-41 (q.v.). All these papers are presented in English.

269 Viking archaeology in Iceland.
Kristján Eldjárn. In: *Third Viking Congress, Reykjavík, 1956.* Edited by Kristján Eldjárn. Reykjavík: Ísafoldarprentsmiðja, 1956, p. 25-38.

A paper presented to the third Viking Congress, Reykjavík by the Director of the National Museum of Iceland. 'For natural reasons Icelandic archaeology is not a very fertile field, and never will be. In this country we have hardly any prehistory at all... our great inheritance is the brilliant mediaeval literature. This fact, however, is no reason why we should neglect such archaeological remains as there are in this country'. Having briefly reflected on pre-Norse remains in Iceland, Dr Eldjárn proceeds to a lucid summary of the two main groups of remains from the Viking age: farm ruins and graves. He concludes with some remarks on the provenance of Icelandic antiquities. The author enlarges on the first of these two groups in 'Two mediaeval farmsites in Iceland and some remarks on tephrochronology' (Gjáskógar in Þjórsárdalur and Gröf in the Öræfisveit), a paper presented to the fourth Viking Congress (York, 1961) and published in its proceedings (Edinburgh: Oliver & Boyd for the University of Aberdeen, 1965, p. 10-19). For further Viking material see History section.

Archaeology

270 **Ruins of the saga time: being an account of travels and explorations in Iceland in the summer of 1895.**
Þorsteinn Erlingsson, with introduction by F. T. Norris, Jón Stefánsson. London: Nutt, 1899. 112p. map. figs.
Reprinted New York: AMS Press, 1978. (Viking Society for Northern Research. Extra Series, vol. 11).

The stimulus for this study was to throw further light on the remains found on the Charles River, Massachusetts, by Cornelia Horsford (see her article 'Dwellings of the saga time in Iceland, Greenland and Vinland' in *National Geographic* vol. 9, no. 3 March 1898. p. 73-84) and thought to relate to settlements of Norsemen in 'Vinland' at the start of the 11th century. Various localities in western Iceland were visited, and examinations made of housing sites, meeting places, grave mounds, cairns, river walls, ditches, etc., for comparative purposes. Includes many line drawings and a map of the route and sites.

271 **The poetic Edda in the light of archaeology.**
Birger Nerman, translated from the Swedish by G. Gosse. Coventry, England: Curtis & Beamish, 1931. 94p. 60 plates. (Viking Society for Northern Research. Extra Series, vol. IV).

A study with a twofold purpose: firstly, to describe the nature of various objects referred to in the Eddic poems, with a view to illuminating certain passages and applying archaeological factors to linguistic interpretations; secondly, to relate the archaeological background of the *Poetic Edda* to the date and legends of its poems. Contains sixty plates.

272 **Carved panels from Flatatunga, Iceland.**
Kristján Eldjárn. *Acta Archaeologica* (Denmark), vol. 24 (1956), p. 81-101. illus.

A detailed description, with illustrations, of the ornamental carved house-timbers to be found at the farm site of Flatatunga in Skagafjörður, northern Iceland. Remains of Norse woodcarving are rare; these panels are to be dated probably in the 11th century, and show strong influence of the Ringerike style with its extravagant tendrils. Their religious character forms the earliest testimony to the Christian faith in Iceland. Dr Eldjárn had earlier presented a paper to the Second Viking Congress at Bergen in 1953 concerning the panels at Flatatunga/Möðrufell, under the title 'Ringerike style in Iceland'.

273 **Thjórsárdalur: Iceland's Pompeii.**
Mats Wibe Lund. *American-Scandinavian Review*, vol. 62, no. 2 (1974), p. 159-65. illus.

A brief illustrated account of the old settlements at Þjórsárdalur, located northwest of Hekla, whose community was destroyed by the Hekla eruption of 1300. Particular description is made of the excavated and now protected farm at Stöng. An earlier account of actual fieldwork centred on Þjórsárdalur and Stöng by a joint Icelandic/Danish/Swedish team is presented by Aage Roussell as 'The archaeological expedition to Iceland in 1939, and its results' in *Le Nord* (Denmark), vol. 6, no. 2-4 (1943), p. 121-32. General conclusions are drawn concerning the character of the Old Norse dwelling, and of the *hof* or temple.

Archaeology

274 Núpsstaður; an old farm in Iceland.
Gísli Gestsson. *Ethnologia Scandinavica*, vol. 8 (1978), p. 41-66. illus. plans.

Núpsstaður is an unusually large farm located to the west of Skeiðarársandur on the south-eastern coast of Iceland. The first documentary record of its existence as a community dates from 1200. The writer of this article presents, in absorbing detail, an historical inventory of the external and internal structure of the farmhouse, the outbuildings and the chapel, by drawing on the evidence of written descriptions, old photographs, and personal recollections. There are many illustrations and plans throughout the text. In archaeological terms, the present buildings are relatively recent (though not by the standards of the Icelandic environment), the 17th century chapel, substantially restored, being the oldest building, and the rest of the buildings, in more or less their present form, dating from the late 19th century. Núpsstaður is still lived in and worked on. This article throws a rare light on the history of the Icelandic farm.

275 The turf farm.
Gísli Sigurðsson. *Atlantica and Iceland Review*, vol. 9, no. 1 (1971), p. 33-41.

The availability of new materials for building at the beginning of this century signalled the end of the most traditional feature of Icelandic rural society - the turf farm. The lack of timber over the centuries made the construction of dwellings with turf a natural procedure, totally in sympathy with the environment. There are still sufficient examples in Iceland (one or two still inhabited) for a detailed picture to be drawn of the history of family life within their walls. This illustrated article is a form of tribute to the long history of the turf farm.

276 Windmills and watermills in Iceland.
A. J. Beenhakker. Reading, England: International Molinological Society, 1976. 12p.

Iceland's contemporary efforts at exploiting the natural energy of water have tended to obscure the historical dimension; the hydropotential has always been apparent, and a proportionately large number of watermills, perhaps 200, were built around the country during the 19th century. The construction of watermills made the windmill a much rarer sight - today only one windmill is to be found in working order, on the small island of Vigur in Ísafjarðardjúp. This publication is a brief but unique survey of Icelandic molinology (sic - the word is not yet recorded in the supplement to the *Oxford English Dictionary*) with a map of the sites, photographs and diagrams. Further information on this topic can be found in an article of the same title by D. G. Tucker in *Industrial Archaeology*, vol. 9, no. 3 (Aug. 1972), p. 278-84.

277 History of industries and crafts in Iceland.
D. G. Tucker. *Industrial Archaeology*, vol. 9, no. 1 (Feb. 1972), p. 5-27.

A survey of the limited range of materials available for the study of industrial archaeology in Iceland. Sectors include fisheries, agriculture, mining, textiles, building, transport and power. An appendix compares the history of technology in Iceland with that of other North Atlantic islands, and indicates some of the relevant objects in the National Museum of Iceland. In the next issue of the same periodical (May 1972), p. 172-77, Tucker contributes further notes on 'The stockfish industry of Iceland: a living industrial archaeology'.

Archaeology

The origin of the Icelanders.
See item no. 300.

Farm abandonment in Eyjafjallasveit, southern Iceland.
See item no. 517.

Genealogy and Heraldry

278 **The genealogist and history: Ari to Snorri.**
Joan Turville-Petre. *Saga-book* (UK), vol. 20, no. 1-2 (1978-79), p. 7-23.
Genealogy was a crucial and pervasive force amongst mediaeval Icelanders in their kinship obligations. This essay is concerned not so much with genealogy in the Icelandic Commonwealth itself as with 'the remoter ranges of ancestry, where the scholar had to proceed from the known to the unknown. At this level, genealogy is an imaginative art, which is nevertheless controlled by rules and techniques formulated in the known area'.

279 **The continuity of Icelandic names and naming patterns.**
Richard F. Tomasson. *Names*, vol. 23, no. 4 (1975), p. 281-89.
Iceland is the only country where the old Scandinavian practice of one's given name being one's primary name persists, through a combination of popular feeling and legislation. (In a check of the Icelandic telephone directory for 1972, the author of this paper found that only 15 per cent of the entries were under a family name rather than a first name followed by patronymic). Among the many points of interest raised in the article is the current preponderance of names which were popular also in saga times. The author presents tables of the rank order of frequency of male and female names from the settlement to the present; he shows Jón and Guðrún to have been the most popular consistently since saga times until 1970 (however, a survey in 1976 showed these to have been overtaken in this year by Þór and the Danish import Kristinn). This article later appears as chapter six of Tomasson's book *Iceland: the first new society* (q.v.). For a broader view of Icelandic onomastics see W. H. Wolf-Rottray's 'Some onomastic and toponomastic aspects of Icelandic traditionalism' q.v.

Genealogy and Heraldry

280 **Our patronymic system.**
Stefán Bjarnason. *Sixty-five Degrees*, vol. 2, no. 1 (winter 1968), p. 13-15+23.

The Icelandic preoccupation with genealogy is here illustrated in a short article on the past and present situation of Icelandic names. The article summarises the legal position concerning names following the parliamentary acts of 1913 and 1925, and includes an example of a lineage traced from Þorfinn Karlsefni, voyager to Vinland in the year 1010, and listed through thirty generations down to the writer of the article. Many Icelanders can claim to be able to do the same.

281 **The coat of arms of Iceland.**
Sven Tito Achen. *American-Scandinavian Review*, vol. 50 (1962), p. 355-58. illus.

A brief description, with colour illustrations, of the three coats of arms in Icelandic history: the first, known from the 14th century, depicting a silver split cod under a golden crown in a red field; the second, adopted in 1903, depicting a silver falcon in a blue field; the third, coinciding with Iceland's independence in 1919, is based on the Icelandic flag, and depicts a blue shield and silver cross superimposed by a red cross (the 'opposite' of the Norwegian flag) surrounded by four creatures and topped with a royal crown - the crown was removed in 1944 when Iceland became a republic.

History

Scandinavian and Viking

282 *Gesta Danorum*. The first nine books of the Danish history of Saxo Grammaticus.
translated by Oliver Eeton. London: Nutt, 1894. 435p.

Saxo Grammaticus, whose original Latin work *Gesta Danorum* was written around 1200, was one of the two continental scholars of the Middle Ages who wrote extensively about the early history of the northern countries (cf. Adam of Bremen in the 11th century). Saxo's account in sixteen volumes is of importance to the historian not so much for the comments which he makes on early Iceland, but for the use which he seems to have made of Icelandic sources to illustrate the history of the Danes. In an appendix to this translation F. York Powell discusses Saxo's methods and sources; the source of Saxo's account of Hamlet the Dane, for example, (Shakespeare in turn used Saxo as his source) is clearly from an Icelandic story telling tradition.

283 **Northern antiquities.**
Paul Henri Mallet, translated from the French by Bishop Thomas Percy. London: Bohn, 1847. 578p. Reprinted New York: AMS Press, 1968.

'... or, an historical account of the manners, customs, religion and laws, maritime expeditions and discoveries, language and literature of the ancient Scandinavians (Danes, Swedes, Norwegians and Icelanders)... revised throughout, and considerably enlarged with a translation of the Prose Edda from the original Old Norse text; and notes, critical and explanatory, by I. A. Blackwell, Esq. To which is added an abstract of the Eyrbyggja saga by Sir Walter Scott' (title page). Enough said, other than that the new material added to the original edition of 1770 comprises well over half of the 1847 edition, and is concentrated on Iceland, particularly the westward discoveries, laws and institutions, manners and customs, and literature.

History. Scandinavian and Viking

284 The heroic age of Scandinavia.
G. Turville-Petre. London: Hutchinson, 1951, 196p.
Reprinted Westport, Connecticut: Greenwood Press, 1976.

This book is, quite simply the best introduction to the early Scandinavian world; no other book in this far-reaching field has quite managed to convey so much within so compact a volume. Each of the sixteen chapters offers the student the basic platform for further study: archaeology, runes and the Old Norse language, legendary and historical heroes, Viking expansion, the discovery and settlement of Iceland, its poets and historians.

285 A history of the Vikings.
T. D. Kendrick. London: Methuen, 1930. 412p.

The first systematic history of the Vikings in English, and the first to treat the Viking presence in all those parts of the world to which it extended. Chapter twelve (p. 336-61) is devoted specifically to Iceland, but the value of this volume, not yet wholly superseded, is its discussion of the similarities and differences of the Viking approach in the various lands. The author became Director and Principal Librarian of the British Museum.

286 Everyday life in the Viking age.
Jacqueline Simpson, drawings by Eva Wilson. London: Batsford; New York: Putnam, 1967. 208p.

A largely successful attempt to bring to life the world of the Viking as farmer, seaman, trader, fighter, homelover, artist and worshipper. An uncluttered and popular presentation directed at the layman, and suitable also for the younger reader, with clear and helpful drawings. Reprinted by the same publishers in 1980 under the changed title *The Viking world.*

287 A history of the Vikings.
Gwyn Jones. London: Oxford University Press, 1968. 504p. 15 maps.

The most scholarly of the many presentations of the Viking world, and the first full-scale treatment in English since T. D. Kendrick (q.v.). This work exhibits a remarkable coherence in pulling together the numerous strands of Viking history into an overall picture of its civilisation. The movement westward to Iceland, Greenland and America is described on p. 269-311. Profusely illustrated, and containing fifteen maps. Issued in paperback format in 1973. The author is a Knight of the Order of the Falcon, a decoration bestowed by the President of Iceland.

288 The Viking achievement: the society and culture of early mediaeval Scandinavia.
Peter Foote, David M. Wilson. London: Sidgwick & Jackson, 1970, 473p. bibliog. (Great Civilisations Series).

The value of this excellent volume lies in its clearly arranged thematic approach, with chapters on the four individual countries followed by chapters on slavery and freedom, the family unit, daily life, administration and justice, trade and transport, warfare, religion, culture, etc. A standard work, detailed but digestible. The co-author of this book, David Wilson, offers a shorter treatment of many of these themes in his *The Vikings and their origins: Scandinavia in the first millennium*, (London: Thames & Hudson, 2nd ed. 1980. 116p. Library of Early Mediaeval

History. Scandinavian and Viking

Civilisations). See his volume with Ole Klindt-Jensen, *Viking art* (London: Allen & Unwin. rev. ed. 1980, 256p.).

289 The age of the Vikings.
P. H. Sawyer. London: Edward Arnold, 1971, 2nd ed. 254p. bibliog.

That this book (unusually in this field) ran to a second edition nine years after it was first published is an indication of its significance. It is very critical of earlier assumptions and interpretations concerning the Viking period: basically, the author seeks to overturn what he sees as a continuation of an historiographic tradition in which the Vikings and their activities have been judged through the same eyes as the Christian society of the west judged them at the time - as pagan, and, therefore, uncompromisingly alien. The fresh approaches to the Viking character which have emerged during the last fifteen years would seem to owe more than a little to this tightly argued and remarkably readable interpretation. *Kings and Vikings A.D. 700-1000* is the title of Sawyer's recent volume, (London: Methuen, 1982) in which the conversion to Christianity is a central theme.

290 Hammer of the north: myths and heroes of the Viking age.
Magnús Magnússon, photographs by Werner Forman. London: Orbis, 1976. 128p.

One reviewer has aptly described this book as 'an act of piety to the spirit of the author's ancestors', and indeed one of the aims of its author is to portray the Vikings in a new and less fierce light. He discusses pre-Viking Scandinavia, the maritime exploits of the Vikings, and the major figures of their cults and legends in an authoritative and enlightening manner. The text is enhanced by some superb photography. The book was reprinted in 1979 under the slightly altered title *Viking: hammer of the north*.

291 The Vikings.
James Graham-Campbell, Dafydd Kydd. London: British Museum, 1980. 200p. illus.

'The Vikings have had a bad press: the British Museum, by means of this book and the exhibition which it illustrates, is trying in some ways to redress the balance'. Those fortunate enough to have visited the spectacularly successful exhibition of the world of the Vikings mounted in 1980 will have got the message; those not so fortunate at least have recourse to this finely produced companion volume with its clearly presented text and excellent illustrations of the exhibits lent from numerous sources.

292 The northern world: the history and heritage of northern Europe.
Edited by David M. Wilson. London: Thames & Hudson, 1980. 248p. illus.

An appreciation of Icelandic cultural history presupposes an awareness of the common roots of northern European civilisation. This volume deserves particular mention, as it synthesises the results of the most recent research, and presents them in a readily appreciable form. Three of the eight contributions to this volume are especially relevant to Viking and early Icelandic cultural history: 'Gods and heroes of the northern world' by Christine E. Fell; 'The Scandinavians

History. Icelandic history. General

at home', by Else Roesdahl; and 'The Viking adventure', by the Director of the British Museum, David M. Wilson. The volume is superbly illustrated.

Icelandic history

General

293 **On the history of Iceland, and the Icelandic language and literature.**
John Hogg. *Transactions of the Royal Society of Literature* 2nd series (1859), p. 324-86.

A paper presented by the eminent Victorian classical scholar and naturalist, in which he offers a synthesis of the historical and cultural character of the Icelandic nation.

294 **The island of fire (Iceland): or, a thousand years of the old Northmen's home, 874-1874.**
Phineas C. Headley. Boston, Massachusetts: Lee & Shepherd, 1875. 339p.

This volume, published to mark the millennial of the settlement of Iceland, is intended, according to its author, to cover the whole field of Icelandic history. In fact, it is a rather rambling account of the older period, laced with literary digressions, notes on excursions, and remarks on 19th-century Icelandic society. Hardly to be recommended as a systematic history, but a number of its observations make it worth a browse.

295 **Iceland: its history and inhabitants.**
Jón Stefánsson. *Journal of Transactions of the Victoria Institute or Philosophical Society of Great Britain*, vol. 34 (1902), p. 164-78; vol. 38 (1906), p. 54-63.

An essay in which the Icelandic author portrays the geographical and environmental influences on the historical development of the Icelandic nation. This two-part paper appeared also in continuous form in the annual report of the Smithsonian Institution for 1906. See Jón Stefánsson's book *Denmark and Sweden with Iceland and Finland* (London: Fisher Unwin; New York: Putnam, 1916).

296 **Concise history of Iceland.**
Bogi Þ. Melsteð, translated by Jón G. Palmeson. Ottawa, Ontario: 1906. 103p. plates.

A modest history, published privately, which for most purposes was to be displaced by the more substantial work of Knut Gjerset (q.v.) but of interest as the first chronological history of Iceland translated into English. Bogi Melsteð was an Icelandic writer (see *A catalogue of the Icelandic Collection*, University of Leeds Library, q.v.), based in Copenhagen, and this translation was motivated by the

History. Icelandic history. Settlement and Commonwealth

late 19th-century emigration from Iceland to Canada, which included the translator. Contains plates of several prominent Icelanders of the later period.

297 **History of Iceland.**
Knut Gjerset. New York: MacMillan; London: Allen & Unwin, 1924. 482p.

Still virtually the only substantial general history of Iceland available in the English language. Although it has no great analytical pretensions, its commendable aim is to record the history of the Icelanders in a way which will help the reader understand the traditional spirit of the nation. It was written shortly after the proclamation of Iceland as a sovereign state in 1918, and up to this point can still be recommended both as a readable history and a scholarly source. Unfortunately, no publishing concern has yet seen fit to reprint this valuable work, despite the lack of a more recent alternative. A decade earlier Gjerset had written his *History of the Norwegian people.*

298 **The origin and development of the Icelandic nation.**
Adam Rutherford. London: Ethnic Study Group, 1938. 29p.

The title of this item is rather grander than its content, but as a potted history of Iceland from the settlement to the eve of the new republic the text of this lecture is well balanced and not without interest. Includes map showing locations of eighteen of the family sagas. In the same year Rutherford also published in both English and Icelandic editions a further booklet entitled *Iceland's great inheritance.*

299 **Iceland's thousand years: a series of popular lectures on the history and literature of Iceland.**
Edited by Skúli Johnson. Winnipeg, Manitoba: Icelandic Canadian Club and the Icelandic National League, 1945. 169p.

A collection of thirteen papers by various writers which together identify and discuss many of the key factors and highlights of Iceland's history and cultural development. Subjects covered include: geographical background; the settlement; early literature; the Old Icelandic Commonwealth; the coming of Christianity; the colonisation of Greenland and the discovery of North America; Snorri Sturluson; *Sturlunga saga;* the 'dark' ages; Hallgrímur Pétursson; the awakening and enlightenment; 19th-century literature; freedom and progress.

Settlement and Commonwealth

300 **The origin of the Icelanders.**
Barði Guðmundsson, translated with an introduction and notes by Lee M. Hollander. Lincoln, Nebraska: University of Nebraska Press, 1967. 173p.

The weight of opinion until well into this century had been in favour of ascribing the settlement of Iceland in the late 9th and early 10th centuries to a Norwegian origin. However, in 1939 at the annual Congress of Scandinavists in Copenhagen,

History. Icelandic history. Settlement and Commonwealth

Barði Guðmundsson, the Icelandic National Archivist, launched his argument that major elements of the settlement were of eastern Scandinavian Danish and Herulian origin, probably via Norway. This book, originally published under the title *Uppruni Íslendinga* (Reykjavík, 1959), is a posthumous collection of eight articles relating to this theory; the main part of the volume on the origins of skaldship in Iceland is a series of scholarly essays on the skaldic poets' treatment of themes such as magic, women's rights, rites associated with the gods Frey and Freyja, genealogies, etc., with which the author illustrates the eastern connection. This is preceded by an introductory essay on the origin of the Icelanders. An important book.

301 On the civilisation of the first Icelandic colonists.
Jón Andrésson Hjaltalín. *Transactions of the Ethnological Society of London*, n.s. no. 6, (1868), p. 176-83.

A short paper in which the Icelandic writer sets out the main features of Icelandic society in its early years, with special regard to its organisation and customs, and its inherently high level of development. Recognition of this degree of sophistication is of fundamental importance to an understanding of Iceland's ability to survive, and latterly to prosper, in the context of over a thousand years of nationhood. Jón A. Hjaltalín was also the joint contributor, with F. York Powell, of the article on Iceland in the renowned edition (the ninth known as the scholars' edition) of *Encyclopaedia Britannica*, published in 1881.

302 The place of Iceland in the history of European institutions.
Charles A. Vansittart Conybeare. Oxford, England: Parker, 1877. 148p. Reprinted New York: AMS Press, 1972.

The Lothian Prize essay for 1877, this volume is an institutional history of the Old Icelandic Commonwealth from the settlement to the fall of the republic, in the course of which the author examines how the continental Norse traditions of administration were translated into Icelandic statehood, with particular reference to the *goðorð*, or system of chieftain-priests, and to the organisation of the Alþing, or parliament; he discusses in detail the operation of the legal system, assesses the impact of the introduction of Christianity, and concludes with a comparative analysis of feudalism in Iceland. In the century since this study was written more detailed knowledge has emerged, but Conybeare's was a significant contribution to the history of the period,and has merited its recent reprinting.

303 Pioneers of freedom: an account of the Icelanders and the Icelandic free state, 874-1262.
Sveinbjörn Johnson. Boston, Massachusetts; Stratford Co., 1930. 361p.

A frequently-cited and substantial volume, motivated by the millennial of the Icelandic parliament, although its approach is serious and analytical rather than merely celebratory. It is directed at the general reader, and succeeds as a well-balanced review of the Old Icelandic Commonwealth, its founders, government and public institutions, legal organisation, social and economic development, and the religious, cultural, educational, recreational and domestic lives of the people. The remarkable flowering of the Commonwealth in Iceland at a time of political and religious absolutism in continental Europe is clearly pointed in this volume.

History. Icelandic history. Settlement and Commonwealth

304 **A history of the Old Icelandic Commonwealth; Íslendinga saga.**
Jón Jóhannesson, translated by Haraldur Bessason. Winnipeg, Manitoba: University of Manitoba Press, 1974. 407p. maps. bibliog. plates. (University of Manitoba Icelandic Studies Series, vol. II).

For eighteen years this work remained available only in Icelandic until this translation. It constitutes a thematic approach to the years 870-1262: government, external exploration, church and religion (the major section), economic history and material culture (including a particularly interesting chapter on class divisions); it also offers an analysis of the factors instrumental in the downfall of the Commonwealth and the loss of independence. Useful appendices include genealogical tables, lists of lawspeakers and bishops, and a bibliography. The volume also includes plates, maps of temple sites and assembly sites, and a folding map of the country showing the administrative divisions of the time. 'Until the middle of the 20th century the biographical form may be said to have dominated Icelandic historical writing. Historians were not only inclined to follow their own time-honoured saga traditions, but also allowed themselves to be unduly influenced by the fact that in a nation as small as their own every individual receives a wider stage for his personal performance than he would find in a more populous society... this is the first major work on Icelandic history in which biographical accounts were carefully subordinated to the analysis of social forces and conditions which shaped the destiny of mediaeval Iceland, and gave the Old Icelandic Commonwealth its own distinctive character'.

305 **Birth of a nation.**
Njörður P. Njarðvík. Reykjavík: Iceland Review, 1977. 96p.

A short and attractive history of early Iceland from the discovery and settlement by Ingólfr Árnason to the dissolution of the Commonwealth. Recommended to the newcomer to Icelandic history of the mediaeval period. Well presented and illustrated. The author has been President of the Writers' Association of Iceland.

306 **Íslendingabók. (The Book of the Icelanders.)**
Ari Þorgilsson, edited and translated by Halldór Hermannsson. Ithaca, New York: Cornell University Library, 1930. 89p. (Islandica, vol. XX).

Ari *fróði* (the wise) lived from 1067 to 1148, and was the first Icelander to write history in the vernacular. Apart from his *Íslendingabók*, he may also have written the original version of the *Landnámabók* (q.v.). *The Book of the Icelanders* in its surviving form is a remarkable document, charting the history of Iceland from the settlement to the year 1000. Ari seems to have been well aware of the art of the historian, particularly in his statement that he is recording only those facts which he has verified, and in the listing of his informants. The influence of Ari's work is clearly acknowledged by the later chroniclers. This translation, with the editor's authoritative introduction, is available in reprint by Kraus. For a more recent (shortened) translation, see Alan Boucher's *A tale of Icelanders* (q.v.).

History. Icelandic history. Settlement and Commonwealth

307 **Landnámabók. (The Book of the Settlements.)**
Translated by Hermann Pálsson, Paul Edwards. Winnipeg, Manitoba: University of Manitoba Press, 1972. 159p. 13 maps. (University of Manitoba Icelandic Studies, vol. I).

There is no other European nation of comparable age which can claim such a remarkable record of the start of its history as can Iceland (the last country in Europe to be settled) in the form of *The Book of the Settlements*, which contains the names, genealogies, and biographical notes of over 400 of the original settlers. This translation, the first into English for over 60 years, is of the earliest of the extant versions, named *Sturlubók* after its compiler Sturla Þórðarson (1214-84). The editors provide a valuable introduction to its antecedents and general background, and append 13 full-page maps showing in detail the areas of the original settlements. The previous translation was by T. Ellwood (Kendal, England: Wilson, 1898.).

308 **Landnámabók: some remarks upon its value as a historical source.**
Jakob Benediktsson. *Saga-book* (UK), vol. 17, no. 4 (1969), p. 275-92.

An examination of the pitfalls of both overestimating and underestimating the historical accuracy of *The Book of the Settlements*, with particular reference to its textual history, and to the identification by Jón Johannesson in 1941 of the versions: two lost (the original from the first half of the 11th century); five extant (three from the 12th-13th, two from the 17th century).

309 **Sturlunga saga.**
Sturla Þórðarson, translated by Julia H. McGrew, introduction by R. George Thomas. New York: Twayne for the American-Scandinavian Foundation, 1970-74. 2 vols. (Library of Scandinavian Literature, vol. 9-10).

Sturla Þórðarson was the nephew of Snorri Sturluson. Among the collection of sagas which make up *Sturlunga saga*, Sturla was responsible for *Íslendinga saga*, a remarkable chronicle of the turbulent age of the Sturlungs, which remains the chief source of information on the last century of the Old Icelandic Commonwealth. It is vivid contemporary history by a writer who was at the centre of the events - Sturla himself was 'lawman' of Iceland. *Íslendinga saga* appears in the first volume of this translation. An early translation of *Sturlunga saga* was made by Guðbrandur Vigfússon (Oxford, England: Clarendon Press, 1878.). For an appreciation of Sturla's work see the Romanes lecture by William Paton Ker entitled *Sturla the historian* (Oxford, England: Clarendon Press, 1906, 24p.).

310 **The age of the Sturlungs: Icelandic civilisation in the 13th century.**
Einar Ól. Sveinsson, translated by Jóhann S. Hannesson. Ithaca, New York: Cornell University Press, 1953. 180p. tables. Reprinted Kraus, 1966. (Islandica vol. XXXVI).

The age of the Sturlungs covers the last two generations of the Old Icelandic Commonwealth from the end of the 12th to later 13th century, which saw the disintegration of the old order of independence and the recognition of Norwegian

History. Icelandic history. Settlement and Commonwealth

sovereignty. The period takes its name from the principal family involved. The concern of the author of this study, who was Professor of Icelandic Literature at the University of Iceland, is with 'the inner life of the Icelanders of this time, their outlook and habits of thought... in an attempt at a unified view of the whole culture'. The Sturlung Age was a time not only of notorious socio-religious and political outrage, but also of towering cultural and intellectual achievement. This book is an authoritative, eloquent and illuminating study of the age. Genealogical tables appended.

311 Goðar and höfðingar in Iceland.
Gunnar Karlsson. *Saga-book* (UK), vol. 19, no. 4 (1977), p. 358-70.

An examination of whether the Old Icelandic Commonwealth 'deserves the name of a democratic society' as has been widely proclaimed. The writer examines the role of the *goðar*, or representative chieftain-priests, in their home districts, their relationships with the farmers, and the changes in their position during the early 13th century. He concludes that the description democratic cannot be sustained in the modern sense, and that the greater independence of the farmers in the 13th century, compared with their dependence on the *goðar* by their predecessors, was an innovation of the age of the *höfðingar* (the newer form of leaders) rather than a remnant of an older freedom.

312 Thraldom in ancient Iceland.
Carl O. Williams. Chicago, Illinois: University of Chicago Press, 1937. 169p. bibliog.

The aim of this study was to 'lay bare the relations between masters and slaves in ancient Iceland'. It is an unusual and stimulating study of social class and dependency as represented in the Eddic poems, the sagas and the laws. The author discusses attitudes and practices, the process of liberation, and what he sees as the withering rather than the abolition of the system. His approach, which is not uniformly valid, is to apply the 20th-century radical conceptions of social class to the workings of an isolated society of a thousand years earlier. For a more recent analysis of 'freemen' and 'slaves' in ancient Iceland, see the article by Kirsten Hastrup in the periodical *Ethnos* (Sweden), vol. 44, no. 3-4 (1979), p. 182-91.

313 Icelandic enterprise: commerce and economy in the Middle Ages.
Bruce E. Gelsinger. Columbia, South Carolina: University of South Carolina Press, 1980. 300p. maps. bibliog. charts. tables.

Considering the geographical isolation of Iceland and the uncompromising nature of the land, it is remarkable how much foreign trading the Icelanders conducted during the mediaeval period. The author of this book, originally a doctoral thesis presented at the University of California, Los Angeles, in 1969, discusses the range of goods which they were able to export, and examines the system of commercial taxes, weights and measures, and prices, in the context of the rise and fall of the Commonwealth. The volume is arranged in three parts: Icelandic prerequisites for foreign trade (resources, institutions and shipping); Iceland's commercial world (continental Scandinavia, the North Atlantic islands, Britain, and deeper into Europe); and a chronological treatment of Icelandic trade. Contains maps, charts and tables. Much use is made of the evidence of the sagas.

History. Icelandic history. Settlement and Commonwealth

314 The Norse traffic with Iceland.
G. J. Marcus. *Economic History Review*, 2nd series, vol. 9, no. 3 (1957), p. 408-19.

A survey of the fluctuating fortunes of Iceland's foreign trade from the late 9th to the early 15th century. Literary and historical sources are drawn upon to identify the principal trading routes and their hazards, as well as the ports and harbours in use. Commodities imported were chiefly timber and meal, while exports included stockfish and wool (both still important exports today), and even falcons. In 1262, when Iceland surrendered her independence to Norway her trading position initially seemed to be vulnerable, but the intervention of the German Hanseatic League, the growing demand for stockfish, and the advances in navigational expertise, in fact led to an expansion of Icelandic traffic at a time when that of Norway was waning. The peak was recorded by the middle of the 14th century, when a combination of natural disasters in Iceland and the decline of Bergen as the administrative centre of Norway resulted in an almost fatal withering of communications between Norway and Iceland. The author writes along the same lines in an article which appeared in *Mariner's Mirror*, vol. 46, no. 3 (1960), p. 174-81.

315 Viking settlers in Greenland and their descendants during five hundred years.
Poul Nørlund, translated by W. E. Calvert. Cambridge, England: Cambridge University Press, 1936. 160p. illus. plans. Reprinted New York: Kraus, 1971.

The Icelandic colonisation of Greenland inspired by Eirík the Red who settled at Brattahlíð in 983 lasted for well over four centuries; neither archaeological remains nor the written evidence of the Icelandic annals offer any hint later than the first decade of the 15th century, at which time this settlement, which at its height numbered over three thousand, must be assumed to have ended, caused perhaps by onward migration to North America, or assimilation with the Eskimo population, or climate, starvation, or extermination by the Eskimo - all of these views have been propounded, the latter two being more widely held. This book is a clearly-presented study, with illustrations and plans, for the history of this settlement: colonisation, navigation, the bishopric of Greenland, the homesteads, the remarkable finding of the Herjólfsnes garments, and the references to the *Skrælings* (Eskimos). A final chapter is a sketch of the forlorn attempts subsequently to discover any survivors of the Icelandic settlement in Greenland; but the mystery remains. See Helge Ingstad's account: *Land under the pole star: a voyage to the Norse settlements of Greenland* (q.v.).

The conversion of Iceland: a survey.
See item no. 359.

Laws of early Iceland: Grágás.
See item no. 442.

History. Icelandic history. 16th-19th centuries

16th-19th centuries

316 Brevis commentarius de Islandia..
Arngrímur Jónsson. In: *The principall navigations...* Richard Hakluyt. London: Bishop, Newberie & Barker, 1598-1600. Enlarged ed. Vol. I.

During the latter part of the 16th century, a period of natural disasters in Iceland, several accounts of the country were circulating which were regarded by others as ill-informed and ulterior in motive. Arngrímur Jónsson (1568-1648) wrote this and two other later accounts of Iceland to counteract the prevailing trend. It was first published in 1593, and appeared in an English translation only five years later. It is now regarded as the first reliable description of Iceland written since the time of the Commonwealth. Arngrím was rector of the Latin School at Hólar. Half a century later there appeared two other Latin accounts of Iceland: *Two treatises on Iceland from the 17th century* by Jakob Benediktsson (Copenhagen: Munskgaard, 1943, 59p. Bibliotheca Arnamagnaeana, vol. III). The Danish authorities, having acquired several earlier accounts of Iceland, despatched them to the bishops of Hólar (Þorlákur Skúlason) and of Skálholt (Brynjólfur Sveinsson) for their comments, which they duly presented in these two treatises. The editor provides an English introduction to the treatises and their authors.

317 The spread of printing: western hemisphere; Iceland.
Benedikt S. Benedikz. Amsterdam: Vangendt; London: Routledge; New York: Schram, 1969. 64p. map. illus.

In spite of, or perhaps because of, Iceland's remoteness, the first printing press reached Iceland as early as 1530 - over a century earlier than the introduction of printing to Norway. This monograph (one of a series on the history of printing outside continental Europe) is the only treatment of this important subject in English, and is a valuable study in historical bibliography. The author traces the development of printing in northern Iceland at Hólar from the first press up to the end of the 18th century, and in southern Iceland at Leirárgarður and on the islands of Hrappsey and Viðey from 1773 to 1844. He relates these developments to the spread of printing in Iceland into the present century. Facsimiles of examples of the history of Icelandic printing accompany the text, and there is a map showing the historical locations of printing presses. 'In no other comparable country has printing become so integral a part of the nation's life, or has been for so long, despite such heavy odds against its survival'. See the illustrated article '16th century book printing' by Kristjana Gunnarsdóttir in *Atlantica and Iceland Review*, vol. 19, no. 1 (1980), p. 49-55.

318 Henry VIII and Iceland.
Björn Þorsteinsson. *Saga-book* (UK), vol. 15 (1957-61), p. 67-101.

'Iceland was not a fatal issue in Henry's foreign policy... but nevertheless he and his consul had Iceland on their agenda more often than any English government down to our own time'. The writer proves this point in his presentation of the factors of contention between England and Denmark, and between the English and Hanseatic merchants in respect of trading activity with Iceland during the first half of the 16th century.

History. Icelandic history. 16th-19th centuries

319 **Piracy in Iceland.**
Mekkin S. Perkins. *American-Scandinavian Review*, vol. 49, no. 3 (autumn 1961), p. 259-65.
During the 16th and 17th centuries international piracy was rife in northern waters. The summer of 1627 was the occasion of the worst such experience for Iceland, when the country was raided by what were popularly regarded as Turks, but were in fact North African moslems with their base in Algiers. Two hundred and forty captives were abducted from the Westmann Islands, and about half that number from the eastfirths, of whom in all only twenty-seven are recorded as having returned to Iceland from Algiers, and that was ten years later.

320 **The old Icelandic land registers.**
Björn Lárusson, translated by W. F. Salisbury. Lund, Sweden: Gleerup, 1967. 375p. plates.
This research work is directed at the specialist in economic history. It comprises a presentation and analytical discussion of the oldest land registers of Iceland, dated 1686 and 1695-98, the former having been compiled on the basis of taxation values, the latter on values according to use. The registers cover more than 4,000 farms listed by *sýsla* (district) and *hreppur* (commune). A particularly valuable chapter for the history of the period is one containing conclusions on the distribution of farm properties by category of owner: Crown, Church, individuals; and on how this distribution had been affected by the coming of the Reformation, with the Crown benefitting at the expense of the Church, and the private sector remaining stable. The volume includes several plates of the original registers.

321 **Arne Magnússon: the manuscript collector.**
Hans Bekker-Nielsen, Ole Widding, translated by R. W. Mattila. Odense, Denmark: Odense University Press, 1972. 70p. illus.
The fullest account in English of Iceland's antiquarian Árni Magnússon (1663-1730) whose activities in the field of manuscript collection had such great implications for Icelandic national culture and its study. Arni Magnússon spent ten years (1702-12) in Iceland in his quest for manuscripts to take to Copenhagen, but two disasters intervened: the sinking of a ship transporting many of these manuscripts, and a fire in Copenhagen which destroyed more than half the collection. What remained, however, was both of early date and important - if it had not been rescued, the history and study of old Icelandic literature could never have conveyed the richness and depth which is nowadays acknowledged. This well-produced biography, with illustrations, covers Árni's education, travels to Iceland, work on the collection in Copenhagen, and the establishment in 1772 of the Arnamagnaean Commission, which for the last two centuries has overseen the preservation and publication of the manuscripts. For a shorter account see co-author Ole Widding's article in *American-Scandinavian Review*, vol. 52, no. 4 (Dec. 1964), p. 429-34. For an article on the vexed question of Danish or Icelandic location of these manuscripts, now well on the way to resolution, see Sigurđur A. Magnússon's 'Return of the Icelandic manuscripts' in the same periodical, vol. 59, no. 4 (Dec. 1971), p. 341-50.

History. Icelandic history. 16th-19th centuries

322 The medieval leper and his northern heirs.
Peter Richards. Cambridge, England: Brewer; Totowa, New Jersey: Rowman & Littlefield, 1977. 178p.

An enlightening study of the social history of leprosy, which is unusual in drawing on records of personal accounts. Although the author is concerned with north-western Europe as a whole, where the disease lingered on for four centuries after its elimination from other parts of western Europe, the situation in Iceland is represented in the text, and the book is notable in this context for including among its appendices two documents relating to Iceland: a translated extract of a letter written by an Icelandic priest suffering from leprosy in 1767; and an English text of the law regarding the isolation of people with leprosy and their confinement in public hospitals in Iceland, proclaimed by the Danish Ministry in 1898. (Hallgrímur Pétursson, the great 17th-century Icelandic hymn writer, suffered from leprosy in later years).

323 The Laki eruption and the famine of the mist.
Vilhjálmur Bjarnar. In: *Scandinavian studies: essays presented to Dr Henry Goddard Leach.* Edited by Carl F. Bayerschmidt; Erik J. Friis. Seattle, Washington: University of Washington Press, 1965. p. 410-21.

The 18th century was a century of natural disasters for Iceland; census figures show a reduction of nearly 7 per cent in the population between the beginning and end of the century. There were climatic deteriorations, epidemic outbreaks, and a series of earthquakes and volcanic eruptions which culminated in the eruption of the Laki craters in south-eastern Iceland in 1783 and 1784. This was the year of the greatest volcanic activity in the history of Iceland; the main phenomenon connected with the Laki eruption was the mist, which was discernible over four continents, and which, combined with the effects of the falling ash, caused widespread famine in Iceland. The author of this contribution vividly describes the battered state of the population even before the eruption, the further misery of the eruption itself, and the *móðuharðindi*, or famine of the mist.

324 The historical works of Jón Espólín and his contemporaries: aspects of Icelandic historiography.
Ingi Sigurðsson. PhD thesis, University of Edinburgh, Edinburgh, 1972. 446p.

A research into the state of Icelandic historiography during the Enlightenment (c. 1760-1830). The author emphasises the essentially pro-monarchic Lutheran attitudes of the Icelandic historians of this period, and devotes the major part of his study to Jón Jónsson Espólín (b. 1769) who is known especially for his history of Iceland from the fall of the Commonwealth in 1262 up to 1832: *Íslenzk árbœkur i söguformi.* The thesis also comprises chapters on Bishop Hannes Finsen and Magnús Stephensen. The author shows Jón Espólín as an occasionally analytical but mainly annalistic historian influenced more by Icelandic tradition than were his contemporaries, who, particularly Magnús Stephensen, positively promoted the Enlightenment. Espólín's life, his method of presenting both Icelandic and world history, and his influence are discussed in detail, and this valuable thesis is complemented with a glossary and bibliography of primary and secondary sources.

History. Icelandic history. 16th-19th centuries

325 Sir Joseph Banks and Iceland.
Halldór Hermannsson. Ithaca, New York: Cornell University Library, 1928, 100p. illus. (Islandica, vol. XVIII).

The only major study of the relationship between Banks and Iceland. Sir Joseph Banks, the naturalist, had first visited Iceland in 1772 (see Roy A. Rauschenberg's *The Journals of Sir Joseph Banks' Voyage...* q.v.), and may be said to have been the founder of Anglo-Icelandic relations. Banks as a political personality later became a key figure in the international events surrounding Britain, Denmark and Iceland during the first decade of the 19th century. Halldór Hermannsson drew upon and reproduces various correspondence between Banks and Iceland held in the British Museum and at Kew Gardens. He also appends to his essay more than twenty sketches made by Banks and his companions on the trip in 1772. Banks' not entirely altruistic advances (though he and the Icelanders shared a mutual respect) which were made between 1801 and 1808 in an attempt to remove Iceland from Danish oppression and place it under the 'protection' of the British Crown, are the subject of a short article by Llewellyn Chanter entitled with some irony 'John Bull's other Iceland' published in *Norseman*, vol. 15 (1957), p. 73-76.

326 An Icelandic revolution.
Alan E. Boucher. *Atlantica and Iceland Review*, vol. 5, no. 3 (1968), p. 15-19.

An illustrated summary of the bizarre events during the summer of 1809, when the Dane Jörgen Jörgensen, whose relations with his own country and with Britain can best be described as ambiguous, sailed to Iceland on a British ship with the London merchant Samuel Phelps, initially to force open the market for British goods against the Danish monopoly, but, in the event, to declare the Danish province of Iceland an independent republic, with himself as protector; this he achieved and sustained for seven weeks until the unromantic intervention of a British naval commander. It is no more than an episode in Icelandic history, but perhaps it has been underplayed in the context of what might have been the subsequent course of the Icelandic nation. The article includes extracts from the journal of William Hooker (q.v.) who was a passenger on the boat with Jörgensen. See the article by Derek McKay 'Great Britain and Iceland in 1809' in *Mariner's Mirror*, vol. 59 (Feb. 1973), p. 85-95.

327 The convict king: being the life and adventures of Jorgen Jorgensson.
James F. Hogan. London: Ward & Downey, 1891. 235p.

'... monarch of Iceland, naval captain, revolutionist, British diplomatic agent, author, dramatist, preacher, political prisoner, gambler, hospital dispenser, continental traveller, explorer, editor, expatriated exile and colonial constable'; with this *curriculum vitae* Jörgen Jörgensen subtitles the autobiography which he wrote in exile in Australia, whither he was sent after his escapades on his home side of the world in Denmark and Iceland (see Alan E. Boucher's *An Icelandic revolution* q.v.). This volume is a translated adaptation of the autobiography, the early part of which contains his own views of the Icelandic episode. His autobiography has also been recently translated into Icelandic. See the article 'King Jörgen Jörgensen: an episode in Icelandic history' by Helgi P. Briem in *American-Scandinavian Review*, vol. 31 (1943), p. 120-31.

History. Icelandic history. 16th-19th centuries

328 Icelandic nationalism and the inspiration of history.
Gunnar Karlsson. In: *Roots of nationalism; studies in northern Europe.* Edited by Rosalind Mitchison. Edinburgh: Donald, 1980. p. 77-89.

A chapter contributed by a lecturer in history at the University of Iceland, in which he traces the origins and development of the nationalist movement in Iceland during the 19th century, and discusses in particular whether it arose from Iceland's own tradition or from cumulative feelings of oppression by the Danish administration. The author's conclusion is that both the awakening and the eventual success of the Icelandic nationalist movement owed almost all to the influence of the nation's cultural heritage.

329 Jón Sigurðsson: Icelandic statesman.
Edward J. Thorlakson. *American-Scandinavian Review,* vol. 32 (1944), p. 17-25.

The occasion of the declaration of the independent republic of Iceland in 1944 is here used to present this appreciation of the man who more than any other Icelander laid the foundations for and fostered the growth of the independent ideal for his country. Jón Sigurðsson was born in Arnafjörður in north-western Iceland in 1811. He enrolled at the University of Copenhagen in 1832 and, considering that he returned to Iceland only occasionally during the rest of his life (he died in 1879), his influence on the political, economic and cultural development of Iceland in the 19th century and beyond was immense. His struggles for Icelandic independence, conducted on Danish soil, are summarised in this article, with particular reference to the annual publication *Ný Félagsrit* of which Jón was the founder and major contributor for thirty years. The birthday of Iceland's national hero was chosen as the country's independence day. Although a multi-volume biography of Jón Sigurðsson has been published in Danish, there is still no major biography available in English.

330 Jón Jónsson of Vogar: his life, 1829-1866.
Jón Jónsson. Nenthead, England; Dick Phillips, 1977. 32p.

In *Fraser's Magazine* for January 1877 there first appeared an astonishing piece entitled 'Jón Jónsonn's (sic) saga: the genuine autobiography of a modern Icelander', edited by G. R. Fitzroy Cole. The recent publisher is to be commended for his enterprise in producing this facsimile edition and bringing the document to a wider audience. Jón Jónsson was born in 1829 and spent most of his life at Vogar, a cottage farm on the shores of Lake Mývatn. He taught himself English from books to a standard sufficient to compose an English account of the first thirty-five years of his life. It falls into three main sections: his childhood; his years in Denmark (1847-51) learning carpentry; and his return to Iceland and Vogar, where he married, had four children, and lived off the land. His autobiography offers an extraordinary insight into the ways of life in rural Iceland during the mid-19th century, and conveys the spirit of the time and place to a degree unmatched by the accounts of any foreign travellers to Iceland at this time (some of whom he recalls entertaining). It is a rare, vivid, and contemporary piece of social history. A parallel Icelandic/English edition was published in Reykjavík by Isafold in 1968.

History. Icelandic history. 20th century

331 A proposed Icelandic colony.
Ted C. Hinckley. *Alaska Journal*, vol. 4, no. 1 (1974), p. 2-9.

The isolated but remarkable story of how, seven years after the Alaska purchase, the territory of Alaska nearly became an Icelandic colony in 1874. This article is an account of the campaign of the Icelandic émigré nationalist Jón Ólafsson, who had settled in Wisconsin three years earlier. He appears to have won wide support in American government circles and in the press, but a combination of factors, including the realisation by some of the Icelandic settlers in North America of the moderate advantages of their existing situation compared with the environmental hazards of the 'promised land' up in Alaska, caused the dream to fade, and Jón Ólafsson, a poet and journalist, who had originally left Iceland to avoid political imprisonment by the Danish authorities, was allowed to return to his native country in May 1875.

332 The distress in Iceland.
Eiríkur Magnússon. London: Truscott, 1882. 54p.

The Mansion House Relief Fund, which had been organised in London by William Morris, sent Morris' friend Eiríkur Magnússon to distribute funds in Iceland, following the severe winter of 1880-81 and the subsequent famine and to report on the situation at first hand. His report, read at a meeting of the Mansion House Committee on 11 December 1882, of which this publication is the full text, is supplemented by the texts of eighty-one letters written between Icelanders from various walks of life, which testify to the prevailing conditions. The report assumed added significance as a counter to the claims made in the *Times* newspaper of 13 October 1882 (one week after Magnússon's departure to Iceland) by another Icelandic scholar based in England, Guðbrandur Vigfússon, that there was no sort of distress in Iceland -a claim which was beginning to undermine the credibility of the relief effort by the time of Magnússon's return nearly two months later. Almost immediately Magnússon issued a pamphlet entitled *Mr Vigfússon and the distress in Iceland*, privately published in Cambridge, in which he refutes the evidence for Vigfússon's claims, and appends the text of a letter to the *Times* of 27 December, signed by seventy-six Icelandic dignitaries in support of the Fund. It should be pointed out that Magnússon and Vigfússon also had their scholastic differences. For an appraisal of the Relief Fund see the article by Richard L. Harris, 'William Morris, Eiríkur Magnússon and the Icelandic Famine relief effort of 1882' in *Saga-book*, vol. 20, no. 1-2 (1978-79), p. 31-41.

20th century

333 The independence of Iceland: a parallel for Ireland.
Alexander McGill. Glasgow: O'Callaghan, 1921. 32p.

A crusading pamphlet in which the author, uniquely, draws the parallel between Iceland's long period of deprivation under the Danish administration before its emergence to independent status, and the situation existing between Ireland and Great Britain. It is a persuasive essay in the historical context. He appends an English translation of the Danish-Icelandic Act of Union of 1918, which designated the two countries as independent and sovereign states united by a common king.

History. Icelandic history. 20th century

334 Nazism in Iceland.
Ásgeir Guðmundsson, translated by Magnús Fjalldal. In: *Who were the fascists? Social roots of European fascism.* Edited by Stein Ugelvik Larsen. Bergen, Norway: Universitetsforlaget, 1980. p. 743-50.

A short but rare account of the emergence of the Icelandic Nationalist Movement, founded in April 1933 in the wake of the depression, and active until March 1939. It includes a summary of the movement's electoral base and its membership figures. 'It is difficult to explain why the Nationalist Party never obtained more support; it is possible that lack of leadership had something to do with it. The Icelandic population seems to have been completely immune to the panacea of national socialism - the tiny Nationalist Party never grew to be more than a strange mixture of immature youths and discontented adults'. A few cell meetings were held until 1944.

335 Recollections of an Icelandic statesman: being a chapter in the autobiography of Sveinn Björnsson.
Sveinn Björnsson, translated by Snæbjörn Jónsson. Reykjavík: Isafoldarprentsmiðja, 1960. 67p. photos.

Sveinn Björnsson (1881-1952) was the first President of the Icelandic Republic, 1944-52, having formerly been Regent. His reminiscences (Icelandic title *Endurminningar*) which cover his life up to 1940 were still being compiled at the time of his death, and were still in rough form. They were subsequently edited by Sigurður Nordal and published with great success in 1957. A full translation into English did not, unfortunately, appear, but this extract, with photographs, is a translation of p. 237-66 of the original Icelandic edition, and covers conferences and meetings, 1938-40, including an account of a visit to Britain during the early months of the war to discuss the trading situation, and a particularly interesting section on German espionage in Iceland and the German application for air bases and other facilities there in March 1939. The translator contributes a preface outlining the character and career of the President. The publisher of the autobiography is the printing office founded by Sveinn Björnsson's father Björn Jónsson, who had himself been a major political figure in Iceland. A shorter version of this extract appeared in *Norseman*, vol. 16 (1958), p. 217-25.

336 Ísland og ófriðurinn. (Iceland and the war.)
Snæbjörn Jónsson. Reykjavík: Snæbjörn Jónsson (The English Bookshop), 1940. 16p.

In September 1940 Snæbjörn Jónsson (of grammar and bookshop fame) contributed an article to the English weekly magazine the *Spectator*. The contents of this article were reported in the Icelandic press, and in his prefatory remarks to this pamphlet, in which he publishes the full text of the article as originally submitted to the *Spectator* plus a translation back into Icelandic, he alludes to the robust reception which the press reports appear to have engendered, and re-offers his piece for people to judge his opinions in context. The theme of this historically interesting and controversial essay is Iceland's difficulty and vulnerability in the home and export markets prior to and intensified by the outbreak of the war. He saw the union with Denmark as severed, Scandinavian cooperation as impracticable, American protection as doubtful. He therefore looks to the British (who were by now occupying Iceland) as the guardians of the future on several fronts, and expresses his support for Icelandic membership of the British Commonwealth. Whether this was to be seen as an advocacy of short-term prag-

History. Icelandic history. 20th century

matism, or as a jeopardising of Icelandic nationalism, is now a matter of the past, though not without its echoes.

337 Iceland in the Second World War, 1939-1946.
Thor Whitehead. PhD thesis, University of Oxford, Oxford, England, 1978. 424p.

A comparative and penetrating study of 'the origins and aims of Icelandic policy and the corresponding British, American and German policies... apart from exploring political relationships, the thesis endeavours to assess the military importance of Iceland during the war' (author's abstract). This thesis was followed by the publication of the author's book (available only in Icelandic) *Ísland i síðari heimsstyrjöld* (Reykjavík: Almennabókafélagið, 1980, 350p.). His approach is the only substantial attempt at placing Iceland's wartime condition in the context of world affairs. Thor Whitehead is now Professor of History at the University of Iceland.

338 The British occupation of Iceland, 1940-1942.
Donald Francis Bittner. PhD thesis, University of Missouri, Missouri, Columbia, 1974. 1,134p. (Available from University Microfilms, Ann Arbor, Michigan).

An exhaustive examination of not only the first two years of Iceland's wartime occupation but also of the British interests and activities concerning Iceland, 1933-46. The thesis is presented as a case study illustrating the British government at war, and, in the author's words, 'provides an excellent example of how a skilled military-diplomatic team, supported by government policy and by conscientious officers and troops, can successfully occupy a foreign state without endangering the objectives of the operation or relations between the occupying power and the host country'. Two articles arising from this research were contributed by Bittner to *Army Quarterly and Defence Journal*, vol. 103, no. 7 (1972), p. 81-90, and *Journal of the Royal United Services Institute for Defence Studies*, vol. 120, no. 4 (1975), p. 45-53.

339 The United States occupation of Iceland, 1941-1946.
John Joseph Hunt. PhD thesis, University of Georgetown, Georgetown, Washington, DC, 1966. 375p. (Available from University Microfilms, Ann Arbor, Michigan and London.).

A detailed study of the 'occupation by invitation', in which the author draws conclusions upon the social, cultural, material, political and economic changes that resulted from the wartime presence of the United States on Icelandic soil, thus effectively ending the previous isolation of centuries.

340 The 'Republic of Iceland' 1940-44: Anglo-American attitudes and influences.
Sólrún B. Jensdóttir Harðarson. *Journal of Contemporary History*, vol. 9, no. 4 (Oct. 1974), p. 27-56.

The municipal airport in Reykjavík and the international airport at Keflavík are tangible reminders of respectively the British and American involvement in Iceland during the Second World War. The purpose of this article is to demonstrate how Britain came to occupy Iceland in a spirit of 'fait accompli' during 1940, before making way for a more 'diplomatic' but controversial period of American presence, 1941-44. This was the period when Icelandic claims for complete

History. Icelandic history. 20th century

independence from the Danish Crown were coming to a head, (in the national referendum over 97 per cent of the votes were cast for abrogation of the Union) and the Anglo-American patterns of involvement are analysed against this background. The public release of the British Foreign Office's wartime archives in 1972 enabled the author to produce fresh and revealing evidence in her assessment. An interesting sidelight on events surrounding the decision to involve the United States is shown in John L. Zimmerman's 'Note on the occupation of Iceland by American forces', *Political Science Quarterly*, vol. 62, no. 1 (1947), p. 103-06.

341 The 1940 occupation.
Pétur Ólafsson, Björn Bjarnason, Björn Tryggvason. *Atlantica and Iceland Review*, vol. 18, no. 2 (1980), p. 13-25.

The British occupation of Iceland on 10 May 1940, one month after the German invasion of Denmark and Norway, was the start of the watershed in modern Icelandic history; for Iceland, through a series of events mainly outside her control, was catapulted into modernity, and simultaneously achieved total independence. In this collection of three articles both the immediate and the long-term impact of wartime events are described: a contemporary report of the Icelanders' reaction to the landing; the strategic importance acquired by Iceland, and the building of the airport at Reykjavík; and a short piece on a few of those Britons who returned to Iceland to live.

342 The northern garrisons.
Eric Linklater. London: HM Stationery Office, 1941. 72p.

Issued for the War Office by the Ministry of Information in its series *The army at war*. Contemporary reflections, by a well-known writer, about British army life on the North Atlantic islands: Orkney, Shetland, Faroe, and especially Iceland (chpts. 4-5). *Garrison in Iceland* is the title of another booklet of contemporary reminiscences reported by C. F. Dunn with photographer Frank Muscroft for the *Yorkshire Post* newspaper which published it in 1941 as a portrait of the Yorkshire Regiment in Iceland.

343 The United States Marines in Iceland, 1941-1942.
Frank O. Hough, edited by Kenneth C. Clifford. Washington, DC: US Marine Corps, Historical Division, 1970. 22p. (Marine Corps Historical Reference Pamphlets).

Like the British War Office, the US Navy Department issued an official series on wartime activities *History of the United States Marine Corps operations in World War II*. This pamphlet is extracted from volume one of the series. The marine occupation of Iceland was known as a 'short of war' operation, and is recorded here solely in terms of its organisation and deployment.

344 No depression in Iceland.
Ernest Watkins. London: Allen & Unwin, 1942. 84p.

This little book is perhaps still not forgotten. Although it had no great pretensions in the first place, it is irreverently funny, and there are still plenty of Britishers around who were stationed in wartime Iceland to appreciate the tongue-in-cheek descriptions of life on duty, and, more importantly in this account, off duty. The book takes the form of a series of letters home between July 1940 and April

History. Icelandic history. 20th century

1942, some of which appeared in *Punch* magazine. Ernest Watkins was also co-editor with Michael Bratby of a collection of pieces written by British servicemen under the title *Iceland presents* (Reykjavík: Snæbjörn Jónsson, 1941, 112p.). Watkins also contributed a more documentary retrospect in an article 'The invasion of Iceland', *Army Quarterly and Defence Journal*, vol. 109, no. 4 (1979), p. 457-66.

345 Vigil in Iceland: a fragment of autobiography, 1940-1942.
Angus Macnaghten. Slough, England: Luff, 1977. 64p.

Written, perhaps strangely, some thirty-five years after the event, this memoir of wartime service in Iceland, based on recollection and re-reading of letters home, offers a subtle contrast in mood to other, more immediate, accounts. Whether this brings the actual experience nearer home is something which only those who served in Iceland can judge. For the rest, this a consciously unassuming piece of personal history in the context of British-Icelandic relations, and, incidentally, a nicely-presented booklet.

346 American soldier in Reykjavík.
Luther M. Choran. *National Geographic Magazine*, vol. 88, no. 5 (Nov. 1945), p. 536-68. photos.

Personal observations by a corporal in the United States Army stationed in Iceland during the war, which it is interesting to compare with British observations, and which sheds some light on American attitudes towards the Icelanders, as well as, more importantly, the Icelanders' reception of the GI's. With hindsight this piece is not without occasional embarrassment, but it is vivid, and accompanied by first-rate colour photography.

347 Midnight Sun: Icelandic series.
Reykjavík: British Force Headquarters, 1940-42. weekly.

The numbers engaged with the British occupying force in wartime Iceland were sufficient to sustain a magazine for their edification. The first issue on Saturday 17 August 1940 appeared fourteen weeks after the date of landing. It contained a mixture of news from home and the warfront, alongside items on Iceland designed to relate the troops to their new environment. When the US force took over, they too were served with a similarly motivated magazine *White Falcon*, 1941-46.

348 Iceland: its importance in an air age.
James Whittaker. *World Today*, vol. 4, no. 7 (1948), p. 297-307.

An interim assessment of Iceland's political and economic situation as a newly-independent republic and shortly after her emergence from the events of the war, which dramatically narrowed both the psychological and the practical divide between herself and the outside world.

They sent me to Iceland.
See item no. 117.

Iceland and the war.
See item no. 493.

Religion

Pre-Christian

349 Norse mythology; or, the religion of our forefathers, containing all the myths of the Eddas.
R. B. Anderson. Chicago, Illinois: Griggs; London: Routledge & Kegan Paul, 1875. 473p. Reprinted Kennebunkport, Maine: Longwood Press, 1977.

Rasmus Björn Anderson was a Norse scholar in the grand tradition of 19th-century learning. In the preface to this work he claims, with some justification, (but see note to Rudolph Keyser's *The private life of the old Northmen* q.v.), that it is the first complete systematic presentation of Norse mythology in the English language. After a long and valuable introduction in which he defines the term 'Norse mythology' from a comparative viewpoint, he proceeds to a descriptive account of the myths in three parts: the creation and preservation of the world; the life and exploits of the gods; the end of the world (*Ragnarök*) and regeneration. He appends a useful glossary of proper names associated with Norse religion. Although the present century has produced more stimulating interpretations of the subject, this work was a pioneering venture in its time, ran to several editions, and is clearly drawn upon by later scholars.

350 The religion of ancient Scandinavia.
W. A. Craigie. London: Constable, 1906. 72p.

The subject of Old Norse religion and its depiction in Old Icelandic literature is vast, and has resulted in volumes of proportionate length describing and analysing its features and relationships. Craigie's book, however, although early, still has much to commend it to the reader requiring a short and sound introduction to the topic. Craigie, one of the most respected scholars on the ancient northern world, writes clearly and with perfect balance about the major deities, the institutions of worship, and the ceremonial practices. 'In the following account... an attempt has been made to exhibit what is really known of the religious beliefs and practices of the people, as distinct from the mythological fancies of the poets'. Therein lies the real value of this admirable little work, in that it helps to illuminate the society of Iceland during its first century and more, rather than a part of its literary tradition.

Religion. Pre-Christian

351 Gods of the north.
Brian Branston. London: Thames & Hudson; New York: Vanguard Press, 1955. 318p. (Myth and Man).

'Mythology is everyman's business; whether it be of the private kind called psychology or the collective kind which manifests itself in stories of the gods... It is not easy to interpret the myths of our own race, for our near ancestors - those of a thousand odd years ago - were persuaded to forget them, or relegate their broken remnants to the nursery. The gods of the north were the gods of our forefathers... if we want to reconstruct their mythology, mainly we must rely on a literature which grew, first orally, then in manuscript, in Iceland. How we should have such close links with the men of Iceland asks for an explanation'. Thus the historical introduction to this respected book forms one of the clearest expositions of the stimulus for studying this subject. The main part of the volume, a journey through the world of Norse mythology, is presented in a manner suitable for both the specialist and the general reader. A later work by Branston is his *Gods and heroes from Viking mythology* (London: Lowe, 1978, 160p.).

352 Gods and myths of northern Europe.
H. R. Ellis Davidson. Harmondsworth, England: Penguin; Santa Fé, New Mexico: Gannon, 1964. 250p.

In her introduction the author makes the telling point that whereas generations of English-speaking children have been brought up on the classical myths of Greece and Rome, we have largely neglected the mythology of our own forebears, the Anglo-Saxons and Vikings, 'whose myths should surely arouse as much curiosity as those of the mediterranean lands'. (Norse deities have, after all, given their names to four days of our week). The author draws on both literary sources and archaeological research for her readable presentation of the characteristics and powers of the deities, whom she describes individually and in groups: Odin; Thór; Freyr, Freyja and the Vanir (the gods of peace and plenty); the gods of the sea; gods of the dead; the 'enigmatic' gods Heimdall, Loki and Baldr. A concluding chapter on the passing of the old gods is a perceptive analysis of the reasons why the heathen religion succumbed to the Christian faith. Other books by this author in the same field include: *The Road to Hel* (Cambridge University Press, 1943); *Pagan Scandinavia* (Thames & Hudson, 1967); and *Scandinanvian mythology* (Hamlyn, 1969.).

353 Myth and religion of the north: the religion of ancient Scandinavia.
E. O. G. Turville-Petre. London: Weidenfeld & Nicolson, 1964. 340p. bibliog. Reprinted Westport, Connecticut: Greenwood Press, 1975.

One of the most respected and frequently-cited of studies on the pagan religion of the north, being both a synthesis of previous research and a stimulating exposition in its own right. An introductory review of the primary sources is followed by substantial chapters on the individual deities. Attitudes and institutions of worship are also discussed in this standard and scholarly work.

Religion. Pre-Christian

354 Gods of the ancient Norsemen.
Georges Dumézil, edited by Einar Haugen. Los Angeles: University of California, Centre for the Study of Comparative Folklore and Mythology, 1973. 157p.

Structuralism, which over the decades has been applied to an increasing number of disciplines, reached the world of Old Norse mythology in 1962 when this work was first published in French. There is little doubt that it stimulated fresh interest in, and threw new light on, the world of the northern gods, although one has to say that the complexities of this method of approach contrast sharply with the magnificent self-statement of the myths as they appear in the old poetry of Iceland. For a critique of this influential work see the article 'Dumézil revisited' by R. I. Page in *Saga-book*, vol. 20, no. 1-2 (1978-79), p. 49-65.

355 Ragnarök: an investigation into Old Norse concepts of the fate of the gods.
John Stanley Martin. Assen, Netherlands: van Gorcum, 1972. 151p. bibliog. (Melbourne Monographs in Germanic Studies, vol. 3).

The fullest study in English of the life force as perceived in the Norse world of pre-Christian times. *Ragnarök*, the 'fate of the gods', or the disintegration of the world order from which would arise the new and perfect creation, is a theme central and in its time unique to Old Icelandic literature. The author of this study defines the concept, examines the literary sources, and makes comparisons with Christian eschatology. He pays particular attention to the battle of the gods, and to the myth of Baldur.

356 The cult of Othin: an essay in the ancient religion of the north.
Henry M. Chadwick. London: Clay, 1899. 82p.

Still the only individual study of Odin, the chief of the northern gods, their ruler, and the 'all-wise'. Contributed by a renowned scholar of the Germanic world, this essay remains a valuable introduction to the many forms of cult and worship surrounding Odin.

357 The golden bough.
Sir James George Frazer. London: MacMillan, 1911-15, vol. 7.

Frazer's monumental study of comparative magic and religion in thirteen volumes includes one 'Balder the beautiful' on analogies and parallels of the myth of the Norse god Baldur, whose story is told in the *Prose Edda*. Baldur, son of Odin, was the best loved of all the gods for a range of qualities, but through the agency of Loki was killed by a branch of mistletoe and burnt on a great funeral pyre. The sub-title of this volume is: 'the fire festivals of Europe and the doctrine of the external soul'. In the one volume abridged edition of 1922 chapters sixty-one and sixty-five are devoted to Baldur. For a more recent study see Cynthia King's book *In the morning of time: the story of the Norse god Balder* (New York: Fourwinds Press, 1970, 257p.).

Religion. Christianity and church history

358 **The problem of Loki.**
Jan de Vries. Helsinki: Societas scientiarum fennica, 1933. 306p.

Loki is the most enigmatic and contradictory of the Norse deities. Many scholars have brought their interpretations to bear on his purpose. De Vries' study is the most exhaustive in its examination of Loki's character, his relationship with Odin, his enmity with the gods, his association with fire, and of the religious parallels in other cultures. The author characterises Loki in a dual rôle of trickster and, especially, 'culture hero' to explain his actions and inconsistent presence in Asgard as a figure of evil.

The Norse myths.
See item no. 641.

The Prose Edda.
See item no. 652.

The saga of Asgard.
See item no. 865.

Christianity and church history

359 **The conversion of Iceland: a survey.**
Dag Strömbäck, translated and annotated by Peter Foote. London: Viking Society for Northern Research, 1975. 109p.

The peaceful conversion of pagan Iceland to Christianity around the year 1000 at the instigation of King Ólaf Tryggvason of Norway is an event difficult to understand without a grasp of the historical, social, political and legal background. This is the only study available in English to place the events surrounding the conversion in their wider perspective, and to render them less arbitrary and fortuitous than they at first appear. It is a remarkably clear analysis, and includes a chapter on the saga of the skaldic poet Hallfred 'vandrædi' (the troublesome), whose story offers illumination for the study of the shift from heathendom to Christendom (see *The saga of Hallfred the troublesome Scald*, translated by Alan E. Boucher q.v.).

360 **Under the cloak: the acceptance of Christianity in Iceland, with particular reference to the religious attitudes prevailing at the time.**
Jón Hnefill Aðalsteinsson. Uppsala, Sweden: University of Uppsala, 1978. 151p. bibliog. (Studia Ethnologica Upsaliensa, 4).

The title of this doctoral thesis is a reference to Þorgeir the Lawspeaker's action in spreading a cloak over himself during his deliberations prior to giving his verdict that Iceland should adopt Christianity, and this action, originally recorded by the historian Ari, is the feature of a detailed section of this study. Its framework consists of an analysis of the sources relating to the pagan religion of the original settlers, followed by an investigation into sources on the acceptance of

Religion. Christianity and church history

Christianity in Iceland, and related missionary activity. The second half is a description and interpretation of the events at the crucial meeting at Þingvellir in the year 1000, and the activities of the protagonists. The author concludes with a particularly interesting chapter on the paradox, perhaps never to be understood fully, of how a committed majority of pagans came to accept and largely abide by the judgment of the lawspeaker in favour of Christianity. (The book is distributed by Almqvist and Wiksell International, Stockholm).

361 Skálholt: the symbol of a common heritage.
Þórarinn Þórarinsson. *American-Scandinavian Review*, vol. 12 (Sept. 1974), p. 228-39.

Skálholt is the elder of the two episcopal seats in Iceland, and the oldest cultural centre in the country. The first bishop of this southern diocese was Ísleif Gizursson, appointed in 1056. It remained an episcopal seat until the end of the 18th century, when ecclesiastical power was transferred to Reykjavík; up to that point it had been the seat of thirty-two Catholic followed by thirteen Lutheran bishops. Skálholt's spiritual, cultural and political luminance faded for a century and a half thereafter, but since the establishment of Icelandic independence a physical and cultural regeneration has taken place through the building by the state of a new church on the old site (consecrated in 1963) and the activities of a restoration society for Skálholt. The historical background and the future development of Skálholt are the subjects of this article. The visitor to Skálholt will also find information in, for example, the booklet *Skálholtsstaður* by Sigurbjörn Einarsson, Bishop of Iceland (Reykjavík: Kirkjustjórnin), which appends a full list of the bishops.

362 Bishop Jón Arason.
Tryggvi J. Oleson. *Speculum*, vol. 28, no. 2 (April 1953), p. 245-78.

Jón Arason (1484-1550) was bishop of the northern seat of Hólar from 1524 until his death. He was the last of the Catholic bishops before the present century, and, as a national leader, was the last champion of the autonomy of Iceland until the national re-awakening in the 19th century. He was executed along with his two sons at Skálholt at the end of a period of flagrant violation of Icelandic rights by the Danish Crown in the context of the Roman Catholic and Lutheran struggle (the term used today to denote the Reformation in Iceland is *siðaskipti*). Jón Arason is a national hero of Iceland, and this article is a well-documented biography. See the play *Bishop Jón Arason* by Tryggvi Sveinbjörnsson (q.v.).

363 The most treasured Nordic bible.
Jónas Gíslason. *Atlantica and Iceland Review*, vol. 17, no. 4 (1977), p. 24-29. illus.

An illustrated article on the first Icelandic Bible, printed at Hólar in 1584, under the supervision of Bishop Guðbrandur Þorláksson. This magnificent example of bibliographic art was originally produced in 500 copies. Its cultural influence on the Icelandic nation was profound: it provided the Icelanders with a vernacular instead of Danish version of the Bible, and thereby contributed to the survival of the Icelandic language and its cultural identity. Facsimile reprints have been published in recent times. The most recent version of the Icelandic Bible was published in 1982, and is a major revision of the previous edition of 1912.

Religion. Christianity and church history

364 Scandinavian churches: a picture of the development and life of the churches of Denmark, Finland, Iceland, Norway and Sweden.
Edited by Leslie Stannard Hunter. London: Faber; Minneapolis, Minnesota: Augsburg, 1965. 200p.

A volume which affords a comparative survey of the religious development of Scandinavia. Chapter six (p. 104-117) contains two contributions on the church in Iceland: one an historical sketch by Magnús Már Lárusson; the other on its contemporary life and structure by Bishop Sigurbjörn Einarsson.

365 Icelandic church saga.
John C. F. Hood. London: Society for Promoting Christian Knowledge, 1946. 241p. Reprinted Westport, Connecticut: Greenwood Press, 1981.

This book is the only full-length account of the history of the Icelandic Church available in the English language, and for this reason deserves its recent reprinting. The treatment is descriptive rather than analytical, but it remains a very useful introduction to the subject. The author starts with observations on pre-conversion Christianity on Icelandic soil, before proceeding to identify the major phases in the development of the Church: the adoption of Christianity; its consolidation through the southern and northern dioceses of Skálholt and Hólar during the following three centuries; the politically paralleled degeneration of the Church over a further three centuries; the Lutheran Reformation; the influence of the mystical poems of Hallgrímur Pétursson, and of the popular sermons of Jón Vidalín, in the late 17th and early 18th centuries; the situation of the church during the natural disasters of the 18th century; and the national awakening during the 19th century. The author was the chief chaplain to the defence forces in Iceland during the last war.

366 State and church in Iceland: past history and present problems.
Patricia Wilson-Kastner. *Lutheran Quarterly*, vol. 28, no. 2 (1976), p. 125-39.

An American theologian's interpretation of the relationship between the institutional Church and the state from the time of the conversion to the present day. The Reformation and the centuries of Danish administration emphasised the ties between the Lutheran Church and the state, and although the 20th century has witnessed a loosening or varying of emphasis in Church-state relations, particularly with the embracing growth of the welfare state, and with the subtle challenge of the newer urban society to the traditional role and relevance of the Church, the interdependence of Church and state remains a firm pattern in the 95 per cent Lutheran, 5 per cent Catholic, society of Iceland. The Church retains, for example, its right to religious instruction in the schools. 'At the very least, the clergy is assured of secure support in a country in which most of the people would probably not actively support the church as a voluntary organisation, and the state can be reasonably sure that organised religion will be a sustainer rather than a critic'. It is a question of 'privileges' and 'perimeters'.

Religion. Christianity and church history

367 **Christianity in Iceland.**
Gunnar Árnason. *Sixty-five Degrees*, vol. 2, no. 3 (summer 1968), p. 11-13.
An Icelandic priest here offers a brief personal view of the development of the Icelandic Church, its place in society, and its current activities. See the article on the Church in Iceland by Bishop Sigurbjörn Einarsson in *Iceland Review*, vol. 5, no. 4 (1967), p. 16-22.

The Lutheran doctrine of marriage in Iceland Society.
See item no. 382.

Customs, Folklore and Beliefs

368 The private life of the old Northmen.
Rudolph Keyser, translated from his posthumous works by M. R. Barnard. London: Chapman & Hall, 1868. 177p.

Keyser, perhaps best known for his scholarship in the field of mythology and religion (his *Religion of the northmen* was translated in 1854), drew extensively on the Old Icelandic sources for this study of daily life in the Norse world. He describes the features of education, marriage, housing, dress, occupations, amusements, and funeral customs. He is concerned mainly with the heathen period, but also touches on some of the changes which, only gradually, took place after the introduction of Christianity. Subsequent commentators have acknowledged the light cast by this book on the domestic background to the sagas. For a later exploration of the daily life and customs of the Norsemen, see the American scholar and feminist Mary Wilhelmine Williams' *Social Scandinavia in the Viking age* (New York: MacMillan, 1920, 451p. bibliog.).

369 Aspects of life in Iceland in the heathen period.
Jón Steffensen. *Saga-book* (UK), vol. 17 (1966-69), p. 177-205.

An interesting miscellany in which the author examines three unusual features which illuminate Icelandic social life and customs prior to and immediately following the introduction of Christianity: the use of nicknames; the practice of charms and cures; the law of baptism and the dispensation concerning the exposure of children, with particular reference to the digest of Christian and civil laws set down in the *Grágás* code.

370 Cult remnants in Icelandic dramatic dances.
Dag Strömbäck. *Arv*, vol. 4 (1948), p. 132-45.

A discussion of the origins and features of songs, dances and plays in Iceland from the mediaeval period and later, drawing on evidence from contemporary sources. Particular attention is paid to the Icelandic *vikivaki*, or 'dance gathering' at festival time, and to the horse-dance *hestleikur*. The author contributes varia-

Customs, Folklore and Beliefs

tions on this theme in a paper 'Icelandic dramatic dances and their west European background' presented to the second Viking Congress at Bergen, 1953, p. 92-99.

371 An old Icelandic medical miscellany.
Henning Larsen. Oslo: Norske Videnskaps Akademi, 1931. 328p.

Research on an Icelandic medical document of the 15th century, discovered amongst the archives held in the Royal Irish Academy, resulted in this unusual volume. Larsen discusses the manuscript, presents his edition of the Icelandic text of eighty pages followed by a full translation into English, and appends a glossary. The text itself comprises charms, a book of simples, an antidotarium, a lapidary, a leechbook, and a cookbook, all reflecting a variety of mediaeval European sources.

372 Icelandic beast and bird lore.
Vilhjálmur Stefánsson. *Journal of American Folklore*, vol. 19, no. 75 (Oct. 1906), p. 300-08.

A selection of popular beliefs concerning animals with a special significance in Iceland. Four creatures in particular are treated in this context: the polar bear; the waterhorse or kelpie *nykur*; the eagle; and the raven.

373 Icelandic feasts and holidays: celebrations past and present.
Árni Björnsson, translated by May Hallmundsson, Hallberg Hallmundsson. Reykjavík: Iceland Review, 1980. 104p.

A very useful guide for the English-speaking reader to the plethora of special days, both religious and secular, in the Icelandic calendar. There is a short introduction to the history of Icelandic calendars and almanacs, and a table of calendar-linked holidays; but the body of the text is devoted to a collection of descriptions of the history and celebrations associated with over sixty special dates in the calendar. The book is therefore useful both as a history of Icelandic customs and as a reference almanac. See the article 'Christmas in Iceland: a long family affair', by Haraldur J. Hamar in *Atlantica and Iceland Review*, vol. 17, no. 4 (1979), p. 14-18.

374 National costume of women in Iceland.
Elsa E. Guðjónsson. Reykjavík: National Museum of Iceland, 1970. 10p. illus.

A pamphlet containing a short history of the development of the Icelandic national dress, with illustrations taken from the exhibits in the National Museum, and text by the curator.

375 Some Icelandic recipes.
Selected by Elín Kristjánsdóttir, translated by Hólmfríður Jónsdóttir. Reykjavík: Örn og Örlygur, 1975. 76p.

What Icelandic cuisine may lack in terms of the range of home-grown produce available, it more than makes up for when it comes to quality and variety on themes, whether in the home or at a restaurant. This enterprising and attractive booklet was compiled for the edification of visitors to Iceland who might wish to try preparing in their own home some of the Icelandic dishes which they have

Customs, Folklore and Beliefs

enjoyed. The two major sections are devoted to recipes involving fish and lamb (the most common staple foods for Icelanders), with ideas on reindeer meat and ptarmigan for the more adventurous (although the pungent shark dish *hákarl* is, understandably, omitted!) Soups, bread and cakes (including the delicious Icelandic pancake with whipped cream) are also represented, as is the ambrosial dish *skyr*, made from skimmed milk, which was brought by the original settlers, and is of a high nutritional value. For a descriptive sketch of the Icelandic diet and traditional recipes see the article 'A cook's tour of Iceland' by Mekkin S. Perkins in *American-Scandinavian Review*, vol. 46, no. 1 (March 1958), p. 41-47.

376 Freemasonry in Iceland.
Einar Loftsson, Sydney Pope. *Ars Quattuor Coronatorum*, vol. 60 (1949), p. 206-10.

The first freemason's lodge in Iceland was established at Reykjavík in 1919 under the Grand Lodge of Denmark. Independence in masonic affairs was gained in 1948. At the time of this article the Icelandic lodge claimed 500 members.

377 Superstitions in the saga island.
Mekkin S. Perkins. *American-Scandinavian Review*, vol. 52, no. 4 (Dec. 1964), p. 415-23.

A description of some of the superstitions which were prevalent in Iceland over the centuries, with indications of their origins, and with particular reference to ghosts and to the most persistent as well as distinctly Icelandic superstition of the *fylgja*, or 'following' guardian spirit.

378 Are we sensitive or superstitious?
Erlendur Haraldsson. *Atlantica and Iceland Review*, vol. 15, no. 4 (1977), p. 30-34.

A summary of the findings of the Department of Psychology at the University of Iceland from a survey and poll concerning the occurrence of psychic experiences amongst the Icelanders. Two thirds of Icelanders claim to have experienced one or more psychic phenomena. For a critique of a related survey from the same source, see the article on Icelandic attitudes to life after death by Haraldur J. Hamar in the same magazine, vol. 17, no. 3 (1979), p. 35-38.

379 An experiment with the Icelandic medium Hafsteinn Björnsson.
Erlendur Haraldsson, Ian Stevenson. *Journal of the American Society for Psychical Research*, vol. 68, no. 2 (April 1974), p. 192-202.

Parapsychology is an established, even popular, pursuit in Iceland, for reasons which may be associated with the comparative ease of establishing genealogical descent within this compact society. This article is a summary analysis of a sitting with the best known Icelandic medium, at which ten 'sitters' were present. Hafsteinn Björnsson is also the subject of a feature article by Ævar Kvaran in *Atlantica and Iceland Review*, vol. 13, no. 1-2 (April 1975), p. 33-37.

Family Life and Organization

General

380 Notes on Icelandic kinship terminology.
Robert T. Merrill. *American Anthropologist*, vol. 66 (1964), p. 867-72.

A useful attempt at an outline classification of the confusing practices relating to kinship terms in Iceland. The writer discusses both the older traditions and the more modern usages, and broadly identifies two parallel systems: informal use of sexual pairs of terms for blood relations, in-laws and fostering; and the system of terms used to group relatives according to their respective responsibilities. These patterns have a strong tradition, and have been subjected to minimal foreign influence, but the dual system is seen as gradually breaking down with the changing social conditions of modern living. This article, which is accompanied by a 'family tree' chart showing the relationships and their Icelandic terms, has been frequently cited in subsequent papers on the Icelandic family organisation.

381 Kinship and economy in modern Iceland.
Ann Pinson. *Ethnology*, vol. 18, no. 2 (April 1979), p. 183-97.

This specialist article is an examination of the terminology of Icelandic kinship as a background to demonstrating how 'patrilineal principles of social organisation have persisted in spite of the abrupt economic development in Iceland'. Concepts of kinship and concepts of property are also discussed. This article is one of a quartet of interrelating articles to appear in the same periodical within five years: two were contributed by George W. Rich under the titles 'Changing Icelandic kinship', vol. 15, no. 1 (Jan. 1976), p. 1-19, and 'Kinship and friendship in Iceland' (with particular reference to family organisation in Akureyri), vol. 19, no. 4 (Oct. 1980), p. 475-93; the third, less readily understandable article, is by Stephen B. Barlau 'Old Icelandic kinship terminology', vol. 20, no. 3 (July 1981), p. 191-202.

Family Life and Organization. General

382 The Lutheran doctrine of marriage in Icelandic society.
Björn Björnsson. Oslo: Universitetsforlaget; Reykjavík: Almennabókafélagið, 1971. 249p. bibliog.

The individual nature of marriage and family life in Icelandic society, together with the almost exclusively Lutheran background of the nation since the time of the Reformation, is the focus of this unique study by the Professor of Social Ethics in the faculty of Theology at the University of Iceland. Within the theological framework of Luther's own teachings on marriage and related subjects, the author presents a variety of data on the legal and sociological aspects of marriage and the family in historical and contemporary Icelandic society, with special reference to surveys conducted in the small town of Akranes on the west coast. He examines the three main types of family organisation, which he calls the engagement family, the cohabitation family, and the marriage family. For outsiders there is the real danger of judging the high rate of illegitimacy in Iceland with reference only to their own society, especially as in most respects Iceland shares the characteristics of western developed societies; in dealing with the question of illegitimacy the author shows why it should be regarded in a different light, and explains the absence of social stigma as attributable in large measure to the institution of 'public engagement'. An historical appendix contains the English text of the marriage rite conducted by Icelandic pastors, which dates from 1565. For a brief sketch by this author, see his article 'Engagement and marriage in Iceland' in *Sixty-five Degrees*, vol. 1, no. 1 (autumn 1967), p. 10-12+33.

383 The domestic cycle in modern Iceland.
George W. Rich. *Journal of Marriage and the Family*, vol. 40, no. 1 (Feb. 1978), p. 173-83.

The author notices no significant change in the patterns of family organisation in Iceland arising from economic growth or industrialisation. He draws the important conclusion that it is the engagement or betrothal which establishes the concept of the formation of the household - marriage symbolises economic and legal independence. He demonstrates how Icelandic society does not conform to the European marriage pattern, and confirms the observations of other commentators that Iceland's traditionally high pre-marital birthrate is to a large degree the result of the association of engagement with the creation of a family unit.

384 Premarital sexual permissiveness and illegitimacy in the Nordic countries.
Richard F. Tomasson. *Comparative Studies in Society and History* (UK), vol. 18, no. 2 (April 1976), p. 252-70.

'The Icelandic case is emphasised in this paper because of the uniquely high level of illegitimacy that has always characterised this most isolated of western societies. This can be viewed as a manifestation of the greater continuity with ancient Scandinavian patterns of family structure and relations between the sexes that has existed in Iceland compared with the other Nordic countries... Also, only in Iceland are specific data on illegitimacy abundantly and publicly available in various directories and genealogical works'. If the level of illegitimacy remains high in Iceland (official figures in 1980 indicated at least 7,000 partners with 4,000 children), so, too, does the tolerance, and for its illumination on such points this investigative article is welcome as an important contribution to the study of continuous patterns of Icelandic social and cultural development.

Family Life and Organization. Women and children

385 **The habits of Icelanders: a survey.**
Pétur Guðjónsson. *Sixty-five Degrees*, vol. 1, no. 1 (autumn 1967), p. 20-34.
The listed findings of a survey conducted by the researcher amongst a sample of 132 persons in Reykjavík concerning attitudes towards premarital sexual relations, illegitimacy and motherhood.

Family organisation in rural Iceland.
See item no. 405.

Women and children

386 **Rights of women among the old Scandinavians.**
Jón A. Hjaltalín. *Journal of Jurisprudence* (Scotland), vol. 16, no. 190 (Oct. 1872), p. 505-26.
A century-old essay about a millennium-old aspect of Icelandic society, yet both the essay and the period which it covers have relevance today. The author examines the evidence of the ancient laws and the sagas in an attempt to establish the status of women in old Norse society, with particular reference to marriage. His conclusion is that while political rights were not granted, and legal rights were limited compared with those for men, there seems to have been an unquestioned equality in terms of social participation, and, indeed, of intellectual respect. He relates these findings to the characteristics of the women in the sagas, where it is significantly rare to find a woman depicted as weak-willed.

387 **Home life in Iceland.**
Thorstina Jackson (Walters). *American-Scandinavian Review*, vol. 16, no. 7 (July 1928), p. 419-26.
A superficial but evocative picture of Icelandic family life between the wars from the woman's point of view, with attention focussed on her influence in the home and upon its organisation. It was during this period that Icelandic women began to divide their attention between home and career; notable examples are described in two articles by Mekkin S. Perkins in the same periodical, vol. 31, no. 1 (March 1943), p. 40-49, and vol. 42 (1954), p. 239-42.

388 **Women and the professions.**
Kristín E. Jónsdóttir, Guðrún Tryggvadóttir, Margrét Guðnadóttir, Sigurlaug Sæmundsdóttir. *Sixty-five Degrees*, vol. 2, no. 2 (spring 1968), p. 22-26.
A quartet of portraits by four Icelandic women who have entered and succeeded in their chosen professions. They comment on the attitudes and problems which they encountered as women in male dominated professions: medicine, dentistry, virology and architecture. The problems of women's employment and family ties are placed in a historical and contemporary context by Anna Sigurðardóttir of the Women's Rights Association of Iceland in an article 'Women's rights and tradition', which appeared in the same magazine, vol. 2, no. 1 (winter 1968), p. 26-28.

Family Life and Organization. Women and children

389 Equal rights for women: the battle still goes on.
Guðrún Erlendsdóttir. *Atlantica and Iceland Review*, vol. 14, no. 2 (1978), p. 14-17.

A brief but helpful review of legislative achievements in the struggles for women's rights, from the decree of 1850, which gave daughters the same claims to inheritance as sons, through to the establishment of the Equal Rights Commission in 1976. Although Icelandic women have full legal parity, the conclusion is that the goal of equal status has not yet been achieved. The article is accompanied by comments from women in five professions: an advertising executive, journalist, television producer, orchestral musician, and parliamentarian (nine out of sixty members of the Icelandic parliament are women). Since this article was written Iceland has elected a woman President, whose campaign was not overdirected towards the female vote, and whose election was neither due to nor dependent upon it. Female suffrage was granted in 1915. The year 1982 saw the 75th anniversary of the Women's Rights Association of Iceland.

390 Growing up in Iceland.
Haraldur J. Hamar. *Atlantica and Iceland Review*, vol. 17, no. 3 (1979), p. 14-20.

A well-written and perceptive feature article which presents an illuminating picture of childhood and adolescence in Iceland. The writer surveys Icelandic youth in various contexts: living standards, family size, medical care, education, summer vacation activity, and the growth of national consciousness in a country increasingly subjected to international influences on the younger generation. 'The smallness of Icelandic society helps more than it handicaps; being a member of such a community makes a young person acutely aware of the role of individuals'. See the article by Alan E. Boucher 'All children are much the same, but... ', *American-Scandinavian Review*, vol. 56, no. 3 (autumn 1968), p. 275-80.

391 La protección a los niños en Islandia. (The protection of children in Iceland.)
Jakob Jónsson. *Revista Mexicana de Sociología*, vol. 21, no. 2 (May 1959), p. 559-68.

In this article (available only in Spanish with English summary) a pastor from Reykjavík sets out the provisions of the Law for the Protection of Children 1932, amended in 1947. Seven areas of child care are enumerated, with indications of the responsibilities of the various institutions for positive approaches to normal, deficient, delinquent and special problem children within the context of family and society. A topic of exceptional importance calling for wider information in English.

Children and television in Iceland: a study of ten to fourteen year old children in three communities.
See item no. 906.

Population and Social Change

Demography

392 Manntál á Íslandi. (Census of Iceland.)
Reykjavík: Hagstofa Íslands / the Statistical Bureau of Iceland.

The earliest census taken in Iceland, indeed, in the modern sense, the earliest taken anywhere in Europe, was in 1703. It was recently presented under the title *Manntál 1703* (Population census 1703) by the Statistical Bureau of Iceland (Statistical Report series II, 21 (1960), 60p.), and includes summaries in English and Esperanto. Also re-issued recently was the census for 1801; this appeared in three volumes, according to region, and was published by Hólar Press, 1978-80. The 20th century has seen seven full censuses, one for each decade; all were published by the Statistical Bureau of Iceland, with the exception of the pre-independence censuses of 1901, which was issued by the Danish Statistical Office, and 1910, which was issued by the Stjórnarráð (Ministry of Iceland) in 1913. Subsequent censuses were taken in 1920 (published 1926); 1930 (published 1937); 1940 (published 1949); 1950 (published 1958); and 1960, at the time of writing the last census to have been fully published (issued by the Statistical Bureau in 1969 under the title *Manntál á Íslandi, 1 December 1960* in the series Hagskýrslur Íslands II, 47, 210p.). No census was taken in 1970, partly because of the time taken to produce the previous one, partly because of the establishment of the National Registry; but a full census, the twenty-second in Icelandic history, was again taken in 1980, some preliminary results of which have been released, although full publication is still awaited. The total population of Iceland at this latest census was 229,187.

393 Population changes in Iceland.
Sigurður Þórarinsson. *Geographical Review* (US), vol. 51 (1961), p. 219-33. maps.

'The settlement of Iceland is unique in being a settlement of the largest habitable area on the globe where no primitive people had ever lived, and where the

Population and Social Change. Demography

Icelanders thus had no possibility of learning anything from natives who had adapted themselves to their environment... to find a counterpart of this large-scale expansion towards the sub-polar areas we must turn to our own century'. The writer proceeds to analyse the changes in the population of Iceland from an environmental rather than economic standpoint, with particular reference to the census of 1703, and to clarify his argument with maps. See Sigurður Þórarinsson's *The thousand years struggle against ice and fire* (q.v.).

394 **Population distribution and standard of living in Iceland.**
Valdimar Kristinsson. *Geoforum* (UK/GFR), vol. 13 (1973), p. 53-62. maps. graphs. tables.

Another useful article on the historical demography of the Icelanders, with special emphasis on the fluctuation in living standards throughout Iceland's history. An improvement of these standards had been one of the motives for the original settlement of Iceland, and the writer of this article traces the successes of the first five centuries, the setbacks of the next two, the disasters of the 18th century, and the profound changes brought about by the initially slow, but increasingly rapid 'urban' evolution of the late 19th and 20th centuries. The text is accompanied by clearly presented maps, graphs and tables.

395 **A millenium of misery: the demography of the Icelanders.**
Richard F. Tomasson. *Population Studies* (UK), vol. 31, no. 3 (Nov. 1977), p. 405-27.

The last of the trio of articles on the population history of Iceland, in which the writer takes a comparative viewpoint by drawing on the census of 1703 (when the population was recorded as totalling 50,358), relating the country's vital statistics to its physical environment, and discussing current population trends, from which he projects a 40 per cent increase in the population for the last quarter of the present century (Iceland has the highest rate of life expectancy in the world). He also makes the unusual calculation that around two million Icelanders have been born during the nation's history. This article re-appears as chapter three of Tomasson's book *Iceland: the first new society* (q.v.).

396 **The Laki eruption of 1783: impacts on population and settlement in Iceland.**
Edgar L. Jackson. *Geography*, vol. 67, no. 1 (Jan. 1982), p. 42-50. map.

The eruption of the Laki craters (q.v.) which resulted in widespread and catastrophic starvation, is here analysed from the standpoint of human geography. Contemporary accounts and statistical data are adduced to demonstrate the numerical recovery of the population and the distribution of new settlements in the area. A map shows the patterns of adjustment.

397 **Emigrant fares and emigration from Iceland to North America, 1874-1893.**
Helgi Skúli Kjartansson. *Scandinavian Economic History Review* (Finland), vol. 28, no. 1 (1980), p. 53-71.

Emigration from Iceland to North America reached mass proportions between 1873 and 1906 - during the quinquennium 1886-90 over four and a half thousand Icelanders, or 13 per cent of the population emigrated. In this very worthwhile piece of historical research the author has collated an extensive series of data

Population and Social Change. Social change

concerning the operations of, and the varying fares charged by, a number of Canadian/American shipping companies in the transport of the emigrants, and analyses their effects on the process of emigration. See the same author's paper 'The onset of emigration from Iceland' in *American Studies in Scandinavia* (Norway), vol. 9 (1977), p. 87-93.

398 **Iceland and the Faroes: a comparative demographic study covering the period 1900-1970.**
Aa. H. Kampp. *Inter-nord* (France), no. 13-14 (Dec. 1974), p. 285-302. maps. graphs. tables.

In this interesting comparative article the reasons for the absolute increases in the populations of Iceland and the Faroes - a trend counter to that in most other 'marginal' regions of the world - are attributed to the people's determination and ability to survive as nations. The author also examines internal regional migration, and changes in age and sex ratios. Illustrated with a variety of maps, graphs and tables.

Social change

399 **Freedom and welfare: social patterns in the northern countries of Europe.**
Edited by G. R. Nelson. Copenhagen: Munskgaard, 1953. 539p.

Sponsored by the Ministries of Social Affairs of Denmark, Finland, Iceland, Norway and Sweden, this wide-ranging volume is still useful for its comparative assessment of social development and welfare organisation in the Nordic countries before and immediately after the Second World War, and for placing Iceland in the context of the Nordic approach. The editorial assistant for the sections on Iceland was Sverrir Þorbjörnsson.

400 **Changes in Icelandic social structure since the end of the eighteenth century.**
Jóhannes Nordal. PhD thesis, University of London, London, 1954. 259p.

This thesis remains valuable as the only study in the English language to examine the social structure of Iceland diachronically. Taking as his starting point the first census of 1703, the author demonstrates that the changes in Icelandic social structure during the 18th and 19th centuries were of an organisational rather than occupational character. The trend towards urbanisation and relative industrialisation during the last two decades of the 19th century and onwards forms the background to the central point of this thesis: the ways in which social mobility has been influenced by social structure, education, career patterns, intermarriage between strata, and the development of the professions. The author enlarges on this last aspect in a paper entitled 'The recruitment of the professions in Iceland' which he presented at the Second World Congress of Sociology, Liège, 1953, and which was included in its *Transactions*, vol. 2 (1954), p. 153-65, originally published in London by the International Sociological Association and

Population and Social Change. Social change

issued in reprint by University Microfilms International, 1981. In this paper he examines the recruitment of doctors, lawyers and the clergy in Iceland.

401 **Social change in Iceland.**
Emory S. Bogadus. *Sociology and Social Research*, vol. 40, no. 2 (Nov. 1955), p. 117-26.

A survey of the major social changes in Iceland during the present century, and particularly of those resulting from the events of the Second World War. Special attention is paid to population, the influence of the co-operative movement, and the development of communications. The author characterises the changes as a 'social revolution'.

402 **Secret of culture: nine community studies.**
Laura M. Thompson. New York: Random House, 1969. p. 150-81.

The Icelanders are one of the national communities investigated by an American anthropologist in this cross-cultural study. She attempts to relate the behavioural patterns of the Icelanders to their historical development and ecological situation. Her broad conclusion is that the persistence and re-emergence of the egalitarian rather than authoritarian structure of Icelandic society has developed from the original relationship between the *goði* and the Þingmenn during the early centuries of Icelandic history - a relationship which she sees as complementary rather than hierarchical; this factor, combined with the unfavourable natural environment, has engendered a spirit of 'first amongst equals' in the social development of Iceland. Although this analysis ignores certain factors, such as the potential effect of international influences during the present century, it is to be respected as a valid contribution to an understanding of the elusive quality of Icelandic society, with its paradox of individual independence and community spirit. The author enlarges on the modern patterns of Iceland's culturally unified community in 'Core values and diplomacy: a case study of Iceland', *Human Organization*, vol. 19 (1960), p. 82-85.

403 **On the myth of social equality in Iceland.**
Þorbjörn Broddason, Keith Webb. *Acta Sociologica* (Norway), vol. 18, no. 1 (1975), p. 49-61.

The sociological approach in this piece of research results in a contrasting view to that of the anthropological approach in Laura M. Thompson's book (q.v.). In their investigation of the popular belief or claim in Iceland and elsewhere that Icelandic society is characterised by a high degree of social equality, they present the results of a survey based on 'occupational prestige groups', and are drawn to the conclusion that not only is the claim largely false, but that Icelandic society is becoming more akin to that of western Europe as industrialisation increases. This sort of sampling investigation attracts greater prestige among sociologists than among empirical observers, whether native or foreign to the communities in question, and the authors underplay the significance of one of their own findings, namely, the lack of consciousness amongst Icelanders of social inequality; they also admit that Iceland is not a class society in the full sense of the term. But there is much perception in the researchers' identification of those factors which have helped to perpetuate the 'myth': kinship networks, linguistic homogeneity, social mobility, relative affluence, and the changing occupational structure. This subject is of exceptional interest in the Icelandic context, and this paper adds strong stimulus to the debate.

Population and Social Change. Social change

404 **Explorations in social inequality stratification dynamics in social and individual development in Iceland.**
Sigurjón Björnsson, Wolfgang Edelstein, Kurt Krappner. Berlin: Max Planck Institut für Bildungsforschung, 1977. 172p.

A specialist research study focussed on Iceland as a nation having undergone rapid modernisation and social evolution since 1945, and one with a high degree of 'socio-cultural homogeneity'. After an examination of some of the contradictions in the egalitarian nature of Icelandic society, the authors explore the structure and content of the class system, and analyse class in relation to intelligence, school achievement, patterns of child-rearing, and mental health. This research produces no major conclusions, but the sociologist will find in it a variety of data hitherto unavailable for the study of contemporary Icelandic society.

405 **Family organisation in rural Iceland.**
Frederick E. Bredahl-Petersen. PhD thesis, University of Edinburgh, Edinburgh, 1977. 378p.

Conclusions drawn from general surveys of Icelandic social structures have resulted in some confusion. It may well be that there is more to be gained from studies such as this thesis, in which the author examines the social changes in a particular *hrepp*, or district, and the way in which the decline in the rural population and the increase in centralised government is rendering the traditional organisation of the *hrepp* less significant; he also deals with the ecological adjustment of the Icelandic farm unit in the context of the social and technological changes which have affected southern Iceland during the present century, but lays emphasis on the continuing strength of kinship. He draws upon census materials, farmers' diaries and reports, oral histories, field-work conducted in the late 1960s, and questionnaires. 'It is the combination of legal and civil administration, householder and kinship expectations, and the subsistence cycle of single and joint farming which give the district of Skeið its unusual character'. Skeið district is located between the valleys of Ölfusá and Þjórsá.

406 **Transhumance and ecology: a study of changing patterns of economic activity and continuities in social organisation in a rural Icelandic township.**
Ann Pinson Gill. PhD thesis, State University of New York, Stony Brook, New York 1978. 278p.

An investigation into the relationships between social organisation and livestock economy in the rural township of Hólarhreppur in Skagafjörður, north Iceland. Evidence is adduced from the present century to show how the political organisation of the community has been maintained in relation to the family hierarchies, and how the changing nature of the agricultural economy has made the family units increasingly dependent upon the contribution of communal labour.

Icelandic sociology: national conditions and the emergence of a new discipline.
See item no. 431.

Health

407 **Health in Iceland.**
Vilmundur Jónsson. Reykjavík: Ríkisprentsmiðjan Gutenberg, 1940. 29p.
English text of the report of the Director of Public Health for Iceland. This is a useful document for a study of Icelandic health service tradition, and for making comparisons with post-war developments (for example, the population has doubled since this report, whereas the number of doctors has trebled). The report covers the training, conditions and activities of medical personnel, hospital administration, health legislation, and a survey of the state of the nation's health. Includes folding graph of birth and death rates from 1700 to 1940, and map of the forty-nine medical districts in 1938 (today these have expanded to fifty-seven).

408 **Disability in Iceland.**
Stefán Guðnason, translated from the Icelandic by Alan E. Boucher. Reykjavík: Prentsmiðja Jóns Helgasonar, 1969. 275p.
This invaluable study was stimulated by the need for the Icelandic State Social Security Institution to provide its medical officers with information on the total situation of the disabled, whether through disease or accident, in Iceland, to facilitate evaluation of social insurance as the law provides. Based on a sample of over one third of the disabled population, this survey contains a preliminary exposition of disability in Iceland and the schemes designed to meet it, followed by an analysis of the various classes of diseases and their occurrence: infectious, neoplasmic, metabolic, haematological, neurological, circulatory, respiratory, digestive, urinary, obstetric, dermatological, skeletal, as well as mental disorders and physical accidents. Appendices tabulate distribution of disabilities according to sex, age, marital status, occupation, hospital admissions, etc.

409 **Perinatal mortality in Iceland.**
Gunnar Biering. *Acta Paedopsychiatrica Scandinavica* (Sweden), vol. 62 (1973), p. 117-20.
A summarised presentation of data concerning perinatal mortality in Iceland during 1970, when the rate was 18.3 per 1,000, and in Reykjavík over the previous decade. No significant variation appears between the capital city and the country

Health

as a whole. A graph also shows the dramatic decline in home deliveries in Reykjavík from 1 in 5 during the early 1950s to 1 in 200 by 1970. For a more detailed survey of this topic see the article by Gunnlaugur Snædal in *Acta Obstetrica et Gynecologica*, suppl. 45 (1975), p. 5-47, in which the author analyses perinatal data from 1881 to 1971, followed by an updating report to 1974.

410 Cancer in Iceland.
Niels Dungal. *Annals of the Royal College of Surgeons*, vol. 16 (1955), p. 211-26.

An inquiry into the incidence and an analysis of forms of cancer in Iceland from a comparative point of view, the findings of which indicate that at mid-century the distribution of the disease differs significantly from that in many other countries, especially in the case of stomach cancer which is frequent in Iceland, and lung cancer which is relatively rare. See the chapter on cancer incidence in Iceland by Ólafur Bjarnason in the volume *Racial and geographical factors in tumour incidence*, edited by A. A. Shivas (Edinburgh: Edinburgh University Press, 1967).

411 Multiple sclerosis in Iceland.
Kjartan R. Guðmundsson, Gunnar Guðmundsson. *Acta Neurologica Scandinavica*, vol. 38, suppl. 2 (1962), p. 1-63.

Another epidemiological study which takes advantage of the relative homogeneity and stability of the population of Iceland. The case-study involved a survey of the prevalence, incidence and geographical distribution of the disease in Iceland, 1946-55. Findings were similar to those for other northern countries. Prevalence of the disease amounted to 80 cases throughout the country, or over 1 in 2,000. No regional variation was detected. Mean age at onset was 25.4 years, and 62.5 per cent of cases were in women.

412 Smallpox in Iceland.
Jón Steffensen. *Nordisk Medicinhistorisk årsbok*, 1977. p. 41-56.

There had been twenty-one epidemics of smallpox recorded in Icelandic medical history. This article is a survey of the history of the disease in Iceland, with particular reference to the severest of the outbreaks, which started in 1707, as a result of which an estimated quarter of the population died. Vaccination was introduced at the beginning of the 19th century, after which time there occurred only one mild epidemic. See in the same yearbook for 1980, suppl. no. 6. p. 76-81, the article on epidemics in Iceland in the 18th century by Olafur Bjarnason, who describes the smallpox outbreaks and the famine resulting from the Laki volcanic eruption in 1783, and makes comparisons between 18th and 20th century mortality in Iceland.

413 Spatial diffusion: an historical geography of epidemics in an island community.
A. D. Cliff (and others). Cambridge, England: Cambridge University Press, 1981. 238p. (Cambridge Geographical Studies, vol. 14).

A specialised research monograph, the substance of which is an examination of the spatial regularities observable in recurrent epidemics of measles in Iceland, where there have been sixteen major outbreaks during this century.

Health

414 Tuberculosis in Iceland: epidemiological studies.
Sigurður Sigurðsson. Washington, DC: US Government Printing Office, 1950. 86p. (Public Health Service Publications, no. 21).

A comprehensive account and analysis of the history and course of tuberculosis in Iceland, the characteristics of the disease and its environment, and the available countermeasures. Between 1929 and 1949 the rate of death from tuberculosis was dramatically reduced by tenfold. The main part of this volume is devoted to the results of mass surveys by districts. Among the major findings is a proportionately lower incidence in rural districts, and among females over 15 years old. The surveys were conducted during the 1940s.

415 Evidence for a food additive as a cause of ketosis prone diabetes.
Þórir Helgason, Magnús R. Jónasson. *Lancet*, no. 8,249 (3 Oct. 1981), p. 716-20.

A specialist medical article by doctors from the diabetic clinic of the University hospital in Reykjavík, whose research into juvenile diabetes brought to light circumstantial evidence of correlation between nitrous compounds in foods, and diabetes. The research commanded attention in international medical circles, but also caused considerable repercussions among the Icelandic public, when it was reported in the press that the findings suggested a direct link between diabetes among boys born during the month of October, and the consumption of smoked lamb, in which nitrite is extensively used as an additive, and which is traditionally consumed in greater quantities during the period of Christmas and the New Year. A further correlation was that the incidence of diabetes in the progeny (not in the consumer) was particularly high in Akureyri, a town shown to have the highest per capita consumption of smoked lamb anywhere in Iceland.

416 Mortality among men alcoholics in Iceland, 1951-74.
Alma Anna Þórarinsson. *Journal of Studies on Alcohol*, vol. 40, no. 7 (1979), p. 704-18.

Per capita consumption of absolute alcohol more than doubled between 1955 and 1974. The purpose of this research-based paper is to compare the mortality of alcoholics in Iceland with that of the country's male population aged 15 years and over. Among the conclusions is the finding that the excess mortality attributable to alcoholism is due largely to violent causes such as accidents and suicides rather than to alcohol-related diseases. Psychiatric data are taken from the Psychiatric Register (1978), and demographic data from the National Register (1979).

417 Psychiatric services and mental illness in Iceland: incidence study.
Lárus Helgason. *Acta Psychiatrica Scandinavica*, suppl. 268 (1977), p. 11-140.

A major research monograph relating to 1966-67, and including the results of a follow-up survey seven years later. It comprises a social, aetiological and clinical analysis of 2,388 Icelanders, correlating demographic with diagnostic, and physical with mental characteristics. Amongst the many findings is a surprisingly high incidence of mental disorder in rural areas. Conclusions are also drawn concerning the effects of mental illness on marriage and divorce, income, migration, and

Health

on the psychiatric hospital services. Earlier supplements to this journal contain two papers of historical and comparative interest related to this problem. In suppl. 173 (1964), 258p., Tómas Helgason's 'Epidemiology of mental disorders in Iceland' is a case-study of 5,395 Icelanders born between 1895 and 1897; in suppl. 162 (1961), p. 81-90, the same author compares the frequency of depressive states in Iceland with that of the other Scandinavian countries.

418 Epidemiological investigation of mental disorders of children in Reykjavík.
Sigurjón Björnsson. *Scandinavian Journal of Psychology*, vol. 15, no. 4 (1974), p. 244-54.

An investigation by a research team from the University of Iceland into mental disorders among 1,000 children in Reykjavík, based on psychological testing and structured interviews with mothers. Correlations are indicated between occurrence of mental disorders amongst 5-15 year-olds and factors such as the educational level of the parents, paternal occupations, maternal attitudes, and the children's schooling.

419 Psychiatry in Iceland.
Esra Pétursson. *International Journal of Social Psychiatry*, vol. 9, no. 3 (spring 1963), p. 154-56.

A short historical account of the development of psychiatry in Iceland, with reference to the original Kleppur hospital, the Icelandic Psychiatric Association, and the training programmes at the University of Iceland.

420 An Icelandic pioneer surgeon.
Guđmundur Björnsson. *Nordisk Medicinhistorisk årsbok*, 1976. p. 146-61.

A paper of interest to both the medical and the social historian. It describes the unique work of Guđmundur Hannesson (born 1865 - see *Körpermasse und Körperproportionen der Isländer: ein Beitrag zur Anthropologie Islands* q.v.), a district medical officer in northern Iceland around the turn of the century. Trained in Denmark, he later became Professor of Medicine and Hygiene at the University of Iceland. He was both a general and an opthalmic surgeon who made a special study of glaucoma in Iceland. He maintained meticulous records of incidence and treatment between 1896 and 1907, and it is these records which have been used as the basis for this paper.

421 Nursing in Iceland.
María Pétursdóttir. *International Journal of Nursing Studies*, vol. 3 (1966), p. 81-87.

An historical survey of the development of the nursing profession in Iceland, in which a President of the Icelandic Nurses Association emphasises the individual character of the early initiatives which has contributed to the independent and self-governing status of the profession today. She traces the origins of organised nursing from the establishment of the leper hospital in 1898, through the foundation of the Icelandic Nurses Association in 1919, to the establishment of the State School of Nursing as part of the new state hospital, Landspítalinn, in 1930, which produced 647 nursing graduates in its first 35 years. She concludes with a summary of the conditions of work of nurses (there are nearly 1,000 nurses in Iceland today). For a student nurse's view, see the enthusiastic and informative report on impressions of training and practical work in the state nursing school

Health

and hospital written by Sigriður Skúladóttir, *Sixty-five Degrees*, no. 9 (March 1970), p. 22-33.

422 Too many doctors for the medical system.
Sonja Diego. *Atlantica and Iceland Review*, vol. 18, no. 2 (1980), p. 46-49.

A feature article presenting a variety of views on the training of doctors in Iceland. Around 30 per cent of Icelandic doctors work abroad, and half of these do not return, for reasons rather different from those in other countries - hitherto the University of Iceland has imposed no limit on the number of medical enrolments, but the question is whether there are too many doctors for the system, or whether the system is insufficiently flexible to accommodate them. In the balance between a high level of health care and the economic facts of life, this article poses the question whether one can talk of a 'right' number of doctors for Iceland.

The medieval leper and his northern heirs.
See item no. 322.

Læknablaðið: the Icelandic Medical Journal.
See item no. 936.

Education and Research

423 History of education in Iceland.
George T. Trial. Cambridge, England: Heffer, 1945. 95p.
The high level of educational development, which, despite long periods of national adversity, has continuously shown through Icelandic society since the time of the settlement is attributable in large measure to the strong tradition of family education. Historically, formal education had been broadly confined to theological study, and, as the elementary school was a very late development, it is fair to say that until well into the present century the formal school had played only a small part in the life of the educated Icelander. It is, therefore, unusually interesting to trace the way in which the institutions of the Icelandic educational system emerged out of this tradition during the 19th and 20th centuries, and paved the way for the post-war system in the republic. This book clearly and concisely describes the Icelandic educational system under Danish administration and influence up to full independence, with emphasis on the predominant sectors of commercial and technical education; it includes a useful chronology of educational landmarks, and a variety of statistical data concerning syllabuses. For a summary account of the state of education in Iceland by the time of full independence see J. C. Jonason's article 'Iceland educates for democracy' in *Elementary School Journal*, vol. 50 (Dec. 1949), p. 212-22.

424 Education in Iceland: its rise and growth with respect to social, political and economic determinants.
Bragi Straumfjord Jósepsson. Nashville, Tennessee: George Peabody College for Teachers, 1968. 2 vols. 956p.
This monumental piece of research was submitted in partial (sic!) fulfilment of the requirements for the degree of Doctor of Education. Traces the educational development of Iceland, 874-1966, identifying eight major periods: colonisation to Reformation (874-1550); Reformation period (1550-1745); educational awakening (1745-1800); nationalistic movement (1800-74); public education movement (1874-1904); formation of an educational pattern (1904-18); consolidation (1918-44); era of modernisation (1944-66). He appends a partially annotated bibliography of English, Icelandic and Danish sources (a version of which, under

Education and Research

the title *Icelandic culture and education: an annotated bibliography*, was issued by the Department of Sociology at Western Kentucky University, 1968, 80p.), a detailed chronology of educational events, a glossary of Icelandic educational terms, and the translated texts of educational laws. Anyone with a serious interest in Icelandic education should gain access to this thesis, now available through University Microfilms International in film, fiche or xerographic format. Also published by the United States Department of Health, Education and Welfare. For a later thesis see George Hanson's *Icelandic education: tradition and modernization in a cultural perspective*. (EdD, Loyola University of Chicago, 1979, 415p.).

425 The literacy of the Icelanders.
Richard F. Tomasson. *Scandinavian Studies*, vol. 47 (winter 1975), p. 66-93.

A discussion of the achievement (unique in Europe) of universal literacy in Iceland during the 18th century, a century of calamity in terms of disease and natural disaster. Evidence is produced from the writings of many travellers to Iceland during the following decades, and from the major study of the subject in Icelandic by Hallgrímur Hallgrímsson in 1925. The author presents the findings of a survey of the bookreading habits and book ownership of Icelanders, as well as of their familiarity with Icelandic literature (ancient and modern) and with foreign writers; the survey was based on interviews with a random sample of 100 Icelanders during 1971. Among the conclusions drawn are that virtually all Icelandic homes at whatever level contain collections of books (with an average of 338 books per household), and that the overwhelming majority of Icelanders actively read books. Such findings, coupled with the unparalleled national per capita publication and sales of books, are contemporary manifestations of the continuity of popular literacy in Iceland, the origins of which may possibly be traced back to the standards of literary interest among the original settlers. This article re-appears as chapter five of Tomasson's book *Iceland: the first new society* (q.v.). An historically related article entitled 'Books owned by ordinary people in Iceland, 1750-1830' was contributed by Sólrún Jensdóttir to *Saga-book*, vol. 19 (1974-77), p. 265-92.

426 In Iceland it's inhuman to send a five-year-old to school.
Laurie MacLennan. *Times Educational Supplement* (UK), no. 2,828 (1 Aug. 1969), p. 23.

A brief feature article in which the reporter identifies the major reasons, mainly social, for the way in which Icelandic schooling is organised.

427 Innovation in foreign language teaching.
Andrí Ísaksson. *English Language Teaching Journal*, vol. 27 (June 1973), p. 288-92.

A brief exposition of the Icelandic Ministry of Education's reasons for lowering the age at which the study of Danish and English is compulsory in Icelandic schools, but at the same time reducing the high number of compulsory languages from five to three. The Icelandic school curriculum has, for obvious reasons, traditionally involved a large element of foreign language study.

Education and Research

428 Teacher education in Iceland.
Þúríður J. Kristjánsdóttir. *Delta Kappa Gamma Bulletin*, vol. 45 (winter 1979), p. 60-63.

A summary of the developments in the training of teachers in Iceland, with particular reference to the requirements of the Education College of Iceland (founded in 1908). In an earlier issue of the same periodical, vol. 44 (fall 1977), p. 10-13, Ingeborg McHaffie presents a portrait of Valborg Sigurðardóttir, Rector of the Fósturskóli in Reykjavík, a college which has pioneered the training of teachers in early childhood education, care and development.

429 The University of Iceland: cornerstone of an expanding society.
Sonja Diego. *Atlantica and Iceland Review*, vol. 18, no. 3 (1980), p. 42-47.

An illustrated introduction to the University of Iceland, which was founded in 1911, and is the centre for virtually all higher education within the country. Includes brief notes on its research, syllabus, tuition and administration. In 1982 the University had over 3,900 students on its register. For an earlier assessment of the state of the University, see the article by the then President of the University, Alexander Jóhannesson, in *American-Scandinavian Review*, vol. 38 (1950), p. 349-54, with particular reference to its removal from the parliament building to its new purpose-built premises.

430 Kennsluskrá. (Háskóli Íslands.)
Reykjavík: Ríkisprentsmiðjan Gutenberg. c. 400p. annual.

The official calendar and prospectus of the University of Iceland, listing academic and administrative personnel, the eight faculties and their departments, syllabuses, supporting services, etc.

431 Icelandic sociology: national conditions and the emergence of a new discipline.
Þórólfur Þorlindsson. *Acta Sociologica* (Norway), vol. 25 (1982), suppl. p. 79-89.

The writer discusses the way in which the discipline of sociology in Iceland has developed in the context of the nation's social situation. He describes the institutional structure of the Icelandic educational system, the division of labour among the social science disciplines in Iceland, and the place of sociology, with reference to its terminology, methodology and research. He comments that Icelandic sociology was originally shaped by British rather than Scandinavian traditions of the discipline.

432 Pioneering political science: the case of Iceland.
Ólafur Ragnar Grímsson. *Scandinavian Political Studies* (Norway), vol. 12 (1977), p. 47-63.

The whole of this issue is devoted to a comparison of the growth and trends in political science in the Nordic countries. The Icelandic contributor discusses the five stages of the development of the discipline in his own country: teaching, research, publication, professionalisation, and international integration. His account is based on the work of the Department of Social Science at the Univer-

Education and Research

sity of Iceland, and a list of the Department's publications, theses and research papers is appended to the article.

433 Reviews of national science policy: Iceland.
Paris: Organisation for Economic Co-operation and Development, 1973. 159p.

This volume is one of a series of country reviews by the OECD, designed to offer the country concerned the opportunity to take stock of its own science policy, and to increase the pool of available knowledge concerning the content of national scientific programmes and their role as an instrument of government. Because of Iceland's special natural environment, the need for a co-ordinated scientific research policy is acute. This review covers the conception of such a policy in Iceland, its technological potential, and the performance of research and development. The second part contains the OECD examiner's report and recommendations, with an account of the meeting between their panel and forty members of relevant organisations in Iceland. Statistical tables accompany the text.

434 Classification of educational systems: Iceland..
Paris: Organisation for Economic Co-operation and Development, 1975. 22p.

A useful tabulation, prepared by the OECD for comparative purposes, of the various types and levels of education within the Icelandic system: nursery, primary, secondary, special, technical, adult, higher, university, research, and teacher training. Each type or level is itself subdivided, and details of length of study, entrance requirements, certificates granted, and full or part-time facilities are systematically listed, with relevant annotations. In the case of teacher training, the OECD had earlier issued a comparative tabulated case investigation entitled *Study on teachers, training, recruitment and utilisation of teachers... Canada, Spain, Iceland*, (1962, 152p.).

Unified curriculum construction: the Icelandic-American comprehensive musicianship project.
See item no. 899.

Statistics

435 Yearbook of Nordic statistics.
Stockholm: Nordic Council, 1962- . annual.

An extremely useful compilation, which draws on the data compiled by the statistical offices of the five Nordic countries. It presents a full range of vital, social and economic statistics in a comparative form, with headings, notes and English text. Iceland figures in all the tables and charts, and can thus be readily compared with the other Nordic countries in a variety of statistical contexts. The compilation includes particularly useful sections on social welfare, transport and the media, plus the latest electoral statistics. Edited by the Nordic Statistical Secretariat, these annual volumes are substantial (the 1981 edition contained 380p.), admirably clear in their presentation, and enhanced by a detailed index of subjects treated.

436 Tölfræðihandbók. (Statistical abstract of Iceland.)
Reykjavík: Hagstofa Íslands / the Statistical Bureau of Iceland, 1976. 253p.

An essential reference tool for any serious statistical study of modern Iceland. The Statistical Bureau, which has responsibility for all official Icelandic statistics except for certain financial data, here presents statistics (mainly for the period 1967-74) on climate, population, labour market, agriculture, fisheries, manufacturing, housing, energy, trade, transport and communications, wages and prices, credit, national accounts, public finance, health and welfare, justice, education and culture, elections, etc. The tables are clearly laid out, with contents pages, headings, sub-headings and explanatory notes in parallel English/Icelandic text. Previous editions were issued in 1967, and in 1930 (the latter under the title *Arbók Hagstofu Íslands*). A more regular appearance would be welcome, but see Statistical Bulletin (q.v.) for updating.

437 Statistical Bulletin.
Reykjavík: Statistical Bureau of Iceland and Central Bank of Iceland, 1932-80. quarterly.

An English language presentation of various social and economic statistics for Iceland, taken from the monthly compilation *Hagtíðindi* (1916-.), and including detailed figures under the following headings: fish catch; foreign trade by country of origin and destination, and by commodity in quantity/value; foreign exchange

Statistics

quotations by the central bank (buying and selling rates); registered motor vehicles; Treasury revenue and expenditure; cost of living index for Reykjavík; banking accounts; tourism; etc. The currency of the information is commendable (figures usually relate to a period only two months prior to publication). From 1980 the Economic Department of the Central Bank of Iceland (Seðlabanki Islands) published this English version in their own right under the new title *Economic Statistics*. It has remained a quarterly publication with a similar content overall, but with the addition of background notes, graphs, and an annual supplement. Extremely useful, and freely distributed.

438 Mannfjöldaskýrslur árin 1961-70. (Population and vital statistics, 1961-70.)
Reykjavík: Statistical Bureau of Iceland, 1975. 140p.

A particularly useful presentation of decennially cumulated statistics, covering population, migration, grantings of citizenship (interesting in the Icelandic context), marriage and divorce, births, adoptions, deaths, and forward projections. Commentaries in Icelandic, but table headings given in English. Volumes in this series were also published for previous decades, e.g. 1951-60 (published 1963), 1941-50 (published 1952); and the earliest volume covered the years 1911-15.

439 Verzlunarskýrslur. (Commercial statistics.)
Reykjavík: Hagstofa Íslands, 1912- . irregular.

The major source of statistics on all aspects of Icelandic commerce, foreign trade and related activities. Issued as one in the series of sectoral compilations by the Statistical Bureau of Iceland. Approximately annual of late, with over 250p. Contents page and main headings in English. Other sectors covered by the serial publications of the Statistical Bureau (available in Icelandic only) include, for example: *Búnaðarskýrslur* (agriculture), *Iðnaðarskýrslur* (industry), *Húsnæðisskýrslur* (housing), all of which are infrequently issued as sub-series.

440 Árbók Reykjavíkurborgar.
Reykjavík: Hagfræðideild Reykjavíkurborgar, 1940- . annual.

The official yearbook of the city of Reykjavík is an enterprising publication offering a mine of statistical information on the country's capital city, plus up-to-date maps. It has appeared regularly since 1940; the 1979 volume contains over 250p.

Manntál á Íslandi. (Census of Iceland.)
See item no. 392.

Vinnumarkaðurinn 1980. (The labour market 1980.)
See item no. 507.

Constitution, Parliament and the Law

The old laws

441 Studies in history and jurisprudence.
James B. Bryce. Oxford, England: Clarendon Press, 1901.
2 vols.
Viscount Bryce remains one of the most perceptive and highly respected analysts of democratic systems in the history of legal and political scholarship. It is fortunate, therefore, that in addition to his valued general impressions of Iceland (see *Memories of Travel* q.v.), he applied his specialism to an analysis of the workings of the Old Icelandic Republic in the brilliant extended essay, 'Primitive Iceland' in volume one (p. 312-58) of his *Studies in history and jurisprudence*. In spite of its age and the fact that it remains available only in this edition, the student with an interest in the law and institutions of the Icelandic Commonwealth will be well advised to seek it out as the best balanced introduction to the subject, and one which offers illuminating comparisons with other ancient and modern constitutions. The author describes 'primitive' Iceland as having produced a constitution 'unlike any other whereof records remain'.

442 Laws of early Iceland: Grágás.
Translated by Andrew Dennis, Peter Foote, Richard Perkins. Winnipeg, Manitoba: University of Manitoba Press, 1980. 279p. (Icelandic Studies, Vol III).
In books and articles on the social history of early Iceland reference to the civil code of laws known as *Grágás* (literally 'grey goose') is sufficiently frequent to have made the lack, hitherto, of a full translation into English surprising. Dating originally from the first quarter of the 12th century, its long and difficult text is

Constitution, Parliament and the Law. Constitutionalism

nevertheless an extraordinary illumination of early Icelandic society. The bulk of the code comprises three major sections: the Christian laws; the Assembly procedures; the treatment of homicide and the wergild ring list (compensation system). The editors have produced this translation from the two extant versions of *Grágás* and its additions, with marginal headings, a glossary of technical terms, and a map of the site of the General Assembly at Þingvellir.

443 **Lawyers in the Icelandic family sagas: heroes, villains and authors.**
Alan Berger. *Saga-book* (UK), vol. 20, no. 1-2 (1978-79), p. 70-79.

A survey of the frequent occurrence of legal conflict in the Icelandic family sagas, in which the author maintains that such episodes have been underrated in their historical significance - some sagas could almost be classed as 'lawyer sagas'. 'The law could be considered a catalogue of conflicts useful to a conflict-hungry literature... narrative could be made convincing with the addition of legal detail. The law was a source of history and for what could pass as history'. For an analysis of a litigation in a particular family saga (*Njáls saga*) see George Clinton's article 'An Icelandic lawsuit of the eleventh century' in *Lincoln Law Review*, vol. 2 (1928), p. 6-13.

444 **Private creation and enforcement of law.**
David Friedman. *Journal of Legal Studies*, vol. 8, no. 2 (March 1979), p. 399-415.

The author of this paper takes some of the individual characteristics of the legal system of the Old Icelandic Commonwealth, in particular the way in which laws were enforced on a private basis, and projects them into the context of modern society, evaluating their potential relevance in terms of their practicality and efficiency.

Constitutionalism

445 **Icelandic law.**
Lester B. Orfield. *Dickinson Law Review*, vol. 6 (1951), p. 42-87.

After an introduction outlining the framework of Iceland's international relations from 874 to 1951, the writer proceeds to an historical survey of the Icelandic legal system. He examines the Norwegian influences on Icelandic law after 1262, and the subsequent Danish influence during the period of protestant reformation and absolute monarchy, through to the constitutional period of the late 19th century, and culminating in the republican constitution of 1944.

446 **Islande: son statut à travers les âges.** (Iceland: her laws through the ages.)
Aage Gregersen. Paris: Sirey, 1937, 462p. bibliog.

A surprisingly seldom-cited work, considering the fact that it is virtually the only full-length treatise in a major language to deal with the constitutional history of

Constitution, Parliament and the Law. Parliament

Iceland up to the time of modern independence. The volume is divided into three 'books' covering the major periods: from the settlement to the fall of the Commonwealth (874-1262); foreign rule, absolutism, and constitutional reform (1262-1918); the establishment of the sovereign state (1918- .). Although the author's treatment is chronological, the thematic constituents of the country's constitutional and administrative development are clearly identified. A substantial work, originally a doctoral thesis, which even now might be worth translating into English.

447 **The constitution of the republic of Iceland.**
Reykjavík: Office of the Prime Minister, 5th printing, 1974. 22p.

The English language text of the Icelandic Constitution which came into force on 17 June 1944, and incorporating certain amendments concerning the composition of the Alþing, and the lowering of the voting age to twenty. (The recent review panel on the Constitution proposes a further lowering to the age of eighteen). The text contains eighty-one articles under seven chapter headings, covering the Republic, the President and Executive, composition of the Alþing (Parliament), powers and procedure of the Alþing, the Judiciary, the Church, civil liberties, etc.

Parliament

448 **The Althing: Iceland's thousand years old parliament.**
Matthías Þórðarson. Reykjavk: Snæbjörn Jónsson (The English Bookshop), 1930. 14p.

The then curator of the National Museum of Iceland presents a short outline of the history and constitution of the world's oldest representative parliament, in an illustrated celebration of its millennium. For another piece of celebration see the article 'Iceland and its one thousand year old parliament' by Clyde Fisher in *Natural History* (*Journal of the American Museum of Natural History*), vol. 30, no. 6 (Nov. 1930), p. 563-76.

449 **The two chambers of the Icelandic Althing.**
Bjarni Benediktsson. In: *Legal essays: a tribute to Frede Castberg*. Oslo: Universitetsforlaget, 1963. p. 394-410.

In this Festschrift for the eminent constitutional lawyer from Norway, the former Prime Minister of Iceland contributed an article of exceptional importance concerning the structure of the Icelandic parliament. During the first 900 years of its history, from its foundation in 930, through its diminution after the loss of independence to Norway in 1262 and subsequently to Denmark, up to its extinction in 1800, the Alþing had been virtually a single chamber. From its restoration in 1843 up to the present time (the period with which this essay is principally concerned) the Alþing has been bicameral. The author examines the reasons for the original decision to divide it into two chambers, and analyses the constitutional and political effects of this division to date. He detects a decline in the importance of this division, as an increasing amount of decision-making has been laid before the united Alþing, and as a greater party politicisation has reduced differences of attitude between the two chambers. The bicameral system he sees as reducing the probabilities of legislative shortcomings, but, on the other hand,

Constitution, Parliament and the Law. Modern justice

as more time-consuming and therefore more expensive. He sees its real justification as lying in the protection which it can afford to minorities.

450 Alþingistíðindi.
Reykjavík: Alþýðuprentsmiðjan, 1845- .

The Icelandic equivalent of *Hansard*, published continuously since the restoration of the Icelandic parliament in the middle of last century. Issued in two main series: the parliamentary documents, and the debates (*Umræður*) with the records of voting. It appears only in Icelandic, and the printed version is in arrears, but any serious student of the Icelandic political process has to be aware of this primary resource, particularly in a country where there are twenty times more members of parliament per (voting) head of population than in Britain. The Icelandic 'Official Gazette' *Stjórntíðindi* is the regular source of information on the enactment of laws, and on other official announcements.

Modern justice

451 The law, the courts and the citizen.
Magnús Þoroddsen. *Sixty-five Degrees*, no. 5 (Feb. 1969), p. 11-14.

A useful article in which the author, himself a judge, sketches the framework of justice in Iceland, with particular reference to the work of the judges, the various types of court, and the cases brought before them. He also comments on the question of court reporting by the media.

452 Policing Reykjavík.
Bjarki Elíasson. *Sixty-five Degrees*, no. 8 (Nov. 1969), p. 12-14.

A personal interview with the chief superintendent of the Reykjavík police force, which touches on several aspects of crime and policing in a capital city noted for its low level of lawbreaking.

453 The national penitentiary: a humanising effort.
Magnús Bjarnfredsson. *Atlantica and Iceland Review* vol. 19, no. 1 (1981), p. 25-29.

An introduction to the character of Iceland's main, and until recently only, prison establishment, which is located near Eyrarbakki on the coast some forty miles south-west of the capital. Serious crime in Iceland, although on the increase, has been markedly rare, and this fact is reflected in the relatively lenient and liberal attitude towards the inmates of *Litla Hraun*, as the prison is called. Another factor, of course, is that Iceland's terrain and sparseness of population render the chances of evading recapture after any escape remote. The state penitentiary is now half a century old - a smaller establishment for minor offences is situated on Snæfellsness.

Constitution, Parliament and the Law. Modern justice

454 **Main features of Icelandic compensation systems.**
Arnljótur Björnsson. *Scandinavian Studies in Law* (Sweden), vol. 25 (1981), p. 11-30.
This article is a survey of the rules of Icelandic tort law. Tort liability is predominantly case law, statute law containing rules applicable only in certain fields. The writer, Professor of Law at the University of Iceland, discusses some of the judgments of the Supreme Court, and outlines the statutory rules; he also touches on the conduct of the aggrieved party. The main part of his paper concerns alternative remedies: social insurance, pension funds, sick pay, collective occupational accident insurance, personal insurance and collateral sources. He concludes that insurance in Iceland is not yet so comprehensive that the tort system can be abolished, but he sees the future progress of insurance cover as of more practical value than reform of tort law.

455 **Labor law and practice in Iceland.**
Franz A. Groemping. Washington, DC: US Government Printing Office, 1970. 38p. (Bureau of Labour Statistics Report).
A useful interim survey of the social factors affecting the Icelandic work-force and their rights, government-labour relations, management-labour relations, and of the various conditions of employment: hours of work, wages, safety, insurance, etc. An appendix lists the twenty-three main laws relating to labour legislation in force in 1968.

Politics

General

456 Nordic democracy..
Copenhagen: Danske Selskab, 1981. 780p. bibliog.
Subtitled 'ideas, issues and institutions in political economy, education, social and cultural affairs of Denmark, Finland, Iceland, Norway and Sweden', this thematically arranged volume forms an excellent comparative study of democracy at work in the Nordic countries; Iceland figures throughout the volume. Three of the thirty chapters are contributed by Icelanders: Sigurður Líndal, lawyer and historian writes on early democratic traditions in the Nordic countries; Gylfi Þ. Gíslason, the Icelandic member of the volume's editorial board, is also co-author of chapters on the political party systems and on the Nordic countries between east and west. The currency of the term 'Nordic democracy' is of interest in itself, and this volume, sponsored by the Nordic Cultural Fund, and which emphasises the influence of Nordic co-operation, goes a long way towards explaining the common democratic traditions of the five countries.

457 The Icelandic power structure, 1800-2000.
Ólafur Ragnar Grímsson. *Scandinavian Political Studies* (Norway), vol. 11 (1976), p. 9-33.
A substantial and stimulating analysis of the past traditions of the élitist elements of the Icelandic political system, and of the recent and likely future weakening of its response to the emergence of new pluralistic pressures. The writer further identifies and discusses the characteristics of the élite, with particular reference to kinship and education. For more detail on the background to this study, see the same author's doctoral dissertation presented to the University of Manchester in 1970 under the title *Political power in Iceland prior to the period of class politics*.

Politics. General

458 **Iceland: a multi-level coalition system.**
Ólafur R. Grímsson. In: *Government coalitions in western democracies.* Edited by Eric C. Browne. New York; London: Longman, 1982. p. 142-86.

Since its formation as an independent republic in 1944, Iceland has seen, during those thirty-eight years, only three brief periods of non-coalition government, in total lasting only eighteen months. Coalition is therefore a core characteristic of the modern Icelandic political system, both inside and outside parliament. In this analytical study (chapter five of the volume), the author, Professor of Political Science at the University of Iceland, examines the various levels of operation of the coalition system and its ramifications, with reference to political policies (foreign policy being particularly important in the context of Icelandic coalition formation), the resources and rules influencing coalition, and, especially interesting, the processes of bargaining and 'payoffs' at cabinet and lower levels. He concludes with a section on the maintenance of coalitions (only two Icelandic post-war coalitions have lasted the full four-year term). He concludes by attributing the integral nature of the coalition system in Icelandic politics to the way in which cabinets influence and are influenced by other levels of the nation's political structure. The text includes tabulated data on Icelandic elections and coalition formations.

459 **The electoral basis of the Icelandic Independence Party, 1929-1944.**
Svanur Kristjánsson. Scandinavian Political Studies (Norway), n.s. vol. 2, no. 1 (1979), p. 31-52.

The Independence Party (Sjálfstæðisflokkur) is the furthest to the right in Icelandic politics. The author examines the electoral basis of the Party in the pre-republican era within the context of Icelandic society, ideology and the moves towards complete independence from Denmark (the Party was formed in 1929 from an amalgam of liberals and conservatives, since when it has always been the largest party in Iceland). He assesses its social composition and support among four major groups: the middle classes, the farmers, the manual workers, and women voters - the first and last of these groups formed the majority of the Party's support. He concludes that, although there has been a certain compromise or shift in the ideology of the Party since 1944, its basic character remains the same. At the present time (1982) the Independence Party is suffering only its third period of non-participation in government since 1944 (1956-59, 1971-74 and 1978- .); in 1978 there occurred the largest turnover of votes for thirty-four years, which nevertheless left the Independence Party as the largest single group in Parliament, but also resulted in a splinter group joining the present coalition, and creating the bizarre situation in which the leaders of both the government coalition and the main opposition group were to be seen at the meetings of the same Party. See the same author's thesis *Conflict and consensus in Icelandic politics, 1916-1944,* PhD, University of Illinois at Urbana-Champaign, 1977, 324p.

460 **Islandsk arbejderbevaegelses historie, 1887-1971.** (History of the Icelandic labour movement.)
Ólafur R. Einarsson. *Meddelelser om Forskning i Arbejderbevaegelsens Historie* (Denmark), vol. 12 (1979), p. 25-31.

An article in Danish (there being no specific treatment in English) in which the Icelandic contributor presents a short survey of the development of trade unionism in Iceland from the founding of the first trade union (for printers) in 1887,

Politics. General

and of the Social Democratic Party (Alþýðuflokkurinn), established in 1916, and other workers' parties.

461 Patterns of Nordic communism.
Trond Gilberg. *Problems of Communism* (US), vol. 24, no. 3 (May 1975), p. 20-35.

A comparative analysis of the Danish, Norwegian and Icelandic Communist Parties. The section on Iceland stresses the individuality of the Party which has 'put together a combination of nationalism, radicalism and unconcern over external debates that augurs well for its ability to continue to play a prominent role on the local political scene'. The People's Alliance (Alþýðubandalagið), founded in this form in 1956, enjoyed, after the Italian Communist Party, the largest percentage vote of any western European communist party in the mid-1970s. For an earlier, somewhat tendentious account of the development of communism in Iceland since the First World War, see the article by Mary S. Olmsted in *Foreign Affairs*, vol. 36 (Jan. 1958), p. 340-47, in which she assigns similar motives to the Icelandic communists as does Gilberg above, but interprets them as strategic rather than ideological.

462 The new régime in Iceland.
Gísli Gunnarsson. *New Left Review*, no. 72 (March-April 1972), p. 54-60.

A committed article, in which the author acknowledges as a positive development the coming to power of the left-wing government in Iceland after the general election of 1971, but tempers his optimism concerning the immediate future of socialism in Iceland by an analysis of the capitalist process in its system, particularly since independence (events since this article was written tend to support the writer's analysis), but his expressed hope is that the continuing absence of radicalism in office will 'contribute to an indispensible ideological and political clarification of the left'. (The leftist coalition survived until the general election of 1974). The article elicits a rejoinder by Jóhann P. Arnason in the next-but-one issue of this periodical (July-Aug. 1972), p. 103-04.

463 European elections: Iceland.
John Madeley. *West European Politics*, (UK), vol. 2, no. 1 (1979), p. 144-46; vol. 3, no. 3 (1980), p. 447-49.

A summary analysis, in two parts, of the eighteen months of electoral activity in the two general elections of summer 1978 and winter 1979; the first of these had resulted in a coalition of the Progressives, the Social Democrats and the People's Alliance; the second, after two months of crisis, resulted in one of the most unusual coalitions, comprising a splinter group of the Independence Party, led by Gunnar Þoroddsen, with the continued representation of the Progressive Party and the People's Alliance. For analyses of earljer general elections in Iceland (1959, 1963, 1967 and 1971) see the articles by Olafur Ragnar Grímsson in *Scandinavian Political Studies*, vol. 6 (1971), p. 195-200, and vol. 8 (1973), p. 193-97.

Pioneering political science: the case of Iceland.
See item no. 432.

Iceland: the Co-operative island.
See item no. 509.

Prime ministers and presidents

464 Bjarni Benediktsson.
Sigurður A. Magnússon. *American-Scandinavian Review*, vol. 58, no. 4 (Dec. 1970), p. 348-51.

A short sketch of the life, career and writings of the Icelandic statesman Bjarni Benediktsson, who, at the time of his tragic death in a fire in 1970 at the age of sixty-seven, was in his third consecutive term of office as Prime Minister (his seven years remain the longest continuous period served by any Prime Minister of the Icelandic Republic), at the head of the coalition led by the Independence Party. For a portrait of the next Prime Minister but one, Ólafur Jóhannesson (born 1913) of the Progressive Party, who held office from 1971 to 1974 and from 1978 to 1979, see the same writer's article in the same magazine, vol. 61, no. 1 (March 1973), p. 16-21.

465 President Ásgeirsson of Iceland.
Benedikt Gröndal. *American-Scandinavian Review*, vol. 42, no. 2 (1954), p. 109-15.

A bibliographical sketch of Iceland's second President, Ásgeir Ásgeirson, whose term of office spanned the years 1952-68. Traces his family background, education, and political career with the Progressive Party up to his appointment as Minister of Education, Prime Minister (1932), and his election as President.

466 Time for a change, says President Eldjárn.
Sonja Diego. *Atlantica and Iceland Review*, vol. 18, no. 1 (1980), p. 19-23.

A portrait of the third President of Iceland, Dr Kristján Eldjárn, who in 1980 announced his retirement from the office after twelve years of residence at Bessastaðir. Although his original election in 1968 was contested, his second and third terms were not, and he proved both a popular and a highly-respected figure both inside and outside Iceland during a period of various political and economic difficulties. He claims that he owed his original election to the fact that he was not a politician, having been curator of the National Museum of Iceland for twenty-one years prior to his presidency. This article offers a brief glimpse of the personality of a man who had been the first citizen of Iceland, as well as his country's foremost archaeologist. He died on 14 September 1982 at the age of 65. For an earlier profile of Kristján Eldjárn shortly after he assumed office as President, see Sigurður A. Magnússon's article in *American-Scandinavian Review*, vol. 57, no. 6 (June 1969), p. 116-22.

467 President Vigdís: her election and first year in office.
Guðjón Friðriksson, Gunnar Elísson. Reykjavík: Örn og Örlygur, 1981. 112p.

A profile in words and pictures of the fourth and current President of Iceland, Vigdís Finnbogadóttir, whose victory in the presidential election of 1980 has been far more popularly received than was suggested by the narrowness of her win over her three male rivals for office. The former Director of the Reykjavík Theatre Company has continued the non-political character of the presidency set by her predecessor, and at the same time is the first woman in the world to have been generally elected as a head of state. The first edition of this volume was entitled *Mrs President*. For profile interviews with the new President, see, for

Politics. Prime ministers and presidents

example, the feature by Sigurður A. Magnússon in *Atlantica and Iceland Review*, vol. 20, no. 1 (summer 1982), p. 24-31; 'Symbol of a nation', *Scandinavian Review*, vol. 69, no. 1 (March 1981), p. 6-17; also the feature in the series 'A life in the day of...', which appears in the *Sunday Times* colour supplements - see the last page of the issue for Sunday 28 Feb. 1982, on the occasion of her state visit to Britain.

Recollections of an Icelandic statesman: being a chapter in the autobiography of Sveinn Björnsson.
See item no. 335.

Foreign Policy

Co-operation and security

468 Treaty of co-operation between Denmark, Finland, Iceland, Norway and Sweden.
Stockholm: Göteborgs Offsettryckeri, 1971. 14p.
An English text of the agreement signed in Helsinki on 23 March 1962, and amended in 1971, covering Nordic co-operation in the fields of cultural development, social affairs, juridical harmonisation, economic progress, and in the work of the Nordic Council. A separate pamphlet from the same source sets out the English text of the related *Treaty concerning Cultural Co-operation*, signed by the five Nordic governments on 15 March 1971.

469 Five northern countries pull together.
Vegard Sletten. Stockholm: Nordic Council, 1967. 92p.
An illustrated publication which traces the historical roots of co-operation between the five Nordic countries, and sets out the contemporary achievements of their co-operation in the fields of interstate relations, freedom of movement, social security, health, justice and cultural affairs. The institutional manifestation of such co-operation, the Nordic Council, was founded in 1953, and its statute and rules of procedure are appended.

470 Foreign policies of northern Europe.
Edited by Bengt Sundelius. Boulder, Colorado: Westview Press, 1982. 239p. tables.
A cross-national treatment of the foreign policies of the five Nordic countries. Iceland figures less than it deserves (indeed there is no Icelandic representative among the six contributors to this volume, five of whom are Swedes). In spite of this, there is much to be gained by the student of Icelandic affairs from this collection of articles, in view of both its up-to-date approach and its comparative view of Nordic foreign policy, which is treated thematically: interdependence, decision-making, strategic perspectives, economic co-operation, policies towards the Third World, and Nordic integration. The articles include many statistical tables in which Iceland figures.

Foreign Policy. Co-operation and security

471 Determinants of Icelandic foreign policy.
Þráinn Eggertsson. *Co-operation and Conflict* (Norway), vol. 10 (1975), p. 91-99.

The author identifies three of the major factors which have determined the development of Iceland's foreign relations: population, location, and economic geography. In this context the author analyses Iceland's foreign policy in relation to national security, European integration, and the question of fishing limits.

472 Iceland: reluctant ally.
Donald E. Nuechterlein. Ithaca, New York: Cornell University Press, 1961. 213p. bibliog. Reprinted Westport, Connecticut: Greenwood Press, 1975.

An invaluable source book, based on a doctoral dissertation submitted to the University of Michigan, which traces in considerable detail the course of defence relations between the highly strategic Iceland and the United States of America, 1940-56, with particular attention to the following aspects: the abandonment of Icelandic neutrality in allowing Allied wartime bases; the rejection of peacetime military bases in the context of the immediate post-war nationalist feeling; the acceptance of collective security; the request for, and the subsequent doubts concerning US protection; the international impact of events in Korea and Hungary; and the influence of internal politics upon external policy. The author draws on primary official sources as well as the Party press to illustrate and explain the fluctuations in Icelandic attitudes towards national defence, and his book remains relevant to the continuing, if rather more polarised, attitudes on defence in Iceland to-day. See the same author's article entitled 'Small states in alliances: Iceland, Thailand, Australia' in *Orbis* (US), vol. 13, no. 2 (summer 1969), p. 600-23.

473 How to throw away an airbase.
Porter McKeever. *Harper's Magazine* (US), (Oct. 1956), p. 39-44.

A vivid piece of 'trumpet-blowing reportage', the interest of which lies not so much in what is written, but rather in the attitudes which it reflects from an American viewpoint vis-à-vis the Icelandic moves to end US presence on Icelandic soil in 1956. A polarised, and in retrospect sometimes misconceived report, which also touches upon British fishing disagreements and Soviet trading with Iceland.

474 Iceland from neutrality to NATO membership.
Benedikt Gröndal. Oslo: Universitetsforlaget, 1971. 105p. (Scandia Books, no. 11).

An Icelander's view of the way in which his country, one with no military history, has tried, not always successfully, to come to terms with recent membership of a military alliance (the North Atlantic Treaty Organisation), albeit remaining unarmed herself. The author speaks from centre stage, so to speak, being currently perhaps the foremost member of Iceland's Social Democratic Party; he was foreign minister, 1978-80, Prime Minister of Iceland in the minority SDP cabinet, 1979-80, and in 1982 was appointed Icelandic ambassador to Sweden. His book is remarkable for its reasoned objectivity concerning a difficult and crucial topic; although other interpretations have been propounded to the right and to the left, this account remains the most concise and helpful introduction to the subject.

Foreign Policy. Co-operation and security

475 Iceland, Europe and NATO.
Ake Sparring. *World Today*, vol. 28, no. 9 (Sept. 1972), p. 393-403.

Another stage in the dispute between Iceland and Britain over territorial waters is here used by the Director of the Foreign Policy Institute in Stockholm to examine from a broader standpoint the shift in Iceland's foreign policy as a result of the swing to the left in the national election of 1971. The article is focussed on relations with the European Economic Community, and on the NATO base at Keflavík.

476 The security of Iceland.
Björn Bjarnason. *Co-operation and Conflict* (Norway), vol. 7 (1972), p. 193-208.

The Independence Party's view of Icelandic security in the 1970s. The author discusses the two major international questions facing the country: the relationship with NATO and fishing limits, in the context of the regional and global implications of Iceland's geographical position. This article forms part of a special issue of the periodical, devoted to the security of the five Nordic states individually, thus affording a comparative regional perspective. Another point of interest is a chart of Soviet military flights recorded off Iceland between 1963 and 1972. The author updates his views in an article entitled 'Iceland's position in NATO', which appeared in *Atlantic Community Quarterly*, vol. 15, no. 4 (winter 1977-78), p. 393-403, and which is preceded by a paper on the same topic by the then Prime Minister of Iceland, Geir Hallgrímsson, p. 389-92.

477 Icelandic security policy: contexts and trends.
Gunnar Gunnarsson. *Co-operation and Conflict* (Norway), vol. 17, no. 4 (1982), p. 257-72.

An analysis of the 'bridgehead' position occupied by Iceland in the Greenland - Iceland - UK gap, and of its relevance to American and Soviet naval strategies. This is followed by a discussion of Iceland's current security policy, and of the cultural, political and military impact of the American presence and the NATO base. The whole issue of the journal is devoted to Nordic security.

478 Iceland and the American presence.
Sigurður A. Magnússon. *Queen's Quarterly*, vol. 85, no. 1 (1978), p. 79-85.

A hardhitting article, and one which gets at the roots of the feelings of many Icelanders about the NATO military base in their country. After a brief review of the background facts, with particular reference to the controversial establishment of the US television station and political ethics, the author broadens his approach into the context of Icelandic national consciousness. An anti-establishment view, which illuminates the whole issue and stimulates further discussion.

Agreement between the European Economic Community and the republic of Iceland.
See item no. 551.

Handbók Útanríkisráðuneytisins. (Manual of the Ministry for Foreign Affairs of Iceland.)
See item no. 948.

Territorial waters and fishing disputes

General

479 Iceland extends its fisheries limits: a political analysis.
Morris Davis. Oslo: Universitetsforlaget; London: Allen & Unwin, 1963. 136p. (North Atlantic Library).
The author uses the occasion of the Icelandic decision of 1958 in favour of extending the country's fishing limits from four to twelve miles as a framework for investigating the decision-making processes involved in the affair. He examines the influences of public opinion, of interest groups such as the fishing lobby and the trades unions, of the political parties, and of the bureaucracy, to present a picture of how the nation governs itself. The event itself is history, but the description of the processes remains relevant to an understanding of Icelandic positions in more recent disputes concerning fishing limits.

480 The law of the sea.
Elizabeth Young, Brian Johnson. London: Fabian Society, 1973. 48p. (Fabian Research Series, 313).
The choice of materials available to the reader wishing to understand the background to disputes over territorial waters is mainly between accounts offered by the protagonists and academic analyses involving legal complexities. This publication, arising from the Icelandic decision of 1972 to extend the fishing limits from twelve to fifty miles, starts from the premise that the law of the sea is a mess, and proceeds to a clear, constructive and objective discussion of the issues, with the Anglo-Icelandic dispute placed in the context of a worldwide problem. A Fabian socialist document. A document of less substance, but again noteworthy for its surprisingly non-protagonist approach, is an occasional paper of the British Conservative Party's Bow Group, infelicitously entitled *Fish and ships: why Britain should support Iceland's 50 mile claim*, contributed by Lawrence Reed, MP, (London: Bow Publications, 1973, 10p.).

481 Iceland's fishery limits: the legal aspects.
E. D. Brown. *World Today*, vol. 29, no. 2 (Feb. 1973), p. 68-79.
An interim evaluation of the jurisdiction of the International Court of Justice in relation to the disputes concerning the extensions of Icelandic fishing limits. The writer's conclusion is not untypical of foreign legal assessments: sympathy for Iceland's predicament, combined with concern at the infringement of international law at the time.

482 Issues arising in the Icelandic fisheries case.
Stephen R. Katz. *International and Comparative Law Quarterly*, vol. 22 (1973), p. 83-108.
A detailed analysis of the major legal issues concerning Icelandic fishing limits, in which the author discusses many of the points of contention for the agenda of the International Court of Justice arising from the Icelandic disputes with Britain up to 1972. Although some of the points raised have been subsequently overtaken by

Foreign Policy. Territorial waters and fishing disputes. General

events, the article is still useful for its consideration of the general legal issues which will surely continue to form the background to developments in North Atlantic waters. The author examines the concepts of duress, self-defence, necessity, and the right to terminate, as well as international practice concerning fishing limits and the continental shelf.

483 Conflicts of interest in territorial waters: Iceland, Ecuador and the straits of Malacca.
Raimo Väyrynen. *Instant Research on Peace and Violence,* vol. 3, no. 3 (1973), p. 123-48.
A comparative analysis of international conflict over territorial waters, in which the case of Iceland is used to illustrate the process which occurs when a small and externally exploited nation attempts to secure its own fishing and other interests by extending its jurisdiction.

484 The Anglo-Icelandic fisheries dispute.
R. P. Barston, Hjalmar W. Hannesson. *International Relations* (UK), vol. 4, no. 6 (Nov. 1974), p. 559-84+628. maps. tables. graphs.
Probably the clearest and most balanced synthesis of the development and state of the fishing disputes between Britain and Iceland in the early 1970s. The authors, one British, one Icelandic, discuss the historical, political and economic background to Iceland's extension of limits to 50 miles, and trace the stages in the agreement reached, albeit temporarily; they also consider the broader international implications. The article is accompanied by relevant tables, graphs and maps.

485 Politics, fish and international resource management: the British-Icelandic cod war.
Bruce Mitchell. *Geographical Review* (US), vol. 66, no. 2 (April 1976), p. 127-38. maps.
A discussion of the political dimensions of the Icelandic fishing question, and an examination of its relation to international considerations involving NATO and the EEC, as well as to the domestic considerations of Icelandic and British politics, with particular reference to public relations and propaganda employed by both countries. Two maps delineate the Icelandic-British agreement of 1973, and the Icelandic-Belgian agreement of the year before. A postscript to this article concerning the subsequent dispute appears in the same periodical, vol. 67, no. 1 (Jan. 1977), p. 105-07, from the same writer.

486 Cod wars and how to lose them.
Sir Andrew Gilchrist. Edinburgh: Q Press, 1978. 122p.
A 'non-official' account written in a spirit of goodwill. Despite its title ('cod war' is a term less liked in Iceland than in Britain) and its breezy style, this book is serious in intent as well as entertaining in presentation. Sir Andrew Gilchrist was British Ambassador to Iceland, 1956-60, and was therefore enmeshed in the first dispute between Britain and Iceland. After introductory chapters on the characteristics of Iceland, he presents his own account of the hostilities of that period, with a retrospect on the two subsequent disputes. He offers several new observations, and his retrospection lends an air of refreshing objectivity: 'I do not show the Icelanders sentimentally as David against Goliath, underdogs with right on

Foreign Policy. Territorial waters and fishing disputes. Texts

their side who achieved an incredible series of victories over Britain. I exhibit them rather as cool, cunning and successful. And courageous - no one who knew the international background and the course of the struggles is likely to deny them a high degree of political and physical courage. The British? I have tried to show them as not so much wrong as misguided'. (A postscript to the book contains a character sketch and appreciation of Bjarni Benediktsson, Prime Minister of Iceland from 1963 until his tragic death by fire in 1970). This book, which was well received in Iceland, was first published in Icelandic (Reykjavík: Almenna Bókafélagið, 1977.).

487 **Friends in conflict: the Anglo-Icelandic cod wars and the law of the sea.**
Hannes Jónsson. London: Hurst; Hamden, Connecticut: Archon Books, 1982. 240p. bibliog.

The most recent and the most substantial examination of all the fishing disputes between Iceland and Britain. The author is a distinguished Icelandic diplomat (currently the Icelandic Permanent Representative at the United Nations), and he analyses the history of the disputes mainly from the standpoint of international law, with particular reference to the Colonial and Progressive schools of thought concerning the law of the sea, the former of which propounds a territorial water strip as narrow as possible (the area outside remaining exploitable by all, subject to agreements on conservation), the latter advocating the continental shelf and its resources as an organic and ecological whole (over which coastal states should have sovereign rights up to a 'reasonable distance') - it is the latter school of thought which has been reflected in the recent evolution of the law of the sea in a way that has extended the limits of coastal states, including Iceland, and to which Britain itself has eventually turned in a broader European context. The author's analysis is well documented from official sources, and includes useful appendices of statistics covering fishstocks, the Icelandic and British fleets, incidents at sea during the disputes, etc. It also includes a summary of the main articles of the Draft Convention of the Law of the Sea, plus a substantial bibliography of the legal aspects of the fishing disputes. A welcome and much needed publication.

Offshore geography of northwestern Europe: the political and economic problems of delimitation and control.
See item no. 157.

Official texts

488 **Fisheries jurisdiction in Iceland.**
Reykjavík: Ministry for Foreign Affairs of Iceland, 1972. 46p.

An official booklet issued during the second of the Icelandic disputes with Britain over fishing limits, which was designed to present the Icelandic case with regard to the importance of fisheries as the mainstay of the Icelandic economy, to the conservation and utilisation of fishery resources, and to the rules regulating the use of the principal types of fishing gear. Appendices include the texts, in English, of official statements made by Icelandic leaders to four international institutions concerned with the question of fishing limits and territorial jurisdiction. Similarly motivated official publications were issued in conjunction with the one previous and one subsequent dispute, and together they offer a good view of the Icelandic stance in these matters during two decades. The Ministry issued two

Foreign Policy. Territorial waters and fishing disputes. Texts

pamphlets during the dispute of 1958-59 (twelve miles), entitled *The Icelandic fishery limits* (December 1958, 14p.), and *British aggression in Icelandic waters* (1959, 43p.). During the third dispute the Ministry issued an updated version of the 1972 publication described above, under the new title *The fishing limits of Iceland: 200 nautical miles* (1975, 46p.), which includes the English texts of further documents and statements from the Icelandic side.

489 **Fisheries dispute between the United Kingdom and Iceland, 14th July 1971-19th May 1973.**
London: HM Stationery Office, 1973. 32p. (Cmnd. 5341).
The British side of the case is officially presented in this Command Paper to Parliament. As with the Icelandic document above, it covers background and current issues at the time of the second dispute, followed by appendices: the first set is documentary, summarising discussions conducted with the Icelandic representation during the period of the dispute; the second set is analytical and tabular. It hardly needs to be said that this item and the Icelandic version, *Fisheries jurisdiction in Iceland* (q.v.) should be studied together, and that there is much to be read between the lines.

490 **Exchange of notes between the Government of the United Kingdom of Great Britain and Northern Ireland and the Government of the Republic of Iceland concerning fishing in the Icelandic fisheries zone (with related documents), Oslo, 1 June 1976.**
London: HM Stationery Office, 1976. 12p. (Cmnd. 6545).
The text of the agreement which entered into force after the fourth and last Icelandic extension of the fishing limits to two hundred miles. The agreement covers the number of British trawlers in action per day, the list of ninety-three named trawlers entitled to fish (with their length and tonnage) the sizes of mesh, and the four areas of conservation. The texts of the agreements following the earlier extensions to twelve and fifty miles were likewise issued as Command Papers: Cmnd. 1482 (1961) and Cmnd. 5484 (1973).

491 **Iceland: Law concerning the territorial sea, the economic zone and the continental shelf.**
International Legal Materials (US), vol. 18, no. 6 (Nov. 1979), p. 1504-07.
The English-language text of the Icelandic Law no. 41 of 1 June 1979, the thirteen articles of which form the ratification of the Icelandic position after the multi-faceted disputes and negotiations of the 1970s. Article one lists the thirty-eight landpoints between which the baseline shall be drawn to calculate the twelve nautical miles delimiting the territorial sea of Iceland. Article two defines sovereignty. Articles three and four define the two hundred mile limit of the economic zone, and the rights of Iceland within that zone. Articles five and six define the continental shelf and associated rights. Article seven deals with the delimitation of areas between states less than four hundred miles distant (i.e. the Faroe Islands and Greenland). Articles eight to thirteen deal with pollution, research, and general provisions. The International Law of the Sea Treaty was finally approved in 1982 and its provisions met virtually all of the Icelandic claims.

Economics

General

492 Economic development of Iceland through World War II.
William Charles Chamberlin. New York: Columbia University Press, 1947. 141p. tables. Reprinted New York: AMS Press, 1968.

This book remains, surprisingly, the only monograph devoted solely to the economic development of Iceland. After an historical introduction, the author sets out the framework of economic organisation in Iceland and traces the country's economic development from the late 19th century to the Second World War ('through' in the title is used in the American sense of 'up to and including'). The most important section, however, in that it identifies many of the reasons why economic 'take-off' became possible as Iceland embarked upon full independence in 1944, is the one dealing with the wartime economy, with particular attention to the foreign reserves which accumulated mainly as a result of the expenditures of the British and, especially, the American forces occupying the country. Appendices include many useful tables of statistics relating to the Icelandic economy in the 1930s and 1940s.

493 Iceland and the war.
Þorsteinn Þorsteinnsson. In: *Sweden, Norway, Denmark and Iceland in the World War.* Edited by E. F. Henkscher; K. Bergendal. New Haven, Connecticut: Yale University Press, 1930, 593p.

This volume is an abridged translation into English from the Scandinavian volume in the series *Economic and social history of the World War.* Part four, p. 559-87, comprises the Icelandic contribution by the then Director of the Statistical Bureau of Iceland. The aim of the series as a whole, which was proposed by the Carnegie Endowment for International Peace, was to conduct an historical survey in an attempt to measure 'the economic cost of the [First] World War, and the displacement which it was causing in the processes of civilisation'. After an introductory chapter, the Icelandic contributor deals with the effect of the First World

Economics. General

War on Icelandic shipping, commerce and imports, prices and wages, banking and state finances, agriculture and fisheries.

494 Report on economic and commercial conditions in Iceland.
J. Bowering. London; HM Stationery Office, 1937. 36p.

One of the world series of economic reports prepared by the Overseas Trade Department of the Board of Trade, this is a useful survey of the pre-war economic state of Iceland. It contains summaries of the conditions in a variety of sectors: finance, trade, industry, nationalisation, co-operatives, fishing, farming, living costs, housing, population, health and education, with statistical appendices on banking, foreign trade, fish stocks, and unemployment. This report is of interest to the economic historian when compared with the very different data from the post-war period.

495 Renaissance of Iceland.
W. R. Mead. *Economic Geography*, vol. 21, no. 2 (April 1945), p. 135-44.

A perceptive analysis of the state of the Icelandic economy by the 1940s, and an examination of the internal and external factors which rapidly led Iceland into a surprisingly strong position from which to develop after the war. The writer clearly shows, using tables, the strands linking the older economy with the newer. Compare this article with 'Iceland's industries' from the same periodical, vol. 7 (1931), p. 284-96, in which S. Axel Anderson assesses the inter-war economy of Icelandic agriculture, fisheries and manufacturing, in relation to the country's adverse natural setting.

496 Economic development in Iceland since World War II.
Ólafur Björnsson. *Review of World Economics/Weltwirtschaftliches Archiv*, vol. 98, no. 2 (1967), p. 218-40.

A substantial examination of and interim report on the first twenty years of the post-war economy of Iceland. After setting the pre-war and wartime background, the writer describes the events leading up to the devaluation of the króna in 1950, the stabilisation programme of 1960 in the context of the quest for a less restrictive economic system, and the appearance of inflationary pressures in the mid-1960s. The vulnerability of the Icelandic economy and its imbalance are stressed throughout.

497 The growth of public expenditure in Iceland.
Gísli Blöndal. *Scandinavian Economic History Review* (Finland), vol. 17, no. 1 (1969), p. 1-22.

A theoretical framework is applied to patterns of Icelandic public expenditure during the 20th century. Fluctuations in public funding are shown to have been far greater than the increase in population and national income. The two World Wars and the Depression are seen as reasons for this discrepancy, as is the post-war tendency for the Icelandic parliament and its succession of coalition governments to spend their way out of periods of crisis. (In 1900 central government expenditure amounted to only 4 per cent of the gross national product - three quarters of a century later this had risen to 28 per cent, and public expenditure as a whole to 35 per cent of GNP).

Economics. General

498 Iceland: a survey of the tax system.
Sigurbjörn Þorbjörnsson. *European Taxation*, vol. 18, no. 10 (1978), p. 328-42.

An article by the Director of the Inland Revenue of Iceland, in which he sets out in detail the full range of taxes and their computations: individual income tax (including that for non-residents) and deductions, corporation tax, net worth tax, municipal taxes, industrial taxes, sales tax, social security contributions, etc. Information such as this has a limited currency in practical terms, but the article presents a clear picture of the general framework within which the Icelandic system of taxation is made to work by the country's nine district tax commissioners.

499 Inflation experience in Iceland.
Jónas H. Haralz. *Journal of Post-Keynesian Economics* (US), vol. 3, no. 3 (1981), p. 312-23.

The writer draws the distinction between the Icelandic economy's creeping inflation during the first twenty-five years after the war and its 'Latin' inflation during the last decade. He examines the reasons for the inflation, the economic and social effects, and the lessons of the Icelandic experience for other nations. His tentative programme for inducing some measure of stability involves reform of institutions, coupled with a long-term policy of economic growth. The contributor is general manager of the National Bank Landsbanki Islands, the largest commercial bank in the country.

500 Housing in Iceland: inflation helps those who help themselves.
Ingi V. Jóhannsson, Jón R. Sveinsson. *Acta Sociologica* (Norway), vol. 24, no. 4 (1981), p. 223-39.

A descriptive analysis of the economics of home ownership in Iceland, based on a survey in the Reykjavík conurbation (see Bjarni Reynarsson's *Residential mobility, life cycle stages, housing and the changing social patterns in Reykjavík* q.v.). Owner occupancy is a staggeringly high 95 per cent for couples aged over 35. The financial problems of the younger families in moving from rented to owner-occupier accommodation are described with reference to the strong tradition of help from the larger family circle, as well as to the activities of the financial institutions. At present, house purchase or house building is mainly an individual enterprise, but the authors of this paper see a current change which will lead to more collective solutions.

501 The new króna/The history of Icelandic currency.
Atlantica and Iceland Review, vol. 18, no. 3 (1980), p. 14-21.

A double feature article presented on the eve of the currency reform introduced in Iceland on 1 January 1981, whereby the new króna assumed a value one hundred times that of the old. The first article is based on an interview with Stefán Þórarinsson of the Central Bank, in which the advantages of the reform are discussed, with reference to administrative streamlining and to the potentially favourable psychological effects in helping to defend the value of the new unit against the frequent successive devaluations which had beset the old króna during the highly inflationary period which commenced in the 1970s (in the event, the psychological effect was overestimated, as there were three devaluations totalling 33 per cent within the new króna's first year of circulation). The second article is an illustrated sketch of the issues of coins and banknotes before and after the authorisation of an independent minting for Iceland in 1922. See Staffan

Economics. Economic monitors

Björkman's *Myntir Íslands, 1836, 1922-1963* (Icelandic Coins, 1836, 1922-1963) q.v.

502 Where on earth will this end anyway?
Jón Baldvin Hannibalsson. *News from Iceland*, no. 60 (Jan. 1981), p. 14-15.
An eloquent and entertaining piece of debunking of economic gurus (Keynesian and monetarist alike) who have sought to apply their theories and policies to the traditional and chronic problems of the Icelandic economy. The writer, who is editor of *Alþýdubladid*, the daily newspaper of the Social Democratic Party (at the time of this article in opposition), may have his tongue in his cheek, but his basic message is worth more than a glance: that if a nation is continuing to enjoy (as Iceland does) virtually full employment, why should it jeopardise this basic component of social equilibrium by trying to control inflation? What a large nation is forced to regard as an overriding problem, a nation of under a quarter of a million people can, with a fair degree of impunity, largely ignore.

503 Iceland: a special report.
Michael Simmons (and others). *The Guardian* (UK), (17 Feb. 1982), p. 20-23.
The state visit to Britain by the President of Iceland, Vigdís Finnbogadóttir, provided the occasion for this special collection of sectoral reports in the British daily newspaper. Together they form a pertinent picture of the Icelandic economy today, and feature the social and political background, the fisheries, inflation, energy reserves, the co-operative movement, foreign trade and tourism, and are flanked by advertising from a variety of Icelandic enterprises. An earlier special report of this nature in the British daily press appeared in the *Financial Times* on 1 Dec. 1976, p. 17-20.

Economic monitors

504 Quarterly economic review: Denmark, Iceland.
London: Economic Intelligence Unit, 1952- . quarterly.
One in a worldwide series of regular reports by an international economic research and management consultancy organisation serving industry and government, which aims to include in the case of each country 'analysis of political developments relevant to an understanding of the economy, government economic policies, trends in investment and consumer spending, performance of key business indicators, evaluation of foreign trade data, and assessment of development plans'. Contains statistical appendices, and the contents of the quarterly issues are synthesised in an annual reference supplement. In general, this is a very useful source of current information on the economic situation and prospects in Iceland.

505 Economic surveys: Iceland.
Paris: Organisation for Economic Co-operation and Development, 1961- . annual.
These detailed surveys, compiled by committees of the OECD for each of its member countries, command considerable attention from government, industry

Economics. Economic monitors

and media for their critical evaluation of the main economic trends during the year, their assessment of the economic policies adopted, and their consideration of the prospects and potential policies for the coming year. Statistical appendices include a wide range of economic indicators, and a chronology of economic events. The Iceland report for 1982 contains 64p. See the Icelandic section in the OECD annual *Review of fisheries in OECD member countries*.

506 Central Bank of Iceland: annual report.
Reykjavík: Seðlabanki Íslands 1961- . annual.

The Central Bank of Iceland was established in 1961, when it took over the central banking functions of the National Bank (Landsbanki Íslands), with responsibility for the issue of banknotes, the setting of foreign exchange rates, etc. An independent, government-owned institution, it is the government's banker, and as such its annual report is a primary guide to the performance of the national economy; the full report is written in Icelandic, but, usefully, an abridged though still substantial version is issued in English. This takes the form of, firstly, the report of the Board of Governors on economic developments, production, prices and incomes, balance of payments, central government finances, investment and pension funds, bond issues and foreign borrowing, external agreements, etc.; secondly, the accounts for the year; thirdly, a statistical appendix, which in the 1981 report contained 36 tables relating to the Icelandic economy and the activities of the Central Bank. This valuable and well-presented report is essential for an appreciation of the current economic situation, and is freely available on request. The 1981 report comprised 76p. For the quarterly publication of the Bank, *Economic Statistics*, see annotation for the *Statistical Bulletin* published by the Statistical Bureau of Iceland and the Central Bank of Iceland (q.v.).

507 Vinnumarkaðurinn 1980. (The labour market 1980.)
Reykjavík: Framkvæmdastofnun Ríkisins, 1982. 105p.

An extremely useful and welcome analysis of the state of the Icelandic labour market. Until the appearance of this report by the Economic Development Institute, manpower statistics for Iceland were difficult to come by - there have been gaps under Iceland in international compilations by the UN and ILO, and the Icelandic census of 1960 had been the most recent source of systematic information on this topic. But now we have up-to-date information on the labour force by age and sex, on its distribution by region and by social-economic sector, on average earnings, hours of work, participation rates, etc., as well as trends and forecasts along these lines. In a country with still only minimal unemployment, such figures are of unusually topical interest to the foreigner. The analytical section of the report is presented in Icelandic, but the foreign reader will find the statistical headings readily translatable with a dictionary. It is to be hoped that in the projected annual editions an English summary and key can be provided.

508 The Icelandic economy: developments, 1980-1981.
Reykjavík: National Economic Institute, April 1981. 81p.

An economic review of the year, with commentary on the economic performance of Iceland in the domestic and international context, accompanied by tabular data on a wide range of economic indicators. The National Economic Institute also published a lecture by Jón Sigurðsson entitled *The Icelandic economy: riches under risk* (1977, 15p.), which can be recommended as an excellent synopsis of the underlying problems and prospects of the country's economy. 'In the long run the major task of economic policy is to secure a balanced development of industries, on the one hand based on marine and other traditional resources, and on the other hand based on industries utilising the country's energy potential... In both cases unhampered access to the markets of the world is of paramount importance'.

Co-operative Movement

509 Iceland: the Co-operative island.
Thorsten Odhe. Chicago, Illinois: Co-operative League of the U.S.A., 1960. 115p.

The only full-length account in the English language of the Co-operative movement in Iceland, which has more members per capita than in any other country, and which is an integral part of the socio-economic fabric of the Icelandic nation. All aspects of the history and development of the movement are treated in this book, which captures the spirit of the whole enterprise in Iceland, and which is written by a Swedish specialist on co-operative organisations in the international economy. The chapter on the Federation of Icelandic Co-operatives (Samband Islenzkra Samvinnufélaga) is of particular importance in the international context.

510 The Co-operative movement in Iceland.
Erlendur Einarsson. *American-Scandinavian Review*, vol. 55 (1967), p. 153-57.

An historical sketch, by the Director of the Federation of Icelandic Co-operative Societies, of the movement which established itself in Iceland in 1882 (centenary celebrations were held in 1982) on the same principles held by the original co-operative society of weavers in Rochdale, England, in 1844. It later developed close links with the agrarian political party, the Progressives, and in organisation of production, distribution and retailing has become the major force in Iceland's internal and external trade. (20 per cent of the population are individual members of Samband, which in 1978, according to the business magazine *Frjálsverzlun*, became the biggest employer in Iceland). The Federation issues its own magazine *Samvinngn*, founded in 1907. For an earlier account from the same periodical, see Ragnar Olafsson's article 'Co-operative Iceland', vol. 27 (1939), p. 23-31.

Agriculture

511 Agricultural policy in Iceland.
Paris: Organisation for Economic Co-operation and
Development, 1976. 26p.
The fact that only 10 per cent of Iceland's terrain is able to sustain agricultural activity (agriculture also engages 10 per cent of the labour force of Iceland) is in itself a challenge to the aims of a national policy. This report is an examination of the productive and trading state of Icelandic agriculture, with reference to the main agricultural indicators, and an evaluation of the policy measures, particularly pricing.

512 A brief survey of the Icelandic farming industry today.
Árni G. Eylands. Reykjavík: Ministry of Agriculture, 1955.
2nd ed. 63p.
Although much of the information in this compilation now has to be updated, it is still a useful source of reference on the organisation of agriculture in post war Iceland. Coverage includes farm administration, crop production, livestock, and a survey of the institutions relevant to agricultural education, extension, conservation, co-operation, administration and banking. The text is interspersed with a range of statistics on production, etc. There is a similar survey from the following decade by Halldór Pálsson and Ólafur E. Stefánsson entitled *Farming in Iceland* (Reykjavík: Agricultural Society of Iceland, 1968, 51p.).

513 Recent changes in the pattern of farming in Iceland.
Ian Y. Ashwell. *Canadian Geographer*, vol. 7, no. 4
(1963), p. 174-80. map. plans.
The post-war movement from the Icelandic countryside to the capital conurbation placed extra strain on the country's farms to provide sufficient home produce to balance the amount of imported foods. This article describes some of the developments in Iceland's primarily grazing agricultural economy, and in particular the supply of fodder for cattle and sheep.

Agriculture

514 Structural changes in the agriculture of Iceland.
F. K. T. Smith. *Journal of the Durham University Geographical Society*, no. 12 (1970), p. 65-79.

A general survey of the changes in Icelandic agriculture during this century, reflecting the country's change from a subsistence to an exchange economy. The article touches on the decline in the agricultural labour market, and on the various sectors: sheep, cattle, crops, greenhouse cultivation, etc. Post-war developments are considered in relation to land reclamation, mechanisation, fertilisers, landholdings and crop processing, plus a brief comparison of Icelandic and Faroese farming. The conclusion emphasises the high degree of differentiation in Icelandic agriculture, the general problem of the harsh environment, and the specific problem of overproduction in the dairying sector.

515 Svarfaðardalur and Dalvík: developments affecting the life of a rural community in mid-north Iceland.
C. Wood. *The Griffin* (Journal of the Geography Department of the North-Western Polytechnic, London), vol. 1 (1970), p. 1-10.

This paper, the outcome of a trip in 1967, is particularly useful for its description of the workings of an actual farm. Svarfaðardalur is a valley in Miðnorðurland, the basalt area between Skagafjörður and Eyjafjörður, which reaches the fjord at Dalvík, a small town with a population of one thousand or so, on the north western shore of Eyjafjörður. A description of the immediate environment is followed by a study of a typical valley farm at Tjörn, where the *tún*, or infield area of cultivation with its farm buildings, covers sixty-five acres. The farm supports cattle, sheep and poultry; the organisation and day-to-day activities of the farm are outlined, with figures, and the impact of the co-operative movement is assessed. The report offers some general conclusions on the prospects for fishing and farming in Dalvík and its dale. Includes a sketch-map of Svarfaðardalur, a plan of the farm at Tjörn, and the projected plan of the town of Dalvík.

516 Changing the face of the land.
Magnús Bjarnfredsson. *Atlantica and Iceland Review* (Iceland), vol. 18, no. 4 (1980), p. 39-45.

A brief illustrated account of the large experimental farm called Gunnarsholt in the vicinity of Hekla volcano. Gunnarsholt is the headquarters of the State Land Reclamation Service; the lessons learned from the successful transformation of Gunnarsholt from a blackened wasteland into a thriving dairy and hay farm are now being applied to other areas of Iceland, in a spirit of repairing the damage done to the land that has supported the Icelanders during eleven centuries of settlement.

517 Farm abandonment in Eyjafjallasveit, southern Iceland.
Guðrún Sveinbjarnardóttir. Birmingham, England: University of Birmingham, Department of Geography (Working Paper Series no. 14), 1982. 36p. maps. photos. plans. tables.

A multi-disciplinary study involving archaeological, historical, climatic, environmental, agricultural and social observation, with the purpose of identifying patterns of farm settlement and abandonment in the district west of Eyjafjallajökull in southern Iceland over the last thousand years. The major periods of abandon-

Agriculture

ment are shown to be pre-12th century, in the 17th century, and since 1850. It was the smaller dependent farms which were abandoned in the earlier periods, whereas modern abandonment is connected with the more general migration from country to town. This paper is illustrated with photographs, maps, plans and tables.

518 I veldi Vatnajökull. (In the domain of Vatnajökull.)
J. D. Ives. *Canadian Geographical Journal*, vol. 72, no. 4 (1966), p. 136-45.

A description of the contest between man and the land in the Öræfi district - a contest being won by the natural forces as farming settlements have been continually reduced over the centuries by climatological factors, volcanic activity, and the phenomenon of glacier bursts which cause the flooding of the Skeiðará river. An article which emphasises the economic effects rather than the physical processes. See Sigurður Þórarinsson's *The thousand years struggle against ice and fire* (q.v.).

519 Glacial control of wind and soil erosion in Iceland.
Ian Y. Ashwell. *Annals of the Association of American Geographers*, vol. 56, no. 3 (Sept. 1966), p. 529-40.

An investigation into certain ice-caps in central Iceland, which demonstrates how winds are affected by the ice-caps, and how the resulting descent of dry air from the Arctic causes severe soil erosion in a belt across southern and central Iceland. This article adds an extra dimension by discussing the contribution of man and animals to land erosion. An earlier issue of the same journal, vol. 50, no. 2 (June 1960), p. 117-22, contains a related article by Vincent H. Malmström entitled 'Influence of the Arctic front on the climate and crops of Iceland'.

520 The soils of Iceland.
Björn Jóhannesson. Reykjavík: University Research Institute, 1960. 140p. map. photos.

A major scientific report from the Department of Agriculture, in which the author examines the formation of soils in Iceland, and their physical and chemical properties. One of the main purposes of this study is to provide the material for a soil map of Iceland - this informative map (enclosed in the end-pocket) delineates in colour on a scale of 1:750,000 the distribution throughout Iceland of twenty-one different soil types, with or without vegetation, in the broad categories of peats, silts, gravels and sands. The second part of the text comprises a regional description of these distributions, with photographs.

521 Iceland reforests.
James P. McWilliams. *American Forests*, vol. 61 (July 1955), p. 17-55 (scattered).

By virtue of its geographical position Iceland should be a part of the global belt of coniferous forest. However, factors such as climatic erosion, centuries of over-grazing by sheep, cattle and horses, and the exploitation of timber for the construction of boats and houses, combined to render Iceland an almost treeless land. What remained was mainly brushwood and dwarf birch, and the irony of the situation is reflected in both the amount of timber which now has to be imported, and the common practice of salvaging driftwood. Reforestation has been discussed for over two hundred years, but not until well into the 20th century was concerted action taken. Today's visitor to Iceland will soon come

Agriculture

across extensive areas of reforestation in various parts of the country - for example, at Hallormsstaðir in eastern Iceland. This article traces the background to and the development of the reforestation programmes up to the mid-1950s. See the article 'Forests for Iceland' by Henry Goddard Leach in *American-Scandinavian Review*, vol. 42 (winter 1954), p. 319-24. For an article emphasising the historical aspects of deforestation, see 'The sagas as evidence of early deforestation in Iceland' by Ian Y. Ashwell in *Canadian Geographer*, vol. 14 (1970), p. 158-66.

522 The reforestation of Iceland.
Hákon Bjarnason. *Sixty-five Degrees* (Iceland), no. 9 (March 1970), p. 28-31.

The Icelandic view of the forestry problem. The long serving Director of the Department of Forestry adduces statistical data relevant to the denudation and reforestation of Iceland, and identifies those species being introduced, with indications of their individual success. The author expanded on this theme at the conference on rehabilitation of severly damaged land, held at Reykjavík in 1976, in a paper 'Erosion, tree growth and land regeneration in Iceland'; the paper was published in the NATO-sponsored conference proceedings which were published under the title *Breakdown and restoration of ecosystems*, edited by M. W. Holdgate and M. J. Woodman (New York: Plenum Press, 1978, p. 241-47.).

523 Grass and grass utilisation in Iceland.
Sturla Friðriksson. *Ecology*, vol. 53, no. 2 (summer 1972), p. 785-96.

It is estimated that the area of Iceland covered by vegetation has been halved since the original settlement. And yet livestock has been continuously important to the Icelanders, who have thus been heavily dependent on the quantity and quality of natural grassland. The writer, from the Agricultural Research Institute of Iceland, examines the historical interdependence of population numbers and grassland coverage, and describes the largely successful attempts during this century to check erosion and reclaim areas for pasture. Half of the fodder for Iceland's proportionately large stocks of sheep, plus cattle and horses, is now provided from cultivated land. See the same author's article 'The importance of grass' in the Icelandic magazine *Sixty-five Degrees*, no. 6 (May 1969), p. 22-27.

524 Sel: Untersuchungen zur Geschichte des isländischen Sennwesens seit der Landnahmezeit.
Egon Hitzler. Oslo: Universitetsforlaget, 1979. 280p. maps. photos. tables.

This unique piece of research, emanating from the Institute for Comparative Research in Human Culture, is a comprehensive investigation into the history and organisation of the Icelandic shielings - the shelters and adjacent pastureland for tending cattle on high ground (the Icelandic word *sel*, literally 'shed', is cognate, and is found as an element in many placenames). The author engaged in interviews with informants from many parts of the country, whom he lists with their districts and dates of birth, to produce an exceptional survey of one of the major features of rural life in Iceland since the time of the settlement. At present the text is available only in German, but is herewith recommended for translation into English. A particular study is made of Sauðadalur in the Húnavatnssýsla district of northern Iceland. Includes photographs, maps and tables.

Agriculture

525 Sheep: providing basic necessities since the settlement.
Magnús Bjarnfredsson. *Atlantica and Iceland Review*, vol. 19, no. 3 (1981), p. 13-19.
A brief illustrated feature on the history of sheep farming in Iceland, with particular reference to the denuding of vegetation, and to the markets for lamb and wool. (There are around a million sheep on Iceland today).

526 The wool industry in Iceland.
Stefán Aðalsteinsson (and others). *Sixty-five Degrees*, no. 10 (June 1970), p. 5-19.
A special feature comprising articles on the background to the Icelandic woollen industry: sheep farming, the tanning process, production (with particular reference to the co-operatives, the Alafoss enterprise, which pioneered the unspun twisted and shrunk technique for softness and flexibility, and the independent knitters), and the merchandising of Icelandic woollens in America. New developments in wool, including the move from small farms to large enterprises, are described by Haraldur J. Hamar in *Atlantica and Iceland Review*, vol. 14, no. 3 (1976), p. 26-31.

The eider farms of Iceland.
See item no. 250.

Fisheries

General reviews

527 Iceland fisheries yearbook.
Reykjavík: Iceland Review, 1981. 60p.
The first issue of a scheduled annual publication reporting on all aspects of the Icelandic fishing industry for the year: conservation, catch, processing, products, exports, the fleet, safety measures, etc. Breakdown by species, plus a section on whaling. List of agencies and sales organisations. This enterprising publication is likely to become a first source of reference for anyone with a commercial interest in North Atlantic fishing.

528 A perspective analysis of the Icelandic fishing industry: a status report and forecast to 1980.
Reykjavík: National Research Council, 1976. 223p.
This report is the work of one of four committees (the others being concerned with agriculture, construction and manufacturing) which were established by the National Research Council (Rannsóknarráðríkisins) as part of a national long-term plan on the scientific and technological future of Iceland's economic development. The report was translated into English in view of the international interest in Iceland's fishing effort. It covers the future of the fleet, the fishstocks and the catch, the fish processing sector, and the economic management of the industry. The main recommendations centre on a complete reappraisal of Icelandic fishing policy, especially in relation to investment, drawn up against a background of conservationist measures. The National Research Council is a governmental body within the Ministry of Culture and Education.

Stocks, the fleet and processing

529 Fishing and the stocks of fish at Iceland.
J. A. Gulland. London: HM Stationery Office, 1961. 52p.

One in the series of fishery investigations conducted for the British Ministry of Agriculture, Fisheries and Food, this research publication is of historical interest for its analysis of the total annual catches of demersal fish in Iceland waters during the first half of this century. Stock levels of cod, haddock and plaice are analysed with regard to previous patterns and to future measures required to control the catch.

530 Icelandic fishing vessels.
Hjálmar Bárðarson. *Iceland Review*, vol. 2, no. 2 (1964), p. 29-36; vol. 3, no. 1 (1965), p. 19-24. illus.

Although much has been written about the stocks of fish and the men who fish them in Icelandic waters, there is little in English on the vessels employed. This article, in two parts, is therefore useful as a survey of the Icelandic fishing fleet up to the 1960s. The figures can be updated from the regular statistical sources. The articles are illustrated.

531 Iceland: how a small country runs a major fishing industry.
Peter Hjul, Peter Brady. *Fishing News International*, vol. 6, no. 11 (1967), p. 24-46.

This article, taken with that mentioned at end of note, forms a useful survey of the Icelandic fisheries during the boom years for the industry in the 1960s. In 1966, Iceland, in spite of the proportionately low number of her workforce, remarkably attained seventh place in the world fishing tables. The reporters discuss the resources in terms of manpower, equipment and investment, and stress the economic imbalance and over-dependence on fishing in relation to the need to conserve the fish stocks, particularly cod and herring. (This article was compiled at around the time of the Nigerian civil war - a distant event, but one which upset the Icelandic stockfish industry and its exports to a degree which served to emphasise the over-dependence on fishing in a small economy). The same reporters' article in the subsequent issue of this magazine, no. 12, p. 24-42, is a survey of the fish processing industry.

532 Iceland stakes her future on 100 freezing plants.
David Glen. *Fishing News International*, vol. 14, no. 12 (Dec. 1975), p. 35-51.

About a third of the total catch of fish is taken for freezing at the hundred or so freezing plants around the coasts of Iceland. Freezing is a cost-beneficial process in the context of demands from foreign markets. Although by the mid-1970s Iceland had all but lost her share of the British market as a result of the fishing disputes, the United States market was being consolidated, and an increasing number of deals were being struck with the Soviet Union. This article stresses the crucial contribution of the fish-freezing effort to the Icelandic balance of payments - 45 per cent of the fishing industry's foreign earnings at this time derived from frozen fish.

Fisheries. Stocks, the fleet and processing

533 **Iceland: more to offer than fish.**
Cedric Dexter. *World Fishing*, vol. 24, no. 8 (Aug. 1976), p. 19-36.

Pressures on the fishing stocks around Iceland, coupled with the uncertainties of the market, have stimulated diversification within the fishing industry. This article is an illustrated assessment of the ancilliary industries: trawler building, trawling equipment (including computerised systems), and various products connected with the processing, packaging and distribution of fish.

534 **Iceland after the cod war.**
J. R. Coull, Sigfús Jónsson. *Geography*, vol. 64, no. 2 (April 1979), p. 129-33.

An interim assessment of the potential economic gains for Iceland as a result of the latest dispute over fishing rights with Britain, following which Iceland enjoyed virtually undisputed control of her own fishstocks. The writers briefly examine the current state of the stocks, the fleet, and the processing sector, to illustrate the challenges that still face the fishing industry of Iceland, notwithstanding her diplomatic success.

535 **Territoriality among Icelandic fishermen.**
Gísli Pálsson. *Acta Sociologica* (Norway), vol. 25 (1982), suppl. p. 5-13.

A paper presented at the 11th conference of the Scandinavian Sociological Association, held in Reykjavík, in which the author discusses the significance of strategies of managing access to fishing grounds: 'The data relate to the indigenous and private strategies used by Icelandic fishermen. Such strategies vary with time and with fishing technology. This article is a discussion of changes in the control of access and their implications for the management of information among skippers. Several scholars have reported claims of territoriality among fishermen, and have referred to them as manifestations of property rights and ownership. It is argued here that territorial claims should be seen as pragmatic attempts to manage the conduct of fishing' (author's abstract).

536 **To dream of fish: the causes of Icelandic skippers' fishing success.**
Gísli Pálsson. *Journal of Anthropological Research*, vol. 38, no. 2 (summer 1982), p. 227-41.

Although this article and the previous one are written from the point of view of the social anthropologist, they are important also in illuminating aspects of the management and success of the Icelandic fishing effort. In this paper the researcher counters the belief in the importance of the 'skipper effect' in determining success, by analysing the size of boats and the number of trips, by demonstrating that there is no correlation between experience and success, and by examining 'risk' hunting and 'safe' hunting. He sees the skipper's prestige not as a game, but as an economic necessity for recourse to larger boats and better crews, which form the real basis of success.

Safety

537 Trawler safety: interim report of the Committee of Inquiry into trawler safety.
Chaired by Admiral Sir Derek Holland-Martin. London: HM Stationery Office, 1968. 11p. (Cmnd. 3773).
Losses of British trawlers in Icelandic waters led to the appointment of this committee of inquiry, whose report and recommendations were presented as a Command Paper to the British parliament by the Board of Trade. The report deals with Iceland, and is specifically concerned with the provision of a special weather advisory service for trawlers operating off northern Iceland during the winter.

538 Focus on the coast guard.
Haraldur J. Hamar. *Atlantica and Iceland Review*, vol. 14, no. 3 (1976), p. 38-40.
An Icelandic view of the country's coastal defences, and their two-fold function: as a rescue service in the troubled seas around Iceland; and as a protective intercepting patrol, seen by the writer as an undermanned police force - he rejects, with some justification the British description of them as 'gunboats', after their involvement in troubled seas of another kind. He sketches the history of the coast guard and describes its capacity (in 1976 it comprised only five vessels).

Local communities

539 Grimsby v. Iceland.
Robert Taylor. *New Society*, (24 May 1973), p. 422.
Politically, the fishing disputes between Britain and Iceland were national in context; economically they were national on the Icelandic side, local on the British. This is reflected in the title of this journalistic piece, which is a character sketch (included here for comparative purposes) of the English east coast fishing port of Grimsby - ironically as Norse a name as one will find in the British Isles - and its 'grim' prospects in the event of the Icelandic stance prevailing. Subsequent events have served only to heighten the impressions recorded here.

540 Fish for survival in Vestfirðir.
Brian John. *Geographical Magazine*, vol. 51, no. 1 (Oct. 1978), p. 63-66. map.
Vestfirðir, the rugged outcrop which forms the north-western peninsula of Iceland, is in many ways a microcosm of the Icelandic problem: the region is relatively prosperous, but this prosperity depends upon its only natural resource, fish. The depopulation and eventual desertion of the village of Hesteyri in 1952 as a result of mismanagement of the herring stock is still fresh in the minds of the population of the area. The article includes a map of the settlements in Vestfirðir.

167

Fisheries. Whaling

Whaling

541 **Whaling.**
Ásgeir Jakobsson. *Atlantica and Iceland Review*, vol. 12, no. 3-4 (1974), p. 24-31.

In view of the fact that in recent years Iceland possessed the largest whaling station on the North Atlantic (at Hvalfjörður on the western coast), and of the international attention focused on whaling activities worldwide, information in English on Icelandic whaling efforts is as scarce as some of the species. This illustrated article, a brief background survey of the development of Icelandic whaling and of research into levels of stock, was written before the recent surge of activism by conservation movements, notably Greenpeace and its vessel *Rainbow Warrior*, which, in 1978-79 conducted an intensive campaign against Icelandic catches of fin whales. (Iceland was one of the seven countries who voted against the ban on whaling which was recently announced by the International Whaling Commission, to take effect from 1986, although it was not one of the four countries to announce non-compliance). For an earlier feature on whaling in Iceland from the same magazine, see Margrét R. Bjarnason's article in vol. 7, no. 1 (1969), p. 12-19.

Natural Resources and Energy

Historical surveys

542 A report on the resources of Iceland and Greenland.
Benjamin Mills Pierce. Washington, DC: US Government Printing Office, 1868. 72p.

The introduction to this historically interesting report for the US State Department is contributed by the Secretary of State, and is worth quoting from as much for its imperialist impertinence as for the light which it sheds on the motives for the report: 'Sir; when you did me the honour to call to my attention the treaty negotiated by you with Denmark, by which we acquired the important islands of St. Thomas and St. John, I ventured to suggest to you the propriety of obtaining, from the same power, Greenland, and probably Iceland also. You thought the suggestion worthy of serious consideration, and requested me to communicate to you my views in writing and the facts, that they might be on the files of the department and ready for use whenever the question might be considered hereafter by the government. In compliance with that request this report is made'. On the basis of the report he concludes 'we should purchase Iceland... the reasons are political and commercial'. Over a century later, the report can be read in a different spirit - in fact it is a randomly presented survey on the natural resources (in the widest sense) of Iceland and Greenland, but its value lies in the many statistics which the author gleaned from primary and secondary sources.

543 Sulphur in Iceland.
C. Carter Blake. London: Spon, 1874, 52p.

The realisation of the value of sulphur as a natural resource with applications in the chemical industries led several of the visitors to Iceland during the 19th century to comment on the potential. This survey of the distribution of sulphur in Iceland, its extractability and market potential, reproduces and enlarges upon previous comments on the topic, with particular reference to the Mývatn district in the north and to Krísuvík on the south-western peninsula. An appendix con-

Natural Resources and Energy. Modern applications

tains the text of a contract for the leasing of the state-owned sulphur mines at Reykjahlíð by the Danish Crown to one Alfred G. Lock of London in 1872.

Modern applications

544 The diatomite industry of Iceland: the development of a sub-Arctic resource.
W. S. W. Novak. *Cahiers de Géographie de Québec*, vol. 20, no. 49 (April 1976), p. 143-62. maps. tables.

The longstanding assumption that Iceland lacked any significant fossil-type resource was challenged in the late 1940s by the realisation that the presence of diatomaceous earth (fossils of microscopic unicellular algae) deposited in the sediment of Lake Mývatn offered commercial possibilities. Diatomite has been shown to have a number of industrial applications, principally as a filtering agent. This article describes the environment of the lake and its deposits, diatoms as a natural resource, and the evolution of the diatomite industry; commercial activity started in 1965, financed substantially by the Johns Mannville Corporation of Denver (which held a 39 per cent stake, but in 1982 became bankrupt - the effects of this on the diatomite plant are at present thought to be only temporary), and by certain Canadian sources. The original company was established by a special enactment of the Icelandic parliament. Some conclusions and forecasts are made concerning the foreign markets for diatomite. Maps and tables accompany the text, and further references to other aspects are appended.

545 The Vestmannaeyjar water scheme, Iceland.
Þórhallur Jónsson. *Journal of the Institution of Water Engineers* (UK), vol. 23 (July 1969), p. 254-58.

Prior to the 1960s water for domestic purposes was provided only by rainfall on roofs collected and stored in cisterns in each house on the island of Heimaey. The increasing demand for water for homes and local industries led to plans for desalination plants or transportation by tanker from the mainland of Iceland. When both of these schemes proved impracticable, it was decided to construct a supply pipeline under the sea. In this article, an Icelandic engineer on the project describes the scheme and its execution: the water source, the pipeline and the pumping station on the mainland; the submarine pipeline, eight miles long and a maximum depth of one hundred metres; and the installation of the fluoridated supply on the island.

546 Completion of Búrfell plant marks major advance in Iceland's hydro programme.
C. K. Willey, E. Briem. *Water Power*, vol. 26, no. 7 (July 1974), p. 246-50. map. photos.

Part of a series of feature articles on hydro-power in Scandinavia, this report is a technical description of the 210 megawatt hydroelectric development on the Þjórsá river in south-western Iceland. A map and photographs illustrate some of the problems involved in harnessing the flow of a glacial river subjected to the temperature variations occurring in Iceland. Búrfell had been projected as a site for exploiting this energy potential as early as 1917, but full realisation of the

Natural Resources and Energy. Modern applications

project came in 1969, executed by Landsvirkjun, the National Power Company of Iceland. The Búrfell power station project was combined with the construction of the aluminium smelter at Straumsvík, which required 120 megawatts of power annually.

547 Geothermal energy and its use for district heating in Iceland.
Gunnar H. Kristinsson, Karl Ó. Jónsson. *Journal of the Institution of Heating and Ventilating Engineers* (UK), vol. 39, (Aug. 1971), p. 103-11.

A technical paper by the Chief Engineer of the Reykjavík Municipal District Heating Service, which covers the development of the nearby thermal areas at Reykir for home heating purposes, including the design, plant, network and distribution of the system, as well as the costing elements of the supply now received by practically every home in the capital. He refers also to the scheme for the small town of Húsavík in the north. This paper is followed by a conference discussion on the topic; it also appears (without the discussion) in the periodical *Steam and Heating Engineer*, vol. 41, no. 479 (Oct. 1971), p. 14-24.

548 Natural heat saves millions of barrels of oil.
Sveinbjörn Björnsson. *Atlantica and Iceland Review*, vol. 18, no. 1 (1980), p. 28-37. photos. diagrs.

In this article the Professor of Geophysics at the University of Iceland presents a readily understandable report on the 'state of the art' in the field of natural heat exploitation, and describes three of the unique procedures developed by Icelandic engineers in the interests of the national economy. He deals with the natural hot water supply to Reykjavík, the process of generating heat and electricity from geothermal brine (which circumvents the problem of silica clogging) exploited on the Suđurnes Regional Heating Project at Svartsengi, near Grindavík, and the heating of homes on the Westmann Islands by tapping heat from the recent lava flow. The article is accompanied by photographs and coloured diagrams illustrating these three techniques, which will shortly be thought of as conventional in Iceland. See the short article 'Nature's hot water heats everything in Iceland' by Helen C. Howes in *Canadian Geographical Journal*, vol. 92 (May 1976), p. 46-49.

549 Geothermal energy in Iceland.
Jane Spooner. *Mining Magazine* (UK), vol. 144, no. 6 (June 1981), p. 543-47.

Nearly 30 per cent of Iceland's energy requirements are now supplied by geothermal sources (hydroelectric power supplies some 40 per cent, and most of the remainder is met by imported oil). The efforts to reduce dependence on oil even further form the topic of this short survey, with particular reference to the Svartsengi power station on the Reykjanes peninsula - see Sveinbjörn Björnsson's 'Natural heat saves millions of barrels of oil' (q.v.).

550 Energy via satellite.
Ívar Guđmundsson. *Scandinavian Review*, vol. 66, no. 3 (Sept. 1978), p. 56-59.

Although Iceland's natural energy resources have been so far only partially harnessed in relation to her own needs, the potential export of non-fossil energy is already the subject of investigation. The Power Relay Transmission System would involve the conversion of electricity generated by geothermal and hydro facilities

Natural Resources and Energy. Modern applications
to microwaves for international transmission by satellite. The theories of one of the pioneers of this concept, K. A. Ericke, are briefly reported in this article, with reference to Iceland's suitability for such a project in terms of its natural energy resources and its geographical location from which a 'hemispherical market for the nation's geothermal energy would be opened'.

Foreign Trade and Tourism

551 **Agreement between the European Economic Community and the republic of Iceland.**
In: *Collection of the agreements concluded by the European Communities.* Luxembourg: Office for Official Publications of the European Communities, vol. 2, 1977, p. 529-759.

Full membership of the European Communities is clearly an impossibility for Iceland for a variety of reasons, not the least of which is the present configuration of the Icelandic economy with its overwhelming dependence on the fishing industry, a sector of considerable controversy within the EEC itself. However, Iceland, in common with many other countries who cannot realistically consider membership, has concluded an agreement with the EEC designed to offer some preferential advantages. This agreement was published as Regulation (EEC) no. 2842/72 of the Council of the European Communities on the 19 December 1972. The text also contains the various protocols. In volume five of the same series, p. 295-312, there appears the text of the agreement between the member states of the European Coal and Steel Community and the Republic of Iceland, also signed in 1972. Both the EEC and the ECSC agreements are also available as HM Stationery Office publications in Command Paper form (Cmnd. 5182 and Cmnd. 5806 respectively).

552 **Icelandic industry at the crossroads.**
Guðmundur Magnússon. *EFTA Bulletin*, vol. 20 (May 1979), p. 6-9.

An interim assessment (shortly before the final elimination of Iceland's protective duties in line with membership of the European Free Trade Association and her trade agreement with the European Economic Community) of the performance and prospects of Icelandic industries outside the fisheries sector. The impact of EFTA on Iceland, the prevailing patterns of Icelandic trade, and the adaptability of the small firm, are each briefly considered in the context of free trade. The article is written by the Rector of the University of Iceland.

Foreign Trade and Tourism

553 Iceland: economic report.
London: Lloyds Bank Group, 1982. 27p.

The Economics Department of the Lloyds Bank Group periodically produces its report on the Icelandic economy for the benefit of its clients engaged or interested in overseas trading with Iceland. Relevant background information and statistics are included concerning the domestic economy, the structure of production, and the external position in relation to opportunities for exporting and importing. Previous edition 1979. Another British bank group to monitor Icelandic trade is Barclay's who occasionally issue a broadsheet on Iceland in the *ABECOR Country Reports Series*.

554 Hints to exporters: Iceland.
London: British Overseas Trade Board. updated. c. 40p.

A practical guide (regularly re-issued) to the major details affecting commercial transactions with Iceland. General information on the country is followed by sections on import and exchange control regulations, and on the methods of doing business in Iceland. Appended information includes a list of authorised interpreters and translators. The booklet is available free of charge to interested parties. Advice for businesses in the United States is given in *Marketing in Iceland*, a regularly updated service prepared by the Commercial Section of the US Embassy in Reykjavík, and published by the US Department of Commerce in its series *Overseas Business Reports*.

555 Tourism policy and international tourism in OECD member countries.
Paris: Organisation for Economic Co-operation and Development, c. 200p. annual.

The growth of the international tourist market in Iceland has made a significant contribution to the country's foreign earnings. As a member country of the OECD, Iceland submits annual reports and statistical data to the Organisation's Tourism Committee, which collates and publishes the details, harmonised with those from the other member countries in this annual compilation. It is a useful starting point for recent information and statistics on tourism policy, tourist flow, expenditure and receipts, transport and accommodation. Another official organisation in Paris, Le Commissariat Général au Tourisme, sent its representative Georges Lebrec to report on tourism in Iceland in 1960. Compiled with the assistance of Ferðamálafélag Reykjavíkur (Tourist Association of Reykjavík) it was issued in Icelandic, under the title *Ferðamál á Íslandi*, and in French. It comprises the results of a survey on all major aspects of the early development of tourism in Iceland.

556 The role of international tourism in Iceland.
D. R. Sterry. *Journal of the Durham University Geographical Society* vol. 12 (1970), p. 80-86.

Although the Icelandic economy can hardly be said to have been transformed by the post-war boom in international tourism, it became clear during the 1960s that such tourism was beginning to contribute to the badly needed diversification of the Icelandic economy. Developments since this article was written have confirmed the trend: visitors to Iceland totalled 10,000 in 1958, 40,000 in 1968, and 77,000 in 1978; however, there was a falling away to 65,000 in 1980. The writer briefly surveys the effects of tourism on the Icelandic balance of payments, the employment opportunities, social benefits, growth potential, and the infrastructure of transport, hotels, etc.

Foreign Trade and Tourism

557 **Law on the organisation of tourism.**
Reykjavík: National Tourist Board of Iceland, 1976. 13p.

In 1976 the Icelandic parliament passed the Law on the Organisation of Tourism. 'The aim of this law is that of furthering the development of tourism and the organisation of tourist services for Icelandic and foreign tourists as an important aspect of the Icelandic economy and social life, both in respect of national economic benefits and protection of the environment'. The thirty-five articles of the Law cover the National Tourist Board, the Iceland Tourist Bureau (Ferðaskrifstofa ríkisins, the state run travel bureau), general travel agencies, the Tourist Fund, and miscellaneous provisions/stipulations. This law is administered by the Ministry of Communications. The text of the Law is here published in the English language.

Verzlunarskýrslur. (Commercial statistics.)
See item no. 439.

Transport and Posts

Transport

558 Transport in Iceland.
Adam Rutherford. Stanmore, England: 1938. 26p.
Published privately by the author, this is a useful booklet for the transport historian, which summarises the main details of communications by sea, air and land (including roads, and mention of two unfulfilled rail projects) as far as they had been developed in Iceland before World War II.

559 Iceland's air pioneers: a saga of enterprise.
Sigurður Magnússon. *Norseman* (Norway), vol. 15 (1957), p. 77-81.
In view of a terrain which precluded inland travel by water or by rail, and which rendered travel by road restrictive, the comparatively sudden transition from horse to aeroplane in Iceland was understandable. This article is a sketch of the early history of Icelandic aviation from the first attempt to establish an airline in 1919, through the founding of the Loftleiðir company by three pilots in 1944, to its first transatlantic scheduled flight in 1947.

560 From Viking ship to super-jet.
Reykjavík: Flugleiðir H. F., 1975. 20p. maps. photos.
An informative booklet which traces the development of commercial aviation in Iceland, and particularly of the country's two international airlines Flugfélag Islands (Icelandair) which flew the European routes, and Loftleiðir Icelandic which operated the transatlantic routes and pioneered cheap fares. The two companies were merged on 20 July 1973 under a new holding company Flugleiðir, whose public relations department issued this booklet which includes historical photographs and domestic/international route maps of the new enterprise. That Iceland can support its own international airline from a population no greater than that of a small European city is increasingly remarkable at a time when oil prices and deregulation are obvious points of vulnerability. Flugleiðir had a staff of 1,800 in 1980. (Indeed, 1979 saw another Icelandic airline, Arnarflug 'Eagle Air' granted licences for scheduled flights to western Europe).

Transport and Posts. Posts

561 **Where buses face air competition.**
W. H. Godwin. *Bus and Coach* (UK), vol. 39 (Oct. 1967), p. 302-04.

The local urban bus system in Reykjavík has long been a successful enterprise, and the long distance network is better developed than the natural conditions would suggest (see *Leiðabók: áaetlanir Sérleyfisbifreiða-scheduled bus timetables* q.v.); however, the indirect routes and extra time which the long distance buses are forced to take by the terrain has been the major reason for the remarkable network of domestic flights linking all the major and some of the minor centres in Iceland. There are over thirty airfields around the country, used by the services of Icelandair and smaller operators.

Posts

562 **Icelandic posts 1776-1919 under Danish administration.**
E. A. G. Carõe. London: Royal Philatelic Society, 1947. 83p.

A collection of articles which originally appeared in the periodical *London Philatelist* between 1944 and 1947. Together they form a remarkably detailed account of Icelandic postal history from the first postal charter of 1776 through to the end of Danish administration. The author makes extensive use of documentary sources in his studies of the international service between Denmark and Iceland, the separate Icelandic Post of 1872, the internal postal routes, the post offices and their marks, postal rates, and of the periodic official reports on the Icelandic postal service. The postal historian and the philatelist will discover much rewarding detail in this survey by Sir Athelstan Carõe, who was Icelandic consul in Liverpool.

563 **Postal service in Iceland, 1776 - 13th May 1951.**
Guðmundur Hlíðdal. Reykjavík: Post and Telegraph Administration of Iceland, 1951. 52p.

The 175th anniversary of the Icelandic post is made the occasion for this account of its early history, written by the former Director of Posts and Telegraphs. He describes and presents the text of the Postal Charter of 13 May 1776 issued by the royal decree of King Christian VII of Denmark. He then sketches the conditions within Iceland at the time of the establishment of the postal service, the origins of the service, the struggles in its early organisation, and the issue concerning Jón Eiríksson as the probable originator of the service. He appends a chronology of important events in the history of the postal service.

Transport and Posts. Stamps

Stamps

564 One hundred years of Icelandic stamps, 1873-1973.
Jón Aðalsteinn Jónsson, translated by Peter Kidson. Reykjavík: Post and Telecommunications Administration, 1977. 471p. illus.

A superbly presented volume commissioned for the centenary of the issue of Icelandic stamps. It is indispensable to the Philatelist with an interest in Icelandic posts. The main part of the work is devoted to a minutely detailed study of the history of Icelandic stamps from their first issue in 1873 (when the use of Danish stamps for postage in Iceland became illegal) up to the early part of this century, including the skilding stamps, aurar stamps, and the over-printings at the turn of the century. The second part is a description of the various issues of commemorative stamps which have been featured from 1911 to the present. Copiously illustrated with plates containing over 600 stamps. A fascinating and definitive examination of the development of the Icelandic posts, and of modern Icelandic history through its stamps. The volume is presented in a protective box case. For the reader requiring only a summary of this topic, the same author contributed an illustrated article to *Atlantica and Iceland Review*, vol. 11, no. 3-4 (1973), p. 38-43.

565 Íslenzk frímerki 1980. (Catalogue of Icelandic stamps 1980.)
Sigurður H. Þorsteinsson. Reykjavík: Ísafoldarprentsmiðja, 1979. 24th ed. 121p. illus.

A handy catalogue of Icelandic stamps, with descriptions and illustrations (in black-and-white only) from 1873 to the present. Includes official, semi-official issues, special cancellations, Christmas seals, local stamps, etc. Items are available at the Frímerkjasalan in Reykjavík.

566 Stanley Gibbons stamp catalogue. Part 11, Scandinavia.
London: Stanley Gibbons, 1980. 150p. illus.

In the long history of the publishing of the philatelist's 'bible' Scandinavia has previously figured in the widely available collective editions, most recently in the three volume edition for Europe. This new edition in separate format will further meet the area specialist collector's needs. 'Scandinavian countries have always ranked high amongst collectors, because of their exemplary philatelic history, their moderate policies, and the outstanding quality of many of their stamps' (prefatory comments). Iceland is featured on p. 65-81, with technical descriptions of and prices for Icelandic stamps issued between 1873 and 1979. (The first official postage stamp actually printed in Iceland dates from 1928). The catalogue contains 165 illustrations of Icelandic stamp issues from all periods. Icelandic stamps of the latter period are noted for their excellent design, making use of Icelandic subjects, and appearing in issues of half a million to three million, to meet postal requirements and philatelic demands. In a related but narrower field of Scandinavian postal history, see the catalogue *Paquebot marks of Norway, Denmark, Finland, Iceland and Sweden* compiled by Edwin Drechsel (Bournemouth, England: Lowe, 1977, 25p.), which contains one or two examples of Icelandic marks.

Transport and Posts. Coins

Coins

567 **Myntir Íslands, 1836, 1922-1963.** (Icelandic coins, 1836, 1922-1963.)
Staffan Björkman. Stockholm: Brolins Boktryckeri, 1965. 17p. illus. tables.

A brief survey of the history of Icelandic coins, from the small coinage struck by Denmark for circulation in Iceland in 1836, through the subsequent use of private tokens and notes, the coinage of the Kingdom of Iceland first struck in 1922, to the republican issues. The text is followed by tables of denominations, dates, alloys, marks and number of pieces struck. Illustrated. See item 501 'The new Króna/The history of Icelandic currency'.

Environment

General

568 The Reykjavík imperative.
John Elkington. *New Scientist*, (23 June 1977), p. 700-02.
A brief report on the Second International Conference on the Environmental Future, held at Reykjavík in 1977. Some of the Icelandic problems in this context are touched upon. The prevailing mood of the conference was not optimistic. The same reporter also comments on some environmental aspects of geothermal energy in Iceland in a subsequent issue of the same weekly, 16 February 1978, p. 439-41.

569 A delicate natural balance in Iceland.
Gunnar G. Schramm. *Scandinavian Review*, vol. 64, no. 4 (Dec. 1976), p. 33-37.
This short article offers some valid generalisations concerning the conflict between Iceland's need to diversify its economy by the exploitation of its cheap energy potential, and the growing awareness of the potential problems for the environment in a country where there has always been, in spite of natural adversities, a certain harmony between man and his surroundings. 'To this one must add the fact that the subarctic environment of Iceland is a highly fragile one, where the biological effects of pollution take much longer to disappear than under more volatile climatic conditions'.

Housing and planning

570 Housing and town planning in Iceland.
Guðmundur Hannesson. *International Federation for Housing and Town Planning Bulletin* (UK), vol. 37 (1937), p. 5-27. illus.

By the 1930s, town planning was compulsory for all communities of whatever size in Iceland - any community numbering more than 500 inhabitants was subject to this condition, which, in the international context, was unique. This article affords an interesting insight into the historical development of housing in Iceland from the time of the settlement through its three stages of construction: turf (the standard material for several centuries), timber (19th century), and concrete (20th century) - at one farm in eastern Iceland the generations are reflected in these three types of building standing alongside each other. By 1930 there were 13,500 dwellings in Iceland, 6,500 of timber, 3,600 of turf, and 3,300 of concrete. The latter part of this article is a description of the town planning situation in Iceland during the 1930s. Committees had been formed a century earlier, but the first full Town Planning Act was passed only in 1931, and its provisions are here described with reference to surveying, supervision of changes, expropriation and compensation, enforcement, etc. Examples of planning in individual communities include Bolungarvík and Isafjörður, accompanied by illustrations of their town plans. For a report from the same period on planning in the capital, see the pamphlet *Rejkjavík: development and town planning* by Hörður Bjarnarson, (Town Planning Board of Iceland, 1939, 25p.).

571 Aðalskipulag Reykjavíkur 1983. (Master plan of Reykjavík.)
Reykjavík: Reykjavík City Council, 1966. 266p. maps. illus.

A Planning Act of 1964 required that all townships in Iceland with a population of more than one hundred inhabitants should prepare a development structure plan. This report on the master plan for the capital city was directed by the Professor of Planning at the University of Copenhagen, Peter Bredsdorff, and comprises a review of the development of Reykjavík from the time of the settlement to date, and plans for the future, which are concentrated on the problems of overcoming the central congestion by means of a new city centre, and decentralisation of the infrastructure. The volume is attractively produced, with illustrations, maps and statistics, and with text in both Icelandic and English (translation by Frederic Stevenson). The report and its recommendations show that the problems of Reykjavík are not peculiarly Icelandic, but reflect the situation that has also affected many larger cities of the world. The report was updated in 1975 to project the plans forward to 1995. The master plan was briefly reviewed by P. D. McGovern in the periodical *Town and Country Planning*, vol. 35 (May 1967), p. 246-49.

572 Style and form in the north.
Gísli Sigurðsson. *Atlantica and Iceland Review*, vol. 6, no. 3 (1968), p. 21-27.

The path to home ownership in Iceland is long and expensive; consequently a great amount of care and labour, often on the part of the prospective owners, is put into the planning and construction of new houses. In this brief article, illustrated with photographs of the exterior and interior designs of three different houses in the vicinity of Reykjavík, an idea is given of the aspirations for house and home among Icelandic urban families. In the same magazine, vol. 17, no. 1

Environment. Nature protection

(1979), p. 10-13, Örnólfur Arnason features some of the older houses in Reykjavík, and the ways in which they are being given a new lease of life.

573 **Residential mobility, life cycle stages, housing and the changing social patterns in Reykjavík.**
Bjarni Reynarsson. PhD thesis, University of Illinois at Urbana-Champaign, Illinois, 1980. 238p.

A study of the ecology and sociology of housing in the capital between 1974 and 1976. The research base was the complete collection of change of address forms submitted to the authorities in 1974. Zonal transfers are analysed in the context of life cycle patterns. The research reveals: a high level of residential mobility; new housing as a dominant factor; non-married households making up over half of the transfers; an up-market trend for houses in central Reykjavík, a down-market trend for suburban flats. The thesis concludes with some observations on the influences of public and private agencies upon the housing market. See Ingvi V. Jóhannsson and Jón R. Sveinsson's 'Housing in Iceland: inflation helps those who help themselves' (q.v.).

574 **Conservation in Iceland.**
Birgir H. Sigurðursson. MCD thesis, Department of Civic Design, University of Liverpool, England, 1980. 116p. plans.

The author's synopsis reads: 'The dissertation examines the practice of conservation in Iceland, primarily through a case study of a part of the capital city. It begins with an outline of the legislative framework of planning and conservation in Iceland. The second part of the work introduces the reader to Reykjavík in general, and to the study area - Grjótaþorp - in particular. In the final section proposals are made for improving the efficiency and effectiveness of conservation in the study area and in Iceland as a whole'. The study is accompanied by a variety of drawings and photographs, and the endpocket contains two folding sheets delineating a site plan and a draft plan for Grjótaþorp on a scale of 1:1,500. A very worthwhile study of conservation in practice in Iceland.

Nature protection

575 **Lög um náttúrvernd no. 47/1971.** (Nature Conservation act no. 47/1971.)
Reykjavík: Ministry of Culture and Education, 1971. 8p.

This important Act, passed by the *Alþing* on 16 April 1971 (superseding the Act of 1956), contains thirty-eight articles dealing with the aims and administration of nature conservation in Iceland, public rights of access and responsibilities to natural areas, protection of natural phenomena, establishment of recreational areas, etc. A supplementary regulation, no. 205/1973, deals with the role of the Nature Conservation Committees elected in each town and country; forty-one articles cover topics as detailed as the building of summer houses and the erection of roadside billboards. Both of these documents are available in English, and throw light on Icelandic official attitudes towards the environment. See *Law on the organisation of tourism* (q.v.).

Environment. Nature protection

576 **The national parks of Iceland.**
Birgir Kjaran, translated by Peter Kidson Karlsson. Reykjavík: Örn og Örlygur, 1969. 100p. photos. figs.

Written by the Chairman of the Council for the Protection of Nature, this book comprises historical and geographical descriptions, with drawings and photographs, of the national parks at Skaftafell in Öraefi and Þingvellir by the Öxará. Skaftafell was the first national park to be established in Iceland, in 1967, although Þingvellir has a longer history of being regarded as a national sanctuary. The parallel text of this very useful guide is in four languages: English, Danish, German and Icelandic.

577 **The national parks of Iceland.**
Ottar Indriðason. *National Parks and Conservation Magazine*, vol. 47, no. 4 (April 1973), p. 4-7.

A further description of the two national parks at Skaftafell and Þingvellir, and of the moves to bring Hornstrandir, the extreme north-western peninsula of Iceland, under environmental protection along the same lines. See the feature article on Skaftafell by one of the projects instigators, Sigurður Þórarinsson, in *Atlantica and Iceland Review*, vol. 6, no. 2 (1968), p. 30-34, and his description of two other protected areas of staggering beauty and variety, Landmannalaugar, in the same magazine, vol. 9, no. 2 (1971), p. 16-22, and Veiðivötn, vol. 19, no. 3 (1981), p. 34-39.

Reforestation of Iceland.
See item no. 522

Sport and Recreation

578 **Chess in Iceland and in Icelandic literature, with historical notes on other table games.**
Willard Fiske. Florence, Italy: Florentine Typographical Society, 1905. 400p. Reprinted New York: Stechert, 1915.

The American benefactor and book collector Willard Fiske is known also for his legacy to the Arctic island of Grímsey, famed for the prowess of its islanders at chess, a game of which Fiske was a devoted student. To this day the Fiske Fund is being used for the benefit of Grímsey's cultural interests, and Fiske Day is celebrated there every 11 November (see Robert Jack's *Arctic living: the story of Grímsey*, q.v.). Fiske visited Iceland, but never Grímsey itself. His book on chess in Iceland is a remarkable work, in which he draws on his philological knowledge to explain the historical development of chess and related table games in the light of the comparative etymologies of their technical terms. The book falls into two parts: the development of chess in Iceland with reference to the sagas and other evidence; and the history and relationships of table games in a world context. The author apologises in his preface for the random nature of his work, and for what he calls his stray notes on the subject, but the volume is a mine of information. Sadly, the second volume, in which Fiske was planning, *inter alia*, a more detailed discussion of the Icelandic game *hnefatafl*, was precluded by his death in 1904.

579 **World chess headquarters in Iceland?**
Freysteinn Jóhannsson. *Atlantica and Iceland Review*, vol. 16, no. 1 (1978), p. 14-19.

A profile of the Icelandic chess grandmaster, Friðrik Ólafsson, at the time of his candidacy for the Presidency of the World Chess Federation, to which, after a tough campaign, he succeeded in 1978. Iceland thereby entered the chess spotlight for the second time in the decade, having staged the Fischer/Spassky world contest in 1972. Friðrik Ólafsson was involved in representations concerning the family of the defected Soviet player Viktor Korchnoi, and this clearly contributed to his failure to be re-elected after some political voting in the election of November 1982.

Sport and Recreation

580 **Icelandic wrestling.**
Jóhannes Jósefsson. Akureyri, Iceland: Þórh. Bjarnason, 1908. 48p. photos.

An historical gem for the person interested in the uniquely Icelandic style of wrestling. Jóhannes Jósefsson was the Icelandic wrestling champion in 1907 and later, and his book, surprisingly issued in English, is a detailed description, accompanied by thirty-seven photographs, of all the attacking and defensive moves practised in this sport. Jóhannes Jósefsson was the first winner of *Íslandsbeltið* (the Iceland belt), and it was on this occasion at Akureyri in 1907 that the first competitive rules in *glíma* were issued. The original Icelandic text of these wrestling rules is reproduced with summary and comments in English by Ingimar Jónsson in *International compilation of sports historical documents, II*, (Leipzig, GDR: Deutsche Hochschule fur Körperkultur, 1978), in the section on the history of sport in Iceland, p. 159-200.

581 **The Icelandic glíma.**
Þorsteinn Einarsson. In: *Third Viking Congress, Reykjavík, 1956.* Edited by Kristján Eldjárn. Reykjavík: Ísafoldarprentsmiðja, 1956. p. 138-41.

Wrestling remains a popular sport in Iceland today, and its Icelandic form is known as *glíma*. This short paper touches upon the origins of the sport in Iceland, and sketches some of its rules.

582 **The bus driver who became a European champion.**
Steinar Júlíússon. *Atlantica and Iceland Review*, vol. 16, no. 2 (1978), p. 33-36.

Iceland's size, isolation and climate are hardly conducive to the emergence of athletes of international status; but in the field of shot-putting, a popular sport in Iceland, two Icelanders have achieved success internationally: Gunnar Huseby was European champion in 1946, and in the 1970s Hreinn Halldórsson became the national sporting hero when he won the European indoor championship in Spain in 1977. This illustrated article traces Hreinn's career up to the point of his preparations for the Moscow Olympics, and touches on the problems of athletic breakthrough from a small nation. He has three times been voted 'athlete of the year' by Icelandic sports writers - in 1981 this title went to another of Iceland's strongmen, the world record-holding weightlifter Skúli Oskarsson.

583 **Goal, goal!**
Steinar J. Lúðvíksson. *Atlantica and Iceland Review*, vol. 18, no. 3 (1980), p. 49-53.

The international appeal of association football had reached Iceland as early as the start of this century - the first championship there was held in 1912. Football is still not a professional sport in Iceland, but in this article the reporter concentrates on the relatively recent trend for Iceland's top players to seek fame and fortune abroad. It was Albert Guðmundsson (a candidate in the country's presidential elections of 1980) who set the example in the late 1940s by establishing himself in European professional soccer as a player in Scotland, England, France and Italy. Today, Icelandic footballers such as the much-travelled Asgeir Sigurvinsson of Standard Liège, Bayern Munich and VFB Stuttgart, Jóhannes Edvaldsson of Glasgow Celtic (now with an American club), Teitur Þórðarson of the 1979 Swedish champions Östers Vaxjö, and, most recently, Pétur Pétursson of Feyenoord Rotterdam and Anderlecht, have become well-known names in a

Sport and Recreation

European context, and, when available from their clubs, have contributed to the gradually rising standard of, and respect for, the Icelandic national side. The same reporter has a piece on the rising popularity of handball in Iceland in the same magazine, vol. 10, no. 3 (1972), p. 55-59.

584 **Golf around the clock.**
Kjartan L. Pálsson. *Atlantica and Iceland Review*, vol. 19, no. 1 (1981), p. 42-47.

A glimpse of the Icelandic golfing scene, which should persuade those visitors with golfing tendencies to take their clubs with them. Midnight golf is an experience unlikely to be forgotten quickly. There are several 9-hole golf courses in Iceland, the only 18-hole course being in Reykjavík (5,700 metres long, par 71), although others are under construction at Akureyri, Hafnarfjörður and Keflavík. As the reporter points out, the lack of trees, at least in this context, is an advantage, and although there are some less familiar hazards to undermine one's confidence, the quality of grass on the fairways and the greens is surprisingly good, considering the environment. Iceland recently won international favour for its efforts in being selected to stage the European Junior Team Championship in 1981.

585 **Rally drivers on the go.**
Sonja Diego. *Atlantica and Iceland Review*, vol. 18, no. 1 (1980), p. 48-51.

Rally driving has only recently been introduced to Iceland, but the growth of interest in the sport has been rapid. In this brief feature the reporter emphasises that the deserted terrain of Iceland makes it an ideal venue not only for domestic competition but also for international rallies certificated by the International Automobile Federation. Iceland roads may not suit the ordinary driver, but they are tailor made (or unmade) for the rally driver.

586 **Gliding in Iceland.**
Gunnar Salvason. *Atlantica and Iceland Review*, vol. 20, no. 2 (winter 1982), p. 27-31.

An interview with Leifur Magnússon, five times winner of the national gliding championships. The first club for gliding in Iceland was founded in 1936, and today the country has about sixty glider pilots.

587 **Swimming.**
Águst Jónsson. *Atlantica and Iceland Review*, vol. 19, no. 3 (1981), p. 40-44.

Swimming has always been regarded as an important activity in Iceland, for two reasons: the dangers of the coastal waters, inland rivers and lakes have always demanded an ability to save life; and the presence of geothermal waters has been a more than adequate substitute for the lack of sunny beaches.

588 **Salmon is supreme.**
Ásgeir Ingólfsson. *Atlantica and Iceland Review*, vol. 9, no. 3 (1971), p. 36-45.

Salmon fishing in Iceland has been popular amongst both Icelanders and foreign visitors since rod fishing was introduced into the country from Britain at the

Sport and Recreation

beginning of this century. In this article the angler is presented with various background information on the rivers (salmon spawn in some sixty rivers in Iceland), on the salmon themselves, the fishing seasons, fishing associations, equipment, conservation and culture measures, and on the number of rods per river. The foreign visitor should, however, check up on the information and current regulations each season. (Iceland was one of the instigators of the North Atlantic Salmon Conservation Organisation in 1982).

589 Rivers of Iceland.
R. N. Stewart. Reykjavík: Iceland Tourist Bureau, 1950. 195p. map. photos.

Stewart, a major-general from Scotland, was a familiar figure in Iceland during the first half of this century, possessing as much knowledge and experience of fishing in Icelandic rivers and lakes as the Icelanders themselves. Indeed, he held a lease of ten years on one particular river in north-western Iceland, Hrútafjarðará. His book, based upon thirty-five seasons' experience of angling in Iceland, remains the only full-length account of, and guide to, Icelandic inland waters for the foreign visitor. He describes several of the major rivers such as the Laxá in some detail, as well as the streams and lakes, with chapters on salmon, char and sea trout, and on the bird life to be found around the waters. He includes further notes on tenancy and the hiring of 'gillies' or local helpers, and on recommended tackle. The volume contains a purpose-drawn folding map delineating the courses of the twenty-three rivers mentioned in the text, plus a further seventeen rivers, and fourteen trout lakes. Also includes photographs.

590 The mountains of Iceland.
Henry A. Perkins. *American Alpine Journal*, vol. 6, no. 1 (1946), p. 1-13.

A mountaineer's view of some of Iceland's notable peaks in their three major categories: fells, volcanoes and ice-caps. He also makes reference to the earlier exploits of mountaineers in Iceland. This article can be read in conjunction with Kenneth A. Henderson's article 'Some Icelandic mountains' in the same journal, vol. 10 (1957), p. 113-20, which contains brief accounts of ascents on Kerlingarfjöll, Hekla, Snæfellsjökull and Herdubreið. In the British counterpart of this periodical, *Alpine Journal*, vol. 48 (1936), p. 1-13, there is a substantial article on Vatnajökull by Andrea de Pollitzer-Pollenghi.

The national parks of Iceland.
See item no. 576.

Language

Norse and Old Icelandic

591 The Scandinavian languages.
Einar Haugen. London: Faber, 1976. 507p. bibliog.
The most substantial comparative treatment of the Scandinavian languages available in English. The overall approach of this scholarly volume is thematic, i.e. there is no specific section on the individual languages. The emphasis is upon the historical development of the languages from their common Norse roots, and although Icelandic is rather underrepresented, the author enables the student to identify the position of the Icelandic language in relation to the other Scandinavian languages. Arising from the research involved in this work, Haugen also produced as chief editor *A bibliography of Scandinavian languages and linguistics, 1900-1970* (Oslo: Universitetsforlaget, 1974, 527p.), an essential tool for the specialist researcher.

592 Icelandic-Norwegian linguistic relationships.
Kenneth G. Chapman. Oslo: Universitetsforlaget, 1962. 200p.
The further west one travels linguistically from continental Scandinavia via the Faroes to Iceland, the more conservative, in terms of the Old Norse standard, the language becomes - as one would expect with the increasing geographical remoteness. In his thesis, however, the author examines the problems of oversimplifying this pattern, and the question of the 'purity' of the Icelandic language, by attempting to show that many shared innovations in Icelandic and in the west Norwegian dialects can be attributed to the history of social interaction between the two countries. This is a work for the socio-linguist.

Language. Norse and Old Icelandic

593 The Viking legacy: the Scandinavian influence on the English and Gaelic languages.
John Geipel. Newton Abbot, England: David & Charles; Totowa, New Jersey: Rowman & Littlefield, 1971. 225p. bibliog.

If Iceland enthusiasts are asked, as the compiler of this bibliography has often been, by those suspecting them of being deliberately esoteric, to justify their interest in this outpost of the Viking world, a useful answer is to illustrate a common heritage of Britain and Iceland by pointing to those lexical and grammatical features of the enquirer's conversation which are Norse in origin, and without which the development of the English language would have been significantly different (the French influence affected the surface of the English language, but the pure Norse influence penetrated to its roots). This book, the only modern generalisation of the topic in English, is an entertaining examination of the common roots, the 'invasion' of Norse into the languages of Britain, and of Scandinavian placenames and personal names to be encountered in the British Isles. Two appendices include selections of Scandinavian loanwords in English, and British surnames of Norse origin.

594 First grammatical treatise: the earliest Germanic phonology; an edition, translation and commentary by Einar Haugen.
London: Longman, 1972. 2nd rev. ed. 83p. (Classics of Linguistics).

The *First Grammatical Treatise*, written by an anonymous Icelander in the middle of the 12th century, is an exceptional document for the reason that at such an early date it applies 'general descriptive principles to a vernacular language'. That the work has survived at all is a result of a scribe having attached the manuscript to that of Snorri's *Edda*, along with three other grammatical treatises of less substance. In this new edition, the English translation is presented in parallel with the Iceland text, and is enhanced by an illuminating introduction to the work itself, an analysis of the First Grammarian's phonology and theory of morphology, and an essay on the unknown author's background and personality. A facsimile of the original manuscript (*Codex Wormianus* 84-90) is appended. This is a unique document for the serious study of the history of the Icelandic language. The *First Grammatical Treatise* was also presented in English by Hreinn Benediktsson (University of Iceland Publications in Linguistics, no. 1, 1972). He had earlier drawn on the First Grammarian's phonology in a paper surveying the history of the vowel system of Icelandic, which appeared in the Journal of the International Linguistic Association, *Word*, vol. 15 (1959), p. 282-312.

595 Early Icelandic script.
Hreinn Benediktsson. Reykjavík: Manuscript Institute of Iceland, 1965. 97p. plates.

A commentary on a selection of Icelandic vernacular manuscript texts dating from the 12th and 13th centuries, as an aid to the study of Old Icelandic palaeography and linguistic features. The volume contains photographic plates of 78 manuscript specimens. For further study of this field, reference must be made to Jón Helgason's prestigious multi-volume series *Early Icelandic manuscripts in facsimile* (Copenhagen: Rosenkilde, 1958- .). Jón Helgason was Professor of Icelandic at the University of Copenhagen.

Language. Norse and Old Icelandic

596 **A grammar of the Icelandic or Old Norse tongue.**
Rasmus Kristian Rask, translated by Sir George Webbe Dasent, new edition with a preface introductory article bibliographies and notes by T. L. Markey. Amsterdam: Benjamins, 1976. 272p. (Amsterdam Classics in Linguistics, vol. 2).

Rask, like Grimm, was one of the founding fathers of comparative historical philology. The original version of this work was published in Danish in 1811, but it was the Swedish version of 1818 which was drawn upon for the English translation of 1843, which in turn is reproduced for this new edition. Although it is the product of painstaking scholarship, Rask's pioneering work is remarkably clear in its presentation of Old Icelandic grammar. The advanced student will find that it still repays browsing, if not cover to cover scrutiny, and should bear in mind that it exercised considerable influence on the work of later grammarians such as Noreen and Heusler. The work is arranged under six main headings: alphabet, inflections, word formation, syntax, prosody, dialects. The original of the English version was published in London by Pickering. Rasmus Rask was a founder member of the new Icelandic Literary Society in 1817.

597 **Icelandic prose reader.**
Gudbrandur Vigfússon, George Powell. Oxford, England: Clarendon Press, 1879. 559p.

This reader is the earliest example of a selective guide to Old Icelandic texts, with the aid of notes, grammar and glossary. Well used in its time, its approach has now been largely superseded, with the availability of more editions of full texts in Icelandic for the foreign student as the interest in Old Icelandic studies has increased. The same can be said for a similar volume compiled by G. N. Garmonsway entitled *An early Norse reader.* (Cambridge University Press, 1928. 148p.).

598 **An Icelandic primer.**
Henry Sweet. Oxford, England: Oxford University Press, 1895. 2nd ed. 110p.

Four years after the publication of his Anglo-Saxon primer in 1882, Sweet first published this primer of Old Icelandic of the period 1200-1350. 'The want of a short and easy introduction to the study of Icelandic has been felt for a long time', and from this point of view it has advantages to this day. The grammar is accompanied by reading texts from prose and verse, and by a basic vocabulary from Icelandic into English. The longstanding availability and maintained use of Sweet's primer has lessened the value of H. M. Buckhurst's *Elementary grammar of Old Icelandic*, (London: Methuen, 1925, 104p.).

599 **An introduction to Old Norse.**
E. V. Gordon, revised by A. R. Taylor. Oxford, England: Clarendon Press, 1957. 2nd rev.ed. 412p.

The first edition of this work appeared in 1927, and from that time, through its second edition and up to its convenient appearance in paperback format in 1980, it has been a standard companion of university students of the Old Norse tongue. A useful introduction is followed by a broad selection of texts from Old Norse (west and east); the second half of the volume comprises a reference grammar of

Language. Dictionaries (Old and modern Icelandic)

Old Norse, including a short section on metre. There is also a substantial glossary of all words found in the reading passages.

600 Old Icelandic: an introductory course.
Sigrid Valfells, James E. Cathay. Oxford, England: Oxford University Press, 1981. 379p.

Students of Old Icelandic language and literature have had to wait a very long time for the appearance of a new and substantial grammar and guide. This course, as its authors correctly claim, represents a departure from the approach of traditional handbooks, which are apt to present ungraded readings followed by a framework of grammar. The readings selected for this course are carefully graded to illustrate the formal grammar, and the authors have constructed drills and translations into Old Icelandic, so that its students, although clearly requiring a reading competence in the language, can monitor the progress of their skills. The course comprises thirty-five lessons, plus keys to the drills and translations, and a substantial glossary. It must be emphasised that this course presupposes a traditional ability in formal language learning, and a familiarity with grammatical terminology. The quick and easy way to a reading knowledge of Old Icelandic does not yet exist, but for the advanced student this course will prove of real value.

601 Graded readings and exercises in Old Icelandic.
Kenneth G. Chapman. Berkeley, California; Los Angeles: University of California Press; Cambridge, England: Cambridge University Press, 1964. 72p.

The first, and in several ways the most successful, attempt at streamlining the beginner's path to a command of the Old Icelandic language. By means of its graded reading passages and exercises it enables those with some general linguistic aptitude to familiarise themselves fairly rapidly with the basics of the formal grammar and with the recurring patterns of Old Icelandic texts. Although primarily designed for use with a teacher, it can be used with some success for self-study, and may initially appear less forbidding than the previous item. It remains in print.

Dictionaries (Old and modern Icelandic)

602 Information retrieval and the Old Norse dictionary.
Pardee Lowe. *Studia Linguistica*, vol. 24, no. 2 (1970), p. 87-113.

A specialist article in which the author examines the failings of Old Norse lexicography, as well as particular pitfalls which are likely to be encountered in any new venture into this field.

Language. Dictionaries (Old and modern Icelandic)

603 Grammatical and lexical materials for modern Icelandic.
Sidney Rufus Smith. *Scandinavian Studies*, vol. 50 (autumn 1978), p. 414-22.

A survey of dictionaries and other linguistic aids available as at 1977 (the situation has changed little since) for those learning the modern Icelandic language at a variety of levels. As the author justifiably claims, the overall picture is not very bright, and he concludes his survey with a table of suggested projects to improve the range and quality. Following on from this see the article 'Modern Icelandic at Colleges and Universities in the United States: materials and instruction' by Stephen Clausing in the same periodical, vol. 53, no. 4 (Aug. 1981), p. 413-19.

604 Isländisches etymologisches Wörterbuch.
Alexander Jóhannesson. Bern, Switzerland: Francke, 1951-56. 1,406p.

A systematic dictionary of the etymology of the Icelandic language. It is designed not as a quick reference work to deal with enquiries about the derivation of particular Icelandic words, but as a specialised tool for the historical linguist. The dictionary, originally issued in *lieferungen* (installments), traces in detail the origin of about 20,000 Icelandic words back to their Indo-Germanic roots, and is arranged by the original root forms. A monumental work, which has remained in print since publication.

605 An Icelandic-English dictionary.
Initiated by Richard Cleasby, subsequently revised enlarged and completed by Guðbrandur Vigfússon, 2nd edition with a suppl. by Sir William A. Craigie. Oxford, England: Clarendon Press, 1957. Reprinted 1975. 883p.

The standard dictionary of the Old Icelandic language. A compendious volume in the great traditions of lexicography, drawing its entries and quoting from texts up to 1850, though the emphasis is heavily upon the mediaeval period. The bibliographical history of the dictionary is of considerable interest: its originator, Richard Cleasby, was an English scholar who settled in Copenhagen and had established the framework for entries from the prose sources before his death in 1847 (although the first Icelandic dictionary was that of Guðmundur Andreæ, published posthumously in 1683, Cleasby's dictionary was the first from Icelandic into English). The work was continued by the Icelandic writer Konráð Gíslason, who completed the basic dictionary by 1854. The Cleasby heirs then entrusted the manuscript to the notable translator Sir George Webbe Dasent in England for negotiation of its publication by the Clarendon Press. The task of revision and enlargement fell to the Icelandic professor at the University of Oxford, Guðbrand Vigfússon, and the dictionary was finally published in 1874. The second edition by Sir William Craigie contains many additional words and references. For an interesting sidelight on the genesis of this dictionary, involving the views of Dasent and Vigfússon see Elizabeth Knowles 'Notes on a first edition of Cleasby-Vigfússon', in *Saga-book*, vol. 20, no. 3 (1980), p. 165-78.

606 Orðasafn íslenzkt og enzkt. (English-Icelandic vocabulary.)
Jón A. Hjaltalín. Reykjavík: Ísafold, 1883. 2 vols. in 1, 355+184p.

Although perhaps of historical interest only nowadays, this two-way dictionary by the eminent Icelandic scholar Jón A. Hjaltalín is remarkable as an early attempt

Language. Dictionaries (Old and modern Icelandic)

at a dictionary of English and Icelandic. The English into Icelandic section is substantial, containing well over 15,000 words.

607 Icelandic-English dictionary.
Geir T. Zoëga. Reykjavík: Bókaverzlun Sigurðar Kristjánssonar, 1942. 3rd ed. Reprinted 1975. 631p.

A straightforward dictionary, with a companion volume from English into Icelandic, which also ran to a third edition in 1954, the original editions having been published at the beginning of this century. Because of their age, they obviously fall short on the more modern terms and idioms, but they were well used during the first half of this century, and with some 15,000 words and half as many compounds in addition included in the Icelandic-English volume, for example, they are still of some practical value. Well used today as an affordable dictionary for students of Old Icelandic is Geir Zoëga's other lexicographical venture *A concise dictionary of Old Icelandic* (originally published in 1910, but reprinted several times by Oxford University Press, 551p.). It remains in print, and for its size is strong on phraseology.

608 Íslenzk orðabók handa skólum i almenningi.
(Icelandic dictionary for schools and for general use.)
Árni Böðvarsson. Reykjavík: Bókaútgáfa Menningarsjóðs, 1963. 852p.

The general dissatisfaction with the state of modern bilingual dictionaries between Icelandic and English necessitates reference to this Icelandic-Icelandic dictionary published by the Cultural Fund, which the practised user will find repays consultation in conjunction with the bilingual dictionaries. It is a popular dictionary in Iceland, not easily found in bookshops, and has proved trustworthy for most purposes. Widely recommended.

609 Ensk-íslenzk orðabók. (English-Icelandic dictionary.)
Sigurður Örn Bogason. Reykjavík: Ísafoldarprentsmiðja, 1966. 2nd ed. 862p.

This dictionary, which was reprinted in 1973, has had a rather bad press amongst English-speaking practitioners. Clearly it has faults, including some mistakes on the English side, and some archaisms on the Icelandic. But it is more serviceable than it is given credit for, and despite its occasional frustrations, it is a substantial dictionary, and, in a field noted neither for quantity nor quality, is at least there to be used. English criticisms will carry rather more weight when someone from the English side gets down to work on producing a top quality dictionary of English and Icelandic.

610 Islenzk-ensk orðabók. (Icelandic-English dictionary.)
Arngrímur Sigurðsson. Reykjavík: Prentsmiðjan Leiftur; New York: Heinman, 1980. 3rd ed. 925p.

Considering the general bemoaning of the narrow range and variable quality of Icelandic dictionaries for the English-speaking user, this dictionary has done well to attract a grudging acceptance, *faute de mieux*. In fact, although it cannot claim to be a specialist's dictionary (it offers neither grammatical nor etymological glosses to the words included), its word for word failure rate for even the most serious student is commendably low, and it includes many phraseological extensions of the commoner words. The dictionary contains around 65,000 words (a high figure by any standard, and exceptional in a case such as Icelandic); the

Language. Dictionaries (Old and modern Icelandic)

layout and presentation are remarkably clear, and its purchase price reasonable in relation to its size and potential market. A rather underrated dictionary which proves itself more than adequate for general purposes, and which includes a fair amount of technical terms. The context symbols appended to many words are a point of interest and usefulness. The only substantial dictionary of Icelandic with an up-to-date orientation.

611 English-Icelandic, Icelandic-English pocket dictionary.
Arnold R. Taylor. Reykjavík: Orðabókaútgáfan, 1972. 384p.

Originally published in two separate volumes (one each way), this dictionary became even handier when it was reprinted in one volume within a durable plastic casing. It is an unpretentious compilation, containing around 5,000 entries in each of the two parts, and can be particularly recommended to the traveller with an ear and an eye to the Icelandic language (it includes indications of the genders of Icelandic nouns in both parts). It is fairly cheap to buy, and, as it really does fit into a pocket, is well worthwhile having about one's person when travelling around Iceland.

612 Icelandic phrasebook.
Henrik Thorlacius. Akranes, Iceland: Prentverk Akranes, 1956. 160p.

It is unfortunate that this guide is not easier to get hold of, because, as far as phrasebooks go, it is more detailed, helpful and relevant than one has a right to expect in the case of a country without a mass tourist market. Compiled by an Icelandic teacher of foreign students, it is divided into two sections: the first is the phrasebook itself, arranged by situation or activity; each sub-section starts with its own short vocabulary, followed by the phrases in English with the Icelandic translation, and pronunciation in phonetic transcript. The second half comprises a short grammar of the Icelandic language.

613 How to say it in Icelandic.
J. G. Shepstone. Reykjavík: Orðabókaútgáfan, 1966. 82p.

Although English is well and widely spoken in Iceland, there are many occasions when some basic Icelandic phrases can be of help to the foreign visitor. Unfortunately, this particular phrasebook cannot really be recommended as a good example of its type. In an Icelandic context, the inclusion of a section on travelling by train is about as relevant as would be a section on rickshaws in London in an English phrasebook; also, phrases such as 'When shall were arrive at the frontier?' would seem to suggest a lack of awareness. That said, this phrasebook can still be of help in certain situations, and is at least fairly readily available. But the market is still open for a really relevant and practical phrasebook for foreign visitors to Iceland.

Language. Modern Icelandic. Grammars and courses

Modern Icelandic

Grammars and courses

614 A primer of modern Icelandic.
Snæbjörn Jónsson. Oxford, England: Oxford University Press, 1927. 282p.

This was the first manual of the modern Icelandic language for the English-speaking student. The narrow range of Icelandic language aids, combined with certain traditional qualities displayed by this grammar, has led to its being reprinted several times during the last fifty years. Its merit is that of the traditional grammar: authoritative presentation of the formal framework of grammar, with exercises and dialogues, a wide range of reading texts, and vocabularies from English to Icelandic and vice versa; its disadvantage is likewise that of the traditional grammar: it communicates the rules rather than the feel of the language, and the day-to-day idioms and vocabulary are underrepresented. It remains useful as a formal reference grammar.

615 Icelandic grammar, texts, glossary.
Stefán Einarsson. Baltimore, Maryland: Johns Hopkins University Press, 1949. Reprinted 1972. 502p.

A part of the original impetus for the compilation of this grammar was the need for a language course for use by American military personnel bound for Iceland during the Second World War. In practice its subsequent use has been far wider, as for over thirty years it remained the most substantial grammar of modern Icelandic available to the English-speaking student, and, indeed, formed the basis for the Linguaphone recorded Icelandic course (q.v.) along with which it is still supplied. However, it is best regarded as the standard reference grammar, rather than as the course for the complete beginner. The section on pronunciation is particularly valuable, and both the inflectional and syntactic features of the language are treated in considerable detail; the selection of passages for reading exercise is varied, if inevitably a little dated in terms of the daily colloquial language of modern Reykjavík. Any serious student of modern Icelandic will require regular access to this grammar.

616 A modern Icelandic reader for foreign students.
Halldór Halldórsson. Reykjavík: Menntamálaráðuneyti, 1957. 150p.

A selection of prose and verse by Icelandic writers of the later period, followed by notes in English explaining points of difficulty. Produced by the Icelandic Ministry of Education mainly for use by students with some knowledge of Icelandic requiring to broaden their vocabulary.

617 Teach yourself Icelandic.
P. J. T. Glendening. London: English Universities Press; New York: McKay, 1961. 190p.

One of the tried, and, on the whole, trusted volumes in the *Teach Yourself* language series. This presentation comprises twenty lessons, appendices illustrating the grammatical features, a rather confusing introduction to pronunciation, a section on idioms and proverbs, exercises with keys, and a basic everyday vocabu-

195

Language. Modern Icelandic. Grammars and courses

lary, plus a rather uneven sketch of the changes from old to modern Icelandic. Students without an awareness of grammatical terminology will, despite the title, need to be guided through this course, but to those with knowledge of another inflected language it can be guardedly recommended for individual study. Provided that the student can survive the first four lessons, which do little to support the author's encouragement that one should not get bogged down by the 'inflectional luggage' of Icelandic, then he or she may well stay the course and be duly rewarded, but even in the first chapter one is confronted with the presentation of strong (as opposed to weak), masculine (as opposed to feminine and neuter) nouns, themselves 'divided into three categories, which have four, three and three subdivisions respectively'. In short, this grammar is worth the considerable effort of study, but must be used in conjunction with other less formal materials, such as newspapers, to counteract the partially inevitable rigidity of its presentation.

618 Icelandic phonetics and pronunciation.
Joseph Kelly, Helga Kress. Reykjavík: Heimspekideild Háskolans, 1972. 40p.

This is a useful booklet for those students with some grounding in modern Icelandic to improve their pronunciation by means of drill patterns. Published by the Philosophical Faculty of the University of Iceland. Sidney Rufus Smith (q.v.) draws the student's attention to another item by Kelly and Kress, which takes the form of a mimeographed course in Icelandic, and which was likewise in use at the University; he saw it only briefly, and the compiler of this bibliography has not managed to track it down at all, for it appears to have been withdrawn by one of its authors, although some copies circulate unofficially.

619 Linguaphone Icelandic course.
London: Linguaphone Institute, 1975.

This course, one in the well-known series of audio-courses in foreign languages, comprises much material from Stefán Einarsson's grammar (q.v.). The original course was produced in 1945, and could not be recommended on account of the self-defeatingly poor quality of the recording. Thirty years later, however, a completely new recording was produced, with the participation of four Icelandic actors, and the course is now a useful and presentable package for the learner suited to this type of self-instruction. It is available either on record or cassette, and the pack includes a copy of Stefán Einarsson's grammar, plus explanatory notes and vocabularies. An expensive acquisition. Another audio-course entitled *Icelandic conversations* was compiled by Kenneth G. Chapman, Pétur Pétursson and Erla Tryggvadóttir, and produced by Harvard University in 1965 in the form of tapes accompanied by mimeographed text, but it is not available through commercial channels.

620 Icelandic in easy stages.
Einar Pálsson. Reykjavík: Mímir Language School, 1975-77. 2 vols.

A very useful and well-constructed course by the Director of the Mímir Language School. This mimeographed course is designed primarily for use with an instructor, and includes graded lessons for practice in colloquial Icelandic, with simple texts and conversations, common phrases, and hints on grammar, plus a very relevant vocabulary arranged by topic. Einar Pálsson describes his methods of teaching Icelandic to foreigners 'as quickly as possible and as painlessly as the language can be taught' in an article entitled 'Spoken Icelandic', *Sixty-five Degrees* (Iceland), vol. 2, no. 2 (spring 1968), p. 18-20+26.

Language. Modern Icelandic. Linguistic theory

621 A course in modern Icelandic.
Jón Friðjónsson. Reykjavík: Tímaritið Skák, 1978. 333p.

The chief advantages of this excellent course lie in its up-to-date approach, and in the way in which it has drawn on the experiences of teaching modern Icelandic to foreign students at the University of Iceland. Its only disadvantages are that it presupposes a familiarity with grammatical terminology, and that it can be used successfully only with accompanying instruction from a teacher. The book is divided into twenty-two chapters, each of which contains a reading text with full vocabulary, a grammar lesson with exercises, and a translation test. There is a useful index of grammatical features, but the lack of a cumulated vocabulary is a hindrance, as retrospective searching for the meaning of a word used previously entails finding the relevant chapter. Given the complexities of the Icelandic language, this course is a commendably clear presentation of the grammatical practicalities, and will repay diligent study. A smaller companion volume contains pattern drills and further vocabulary. Not cheap to buy, but an investment in terms of its linguistic value.

Linguistic theory

622 On complementation in Icelandic.
Höskuldur Þráinsson. New York: Garland, 1979. 507p.

A highly-specialised research study, originally submitted as a doctoral dissertation to Harvard University, of an aspect of the syntax of the verb in modern Icelandic. The work is directed at the theoretical linguist, and draws on the framework and arguments associated with transformational generative grammar. The author applies a branch of linguistic theory to the Icelandic language, and, conversely, draws lessons from Icelandic syntax for the theory of linguistics.

623 Quantity in historical phonology: Icelandic and related cases.
Kristján Árnason. Cambridge, England: Cambridge University Press, 1980. 234p. bibliog.

This specialised research monograph comprises an examination of Icelandic phonology, in which the findings are used to pose more general questions of linguistic theory. The Icelandic language is analysed in this respect from 1200 to the present; the chapter on the phonological transition from early to modern Icelandic is a particularly valuable exposition. Reference may also be made to a related work by Sarah Garmes, based upon a doctoral dissertation presented to the Ohio State University in 1974, and published under the title *Quantity in Icelandic* (Hamburg, GFR: Buske, 1976. 287p).

State of the language

624 Modern Icelandic: an essay.
Halldór Hermannsson. Ithaca, New York: Cornell University Library, 1919. 66p. (Islandica vol. XII).

An extended essay on the development of the modern Icelandic language. The author examines its natural development, and the ways in which grammarians and administrators have sought to influence it, as well as its prospects for survi-

Language. Modern Icelandic. State of the language

val. The only cursive treatment of the topic in English. Still available in reprint by Kraus.

625 How 'archaic' is modern Icelandic?
Ulrich Grönke. In: *Studies for Einar Haugen.* The Hague, Netherlands: Mouton, 1972. p. 253-60.

Parallel with the concept of the unity of the Icelandic language is that of its stability stemming from its isolation from developments in the other Norse languages. A popular generalisation is that of modern Icelanders reading the old sagas with only little less ease than they would a contemporary novel. The purpose of this paper is to show that this diachronic stability is only relative. The author concludes that Icelandic linguistic archaism is counterbalanced by a good deal of modernism: 'this may disappoint the romantic; it will not surprise the linguist'.

626 Growth of vocabulary in modern Icelandic.
R. J. McClean. London: Birbeck College, 1950. 30p.

The text of an inaugural lecture which briefly deals with the transition from early to modern Icelandic, before concentrating on the response of the modern language to new lexical concepts. Particular attention is paid to the way in which it has absorbed, adapted or substituted foreign words in the fields of commerce, transport, technology and sport.

627 Icelandic dialectology: methodology and results.
Hreinn Benediktsson. *Íslenzk tunga* (Iceland), vol. 3 (1961-62), p. 72-113.

There has long existed a paradox whereby the Icelanders' own view of their language as exhibiting no dialects has contrasted with the views of some foreign linguists who have claimed otherwise. Hreinn Benediktsson's article was really the first systematic examination of the question, and has since been frequently cited as the core paper; it is fitting that it should have appeared in Iceland's leading linguistic periodical, and convenient that it appears in English. He discusses regional differences in vocabulary, morphology, pronunciation, etc., the differences between *harðmæli* and *linmæli* ('hard' and 'lax' speech), and the age of certain differences, especially the generally acknowledged variation between *hv* and *kv*. He also considers recent and possible future changes. Throughout the article, one is aware of the author's initial caveat in defining the term dialect, particularly when one may mean only 'regional variation', but on this basis he concludes that, in spite of Iceland's comparative homogeneity, there are internal factors which would lead one to except greater linguistic variation than is in fact found.

628 On standard, substandard and slang in Icelandic.
Ulrich Grönke. *Scandinavian Studies*, vol. 38 (1966), p. 217-29.

A discussion of the status of *sletta* (*að sletta* means 'to splash about') or the generally acceptable substandard, whereby a Danish word is adapted to the phonetic structure of Icelandic, and of *götumál* ('street language') or slang in its more usual sense, the origins of which are to be found mostly in American-English through the dual influence of the NATO base and of American media distribution in Iceland, and which is to be heard in words such as *óboj* (oh boy!), *gæi* (guy), *pæja* (pie = sweety pie), etc. The unity of the Icelandic language may still be virtually intact from the dialectal point of view, and the purist movement

Language. Modern Icelandic. State of the language

has been successful in restricting conventional loanwords in Icelandic to a proportion lower than in any other Germanic language. Grönke presented further examples of these features in a paper entitled 'Sletta and Götumál' at the Second International Conference of Nordic and General Linguistics, and which was published in the conference volume *The Nordic languages and modern linguistics, vol. 2* (Stockholm: Almqvist & Wiksell, 1975, p. 475-85.). *Götumál* expressions are also described by Oscar F. Jones in an article in an earlier issue of *Scandinavian Studies*, vol. 36 (1964), p. 59-64.

629 Foreign words in Icelandic.
Árni Böðvarsson. *Sixty-five Degrees* (Iceland), no. 10 (June 1970), p. 31-38.

An Icelandic lexicographer (see Árni Böðvarsson's *Íslenzk orðabok handa skólum i almenningi* q.v.) here writes for the general reader about the ways in which the Icelandic language, perhaps more in its spoken than its written form, has, with some reluctance, borrowed or adapted foreign words and rather more ingeniously, found native words or roots to convey the new concepts arising from social and technological developments on the international scene. He presents many of the commonly encountered examples.

630 Some onomastic and toponomastic aspects of Icelandic traditionalism.
W. H. Wolf-Rottray. *Names*, vol. 19, no. 4 (1971), p. 229-39.

'The strictures of later measures to ward off foreign word influences - an attitude eventually hardened into an unparalleled official, government-supported protectionism, bears witness to the fact that Icelanders, in view of the nation's paucity in numbers and her geographical situation, not only consider their language to be the criterion of their national existence to a much higher degree than other nations would theirs, but also to deem the preservation of its continuity to be of vital importance'. Against this background, whereby the unmodified intrusion of foreign words has been held to be the main threat to the traditional purity of a language in all respects remarkably stable, the author discusses the popularisation of foreign names in Icelandic (both placenames and personal names), with copious examples. See Richard, F. Tomasson's 'The continuity of Icelandic names and naming patterns' (q.v.).

631 Zur Sprachpolitik und Sprachpflege in Island.
Jón Hilmar Jónsson. *Muttersprache*, vol. 88, no. 6 (1978), p. 353-62.

An Icelandic view of how the historical advantages bestowed upon the Icelandic language in relation to its linguistic purity are being diminished by the pressures of internationalisation. The author of this article discusses language policy and 'care' of the language in the face of neologisms, whether imported or internally generated. An earlier article in the same vein by the Belgian, Pierre Halleux entitled 'Le purisme islandais' appeared in the French periodical *Études germaniques*, vol. 20 (1965), p. 417-27.

Language. Modern Icelandic. State of the language

632 Icelandic purism and its history.
Halldór Halldórsson. *Word* (US), vol. 30, no. 1-2 (April-Aug. 1979), p. 76-87.

A paper full of interesting points concerning attitudes towards the character of the Icelandic language over the centuries. In his discussion of new words, which the author sees as more likely to be accommodated by highly inflected languages with their capacity for word formation (he contrasts the significance and popularity of new coinages in Icelandic compared with Danish, Norwegian and Swedish) he traces the first awareness of the purity of Icelandic back to the 17th century, with reference to the scholar Arngrímur Jónsson, then to Jón Olafsson and the lasting movement for new formations instead of loanwords, the stance of the Icelandic Society for the Learned Arts in the late 18th century, and the 19th century views in the context of the nationalist and romantic movements in which language policy was spearheaded by the Latin school at Bessastaðir and the editors of the periodical *Fjölnir*; he discusses removal of the significance and popular-acter of the dictionaries. He concludes by identifying four principles upon which Icelandic purism is based: the speech of ordinary educated people from rural areas; the patterns of speech in Old Icelandic literature; the patterns of the best modern authors; and the avoidance of loanwords except when they can be easily adapted to the Icelandic inflectional and phonetic system - the so-called *nýyrdastefna*. He appends notes on orthography, with reference to the controversial abolition of the letter z, and a useful list of seven committees and institutions concerned with language planning in Iceland.

633 The pronouns of address in present-day Icelandic.
Oscar F. Jones. *Scandinavian Studies*, vol. 37 (1965), p. 245-58.

A discussion of the state of usage of the 'familiar' and the 'polite' forms of the second person pronoun in Icelandic. Evidence suggests a continuing punctiliousness amongst some people in using Þér to strangers and Þú to friends or acquaintances, but also a weakening of the distinction among others which could lead to the elimination of the formal pronoun. See the specialist review article by Einar Haugen entitled 'Pronominal address in modern Icelandic: from 'you two' to 'you all', *Language in Society* (UK), vol. 4 (1975), p. 323-39, concerning the change from the use of the dual pronoun to the polite singular.

634 Modern Icelandic personal bynames.
Christopher S. Hale. *Scandinavian Studies*, vol. 53, no. 4 (autumn 1981), p. 397-404.

The Old Norse practice of the byname (a form of nickname) has survived in Iceland probably because of the continued use of the patronymic system. Although the use of personal bynames is virtually extinct in the urbanised areas of the country, it persists to a degree in rural areas. The contributor of this interesting paper examines the practice and cites numerous examples.

635 Use of Reykjavík streetnames.
Oscar F. Jones. *Scandinavian Studies*, vol. 42, no. 2 (May 1970), p. 190-96.

A paper identifying and giving the meaning of many of the frequently occurring words which form part of the compound names of streets in the capital city; these can be appreciated by the person who speaks no Icelandic. For the foreigner requiring to use the street names in conversation, the writer sets out, with examples, the way in which street names are used with prepositions.

Language. Modern Icelandic. State of the language

636 **Abbreviation rules in modern Icelandic.**
Pardee Lowe. *Scandinavian Studies*, vol. 42, no. 3 (Aug. 1970), p. 334-42.

Abbreviated forms are no less of a nuisance in Icelandic than in other languages. Dictionaries of abbreviations are notoriously prone to user failure, because of the often arbitrary, idiosyncratic or pressurised nature of modern abbreviations. This article, for the linguistic specialist, is an attempt to formulate a set of rules observable in Icelandic abbreviation, using a generative approach. The rules themselves may be of linguistic interest, but are hardly worth mastering for any practical purposes.

637 **The awful Icelandic language.**
Brendan Glacken. *Atlantica and Iceland Review*, vol. 11, no. 3-4 (1977), p. 46-62.

An Irish sense of humour is here brought to bear upon the familiar frustrations associated with learning the Icelandic language. A divertissement, but one which will bring a wry and knowing smile to the faces of those foreigners who have made the attempt, whether successfully or unsuccessfully. A fitting last word on this section!

Notes on Icelandic kinship terminology.
See item no. 380.

Literature, Old Icelandic

Texts and translations

Anthologies

638 **Translations from the Icelandic.**
Translated and edited by W. C. Green. London: Chatto & Windus, 1908. 260p. (The King's Classics). Reprinted Totowa, New Jersey: Cooper Square Press, 1966.
A modest but well-balanced selection of introductory passages from Old Icelandic literature, containing prose from the *Prose Edda* and the sagas, verse from the *Poetic Edda* and the sagas, as well as some of the passion psalms and other sacred poetry of the 17th century father-figure Hallgrímur Pétursson. The translations are close rather than creative, but the translator attempted, with some success, to preserve the rhyming, alliterative and other features of the poetic selections. Later anthologies may display more imagination, but this volume has a 'period' feeling which may still appeal to the bibliophile, and was considered to be worth reprinting half a century later.

639 **A pageant of old Scandinavia.**
Edited by Henry Goddard Leach. New York: American-Scandinavian Foundation, 1946. 350p. bibliog.
'Pageant' is a fair description of this volume: it comprises a varied and balanced selection of extracts from Old Norse prose and poetry in English translation by several hands. The themes of this anthology embrace the Scandinavian world, but 'it was in Iceland that the literary genius of old Scandinavia was concentrated as Icelandic became the Athens of the north... the concentrated metrical testimony of runic inscriptions, the lyric and dramatic passages of the Poetic Edda, the passionate intensity and elaborate skills of the untranslatable skaldic verse, the lucid and selective histories of Snorri Sturluson, and the dramatic records of fact

Literature, Old Icelandic. Texts and translations. Poetry

in the sagas of Iceland, make the production of ancient Scandinavia highly important in the golden treasury of letters'. This volume offers a rewarding opportunity for the uninitiated to introduce themselves to the total atmosphere of Norse literature. The analytical list of sources appended is useful.

640 The northmen talk: a choice of tales from Iceland.
Translated and with an introduction by Jacqueline Simpson. London: Phoenix House; Madison, Wisconsin: University of Wisconsin Press, 1965. 290p.

A selection which can be highly recommended as an introduction to the spirit of Old Icelandic literature. The choice of texts is imaginative, the translation sympathetic and the introduction helpful. The anthology comprises tales from the Eddic lays of gods and heroes; biographical, chronicle and semi-historical narrative; realistic and fantastic tales; and the imported ballads. The family sagas are perhaps underrepresented, but this volume is an excellent appetiser.

641 The Norse myths.
Introduced and re-told by Kevin Crossley-Holland. London: Deutsch; New York: Pantheon Books, 1981. Harmondsworth, England: Penguin, 1982. 296p. bibliog.

An attractive and lively re-telling, in English prose, of thirty-two of the Norse myths, taken from the *Poetic Edda* and *Prose Edda*. The style has a considerable spirit, and with occasional explanatory passages and aspects from other sources worked into the stories, the aim, successfully accomplished, is to present the myths in a form which will appeal to a general readership. The translator, himself a poet and an author with a reputation in writing books for the younger reader, has written a stimulating introduction with a broad canvas, and appends background notes to each myth, a glossary of proper names, bibliography and index. Kevin Crossley-Holland also edited the *Faber Book of Northern Legends* (1977), in which stories from the *Eddas* and sagas are translated by various hands.

Poetry - Eddic, skaldic, early Christian

642 Corpus poeticum boreale: the poetry of the old northern tongue from the earliest times to the thirteenth century.
Edited and translated by Guðbrandur Vigfússon, F. York Powell. Oxford, England: Clarendon Press, 1883. 2 vols. Reprinted New York: Russell, 1965.

The pioneering work on Old Norse poetry, to which all subsequent editors and translators have had to refer in depth. The first volume comprises the Eddic poems, the second comprises the skaldic or court poetry. The fact that a century after its original appearance this work is still held in esteem is a testimony to its scope and scholarship. Vigfússon and Powell also edited the corpus of Old Icelandic prose (q.v.).

Literature, Old Icelandic. Texts and translations. Poetry

643 **The poetic Edda.**
Translated from the Icelandic with an introduction and notes by Henry Adams Bellows. New York: American-Scandinavian Foundation, 1923. 583p. Reprinted New York: Biblo & Tannen, 1969.

Perhaps the most influential of the 20th century translations of the *Poetic Edda* (sometimes referred to as the *elder Edda* or the *Edda of Sæmund the Wise*). From previous centuries there are the translations by A. S. Cottle in 1797, Benjamin Thorpe in 1866, and Vigfússon/Powell (q.v.). Bellow's translation has served well through a number of reprintings. From a similar date is another fine translation by Lee M. Hollander, (Texas University Press, 1928. 2nd ed. 1962). More recent is Patricia Terry's translation *Poems of the Vikings: the Elder Edda*, (Bobbs Merrill, 1969).

644 **The poetic Edda. Volume I: heroic poems;**
Edited with translation introduction and commentary by Ursula Dronke. Oxford, England: Clarendon Press, 1969. 251p.

Having relied on the Vigfússon/Powell edition for the best part of a century, the Clarendon Press embarked upon the first full critical edition of the *Poetic Edda* for the English-speaking student - it came too late to aid a generation of students (the present compiler included) who were usually referred to the German edition by Neckel, revised by Hans Kuhn in 1962. The four heroic poems in this volume are: *Atlakviða, Atlamál in Grænlenzko, Guðrúnarhvöt,* and *Hamðismál.* The later heroic poems and the mythological poems were planned for three further volumes, which, regrettably, in view of the high degree of scholarship exhibited in this first volume, have not yet appeared. Failing completion of this set, the reader requiring access to the mythological poems can be referred to the previous items in this section, or, specifically, to Olive Bray's edition *The Elder or Poetic Edda, part I: The mythological poems*, illustrated by W. G. Collingwood (London: Viking Club Translation Series, 1908. Reprinted New York: AMS Press, 1979).

645 **Norse poems.**
W. H. Auden, Paul B. Taylor. London: Athlone Press, 1981. 256p.

Old Icelandic poetry at first sight seems to have certain features which make it suitable for straightforward translation into English; hence the many attempts over the last two centuries. However, a comparison of these attempts with the original and with each other, however respectable, encourages deeper thought. Can it be translated at all without failing to convey its towering qualities and its unique spirit? It has taken a poet of the stature of Auden to do it the highest degree of justice in translation that it will probably ever achieve. Taylor has done the editorial spadework from which Auden himself has worked, although Auden could read Icelandic and also worked from the original. This volume, the complete collection of Auden's translations from the *Poetic Edda*, contains the twenty-nine poems of the *Codex Regius*, plus further associated poems; it is divided into three sections:- the Viking poems, the Niflung poems, and the mythological poems (which include his magnificent translation of *Hávamál*). Some readers may regret the absence of an introductory essay to this collection, or of any explanatory notes, but this uncluttered and attractively produced presentation allows the poems, through Auden, to speak for themselves - there is nothing to distract, all to appreciate. The earlier collection of Auden and Taylor, which was published under the title *The Elder Edda* (London: Faber; New York:

Literature, Old Icelandic. Texts and translations. Poetry

Random House, 1969. Paperback ed. 1973), served admirably for twelve years, and may still do so in view of its introduction, notes and glossary, but the further twenty or so poems in the new collection, itself reasonably priced for its quality, commend it as one of the first books to show up on the bookshelves of anyone with a feeling for the heritage of Iceland.

646 **The Hávamál, with selections from other poems of the Edda, illustrating the wisdom of the north in heathen times.**
Edited and translated by D. E. Martin-Clarke. Cambridge, England: Cambridge University Press, 1923. 124p.

Hávamál (*Sayings of the High One*) is the longest of the Eddic poems, and is a remarkable piece of humanistic literature, offering counsel on the conduct of life. As a poem it has the unwavering quality of not wasting a single syllable, being taut, pithy and transporting. Only Auden has matched it in translation, although as a more conventional version this edition, and its notes, has still some help to offer.

647 **Völuspá.**
Edited by Sigurđur Nordal, translated by B. S. Benedikz, John McKinnell. Durham, England: University of Durham, Department of English Language and Medieval Literature; St. Andrews, Scotland: University of St. Andrews, Department of English, 1978. 165p. (Durham and St. Andrews Medieval Texts, no. 1).

Völuspá (*Song of the Sybil*) is perhaps the most magnificent of the mythological poems of the *Poetic Edda*. It is a visionary poem, which traces the shifts in the course of the world from its creation out of chaos to its destruction and ultimate re-creation when gods and men will live in harmony. This enterprising edition, the first of a series which will concentrate on texts, 'which are either not readily available in adequate editions in English, or which can be obtained only at a price which puts them out of reach of most undergraduates', is an English version of the commentary and notes of Professor Sigurđur Nordal's classic edition of *Völuspá* published in Reykjavík in 1923 (rev. ed. 1952). A glossary has been added. See Sigurđur Nordal's essay 'The author of Völuspá', likewise translated by Benedikz in *Saga-book*, vol. 20, no. 1-2 (1978-79), p. 114-30, in which he attempts to deduce the traditions, motivation and character of the unknown author from the language and images of the poem.

648 **Old Norse poems: the most important non-Skaldic verse not included in the Poetic Edda.**
Lee M. Hollander. New York: Columbia University Press, 1963. 115p. Reprinted Kraus, 1973.

The title perhaps has to be read twice, but its implication is clear: it is possible to forget that, in addition to the two major poetic corpuses in Old Icelandic literature (the *Poetic Edda* and the skaldic poems), there remains a considerable collection of lays of quality and variety; earlier heroic lays such as *Bjarkamál*, later romantic or elegiac lays such as *Hjálmar's death song*, and celebratory lays such as the *Lay of Harald* (Fairhair). Sixteen poems are introduced and translated in this collection, including the later Christian poem *Sólarljóđ* or *Lay of the Sun*.

Literature, Old Icelandic. Texts and translations. Poetry.

649 **The Skalds: a selection of their poems.**
Introduction and notes by Lee M. Hollander. Princeton, New Jersey: Princeton University Press for the American-Scandinavian Foundation, 1945. 216p.

An admirable introduction to the work of thirteen of the skaldic poets. One of the major differences in our knowledge of the Eddic and skaldic poems is that in many cases we know who the skaldic poets were. Each of them is separately introduced, and the translations, remarkable in themselves, are clearly presented within the context of the events described in the poems. The general introduction covers the place of the skald within the court circle, and the complex technical framework of the poems. Hollander advanced the study of the skalds still further with his compilation *A bibliography of Skaldic studies* (q.v.).

650 **Icelandic Christian classics.**
Translated in whole or part with introduction by Charles Venn Pilcher. Melbourne, Australia: London: Oxford University Press, 1950. 60p.

Translations in the original metre from two of the mediaeval sacred poems of Iceland, which are renowned for their spiritual force and exquisite composition. The anonymous *Lay of the Sun* (*Sólarljóð*) dates from the early 13th century and is in many ways a culmination of Eddic poetry: 'it baptises this older poetry (i.e. *Hávamál, Völuspá*) into Christ'. The core of the poem concerns the return of a dead father to tell his son of the horrors of hell and of the joys of heaven. It has been seen as an allegorical commentary upon the age of the Sturlungs and its earthly intrigues. The second poem, *Lily*, is from the following century and is described in *Lilja: an Icelandic religious poem of the fourteenth century* (q.v.). This collection also contains translated extracts from the *Passion hymns of Hallgrímur Pétursson* (q.v.), and of the millennial hymn by Matthías Jochumsson.

651 **Lilja (The Lily): an Icelandic religious poem of the fourteenth century.**
Eystein Ásgrímsson, edited with a metrical translation notes and glossary by Eiríkr Magnússon. London: Williams & Norgate, 1870. 124p.

If the *Lay of the Sun* is a baptism of Eddic poetry, *The Lily* is a baptism of skaldic poetry. Written around 1350, it is a jewel of Icelandic literature of any period. Representing the mediaeval world-view of the Bible story it exerted a profound influence on the Icelandic people during the dark centuries, through its sublime vision and the beauty of its poetry. Eiríkr Magnússon was first to bring it to the attention of English readers with this parallel text edition, which he illuminates with an introduction to the poem and its author.

The North American book of Icelandic verse.
See item no. 776.

Literature, Old Icelandic. Texts and translations. Prose Edda

Prose Edda

652 The Prose Edda.
Snorri Sturluson, translated with an introduction by Arthur
G. Brodeur. New York: American-Scandinavian
Foundation, 1916. 266p. Reprinted 1960.

The so-called *Prose Edda* (otherwise known as the *younger Edda* or *Snorra Edda*) dates from the early 13th century, and is a remarkable work which is arranged in four sections: a *prologue*; *Gylfaginning* (the deluding of Gylfi), in which a wise king travels in disguise to Asgard, the home of the gods, to learn the secrets of the world (presented by Snorri in the form of questions and answers), whereby the reader is offered an exposition of the Norse mythology of the *Poetic Edda*; *Skáldskaparmál* (the language of poetry) is a form of textbook of the complicated diction of poetry, particularly skaldic poetry, in which Bragi, the god of poetry, reveals his art; the final part, *Háttatal* (metrical list) is an ingenious rather than creative poem to King Hákon, composed in a hundred metrical variations, and illustrating the points made in the previous section. Brodeur's edition has lasted well (see his explanatory work *The meaning of Snorri's categories* (University of California Press, 1952). An early translation of Snorri's *Edda* was that by Sir George Webbe Dasent, (London: Pickering, 1842). For a more recent translation (in part only) see *The Prose Edda of Snorri Sturluson: tales from Norse mythology*; selected and translated by Jean I. Young, with an introduction by Sigurður Nordal (Cambridge: Bowes & Bowes, 1954, 131p. Reprinted Berkeley, California: University of California Press, 1964). An important new edition of two parts of Snorri's *Edda*, the *prologue* and *Gylfaginning* (Oxford, England: Clarendon Press, 1982, 177p.) was edited by Anthony Fawkes, Reader in Old Icelandic at the University of Birmingham. The text is accompanied by an introduction to the background of its author, contents, sources and manuscripts, plus notes, glossary and bibliography.

Sagas

653 Origines Islandicae..
Edited and translated by Guðbrandur Vigfússon, F. York
Powell. Oxford, England: Clarendon Press, 1905. 2 vols.
Reprinted Kraus, 1976.

The subtitle of this pioneering work of traditional scholarship defines its scope: 'a collection of the more important sagas and vernacular writings relevant to the settlement and early history of Iceland'. For nearly half a century this work with its companion set covering the poetic corpus - *Corpus poeticum boreale: the poetry of the old northern tongue from earliest times to the thirteenth century* (q.v.) - was the foreign student's bible for the study of Old Icelandic texts: one reason for its popularity among students was its page arrangement, which presents the Icelandic text at the top and the English version immediately beneath. The convenience, if not the scholarship, of these volumes has now been superseded with the appearance of many more texts of individual prose works in modern editions, but the cumulative index of persons and places mentioned in the sources remains of value. Other Icelandic sagas relating to the Viking settlements were also presented by Guðbrandur Vigfússon in *Icelandic sagas and other historical documents relating to the settlements and descents of the Northmen on the British Isles* (London: HM Stationery Office, 1887-94. 4 vols.). These were issued by the Public Record Office in its series of mediaeval writings on Britain,

Literature, Old Icelandic. Texts and translations. Kings' sagas

and contain facsimiles of *Orkneyinga saga*, with *Magnús saga* and *Hákonar saga*, plus translations by Sir George Webbe Dasent. Reprinted by Kraus in 1964.

Íslendingabók. (The Book of the Icelanders.)
See item no. 306.

Landnámabók. (The Book of the Settlements.)
See item no. 307.

Sturlunga saga.
See item no. 309.

Kings' sagas

654 **Heimskringla.**
Snorri Sturluson, translated by Samuel Laing. London: Dent; New York: Dutton, 1914-30. rev. ed. 1961-64. 3 vols. (Everyman's Library).

Snorri's *Heimskringla* (*Circle of the World*) can be placed amongst the most eminent historical works written anywhere during the mediaeval period. In this work, Iceland's greatest writer displays both the artistic and the scientific facets of the true craft of the historian. *Heimskringla* is basically concerned with the history of the kings of Norway from the earliest times up to 1177, the year before Snorri's birth. The core of the whole work is formed by the two *Ólaf sagas* (King Ólaf Tryggvason and King Ólaf the Saint), which in this edition makes up the two volumes of part one. Part two comprises the sagas of the other Norse kings. The later edition is revised with an introduction by Peter Foote and Jacqueline Simpson. Laing's original translation appeared in 1844. Another translation to be recommended is that by Lee M. Hollander (Austin, Texas: University of Texas Press, 1964, 854p.). This edition also offers a valuable introduction. Erling Monsen's translation (Cambridge, England: Heffer, 1931, 770p.) is also noteworthy. A shortened version was published in Stornoway, Scotland by Thule Press in 1980.

655 **King Harald's saga, from Snorri Sturluson's Heimskringla.**
Translated with an introduction by Magnús Magnússon, Hermann Pálsson. Harmondsworth, England: Penguin, 1966. 180p. maps. table.

This 'saga history', written about 170 years after the death of Harald Harðraði of Norway, tells, in Snorri's fluent style, the violent story of Harald's adventures throughout Europe until his defeat and death at the battle of Stamford Bridge in 1066 against King Harold Godwinsson of England, which effectively ended the Viking era. This fast moving translation is accompanied by a substantial introduction, glossary of proper names, chronological table and maps.

656 **Sverrissaga, the saga of Sverrir of Norway.**
Translated by John Sephton. London: Nutt, 1899. 310p. 8 maps. (Northern Library).

The saga of King Sverrir of Norway, who died in 1202, is probably the oldest of the Kings' sagas, and was composed in the monastery at Þingeyrar, perhaps three-quarters of a century after his death. It is somewhat surprising that this is

Literature, Old Icelandic. Texts and translations. Sagas of Icelanders

the only full translation of this saga from Icelandic into English, as it is the most impressive of the Kings' sagas outside *Heimskringla*, both in its form and its artistic style. Chronologically, it continues the events from where Snorri stopped, and it reflects some of Snorri's qualities. Written shortly after Iceland's capitulation to Norway.

657 The saga of the Jómvíkings.
Translated from the Old Icelandic with introduction and notes by Lee M. Hollander, illustrated by M. Thurgood. Austin, Texas: University of Texas Press, 1955. 116p.

A saga somewhat on its own in style and subject matter, but usually classified with the Kings' sagas. It is known that this saga left an impression on home-based Icelanders in its depiction and semi-historical recording of the activities of the band of Baltic warriors known as the *Jómsvíkings*, which culminated in the invasion of King Hákon's Norway, and their defeat in the naval battle of Hjörunga Bay in 986. Five Icelandic skaldic poets at the Norwegian court are known to have participated in the events described, and to have composed verses accordingly. Although not strong on characterisation, this saga is simply and skilfully told, and is, above all, an action-packed story. A parallel Icelandic/English text edition of this saga, translated with introduction, notes and appendices by N. F. Blake, was published in Nelson's Icelandic Texts Series (London, 1962. 56p.).

Sagas of Icelanders

658 The saga library.
Translated by William Morris, Eiríkr Magnússon. London: Quaritch, 1891-1905. 6 vols.

The Morris/Magnússon collaboration on the translation of the Icelandic sagas has its admirers and detractors, but what must be generally conceded is its profusion, its enthusiasm, and its effect upon the furtherance of the study of the country and its heritage. These colleagues did perhaps their best work on the legendary sagas (q.v.), and this collection is somewhat unbalanced: the last four of the six volumes comprise a translation of Snorri's *Heimskringla*, but the first two volumes contain a selection of sagas of Icelanders: *Bandamanna saga, Howard the Halt,* and *Hen Thórir* in volume one; *Eyrbyggja saga* and *the Saga of the Heath-Slayings* in volume two; these first two volumes were reprinted in facsimile by Prior of London in 1981. See the same colleagues' anthology *Three northern love stories and other tales* (London: Ellis & White, 1875, 256p.), which includes four sagas/tales of Icelanders: *Gunnlaugs saga, Hávarðar saga (Howard the Halt), Þorsteinn Staff-struck,* and *Víglundar/ Þorgríms saga,* as well as two mythical-heroic tales, *Friðjófs saga, Heðins saga ok Högna,* plus one King's saga, *Roi the Fool.*

Literature, Old Icelandic. Texts and translations. Sagas of Icelanders

659 Four Icelandic sagas.
Translated with an introduction and notes by Gwyn Jones. Princeton, New Jersey; Princeton University Press, 1935. 163p.

Published for the American-Scandinavian Foundation, this collection includes *Hrafnkels saga Freysgoða, Vopnfirðinga saga* (both from the eastern part of Iceland), *Kjalnesinga saga*, and the story of *Þorsteinn the White*. Gwyn Jones' translation of *Vatnsdæla saga* was issued by the same publishers in 1944 (reprinted 1970, 156p.).

660 Three Icelandic sagas.
Translated by M. H. Scargill, Margaret Schlauch. Princeton, New Jersey: Princeton University Press for the American-Scandinavian Foundation, 1950. 150p.

Another set of translations sponsored by the American-Scandinavian Foundation, an organisation which, over the decades, has performed a valuable service in instigating many translations from Icelandic literature for the English reader. This illustrated collection includes the popular *Gunnlaugs saga Ormstungu* (*Wormtongue*), the satirical *Bandamanna saga*, and the perhaps underrated *Droplaugarsona saga*. The volume was reprinted in 1970. A further two sagas of Icelanders were brought together by the ASF in the volume containing Lee M. Hollander's translation of *Kormáks saga* and *Fóstbræðra saga* (*Sworn Brothers*), (1949, 217p.). Both of these sagas are early compositions.

661 The Confederates, and Hen Thórir: two Icelandic sagas.
Translated with an introduction by Hermann Pálsson. Edinburgh: Southside, 1975. 139p. (UNESCO collection of representative works. Icelandic Translations Series).

Two sagas from western Iceland which share a common quality of structural unity and precision, in which every detail contributes to or derives from the major action or central incident. *The Confederates* (*Bandamanna saga*) has acquired the wider reputation of the two because it is the only example of a 'comedy' amongst the sagas - W. P. Ker, in his excellent essay on this saga (q.v.), describes it as 'the first realistic comedy of modern Europe', and, indeed, although many of the sagas display comical or satirical features in passages, *Bandamanna saga* is conceived in its entirety as a satirical exposition of the authority and motivations of the age, as eight 'confederate' chieftains attempt to manipulate the law. *Hen Thórir's saga* (*Hænsna Þóris saga*) is a tapestry of clearly and concisely drawn characters, none of them dominant in the story line, but all of them 'geared' to the causes and consequences of the burning to death of Blund Ketil. The edition of *Bandamanna saga* by the Norwegian scholar Hallvard Magerøy has been re-issued with an English translation by Peter Foote of the introduction and notes (Viking Society for Northern Research, 1981, 105p.).

Literature, Old Icelandic. Texts and translations. Sagas of Icelanders

662 Eirík the Red, and other Icelandic sagas.
Selected and translated with an introduction by Gwyn Jones. London: Oxford University Press, 1961. 318p. Reprinted 1980. (World's Classics, 582).

For the newcomer to Icelandic saga literature this selection is particularly suitable. Of the nine stories included, eight are taken from the shorter sagas of Icelanders: *Hrafnkels saga, Gunnlaug Wormtongue, Hen Thórir, Vapnfjord Men, Eirík the Red*, plus the three even shorter tales of *Thorstein Staff-struck, Auðunn and the Bear*, and Þiðrandi. The ninth story is *Hrólfs saga kraka*, one of the so-called 'legendary' sagas. Apart from some omissions of genealogical passages these stories are here presented in their complete form. The translations are in keeping and readable, and the format of the volume convenient and attractive. Reprinted as a paperback in the same series in 1980.

663 The Vinland sagas: the Norse discovery of America.
Harmondsworth, England: Penguin; New York: New York University Press, 1965. 124p. maps.

A clearly translated presentation of the two Icelandic sagas which tell us so much about the attempted colonisation of North America from Iceland via Greenland at the end of the 10th century: *Grœnlendinga saga*, and *Eiríks saga rauða*, the latter seeming to be a revision of the former. This edition is particularly helpful for its lucid introduction to the problems of understanding the Vinland question; also for its descriptive list of proper names of characters and places in the sagas. Maps are also appended. For earlier translations of these two sagas those by Einar Haugen (based on A. M. Reeves) *Voyages to Vinland: the first American saga* (New York: Knopf, 1942, 181p.); and by Halldór Hermannsson *The Vinland sagas* (Ithaca, New York: Cornell University Press, 1944. Islandica, vol. XXX). Translations are also included in Gwyn Jones' valuable work *The Norse Atlantic saga (q.v.)*.

664 Egils saga.
Translated with an introduction by Hermann Pálsson, Paul Edwards. Harmondsworth, England: Penguin, 1976. 254p. maps.

Egils saga Skallagrímssonar is a saga of such compelling variety that it appeals to all in some measure. There is good reason to believe that it was written by Snorri Sturluson, around 1230, and this would undoubtedly help to explain both the peculiar power and the strikingly effective paradoxes of the saga. The character of Egil is unique - in their illuminating introduction the translators identify the major enigmas of Egil's individuality: he is a ruthless viking, but a poet of passion and sensitivity (the saga contains Egil's own poem *Sonatorrek*, a magnificently moving lament for the death of his sons); he is a runic sorcerer, but for both good and evil; a lawyer, but a drunkard; a compulsive wanderer, but an established farmer; generous at times, but at others miserly. 'He is never dull, and though we may not like some of the things he does, we are never allowed to settle into a fixed attitude towards him'. All modern environmental influences must be suppressed in the evaluation and appreciation of this saga in its kaleidoscopic ranging between the vast Viking world and the family farm at Borg in western Iceland. Appendices include a glossary of proper names, and four maps. This saga has attracted several notable attempts at English translation. One early translation was that by W. C. Green, (London: Stock, 1893). Cambridge University Press has published two translations, by E. R. Eddison in 1930 (reprinted by Greenwood Press, 1968), and by Gwyn Jones in 1960 (especially recommended).

211

Literature, Old Icelandic. Texts and translations. Sagas of Icelanders

Another version, commendably uncluttered, is that by Christine Fell (London: Dent, 1975).

665 Eyrbyggja saga.
Translated by Paul Schach, introduction and verse translations by Lee M. Hollander. Lincoln, Nebraska: University of Nebraska Press for the American-Scandinavian Foundation, 1959, reprinted 1977, 140p. map.

Of the longer sagas of Icelanders, *Eyrbyggja saga* is the least unified in that there is no character central to the saga as a whole, nor, indeed, a central story line. It is, rather, a history of events in a particular locality, the Snæfellsness peninsula, in the first two centuries after the settlement of Iceland, and, as such, is rich in information concerning the early practices of the Icelanders. The author of this saga, however, is more than an annalist, for he draws some vivid characters, particularly in the case of Snorri Goði the chieftain. This edition can be recommended for its introduction and lively translation. Includes map of the locality. Another recent translation to be specially noted is that by Hermann Pálsson and Paul Edwards (Edinburgh: Southside Publishers, 1973, 200p. New Saga Library), which is one of the texts in the UNESCO sponsored series of Icelandic translations.

666 The saga of Gísli.
Translated by George Johnston, with notes and essay by Peter Foote. London: Dent; Toronto: Toronto University Press, 1963, paperback, 1973. 146p. maps.

Gísla saga Surssonar is one of the few sagas where there is a clear purpose on the part of the storyteller to move the audience emotionally. It is a genuinely tragic story of death, vengeance, outlawry, blood ties, conflicting loyalties, and, above all, the force of destiny. However, its author is not concerned solely with the telling of a violent tale, for there are tender and humourous moments, and he has clearly mastered the art of cathartic release at the conclusion. The cinematic possibilities of this powerful yet subtle saga were realised in 1981 with the production of a full-length feature film by an Icelandic company (see Árni Þórarinsson's *The outlaw: a saga becomes a screen success*, q.v.). Earlier translations of this saga include the pioneering version by Sir George Webbe Dasent (Edinburgh: Edmonston & Douglas, 1866); a translation entitled *The Outlaw* by Maurice Hewlett (London: Constable, 1919), in the series *The sagas re-told*; also an illustrated edition by Ralph B. Allen (New York: Harcourt, Brace, 1936). For a dramatised version see Beatrice Helen Barmby's *Gísli Súrsson*, a play in three acts, (Westminster: Constable, 1900, 206p.). (This play was accorded the honour of a translation back into Icelandic by the Icelandic national poet Matthías Jochumsson.)

667 Grettir's saga.
Translated by Denton Fox, Hermann Pálsson. Toronto: University of Toronto Press, 1974. 199p.

Grettis saga is one of the great tragic sagas. It falls into three parts: the first part (sometimes identified separately as the *Saga of Önund Treefoot*) concerns the activities of Grettir's ancestors in Norway and Iceland; the second part tells of the life and heroic adventures of Grettir himself, under the dying curse of the unearthly Glámr, which turns Grettir from hero to outlaw (the Glámr episode is one of the purple passages of saga literature); the third part deals with the avenging of Grettir's death. Grettir's saga is generally considered to be the last of

Literature, Old Icelandic. Texts and translations. Sagas of Icelanders

the classical sagas. *Grettla* was a popular saga for translators in the late 19th and early 20th centuries: William Morris and Eiríkr Magnússon's famous version was published in the 1860s (London: Ellis, 2nd ed. 1869), and has retained appeal sufficient to warrant a facsimile reprint (London: Prior 1980); this was followed by that of another Victorian traveller to Iceland, Sabine Baring-Gould. (London: Blackie, 1890); a simplified version taken from Morris and Magnússon was composed by Allen French (New York, Dutton 1908 and reprints); and there is a fine translation by George Ainslie Hight (London: Dent, 1914. Everyman's Library), which merited its new edition in 1965, edited by Peter Foote.

668 Gunnlaugs saga Ormstungu. (The story of Gunnlaug Serpent-Tongue.)
Edited with introduction and notes by P. G. Foote, translated from the Icelandic by R. Quirk. London: Nelson, 1957. 47p. map. (Icelandic Texts Series).

Gunnlaugs saga marks the turning point in the development of the Icelandic saga; whilst retaining some of the spirit of the older sagas, it contains even stronger elements of the later romantic stories which signalled the decline of the 'classical' saga tradition. It is also a short saga and somewhat derivative; one critic has described it as a 'slick best-seller'. But is has remained a very popular saga amongst Icelanders, and has much of interest to offer both in content and in style. This parallel Icelandic/English text edition is accompanied by a helpful introduction, and a map of the Borgarfjörður district, scene of the saga. William Morris and Eiríkr Magnússon included a translation of this saga in their *Three northern love stories* (London: Ellis & White, 1875, p. 1-63).

669 The saga of Hallfred the troublesome Scald.
Translated and introduced by Alan E. Boucher. Reykjavík: Iceland Review, 1981. 96p. (Iceland Review Saga Series).

Hallfreðar saga was composed in the early 13th century, probably in north-western Iceland, and deals with events either side of the year 1,000. Although not generally placed in the forefront of the saga literature, its central character, Hallfred Óttarsson, is one of the most memorable from any saga. Hallfred was court poet, or skald, to King Ólaf Tryggvason of Norway, and he was thus drawn into the debate and action concerning the change from heathendom to Christendom in Iceland. His nickname *vandræði* (troublesome) could be applied to most of his activities, but he is above all an individualist, whose ambivalent attitudes lead the translator to describe him as 'a kind of Hamlet of his times'. The translator's introduction is useful for background information on the saga itself, and for elucidating Hallfred's skaldic verses, over thirty of which are to be found within the story. An appendix contains a translation of Hallfred's long poem *The lay of Ólaf. Hallfreðar saga* is an enjoyable story, and this rare translation is presented in an attractive format for the general reader.

670 Hrafnkel's saga, and other stories.
Translated with an introduction by Hermann Pálsson. Harmondsworth, England: Penguin, 1971. 135p.

If *Njáls saga* is the crown of Old Icelandic literature, *Hrafnkels saga* is the gem. Sigurður Nordal (see *Hrafnkels saga Freysgoða: a study by Sigurður Nordal*, q.v.) described it as one of the most perfect short novels in world literature. It was written in the third quarter of the 13th century, and is set in eastern Iceland. Its structure is the tightest of all the Icelandic sagas, and it is one of the few sagas to concern itself with the development of character, in its story of Hrafnkel

Literature, Old Icelandic. Texts and translations. Sagas of Icelanders

Freysgoði ('the Priest of Frey'), whose arrogance is repaid by his humiliation and is supplanted by moderation. The general reader of today will find this the least cluttered of the sagas and unflaggingly absorbing. In this volume there are also two shorter stories set in Iceland, *Thorstein Staff-struck*, and *Alehood*, plus four further adventures of Icelanders at the royal courts of Scandinavia: *Hreiðar, Halldór Snorrason, Auðunn* and *Ívar*. An English edition, though no translation, of the text of this saga was prepared with introduction and glossary by Frank Stanton Cawley, (Harvard University Press, 1932, 82p).

671 **Laxdæla saga.**
Translated with an introduction by Magnús Magnússon, Hermann Pálsson. Harmondsworth, England: Penguin, 1969. 267p.

This saga, written around 1245, is perhaps the most European in feeling of the Icelandic family sagas. Two features of its style have helped to earn it this description: firstly, it is unusual in being a love story, with its culminating theme of the love of Guðrún Ósvífsdóttir, the most vivid female character of the sagas; secondly, it contains elements of chivalric sentiment, at a time when the age of chivalry was flowering in continental Europe. And yet it retains all the traditional elements of the classical Icelandic family saga, and is firmly within that tradition, rather than in the tradition of the later romances. The saga is set in the district of the Laxá river which flows into Hvammsfjördur in western Iceland, and the time-span is from the settlement of Iceland up to the early 11th century. This edition is notable for its flowing translation, illuminating introduction, and helpful appendices which include genealogical tables, glossary of proper names, and maps of the district. It was selected for presentation in the series of fine book editions published by the Folio Society. This is another saga with an impressive tradition of English versions: William Morris re-worked the story of Guðrún as part of his great work *Earthly Paradise*; Muriel Press' translation of 1899 appeared in a new edition by Peter Foote, (London: Dent, 1964 Everyman's Library); Thorsten Veblen's translation was published in New York by Viking Books in 1925; and there is a more recent and excellent translation by A. Margaret Arent (University of Wisconsin Press) for the American-Scandinavian Foundation, 1964.

672 **The story of Burnt Njal.**
Translated by George W. Dasent. Edinburgh; London: Dent, 1861. 2 vols. Reprinted 1971 in 1 vol.

By common consent the greatest of all the Icelandic sagas, and arguably the finest work in the history of Icelandic literature - it has certainly attracted more study and critical assessment than any other example of Norse literature. Written around 1280, but referring to events of 300 years earlier, it is brilliantly conceived, finely structured, and engrossingly narrated. Its theme of vengeance and fate is universal, its character unmistakably Icelandic, and its author unknown. Sir George Dasent's translation is, by the standards of today, rather archaic and occasionally turgid, but it was a scholarly translation, and possesses a certain powerful dignity which has prompted subsequent translators to acknowledge it as a pioneering effort in the striving to preserve the character and the spirit of the original; hence its frequent reprintings, the later one having the benefit of a valuable introduction by G. Turville-Petre. The reader with a deep interest in *Njála* will find an acquaintance with Dasent's translation worthwhile, but there are two more recent translations which can be more generally commended: that by Carl F. Bayerschmidt and Lee M. Hollander (New York University for the American-Scandinavian Foundation, 1955, Library of Scandinavian Literature vol. 3); and that by Magnús Magnússon and Hermann Pálsson, an authoritative and persuasive edition in convenient (paperback) format. (Harmondsworth, England:

Literature, Old Icelandic. Texts and translations. Sagas of Icelanders

Penguin 1960, 375p.). Both of these volumes include notable introductions, and the latter a helpful glossary of proper names, plus genealogical tables.

673 Víga-Glúms saga.
Translated from the Icelandic by Lee M. Hollander. New York: Twayne for the American-Scandinavian Foundation, 1972. 143p. (Library of Scandinavian Literature, vol. 14).

A biographical saga set in northern Iceland, revolving around the character of Glúmr Eyjólfsson, whose rise, fall and final peace with an acceptance of Christianity are portrayed against a background force of personal destiny, which is a distinguishing feature of this highly developed family saga. The volume also includes the story of Ögmund Dytt. There are certain difficulties in this saga, which may explain the fact that there is only one other unabridged translation into English, and that is from the last century - Sir Edmund Head's translation (London: Williams & Norgate, 1866), stands up well to the passage of time. Interest in the saga was re-kindled by G. Turville-Petre's edition of the Icelandic text, which he illuminates with an introduction to the composition of the saga (Oxford University Press, 1960, 2nd ed. 158p.).

674 Tales from the Eastfirths. (Vopnafirðinga saga...).
Translated by Alan E. Boucher, with a special introduction by Óskar Halldórsson. Reykjavík: Iceland Review, 1981. 96p. (Iceland Review Saga Library).

One of the volumes with which this enterprising series is being launched, a series designed to present in English translation a selection of Icelandic sagas and related materials, each in an attractive and convenient format. This volume contains four stories relating to the families of Vopnafjörður in north-eastern Iceland. *Vopnafirðinga saga* itself is the main story, followed by three shorter stories in which several characters from the same family line appear: Thorstein the White, Thorstein Rod-Stroke, and Gunnar Þiðrandi. Also included is the related heroic poem *Íslendingadrápa* (*Lay of the Icelanders*) written by Hauk Valdísarson in the 12th century. The translation of these pieces is straightforward and flowing, and the introduction contains the right level of background information for the general reader, at whom the series is directed.

675 A tale of Icelanders.
Translated and introduced by Alan E. Boucher. Reykjavík: Iceland Review, 1982. 104p. (Iceland Review Saga Series).

The sagas of Icelanders have tended to overshadow the shorter tales, or þættir, and yet, as the translator of this collection affirms, the þættir are distinguished from the sagas only by their brevity. Many of them are miniature gems, and in some cases may well have been the forerunners of the longer sagas. This collection, virtually the only English translation devoted specifically to the genre, contains twelve examples, including the tales of *Auðunn and the bear*, *Ale-Cap*, *Halldór Snorrason*, *Hreiðar* and *Stub*. The collection is given an historical prologue in the form of a slightly shortened version of Ari's *Book of the Icelanders*, and includes brief notes on each þáttur. An enterprising and appealing introduction to these varied and entertaining pieces.

Literature, Old Icelandic. Texts and translations. Sturlunga saga

676 **Auðunn and the bear.**
Arnold R. Taylor. London: Viking Society for Northern Research, 1948. 20p.
One of the most popular of the þættir, (see A tale of Icelanders q.v.) Auðunar páttr vestfirska is a beautifully told little story of how Audunn, an Icelander from the western fjords buys a Greenland bear at great cost, and travels to Norway and Denmark to offer it to King Harald and King Svein. Composed around 1200, it is meticulously structured, and acutely observed in its characterisation. It is five minutes of reading pleasure. This pamphlet, reprinted from the Viking Society's periodical *Saga-book*, vol. 13, no. 2, comprises the text of the story and an essay in appreciation of its qualities. The story's popularity is measured by its inclusion in a number of collected translations (see index).

Sturlunga saga

677 **Þorgils saga ok Hafliða.** (The saga of Þorgils and Hafliði.)
Edited by Ursula Brown (Dronke). London: Oxford University Press, 1952. 100p. maps. tables. (Oxford English Monographs).
The collection of sagas collectively known as *Sturlunga saga* is often classified as a group in itself. *Sturlunga saga* is characterised by its detail and realism in relation to the momentous events of the 12th and 13th century in Iceland, of which it is a contemporary historical record, and about which there is a remarkable degree of impartiality displayed, considering the authors' often direct or indirect involvement. The *saga of Þorgils and Hafliði* is one of these sagas, dating from the late 12th century, and referring to events between 1117 and 1121. It is a vividly narrated saga concerning the quarrels and lawsuits engaged in by two chieftains, and their eventual reconciliation. The Icelandic text has here been scrupulously edited for English-speaking students, and is accompanied by a valuable introduction dealing with date and composition of the saga, its relationship to oral and written sources, its authorship, and the manuscripts. Also included are maps, and the indispensable genealogical tables. This saga had been previously edited with introduction and notes by Halldór Hermannsson in the annual *Islandica*, vol. XXXI, (Ithaca, New York: Cornell University Press, 1945).

Sturlunga saga.
See item no. 309.

Bishops' sagas

678 **Stories of the bishops of Iceland.**
Translated from the Icelandic by Mary Disney Leith. London; Masters, 1895. 126p.
This volume comprises a selection of chronicles taken from the Bishops' sagas, including the stories of Þorvald the Farfarer, Bishop Ísleif, and Þorlák the Saint, and the short but important piece known as *Húngrvaka* (*Hunger-waker*) in which the writer aims to awaken the appetite for knowledge about the lives of the first five bishops of Skálholt (the southern and earlier of the two episcopal sees of mediaeval Iceland) and about the origins of the Icelandic church. Þorvald

Literature, Old Icelandic. Texts and translations. Sagas of ancient times

Kodransson's story is interesting in that it records the missionary work undertaken before the adoption of Christianity in Iceland in the year 1000. Isleif Gizursson was the first native Icelandic bishop, appointed in 1055, and it was he who built the first church at Skálholt. Þorlák Þórhallsson's bishopric lasted from 1178 to 1193, and he was venerated as a reformer.

679 The life of Guđmund the Good, Bishop of Hólar.
Translated from the original Icelandic sources by G. Turville-Petre, E. S. Olszewska. Coventry, England: Curtis & Beamish for the Viking Society for Northern Research, 1942. 112p.

The saga of Guđmund Arason is arguably the most interesting of the bishops' sagas. Guđmund lived from 1161 to 1237, and came from a humble but established family in northern Iceland. His early years of priesthood earned him a reputation for austerity and charity, and he was consecrated Bishop of Hólar (the northern and later of the two episcopal sees of Iceland) in 1203. His eventful and often interrupted tenure forms the backbone of this story. As the translators comment 'Guđmund's unyielding struggle to uphold the rights of the Church against the national rights of the chiefs had made his life as Bishop one of continual suffering and humiliation for himself'. In many ways he recalls the example of Thomas à Becket of Canterbury, and the events surrounding Guđmund's life can be seen as a microcosm of the forces which led to the downfall of the old independent Icelandic Commonwealth in the 13th century. The life of the first Bishop of Hólar after the fall of the Commonwealth is told in *The life of Laurence, Bishop of Hólar* (Laurentius saga), compiled by Einar Haflidason, and translated from the Icelandic by Oliver Elton (London: Rivington, 1890, 152p.).

Sagas of ancient times

680 The story of the Volsungs and Niblungs, with certain songs from the elder Edda.
Translated from the Icelandic by Eiríkr Magnússon, William Morris. London: Ellis, 1870. Facsimile reprint, London: Prior; Totowa, New Jersey: Cooper Square Press, 1980.

In his preface Morris describes *Völsunga saga* as 'the Great Story of the North, which should be to all our race what the Tale of Troy was to the Greeks'. This was the first translation of this legendary saga into English, and it remains famous. It was the inspiration for some of Morris' primary works, including *Sigurd the Volsung*, which he composed six years later. To those songs from the *Elder Edda* inserted into the prose text by the 12th century author, the translators have added many of the remainder in the second part of the volume 'in the order of the story and forming a metrical version of the greater portion of it'. For a later, more conventional translation, see that by Margaret Schlauch in the volume *The saga of the Volsungs, and the saga of Ragnar Lodbrok, together with the lay of Kraka* (New York: American-Scandinavian Foundation, 1930. Reprinted New York: AMS Press, 1976). See the translation by R. G. Finch (London: Nelson, 1965), a scholarly edition with parallel Icelandic/English text.

Literature, Old Icelandic. Texts and translations. Sagas of ancient times

681 The saga of King Heiðrek the Wise.
Translated from the Icelandic with introduction notes and appendices by Christopher Tolkien. London: Nelson, 1960. 100p. (Icelandic Texts Series).

Apart from *Völsunga saga, Heiðrek's saga* (or *Hervarar saga*) has been one of the most studied of the *fornaldarsögur*, or sagas of ancient times - those sagas of a more mythical nature with little historical authenticity, which make use of the old heroic poetry and continental themes. This translation, presented in parallel with the Icelandic text is commendably straightforward, and the translator's introduction is helpful in placing the many various strands of the saga in their wider context. This saga is notable for its inclusion of the haunting poem *The waking of Angantýr* and *Hjálmar's death song*. Tolkien also contributed the introduction to G. Turville-Petre's edition of this saga *Hervarar saga ok Heiðreks* (London: Viking Society for Northern Research, 1956. Reprinted with additions in 1976, 145p.).

682 The saga of Hrolf Kraki.
Stella M. Mills, with an introduction by E. V. Gordon. Oxford, England: Blackwell, 1933. 101p.

Hrólfs saga Kraka is one of the most typical and popular of the legendary sagas of ancient times. Based on handed down tales about the kings of Denmark in the 6th century, it is an episodic saga of family destiny, adventure and violence, liberally laced with fictional elements from fairy-tales and folklore. A later translation is included in *Eirík the Red, and other Icelandic sagas* (q.v.).

683 Gautreks saga, and other medieval tales.
Translated with an introduction by Hermann Pálsson, Paul Edwards. London: University of London Press; New York: New York University Press, 1968. 156p. map.

In 13th and 14th century Iceland, the Icelanders' perception of the pre-settlement world was hazy, both historically and geographically, and was based on a variety of sources; in a way this seems to have acted as a stimulus for the composition of the mythical-heroic sagas and other tales, and for recreating a world of romance and imagination, at the same time reflecting the survival of pagan values long after the acceptance of Christianity. The *saga of Gautrek* (King of Gotaland) and the four other tales in this book - *Bósi and Herraud, Egil and Ásmund, Thorsteinn Mansion-Might*, and *Helgi Thórisson* - collectively illustrate many of the essential features of the genre. The translators include a substantial glossary of proper names, which aids an understanding of these pieces, and a map of the northern world as perceived by their authors. The same translators also worked on what can be regarded as a sort of sequel to *Gautreks saga*, which records the exploits of Gautrek's son - *Hrolf Gautreksson: a Viking romance* (Edinburgh: Southside, 1972, 148p., UNESCO series of representative works). This saga is notable for its final passage, in which its author reveals clues as to the aims and audiences of these legendary romances.

Literature, Old Icelandic. Texts and translations. Sagas of ancient times

684 Göngu-Hrolf's saga: a Viking romance.
Translated by Hermann Pálsson, Paul Edwards. Edinburgh: Canongate; Toronto: University of Toronto Press, 1980. 128p.

Essentially a romance, beyond the Icelandic tradition, and possessing neither the impact of character nor the vivid realism of the traditional sagas of Icelanders. However, the translators argue persuasively that this saga, written in the 14th century, and which has always been popular, should be judged on its own merits (a strong and adventurous storyline is one of these) and not be seen merely as a 'degenerate offspring' of the classical sagas. Hrolf the Tramper (Rollo was the first Viking to settle permanently on the continent) is here portrayed as a hero only in the romantic sense, but his story (which bears little relation to what is known of him) can be read with some pleasure and escapism. This book was accepted in the Icelandic Translations series of UNESCO's collection of representative works. The pioneering work on this saga was by Jakob W. Hartmann in his *Göngu-Hrolfs saga: a study in Old Norse philology* (1912. Reprinted New York: AMS Press, Columbia University Germanic studies. Old Series, no. 14).

685 Arrow-Odd: a medieval novel.
Translated with an introduction by Hermann Pálsson, Paul Edwards. New York: New York University Press; London: London University Press, 1970. 136p.

In many ways this saga is a culmination of the features and style of the romantic hero tales of the northern world composed by Icelanders. *Örvar-Odds saga*, as it is called in Icelandic, is a typically fast-moving tale, trans-European in location, and continental European in spirit. Like *Göngu-Hrolf's saga* (q.v.), it dates from the 14th century, but has an even stronger element of the picaresque.

686 The saga of Tristram and Ísönd.
Translated with an introduction by Paul Schach. Lincoln, Nebraska: University of Nebraska Press, 1973. 148p.

Tristrams saga is significant because it was probably the earliest of the romantic tales from the south to be commissioned for translation by the Norwegian court, and because its success opened the floodgates for further translations, which in turn were imitated by Icelandic writers - well over two hundred of these Icelandic *riddarasögur* (knightly tales) and the related *lygisögur* (lying tales) are known to have been composed, by far the largest group of saga types. Although their merit has been generally questioned, their popularity at the time has not.

687 Hamlet in Iceland.
Israel Gollancz. London: Nutt, 1898. 284p.

The earliest reference to Hamlet appears in the *Skaldskaparmál* section of Snorri's *Edda*. In his long and valuable introduction Gollancz is concerned with 'diagnosing Iceland's long and painful struggle for a Hamlet saga'. He presents the full text with an English translation of the *Ambáles saga*, a late romance dating from the early 17th century, plus extracts from the five extant *rímur* on the Hamlet theme, and other relevant texts.

Literature, Old Icelandic. Texts and translations. Legends

Legends and folk-tales

688 Icelandic legends.
Collected by Jón Árnason, translated by George E. J. Powell, Eiríkr Magnússon. London: Bentley, 1864-66. 2 vols. illus. Reprinted New York: AMS Press, 1980.

Originally published in Leipzig (1862-64) under the title *Íslenzkar þjóðsögur og Æfintyri (Icelandic folk-tales and fairy stories)* this compilation owed its impetus to the nationalistic movements of Europe in the 19th century, and to the attendant re-awakening of interest in national cultures, as exemplified by the Grimm brothers' *Kinder und Hausmärchen* with which Jón Arnason was fully acquainted. Jón Arnason was librarian of the National Cathedral Library in Iceland, 1848-81, and with the early collaboration of Magnús Grímsson he set about appealing to the public for help in recalling and recording the folk-tales of Iceland. His collection, therefore, is one of national tales as well as folk-tales, and its value lies in bringing to the fore this separate strand of traditional Icelandic narrative creation. This translated edition omits the original introduction by Guðbrandur Vigfússon, nor does it include all the tales presented in the Icelandic edition (which itself did not represent Jón's entire collection); but the stories of elves, water monsters, trolls, ghosts, etc. form a remarkable anthology, and afford fascinating comparisons with folk-tales from elsewhere. The volumes are illustrated, and the recent reprint has happily ensured easier accessibility.

689 Icelandic folktales and legends.
Jacqueline Simpson. London: Batsford; Berkeley: University of California Press, 1972. 206p. bibliog.

The value of this translated selection from Jón Árnason's volumes (q.v.) is fourfold: its illuminating introduction; the lively but close translation when compared with that of Powell and Magnússon; the inclusion of some tales not in their collection; and the explanatory notes to each tale which identify parallels in other Germanic sources. This selection represents a full range of the various moods to be encountered in the Icelandic folk-tales. Further tales are presented by the same translator in her book entitled *Legends of Icelandic magicians* (Cambridge, England: Brewer for the Folklore Society; Totowa, New Jersey: Rowman & Littlefield, 1975, 120p.). This selection is helpfully introduced by B. S. Benedikz.

690 Icelandic folktales.
Translated by Alan E. Boucher. Reykjavík: Iceland Review, 1977. 3 vols.

An attractively produced selection of tales from the legends and folklore of Iceland, arranged thematically by volume: volume one, 'Ghosts, witchcraft and the other world'; volume two, 'Elves, trolls and elemental beings', and volume three, 'Adventures, outlaws and past events'. Alan Boucher translated more tales in a collection entitled *Mead Moondaughter and other Icelandic folktales*, with illustrations by Karolína Lárusdóttir (London: Hart-Davis, 1967, 159p.).

Scandinavian legends and folk-tales.
See item no. 864.

History and criticism

General

691 Scandinavian studies: essays presented to Dr. Henry Goddard Leach on the occasion of his 85th birthday.
Edited by Carl F. Bayerschmidt, Erik J. Friis. Seattle, Washington: University of Washington Press for the American-Scandinavian Foundation, 1965. 458p.

Leach acquired a wide reputation for his scholarship in the field of Scandinavian culture (see, for example, his *Angevin Britain and Scandinavia*, Harvard, 1921). This Festschrift, which includes a bibliography of Leach's writings from 1909 to 1963, offers several articles which are of interest in a specifically Icelandic context: 'Some parallels in Norse and Indian mythology', by Stefán Einarsson; 'The location of Ginnunga-gap', by Vincent H. de P. Cassidy; 'The element of the supernatural in the sagas of Icelanders', by Carl F. Bayerschmidt; 'The angry old men (a comparison of the Icelander Egil Skallagrímsson and the Welshman Llywarch the Old in their respective sagas)', by Gwyn Jones; and 'The style and structure of Tristrams saga (an Icelandic derivative saga)', by Paul Schach. The volume also includes two contributions relating to more modern times: 'The Laki eruption and the famine of the mist (1783-84)', by Vilhjálmur Bjarnar (q.v.); and 'Gunnar Gunnarsson (the 20th-century Icelandic novelist),' by Richard Beck.

692 Old Norse literature and mythology: a symposium.
Edited by E. C. Polomé. Austin, Texas: Texas University Press, 1969. 347p.

A Festschrift for Lee M. Hollander, Chairman of Germanic Studies at the University of Texas, a prolific translator from Old Icelandic and a distinguished critic, Knight of the Order of the Icelandic Falcon. Several of his colleagues from Texas, and two from abroad, contribute papers: E. Haugen on translating, E. Wahlgren on Vinland, P. Schach on Tristram, A. M. Arent on *Grettla*, K. Reichart on skaldic poetry, W. P. Lehmann on Eddic poetry, G. Turville-Petre on fertility myth, and E. C. Polomé on *Völuspá*. Includes bibliography of Hollander's writings.

693 Iceland and the mediaeval world: studies in honour of Ian Maxwell.
Edited by Gabriel Turville-Petre, John Stanley Martin. Melbourne, Australia: University of Melbourne, 1974. 176p.

A Festschrift to mark the retirement of the Professor of English at Melbourne University, and also to co-incide with the 1100th anniversary of the settlement of Iceland. Contributions on specifically Icelandic themes include articles by Peter Foote on the audience and vogue of the sagas of Icelanders, and by John Stephens on the Eddic lay *Atlakviða*, plus an edition by Turville-Petre of the *Sonatorrek*, the deeply moving poem from *Egils saga*, in which Egil laments the death of his sons. Gabriel Turville-Petre, the editor of the above volume, who died in 1978 after a uniquely distinguished scholastic involvement in Old Norse studies, was himself the figure of honour in a commemorative volume entitled *Speculum Norroenum: Norse studies in memory of G. Turville-Petre* (Odense, Denmark:

Literature, Old Icelandic. History and criticism. General

Odense University Press, 1981, 508p.). The volume contains thirty specialist articles by various contributors, and is accompanied by a bibliography of Turville-Petre's writings. Edited by Ursula Dronke, Guðrún P. Helgadóttir, G. W. Weber and Hans Bekker-Nielsen. Turville-Petre was another holder of the Icelandic honour of Knight of the Order of the Falcon.

694 Edda: its derivation and meaning.
Eiríkr Magnússon. London: Viking Club, 1896. 23p.

The term *Edda* is so pervasive in the study of Old Icelandic literature that one can forget that its meaning and derivation are by no means undisputed. Eiríkr Magnússon, the 19th-century Icelandic scholar noted for his controversial and often convincing interpretations of Old Norse topics (see, for example, his paper on Yggdrasill as the world-tree, presented to the Cambridge Philosophical Society in 1895) here considers the traditional derivation of the word *Edda* and its interpretation as a literary title associated with Sæmund and Snorri. Not for the only time does he cross swords with the other leading Icelandic scholar of this period, Guðbrandur Vigfússon.

695 Epic and romance: essays on mediaeval literature.
William Paton Ker. London: MacMillan, 1897, 451p.
Reprinted New York: Dover Publications, 1957.

No serious critic or historian of northern literature can fail to have been influenced by this seminal work; nearly a century on, it is still frequently cited and acknowledged, and its freshness and insight have maintained it as a standard work on the place of Icelandic literature within the mediaeval tradition. The book is divided into five major sections: a general introduction to epic and romance; the Teutonic epic; the Icelandic sagas; and two sections on Old French and its influences. The section of over a hundred pages on the Icelandic sagas describes their content and form, the heroic ideal, tragedy, the rarely discussed aspect of comedy (with particular reference to *Bandamanna saga*), and the northern prose romances. 'While the life represented in the sagas is more primitive, less civilised, than the life of the great southern nations in the Middle Ages, the record of that life is by still greater interval in advance of all the common modes of narrative then known to the more fortunate or more luxurious parts of Europe. The conventional form of the saga has none of the common mediaeval restrictions of view. It is accepted at once by modern readers without deduction or apology on the score of antique fashion, because it is, in essentials, the form with which they are acquainted in modern story-telling (and, more especially, because the language is unaffected and idiomatic)'.

696 Iceland and the humanities.
William Paton Ker. *Saga-book of the Viking Club*, vol. 5 (1906-07), p. 341-53.

The proceedings of the Viking Society for Northern Research, as recorded in the volumes of its periodical *Saga-book* over the decades, have produced a wide variety of stimulating articles relating to Old Icelandic studies. One of Ker's (sometime President) contributions is this perceptive and eloquent essay on the background and concept of the humanities in Iceland, and the individual approach of the Icelanders to history and literature. 'There is a self-conscious principle of style and good grammar in Iceland by which the people are kept together as articulate speakers, through all the difficulties of their climate and their history... the Icelandic settlement was (and remains in history) a protest against all the successful commonplaces of the world'.

Literature, Old Icelandic. History and criticism. General

697 Notes on the intellectual history of the Icelanders.
G. Turville-Petre. *History*, n.s. vol. 27, no. 106 (Sept. 1942), p. 111-23.

A stimulating essay on a number of controversial topics in Old Icelandic literature. The author discusses the question of when the Icelanders began to write, the growth and range of their writings, the use of oral tradition in the family sagas, and the problem of saga style.

698 Origins of Icelandic literature.
G. Turville-Petre. Oxford, England: Clarendon Press, 1953. Reprinted with corrections 1967, 260p.

'Although much has been written about the great sagas of the 13th century, most English scholars have neglected the literature of the 12th century. The classical literature can be appreciated better if that of earlier generations is also considered'; thus the author justifies this still standard work on 'pre-classical' Icelandic literature. He discusses the pagan poetry, the conversion to Christianity, early religious literature, the influence of the historian Ari, the synoptic historical literature of the late 12th century, and ends with an epilogue on the classical age. It is a remarkably lucid and cogently argued work, which is essential for an understanding of how the classical prose of Iceland developed from pre-Icelandic roots, acquired its unique style through three centuries of Icelandic social progress, and finally flowered into a golden age at a time when almost all other European literatures were comparatively barren. 'Prose develops later than poetry, and, however important the poetry of the Icelanders, their greatest achievements were in prose'.

699 The emergence of vernacular literature in Iceland.
Theodore M. Andersson. *Mosaic* (Canada), vol. 8, no. 4 (1975), p. 161-69.

When can one begin to talk of a uniquely Icelandic literature? The author of this paper emphasises the common Germanic tradition of Eddic poetry, the Norwegian origins of skaldic verse, and the pre-settlement orientation of the legendary forms of saga. These three strands are seen as only partly belonging to the Icelandic tradition. But it is in the narratives of *Sturlunga saga*, in the sagas of Icelanders (often called the family sagas) and in their oral antecedents that an exclusively Icelandic vernacular tradition can be said to have established itself.

700 Edda and saga.
Bertha S. Phillpotts. London: Thornton Butterworth, 1931. 256p. Reprinted Kraus, 1973.

One of a trio of books by this respected author which have maintained a strong influence on the subsequent appreciation and study of early Icelandic literature and its antecedents, *Edda and saga* is one of the best introductions to the subject, being clear, concise and readable. It is helpful to the newcomer and stimulating to the specialist. The author deals first with the Eddic poems, their style and verse form, and their contents seen separately as the world of men and the world of gods. Her second part is a discussion of the sagas of Icelanders, their social background, composition and characterisation, followed by a chapter on the historical and legendary sagas. The advanced student can also refer to Bertha Phillpotts' earlier study *The Elder Edda and ancient Scandinavian drama* (Cambridge University Press, 1920, 216p.), in which she introduced her 'seasonal theory' relating to some of the myths; also her *Kindred and clan in the middle*

Literature, Old Icelandic. History and criticism. General

ages and after: a study in the sociology of the Teutonic races (Cambridge University Press, 1913).

701 Snorri Sturluson.
Marlene Ciklamini. Boston, Massachusetts: Twayne, 1978. 188p. bibliog. (Twayne's World Author Series, 493).

Remarkably, this is the first and only full-length study in English devoted to the work of Snorri Sturluson (1178-1241), one of the great figures of the mediaeval world in general, and the greatest figure of the Old Icelandic Commonwealth. It should be emphasised that this book is a study of Snorri the writer rather than Snorri the politician, of the structure and art of his writings rather than their historicity and influences, of *Heimskringla* and saga writing rather than his *Prose Edda*. As such it is a valuable and illuminating study for the specialist student. However, the fully-rounded study of the man, his career and his literary output remains to be presented to the English-speaking reader.

702 Creator of documentary fiction.
Njörður P. Njarðvík. *Atlantica and Iceland Review*, vol. 17, no. 4 (1979), p. 34-39.

For the more general reader, a concise and well-balanced introduction to the writings of Snorri Sturluson, contributed in commemoration of the 800th anniversary of Snorri's birth, and suggesting the motives for Snorri's two major works: in the case of the *Prose Edda* (in which Snorri, a Roman Catholic, revives the study of pagan lore some two centuries after Iceland's conversion to Christianity) he is seen as striving to preserve his country's cultural heritage; in the case of *Heimskringla* (where Snorri records the history of the kings of Norway) he is seen as amassing evidence from which the Icelanders could draw evidence in support of their struggle for national independence. This illustrated article also touches on Snorri's political career.

703 Icelandic sagas and manuscripts.
Jónas Kristjánsson. Reykjavík: Iceland Review, 1970. 96p. illus.

A finely illustrated volume in which the Director of the Manuscript Institute of Iceland discusses the roots of the Eddic poems and the sagas, their character and purpose, and, especially, how they were transmitted, recorded and preserved. He includes an account of how a great corpus of saga manuscripts was collected in Iceland and taken to Denmark in the early 18th century to form the Arnamagnaean Collection (for this aspect see specifically the book 'Arne Magnússon the manuscript collector' by Hans Bekker-Nielsen and Ole Widding q.v.). See the article by Sigfús Blöndal 'Iceland, a treasure trove of manuscripts' in *American-Scandinavian Review*, vol. 18, no. 5 (May 1930), p. 275-81, in which the vernacular character of the manuscripts is emphasised.

A history of Icelandic literature.
See item no. 770.

Literature, Old Icelandic. History and criticism. Poetry

Poetry

704 Old Icelandic poetry: Eddic lay and Skaldic verse.
Peter Hallberg, translated with a foreword by Paul M. Schach, Sonja Lindgrenson. Lincoln, Nebraska: University of Nebraska Press, 1975. 219p. bibliog.

A definitive study, originally published in Swedish in 1962, in which the author takes Snorri's treatise on poetics as the point of departure for a thorough yet lucid exposition of all forms of Old Icelandic poetry. He summarises the characteristics, style and metre of Eddic and skaldic verse, before examining both forms in detail, with an analysis of the way in which they reflected the transition from the pagan to the Christian environment. He concludes with a chapter on the later form of poetry known as *rímur*.

705 The Elder Edda and ancient Scandinavian drama.
Bertha S. Phillpotts. Cambridge, England: Cambridge University Press, 1920. 216p.

An early and still-respected study of Eddic poetry, and of its heroic and mythical elements. The main purpose of the work is to relate the development of the Eddic poems to the general Scandinavian context, and the volume is often cited for the author's theories concerning ancient fertility dramas, in particular her 'seasonal theory', applied to the Eddic poem *Skírnismál*: see Ursula Dronke's 'Art and Tradition in Skírnismál' (q.v.).

706 Art and tradition in Skírnismál.
Ursula Dronke. In: *English and mediaeval studies presented to J. R. R. Tolkien.* Edited by N. Davis; C. L. Wrenn. London: Allen & Unwin, 1962. p. 250-68.

Criticism of the Eddic poems has tended to concentrate upon explanation of the mythological context, rather than on their artistic qualities. This short study is an example of how best to appreciate the poems, by looking at the way in which the poet uses the traditions to create the work of art. *Skírnismál*, the story of Freyr, god of peace and plenty, Gerðr, the giant's daughter and Frey's exclusive desire, and Skírnir, Frey's messenger, is one of the finest and most sophisticated of the thirty-five Eddic poems which survive, and has its roots in the mythology of the seasons and fertility dramas. 'The poet of Skírnismál plays with a mythological theme and, at the same time, shows its reality. It is a serious poem, delivered with the speed and lightness of a jeu d'esprit'.

707 Scaldic poetry.
E. O. G. Turville-Petre. Oxford, England: Clarendon Press, 1976. 102p.

A scholarly work in two parts: the first comprises a technical introduction to skaldic poetry and the *dróttkvætt* (heroic or court metre), its style of diction and the unique kennings; the second part is a selection of verses from twenty-three of the best known skaldic poets of the 9th to 11th centuries, including Bragi the Old (the first skald of whom we have real knowledge) and Egil Skallagrímsson . Most of the verses are found in the sagas, and hence have an historical relevance in relation to the events which they describe. The texts are here presented with parallel translation into English, notes on the verses and on the poets themselves. A welcome textbook for the student of Old Icelandic poetry. The advanced spe-

Literature, Old Icelandic. History and criticism. Sagas

cialist in this difficult form may refer to *Islandica: an annual relating to Iceland and the Fiske Icelandic Collection*, vol. XLII (q.v.). See Turville-Petre's concise article on skaldic poetry in the journal *Mediaeval Scandinavia* (Denmark), vol. 7 (1974), p. 7-14.

708 Riddles, kennings and the complexity of skaldic poetry.
John Lindow. *Scandinavian Studies*, vol. 47, no. 2 (summer 1975), p. 311-27.

One of the main features contributing to the complexity of skaldic verse is the kenning. The writer of this article quotes a generally accepted definition of the term kenning as a 'metaphor consisting of two or more parts, where one part (baseword) is modified by another part or parts (modifiers) so as to provide the meaning of the entire expression': a simple example would be 'hail of weapons' to denote 'battle'. He examines this definition by comparing it with definitions of the riddle, and by indicating the type of audience for whom the early skaldic poetry, especially the so-called *dróttkvæði* verse, functioned as a form of secret language.

709 The romantic poetry of Iceland.
William Craigie. Glasgow: Jackson for University of Glasgow, 1950. 30p.

A clearly presented description of the Icelandic *rímur*, a form of verse cultivated by the Icelanders from the 14th century, whereby popular ballads and other poetry from mediaeval Europe were laced with many of the major elements of the earlier Icelandic skaldic poetry. This elaborate form of verse has survived to the present day as a popular art form. This paper was presented as the 11th W. P. Ker Memorial Lecture to the University of Glasgow. Another of Craigie's lectures is in print, the Taylorian Lecture, *The art of Icelandic poetry* (Oxford, England: Clarendon Press, 1937, 34p.).

710 Report on rímur, 1980.
S. F. D. Hughes. *Journal of English and Germanic Philology*, vol. 79, no. 4 (Oct. 1980), p. 477-98.

A review article, surveying the study and state of the art of the *rímur* verse form, which, apart from its intrinsic interest, has relevance for the recent revival of interest in the legendary sagas and chivalric tales. This article continues the survey of *rímur* in Stefán Einarsson's review in the same journal, vol. 54 (1955), p. 255-61.

The poetic Edda in the light of archaeology.
See item no. 271.

Sagas

711 The Icelandic sagas.
William Craigie. Cambridge, England: Cambridge University Press, 1913. 120p. Reprinted Kraus, 1968; Norwood, Pennsylvania: Norwood Editions, 1976.

This is not the only work by this respected scholar in which a great deal is conveyed within a short space. Considering the canvas of the subject, the treat-

Literature, Old Icelandic. History and criticism. Sagas

ment is remarkably concise, and its subsequent influence can be judged by its reprintings over half a century later. The author discusses the origins of the sagas, and their different forms: the historical sagas, the family sagas, the legendary and romantic sagas. He also assesses their translations into English up to the early 20th century. The book was originally issued as a Cambridge manual of literature.

712 The Old Norse sagas.
Halvdan Koht. New York: American-Scandinavian Foundation; London: Allen & Unwin, 1931. 191p.

A straightforward and occasionally original history and criticism of the Icelandic sagas in their different forms, in which the author discusses their origins, historical value and artistic creation. Particular attention is paid to the family sagas, and there is a separate chapter devoted to Snorri Sturluson as a saga writer. There have since been deeper studies of the sagas than this, but it remains well cited and worth reading.

713 European sources of Icelandic saga writing: an essay based on previous studies.
Lars Lönnroth. Stockholm: Boktryckeri Aktiebolaget Thule, 1965. 38p. bibliog.

A persuasive essay, the theme of which is that Old Icelandic saga composition should be seen as a 'branch of European literature, and not as a product of an isolated Germanic culture'.

714 What was before the saga? A jubilee discourse.
Halldór Laxness. *Scandinavian Review*, vol. 62, no. 4 (Dec. 1974), p. 339-61.

To mark the 1100th anniversary of the settlement of Iceland, Laxness contributed this provocative article on the reasons why the Icelandic sagas were written. He discusses chronologically the course of Old Icelandic literature: the historical work of Ari, and *The Book of the Settlements*; the skaldic poetry; ecclesiastical writings; and the age of the saga in the 13th century. He questions the accuracy of the first, the ethos of the second, the motives of the third, and the need to establish the factual basis of the fourth - all this by way of illustrating the notion that there may have been an underlying need of the saga writers to conceal or disguise the pagan and allegedly illiterate origins of the Icelanders. Laxness' article is typically compelling and laced with humour - in many ways it is an antidote to the scholastic approach to Icelandic cultural history, but one feels that his instinct and intuition as an Icelander, allied to his experience as a giant of modern Icelandic letters, may carry as much conviction as the more conventional forms of interpretation. In this article, which tells us as much about the man as about his subject, Laxness quotes the words of a scribe written at the foot of a page of saga vellum: 'As nobody is bound to believe more of a book than he himself likes, neither this nor any other book can be made to suit everybody. The best and wisest thing to do is to listen, and preferably in a cheerful rather than a sulky mood...'. Laxness suggests that this may be wisdom itself - his article can be read in the same spirit.

Literature, Old Icelandic. History and criticism. Family sagas

Sagas of Icelanders (family sagas)

715 The origin of the Icelandic family sagas.
Knut Liestøl, translated from the Norwegian by A. G. Jayne. Oslo: Instituttet for Sammenlignende Kulturforskning, 1930. 261p. Reprinted Westport, Connecticut: Greenwood Press, 1974.

An important work, which has rarely missed citation by subsequent literary historians of the field. Liestøl's study comprises an analysis of the pre-Icelandic Norse literary traditions, and of the style and variants of the Icelandic sagas as clues to the form and development of their oral precursors. He discusses the authors, or 'storytellers', the unique features of the sagas arising from the social conditions of Iceland, the outside influences, and the question of the historicity of the family sagas.

716 The Icelandic saga.
Peter Hallberg, translated with introduction and notes by Paul Schach. Lincoln, Nebraska: University of Nebraska Press, 1962. 179p.

A translation from the original Swedish of a work which stands among the most illuminating analyses of the Icelandic sagas. Within a perceptive historical framework the author has placed a core of chapters which form a thematic approach to an understanding of the sagas, and which point to the philosophical and emotional drive behind their construction; he examines the concept of destiny, the values of life, and the humour revealed in the sagas, which he illustrates with examples drawn from a wide range of classical saga literature. 'In choice of subject matter, in character portrayal, and in style, these sagas are entirely and uniquely an Icelandic creation'. The main value of this book lies in the way in which its author proves his point by relating the ideals of the early Icelanders to the literature which they created.

717 The Icelandic family saga: an analytic reading.
Theodore M. Andersson. Cambridge, Massachusetts: Harvard University Press, 1967. 315p. (Harvard Studies in Comparative Literature, 28).

A comparative study of the family sagas. It is divided into two parts: the first is a descriptive account of the basic structure and rhetorical patterns of the sagas; the second is analytical, and by means of synopses of, and comments on, twenty-four family sagas, illustrates the author's general conclusion: 'The written family saga is a gradually mounting conflict culminating in a dramatic climax, followed by some form of revenge, and ultimately resolved by a reconciliation between the conflicting parties'. An earlier and more specialised work by the same author is entitled *The problem of Icelandic saga origins* (New Haven, Connecticut: Yale University Press, 1964, 190p. Yale Germanic studies, 1).

718 Dating the Icelandic sagas: an essay in method.
Einar Ól. Sveinsson. London: Viking Society for Northern Research, 1958. 127p.

An important study, the first approach to the problem of when the family sagas were transcribed since Finnur Jónsson's researches at the beginning of this cen-

Literature, Old Icelandic. History and criticism. Family sagas

tury. The author analyses several types of evidence: palaeographic, historical, linguistic, literary and stylistic. His view is understandably cautious, and is concentrated on establishing a method for dating the sagas, rather than on finding final solutions.

719 The Icelandic family sagas and the period in which their authors lived.
Einar Ól. Sveinsson. *Acta Philologica Scandinavica* (Denmark), vol. 12 (1937-38), p. 71-90.

The degree of historical authenticity which can be assigned to the family sagas has tended to be cheerfully ignored by the purely pleasure-seeking reader, and to be excessively researched by the specialist analyser. The 'fact versus fiction' debate, to put it in crude terms, is nevertheless important for a serious understanding of the family sagas, even if irrelevant to their entertainment value. In this article, the writer offers a clear and balanced view of one of the chief factors to be taken into account, namely, the potential effect of the saga writer's own contemporary environment upon his presentation of a story and subject matter relating to a period of two centuries earlier. The author's feeling is that the most valued qualities of the family sagas are apparent 'when the old subject matter and the old ethical outlook is blended with the artistic abilities of the age of writing and with its material knowledge of life'. See the same author's article 'The value of the sagas' in *Saga-book*, vol. 15, no. 1-2 (1957-61), p. 1-16.

720 The historical element in the Icelandic family sagas.
Sigurður Nordal. Glasgow: Jackson for the University of Glasgow, 1957. 35p.

A lucid and eloquent paper, whose author, with reference to the family sagas in general and to *Njáls saga* in particular, definitively expresses the spirit of enquiry into their historical content: 'It was inevitable that scholarship should react against the credulity which has taken the historicity of the family sagas too literally... but let us not, in our zeal of criticism, be carried to the other extreme, so that we overlook the tremendous importance of the historical element, rightly defined, nor forget how the art of the sagas very soon decayed when it was neglected. And let us not either forget, in our gratitude to the authors, that we owe them the courtesy to detect rather too little than too much of what they themselves wanted to be hidden'. This paper was presented as the 15th W. P. Ker Memorial Lecture to the University of Glasgow.

721 An anthropological approach to the Icelandic saga.
Victor W. Turner. In: *The translation of culture: essays to E. E. Evans-Pritchard.* Edited by T. O. Beidelman. London: Tavistock, 1971. p. 349-74.

Perhaps because Iceland was never a primitive society in the usual sense, it has attracted comparatively little attention from historical anthropologists. The Icelandic family sagas, however, reveal an unparalleled range of information about the way in which Icelandic society was organised. The author of this essay devotes his attention to *Njáls saga*, which he describes as an 'anthropological paradise', and claims that, whereas the literary critic tends to accept rather than enthuse about the amount of genealogical detail set forth in the family sagas, the anthropologist is seeking precisely this type of information on kinship and social relationships to interpret the structure of Icelandic society, a knowledge of whose workings would naturally have been assumed by an original audience, but which to the modern reader is only implicity indicated. The essay contains certain anthropological

Literature, Old Icelandic. History and criticism. Family sagas.

jargon which obscures some straightforward observations, but is an unusual approach to an understanding of the vivid world of the sagas.

722 Beginnings and endings in the Icelandic family sagas.
Kathryn Hume. *Modern Language Review*, vol. 68, no. 3 (July 1973), p. 593-606.

'As modern readers, we react negatively to saga beginnings and endings because we are neither conditioned to respond to the conventions of this form, nor aware of personal genetic connexions to the actors. Seen in the light of this analysis, though, perhaps future readers will recognise the original function which opening and closing material performed, and value its intrinsic significance as a highly original attempt to relate art to the continuum of human experience'. This article is a useful counterbalance to traditionally critical attitudes towards the genealogical introductions and epilogues to the sagas, which critics have often tended to disparage, apologise for, ignore, and even omit from translations.

723 The saga mind.
M. I. Steblin-Kamensky, translated by Kenneth H. Ober. Odense, Denmark: Odense University Press, 1973. 171p.

Particular service was rendered in translating this book by the respected scholar from Leningrad who died in 1981. What O. I. Senkovskii had done for Icelandic studies in the first half of the 19th century, Steblin-Kamensky emulated in the present century, having translated both *Eddas* and many of the family sagas into Russian. Originally published in 1971 under the title *Mir sagi*, this book offers perhaps because of its provenance, an unusually fresh approach to the understanding of the Icelandic family sagas. It is a stimulating attempt to portray the 'spiritual' world of the sagas by considering concepts such as truth, good and evil, time and place, life and death, as well as form, character, etc., all from the point of view of the listener and the 'teller' (the author of this book draws inferences from the lack of an Old Icelandic word for 'authorship'). The effects of the sagas on the modern reader are varied and personal, but this study possesses the capacity to cause re-thinking.

724 How pagan are the Icelandic family sagas?
Bernadine McCreesh. *Journal of English and Germanic Philology*, vol. 79, no. 1 (Jan. 1980), p. 58-66.

Numerous critics have addressed themselves to the question of why the Icelandic family sagas, written two centuries or more after Iceland's conversion to the Christian faith, should fail to reflect through their transcribers significant strands of a Christian tradition. The author of this article re-examines some of the evidence to point the contrary view that the pagan nature of the sagas is 'more apparent than real', and that the saga writers are, moreover, to be found 'Christianising' their stories in certain instances. The pagan or 'un-Christian' tone of the family sagas is argued by Peter Foote in an article entitled 'Secular attitudes in early Iceland' in the annual *Mediaeval Scandinavia*, vol. 7 (1974), p. 31-44, in which he considers developments in Norway and Iceland prior to the age of the saga to throw light on the 'predominantly secular... earthbound, humanist nature of such story-telling'. The debate continues.

Literature, Old Icelandic. History and criticism. Family sagas

725 Ethics and morals in Icelandic saga literature.
M. C. van den Toorn. Assen, Netherlands: van Gorcum, 1955. 153p.

A scholarly examination of an aspect of saga study which has received relatively little attention, considering the potential light which it can throw upon the society of the period. By 'ethics' the author understands 'the delimitation of the concepts of good and evil, and the applications of these standards in daily life'; the term 'moral' he sets apart for 'the intention which an author incorporates into his work in order to edify his readers or hearers'. He examines, with copious examples from the literature, both the pagan and the Christian manifestations of human conduct.

726 The displacement of the heroic ideal in the family sagas.
Theodore M. Andersson. *Speculum*, vol. 45, no. 4 (1970), p. 575-93.

An interesting discussion of the ethics of the Icelandic family saga, and of the balance between the heroic ideal and contemporary morality. As the title of the article implies, the writer considers that the family sagas do indeed reflect heroic attitudes, but that the conclusions of these sagas always resolve into a 'restoration of the social balance', thus reflecting their portrayal of a normal society with a familiar set of values and morals. He adduces many examples from the family sagas, and a knowledge of these sagas is necessary for an appreciation of this article. For an affirmation of the heroic ideal, however, with particular reference to *Njáls saga*, see Alan E. Boucher's article 'The Icelandic hero' in *The Listener*, 18th Sept. 1969, p. 367-69.

727 Patterns in Old English and Old Icelandic literature.
A. C. Bouman. Leiden, Netherlands: Leiden University Press, 1962. 159p.

In this comparative study of the conscious and unconscious use of patterns in mediaeval literature - patterns associated with traditional themes, forms and emotions - three of the author's five chapters comprise essays on aspects of major sagas of Icelanders - 'Literature and myth: the picture of Hallgerðr Höskuld's daughter' (*Njáls saga*); 'Egil Skallagrímsson's poem *Sonatorrek*' (*Egils saga*); 'Patterns in *Laxdœla saga*' - portraits, dreams, heroic influences and Christian colourings.

728 The relation and development of English and Icelandic outlaw traditions.
Joost de Lange. Haarlem, Netherlands: Tjeenk Willink, 1935. 138p.

Another comparative study of mediaeval English and Icelandic literature, in which an interesting attempt is made to correlate the tradition of the outlaw in both literatures, and to determine their common sources or mutual influences. On the English side particular attention is paid to Hereward the Wake and the ballads of Robin Hood; on the Icelandic side the author examines four sagas of outlawry - three from the sagas of Icelanders: *Gísla saga*, *Grettis saga* and *Harðar saga*; also *Áns saga Bogsveigis*, one of the sagas of ancient times, which he sees as constituting the link between English and Icelandic outlaw tradition.

Literature, Old Icelandic. History and criticism. Family sagas

729 Character delineation of women in the old Icelandic sagas.
Loftur L. Bjarnason. *Scandinavian Studies*, vol. 28, no. 4 (Nov. 1956), p. 142-53.
'One can scarcely call to mind a single major saga that does not have at least one woman of heroic stature'. This article is an elaboration of the point, with emphasis upon the skill of the saga tellers in drawing the characters of women: physical description plays little part; overt emotion and speech seldom provide the key to their character; but their actions and especially their influences are purposefully described in such a way that women come across as forces rather than portraits. Particular reference is made to *Fóstbrœðra saga*, *Heiðarvíga saga*, *Laxdœla saga* and *Njáls saga*. For a rather less serious piece, the tone of which is summarised by the concluding remark 'Of all mediaeval cultures, American women would feel themselves most at home in this [Icelandic] one', see the article 'The women of the Icelandic sagas', by Margaret Schlauch, in *American-Scandinavian Review*, vol. 31, no. 4 (Dec. 1943), p. 333-40.

730 The portrayal of women in the Icelandic family sagas.
Shang-Lan Sophia Yeh. PhD thesis, University of Iowa, Iowa, 1974. 301p.
A substantial analysis of the characterisation of women in the sagas and shorter stories. The author identifies several categories of characters: instigators or troublemakers, peacemakers, lovers, prophetesses, sorceresses, etc. She makes comparisons between the portrayal of women in the *Poetic Edda* and in the sagas. In her conclusion she stresses the vital and positive character of women in the sagas, and relates these features to a picture of the actual situation of women in Icelandic society of the 10th and 11th centuries.

731 The comic in the Icelandic family saga.
Fritz H. König. PhD thesis, University of Iowa, Iowa, 1972. 182p.
The only full-length study in English of the comic elements in the sagas, a feature which the author of this thesis analyses and also illustrates with copious examples to show that comedy is a richer characteristic than critics had hitherto implied. He concludes that certain aspects of humour, such as the grim or the laconic, are essential factors in the composition of the saga as a distinctive genre.

Individual family saga studies

732 Studia Islandica.
R. George Thomas. *Modern Language Quarterly*, vol. 11 (1950), p. 281-97+391-403.
Although this two-part article is intended as an evaluation of the work of one of Iceland's foremost scholars, Sigurður Nordal, who, amongst many other achievements, edited the Old Icelandic Texts Society's series *Íslenzk fornrit*, and wrote a definitive work on Snorri Sturluson in 1920, it is largely an appreciation of Professor Nordal's studies of two of the sagas of Icelanders: *Egils saga* (with the question of Snorri's authorship), and *Hrafnkels saga Freysgoða* (q.v.); both of these studies have proved influential. For a brief general appreciation of Sigurður Nordal, see Stefán Einarsson's article in *American-Scandinavian Review*, vol. 49, no. 4 (1961), p. 374-79.

Literature, Old Icelandic. History and criticism. Family sagas

733 Egil Skallagrímsson in England.
Gwyn Jones. *British Academy Proceedings*, vol. XXXVIII (1953), p. 127-44. (Sir Israel Gollancz Memorial Lecture).

A lecture in praise of the eponymous hero of *Egils saga*, the 'bóndi of Borg' who became the 'skald in England' by his presence at Brunanburh in 937 and York in 948, the later visit resulting in the magnificent poem *The Lay of Arinbjörn*. This lecture is available as an offprint.

734 The construction of Gísla saga.
Taylor Culbert *Scandinavian Studies*, vol. 31, no. 4 (Nov. 1959), p. 151-64.

The design of *Gísla saga* has been highly praised by many respected scholars in the field. The author of this paper is concerned with investigating the reasons for its reputation, and with the apparent lack of adjustment required by the modern reader for an appreciation of its qualities. Upon a saga which is almost completely biographical its composer has structured a classical framework: a threefold crescendo of relationships, firstly between Gísli and his immediate adversary, secondly between Gísli and society, thirdly between Gísli and his fate - all of which are 'resolved' by the saga's climax. Sufficient evidence is presented in this paper to demonstrate the conscious design on the part of the saga writer.

735 The thematic design of Grettis saga.
Kathryn Hume. *Journal of English and Germanic Philology*, vol. 73, no. 4 (Oct. 1974), p. 469-86.

An article with a similar, if rather more difficult, aim to that in Taylor Culbert's *The Construction of Gísla saga* (q.v.). *Grettis saga* has achieved its status in the front rank of Icelandic sagas because of its highlights, which, for many critics, have been bright enough to outshine the apparent incongruities both in the form of the story and in the character of Grettir himself. But in this essay the writer argues persuasively for a more constructive approach to these anomalies, which she sees to be in large measure part of the total thematic and artistic design of the saga.

736 The character of Gunnlaug Serpent-Tongue.
Robert S. Cook. *Scandinavian Studies*, vol. 43, no. 1 (winter 1971), p. 1-21.

Gunnlaugs saga Ormstungu is a saga which has always been popular, and yet has suffered frequent critical disapproval on the grounds that it contains many elements which heralded the decline of the Icelandic family saga with the onset of romance. But this article offers a spirited critical defence of those very qualities, in particular the character of the eponymous figure, which have made it popular.

737 Hrafnkels saga Freysgoða: a study.
Translated by R. George Thomas. Cardiff: University of Wales Press, 1958. 75p.

Originally published in Icelandic in 1940, this study, and its welcome translation into English, regenerated great interest in, and respect for, *Hrafnkatla*. Nordal's study is penetrating, lucid and, above all, an aid to the uncluttered appreciation of this fine and tautly composed saga. He surveys the theme of the saga, its historical 'truthfulness', its sources, its composition and manner of narration, and its characterisation. He sees it as 'one of the most completely developed short novels in world literature... of all the Icelandic sagas, Hrafnkatla seems to me to

Literature, Old Icelandic. History and criticism. Family sagas.

be the easiest to remember, and to repeat for amusement'. The latter part of this statement is the most brilliantly simple justification of the appeal of any saga, and is worth reams of the convoluted critical effort expended on 'appreciation' of the Icelandic sagas. Nordal's study has not totally overshadowed an almost contemporary article by E. V. Gordon 'On Hrafnkels saga Freysgoða', which appeared in the journal *Medium Aevum*, vol. 8 (1939), p. 1-39.

738 Art and ethics in Hrafnkel's saga.
Hermann Pálsson. Copenhagen: Munskgaard; New York: Humanities Press, 1971. 83p. bibliog.

Another excellent and concise study of *Hrafnkels saga*, in which the saga is viewed synchronically in relation to what it is saying as contemporary history, and particularly for what it reveals of the moral values which it incorporates. After a introduction to the structure of the saga and its landscape, there is a series of essays on freedom, justice, self-awareness, emotions and heroic attitudes.

739 Hrafnkel's character re-interpreted.
Pierre Halleux. *Scandinavian Studies*, vol. 38 (1966), p. 36-44+98-101.

The regeneration of interest in *Hrafnkels saga*, after the work of Nordal (q.v.), is exemplified by a spate of articles in this journal over the span of a decade. *Hrafnkatla*, perhaps more than any other saga, speaks for itself, and the point comes where one may suspect critical overkill. Nevertheless, some respected names have contributed to the debates in honour of this saga, and so the student may wish to follow up these further contributions to the same journal: Anne Saxon Slater, vol. 40 (1968), p. 36-50; W. F. Bolton, vol. 43 (1971), p. 35-52; F. J. Heineman, vol. 46 (1974), p. 102-19 and vol. 47 (1975), p. 448-52+453-62; and Peter Hallberg, vol. 47 (1975) p. 442-47+463-66.

740 On civilizing Hrafnkell.
Edward I. Condren. *Modern Language Notes*, vol. 88 (1973), p. 517-34.

The author of this article rightly claims that *Hrafnkels saga* has attracted an imbalance of criticism concerning its historical accuracy or lack of it (it is not alone among the family sagas in such treatment). The ordinary reader, and, one ventures to suggest, the original author of the saga, share the overriding purpose of entertainment. This article is welcome in that it attempts an artistic appreciation of the saga and its integrity - 'Hrafnkell becomes by the end of the saga the very symbol of Iceland'.

741 The topography of Hrafnkels saga.
O. D. MacRae-Gibson. *Saga-book* (UK), vol. 19 (1974-77), p. 239-63. maps.

In recent years, a particularly popular form of conducted tour around Iceland has been the 'saga-tour', on which the participants, armed with texts of the sagas, visit the locations of individual sagas, in the usually fulfilled hope of finding the settings little changed since saga times, and thereby enhancing appreciation of the story. *Hrafnkels saga* is generally recognised as having made particularly significant use of the topography of its setting in eastern Iceland. This article is precisely concerned with relating the saga to its setting, and includes two maps.

Literature, Old Icelandic. History and criticism. Family sagas

742 The greatest of sagas.
Gwyn Jones. *Times Literary Supplement* (UK) (24 Dec. 1954), p. 836-37.

The publication of the *Íslenzk Fornrit* edition of *Brennu Njáls saga*, edited by Einar Ól. Sveinsson, provided the occasion for this essay, which is an eloquent appraisal of the greatness of this saga. 'Far more than any of its rivals it has claims to be the national epic of Iceland... Njála is a book big enough and rich enough to be most things to most men'.

743 Fatal fascination: a choice of crime.
Nigel Balchin. London: Hutchinson, 1964. 200p.

In his chapter 'Burnt Njál: the irredeemable crime', p. 9-57, this well-known English writer gives an outsider's (in the sense of non-specialist) view of the tragedy of Njál and analyses the 'crime' as a product of the society of the time, and projects it into the wider context of the modern world view of crime. It is an unusual and interesting essay which emphasises the timelessness of the saga's inner tension.

744 Njáls saga: a literary masterpiece.
Einar Ól. Sveinsson, edited and translated by Paul Schach. Lincoln, Nebraska: University of Nebraska Press, 1971. 210p.

The best book about the best known saga. The author is widely recognised as the foremost authority on *Njála*, a reputation stemming from his work *Á Njálsbúð* which was written in 1943, and which led to the volume translated here. He analyses clearly and convincingly the roots of the saga, its art and ideals; but the core of this study concerns the saga's portrayal of character; separate chapters are devoted to Njál himself, his eldest son Skarp-Heðin, and Hallgerð wife of Gunnar. In contrast to many studies of sagas, in which the critic takes them apart and leaves the reader to put them together again, this appraisal keeps *Njáls saga* intact and fortifies appreciation of its immense qualities.

745 Fire and iron: critical approaches to Njáls saga.
Richard F. Allen. Pittsburgh, Pennsylvania: University of Pittsburgh Press, 1971. 254p. bibliog.

A stimulating series of critical essays, which comprise an examination of *Njáls saga* in the light of modern critical approaches. The overall purpose of the book is to explain the essential unity of the saga in the face of its complexity. The author discusses various elements, including its rhetoric, and its formal and thematic structure. He introduces his studies with an exposition of the problems of saga criticism in general, and appends a substantial bibliography of critical writings relevant to *Njáls saga*.

746 Njáls saga: a critical introduction.
Lars Lönnroth. Berkeley; Los Angeles: University of California Press, 1974. 275p. bibliog.

The third of the full-length studies of *Njáls saga* available in English. This work, which presupposes some familiarity with saga study by its readers, is to some extent a synthesis of previous scholarship on the sagas, but presented in a new light, especially in its identification of both the Norse and wider European influences on *Njáls saga* (see Lars Lönnroth's *European sources of Icelandic saga*

Literature, Old Icelandic. History and criticism. Kings' sagas

writing q.v.). Includes a substantial bibliography. An article which likewise places *Njáls saga* within the broader western literary tradition was contributed by Denton Fox to the periodical *Comparative Literature* (US), vol. 15, no. 4 (fall 1963), p. 289-310.

747 Historicity and oral narrative in Njáls saga.
Walter Scheps. *Scandinavian Studies*, vol. 46, no. 1 (spring 1974), p. 120-33.

The author of this article advances the plausible view that *Njáls saga*, which he regards as unsurpassed in the context of mediaeval narrative fiction, is not so much a product of oral tradition as a transcendence of it: 'a conscious and deliberate imitation of oral narrative by a brilliant author whose own language did not contain the words to describe what he was doing'. He recommends that, pending further evidence, critical approaches to the saga should be concentrated not on the question of its genesis and historical veracity, but upon its language, structure, characterisation, symbolism, and relationship to other literary works.

748 The Sturlung age as an age of saga writing.
R. George Thomas. *Germanic Review*, vol. 25, no. 1 (Feb. 1950), p. 50-66.

An essay in how to come to terms with the essential contrast, even paradox, of Iceland in the 13th century - the flowering of saga literature in an age of violence, a mixture of 'culture and brutality'. The writer is concerned chiefly with *Sturlunga saga* and Sturla Þórðarson's contribution to it. He throws light on the motives and methods of the saga writers of the time, by seeing Sturla as a pivotal figure, an historian and an artist, drawing on his heritage, refining its presentation, and setting a standard for the future. And yet the fall of the Old Icelandic Commonwealth turned the Icelanders in on themselves, and the insular inbreeding signalled the end of the golden age of saga writing.

Kings' sagas

749 Oratory in the Kings' sagas.
James E. Knirk. Oslo: Universitetsforlaget, 1981. 247p. bibliog.

An extraordinarily detailed specialist study, based on a doctoral dissertation, comprising an investigation into the speech patterns of the so-called Kings' sagas. The author is concerned with comparing the oratory of these sagas (a frequent feature because of their character) with the oratory of other mediaeval literature of Europe, with other Icelandic literature of the period, and between the Kings' sagas themselves. Particular attention is paid to the style of *Heimskringla* and *Sverris saga*.

750 The legendary history of Ólaf Tryggvason.
Gwyn Jones. Glasgow: Jackson for the University of Glasgow, 1968. 38p.

An attempt to salvage historical fact from the mass of legend surrounding King Olaf Tryggvason of Norway, the man behind the conversion of Iceland to Christianity in the year 1000, but described in this lecture as 'Christ's best hatchetman'. Olaf inevitably figures in a number of Icelandic sources covering the end of

Literature, Old Icelandic. History and criticism. Sagas of ancient times

the 10th century: he is recorded by Ari, features in *Hallfred's saga*, and is finely dealt with by Snorri in *Ólafs saga Tryggvasonar* (part of *Heimskringla*). Three other sagas of King Ólaf are known, two having been composed at the monastery of Þingeyrar. This paper was presented as the twenty-second W. P. Ker Memorial Lecture to the University of Glasgow.

751 East Yorkshire in the sagas.
A. L. Binns. York, England: East Yorkshire Local History Society, 1966. 40p. (EYLHS Series no. 22).

A topographical aid to the reading of two Kings' sagas and one legendary saga, comprising an anthology of passages from *Ragnars saga Loðbrókar*, *Jómsvíkinga saga* and *Haralds saga harðráða* is an attempt 'to make available in a small space to the English reader most of the material on which a first-hand judgement of the Old Icelandic sagas about events in Yorkshire can be based'. (See Gwyn Jones' 'Egil Skallgrímsson in England' q.v.). The same author contributed a more general survey *The Viking century in East Yorkshire* (York, England: East Yorkshire Local History Society, 1963. 54p. EYLHS Series no. 15).

Sagas of ancient times

752 Kings, beasts and heroes.
Gwyn Jones. London: Oxford University Press, 1972. 176p.

For the student of comparative mediaeval literature this study is an interesting comparison of narrative techniques in three legendary tales: the Old English *Beowulf*, the Old Welsh *Culhwch and Olwen*, and the Old Icelandic *Hrólfs saga kraka*. See the article 'Fornaldur sögur Norðurlands: a structural analysis' by Ruth Richter-Gould in *Scandinavian Studies*, vol. 52, no. 4 (autumn 1980), p. 423-41, which identifies five main features common to the narrative structure of the legendary sagas.

753 Legendary fiction in mediaeval Iceland.
Hermann Pálsson, Paul Edwards. *Studia Islandica/Íslenzk fræði* (Iceland), vol. 30 (1971), 120p.

A valuable contribution to the study of the *Fornaldarsögur Norðurlanda*, or the legendary sagas of ancient times. The authors' introduction defining the nature of such sagas and their place in Icelandic literature is worth particular attention for its clarity. They proceed to a description of the northern European settings of these sagas and to a discussion of the heroic, romantic and sometimes comic elements which are their hallmark. Popular in their time and since, they have suffered critically only in comparison with the family sagas of Icelanders. They can be happily read in their own right.

754 Romance in Iceland.
Margaret Schlauch. Princeton, New Jersey: Princeton University Press for the American-Scandinavian Foundation; London: Allen & Unwin, 1934. 201p. Reprinted New York: Russell, 1973.

The romantic sagas which were poured out by Icelandic storytellers from the mid-13th century to the late 14th century and even later are generally regarded

Literature, Old Icelandic. History and criticism. Folklore

as a dissolution of the classical saga form. Over 250 of them survive, and many more are known to have existed. The author of this definitive critical work does not attempt to compare them with the sagas of Icelanders, but concentrates on their own traditions, influences and qualities. The interest of these *riddarasögur* and the related *lygisögur* lies in the very variety of these influences, and in the 'cavalier' way in which they reveal themselves. Classical saga strands do appear, but the rest is a medley of oriental fantasy, Greek and Roman echoes, French romance, miscellaneous mythology and folklore, magic and superstition. The realism of old has gone, and romance reigns.

Folk-tales and folklore

755 Icelandic folktales or national tales.
Melinda Babcock. *Journal of the Anthropological Society of Oxford*, vol. 7, no. 2 (1976), p. 78-86.

With particular reference to Jón Árnason's famous collection of folk-tales (see *Icelandic legends*, collected by Jón Arnason, translated by Powell and Magnússon q.v.), this article is an attempt 'to explain how the Icelandic tales came to have an added significance, beyond their "folk" origins, as the nexus of a number of nationalistic movements in 19th-century Iceland'. The author's conclusion is that these tales, in language, style and subject matter, were Icelandic in identity and clearly distinguishable from Danish influence; hence their appeal to Icelandic writers with a nationalist cause to propound.

756 Icelandic folktales.
Steingrímur J. Þorsteinsson. *Scandinavica*, vol. 12, no. 2 (1973), p. 85-99.

The text of a lecture by an Icelandic professor which discusses the enterprise of Jón Arnason and others in collecting popular tales, the motifs and features of Icelandic folk-tales, their relevance to the sagas, and their influence upon some Icelandic creative artists of the 20th century. In the previous volume of this periodical, vol. 11, no. 2 (1972), p. 127-36, there is an article on folklore and literature in Iceland and the problem of literary progress, in which the Russian scholar M. I. Steblin-Kamensky discusses oral literature and its effect on romantic and contemporary literature, and distinguishes between 'conscious' and 'unconscious' authorship.

757 Basic themes in Icelandic folklore.
B. S. Benedikz. *Folklore* (UK), vol. 84 (spring 1973), p. 1-26.

A clearly-presented commentary and guide to the many and varied features and themes to be found in the traditional Icelandic folk-tale, in which the reader is taken through the classification drawn up by the collector Jón Arnason, and orientated in this fertile field. See the same writer's more specific article 'The master magician in Icelandic folk-legend', *Durham University Journal*, vol. 26, no. 1 (Dec. 1964), p. 22-34.

Literature, Old Icelandic. History and criticism. Folklore

758 **Dreams in Old Norse literature and their affinities in folklore.**
Georgia Dunham Kelchner. Cambridge, England: Cambridge University Press, 1935. 154p. Reprinted Folcroft, Pennsylvania: Folcroft Library Editions, 1977.
Dreams, both direct and symbolic, are a frequent feature of Old Icelandic literature - more than 500 occurrences have been noted. This book, which is the only detailed examination of the subject, is arranged in two parts: the first is a general study of the dreams and their themes related to folklore; the second is an index and brief description of individual dreams occurring in the literary sources (e.g. the dreams in *Sturlunga saga*). See the illuminating paper by G. Turville-Petre entitled 'Dreams in Icelandic tradition', which appeared in two sources: *Folklore*, vol. 69 (1958), p. 93-111; also in *Nine Norse studies* (Viking Society for Northern Research, 1972, p. 30-51.).

759 **The craftsman in the mound.**
Lottie Motz. *Folklore* (UK), vol. 88 (spring 1977), p. 46-60.
For the student of comparative folklore this is an unusual article in which the writer examines the legendary figure of the dwarf as depicted in Old Icelandic literature, with particular reference to his work and dwelling places in comparison with his counterparts in the folklore of north-western Europe. A wider treatment of the supernatural element, which is one of the most frequent features distinguishing the mediaeval romances from the classical sagas, is given by Kathryn Hume in an article entitled 'From sagas to romance: the use of monsters in Old Norse literature', *Studies in Philology*, vol. 77, no. 1 (Jan. 1980), p. 1-25.

760 **Thor's hammer.**
H. R. Ellis Davidson. *Folklore* (UK), vol. 76 (spring 1965), p. 1-15.
A comparative analysis of one of the most vivid themes of the supernatural in Old Icelandic literature - the hammer of the god Thór (Mjöllnir) and its various powers as a missile, thunderbolt, etc. A related article by Jacqueline Simpson entitled 'The king's whetstone' appeared in the periodical *Antiquity*, vol. 53 (1979), p. 96-101, in which she interprets the whetstone in Old Icelandic literature as a thunderbolt of the sky-god, and relates it to the whetstone sceptre from the Sutton Hoo ship burial.

761 **Celtic elements in Icelandic tradition.**
Einar Ól. Sveinsson. *Béaloidas*/Journal of the Folklore of Ireland Society (Eire), vol. 25 (1957), p. 3-24.
A paper read at the International Congress of Celtic Studies. The anthropological influence of Celts on Iceland, a country which the Celts had discovered, without permanently settling, perhaps a century before the arrival of the Norsemen, is not in doubt; both anthropological and linguistic observations have established the connection. However, the extent of this influence is differently interpreted. In this paper the writer considers the evidence of Celtic motifs in Icelandic literature, whether directly or indirectly received. Themes from different periods of Irish and Icelandic literature are compared, such as the representation of magic spells. 'What the Norsemen brought with them to Iceland is Icelandic inheritance; but the Irish settlers in Iceland were also one of the constituent parts in the making of the Icelandic nation, and what they brought with them has since played a rôle

Literature, Old Icelandic. History and criticism. Influence.

in Icelandic culture which is not something foreign to the Icelanders but rather a legacy.'

Influence on English literature

762 The influence of Old Norse literature on English literature.
Conrad Hjalmar Nordby. New York: Columbia University Press, 1901. Reprinted New York: AMS Press, 1966.

A still relevant essay on the influence of mediaeval Icelandic culture on English authors of the 18th and 19th centuries, including those, from Thomas Gray to Walter Scott, whose acquaintance with the Old Icelandic sources was formed via the Latin, and others whose knowledge came more directly from the Old Icelandic language itself, such as Thomas Carlyle, Henry Longfellow, Matthew Arnold, Charles Kingsley and William Morris. For a later study, which advances this approach, see Dorothy M. Hoare's *The works of Morris and Yeats in relation to early saga literature* (Cambridge University Press, 1937, 179p. Reprinted New York: Russell, 1971). The author draws the conclusion with which many would agree, that Morris lacks the art of the translator, but flourishes as a re-teller (see especially chapter three 'The dreamer in contact with the Icelandic saga').

763 The sage and the sagas: the brothers Carlyle and 'Early Kings'.
Edward J. Cowan. *Bibliotheck* (Scotland), vol. 9, no. 5 (1979), p. 161-83.

Thomas Carlyle, the essayist, and his younger brother John both had an enthusiasm for the Norse world, the latter's being somewhat more assiduous than the former's. Thomas in fact wrote what he called 'that long rigmarole upon the Norse kings... uncertain what to do with it, if not at once throw it on the fire'. It was in fact published in 1875 by Chapman & Hall of London, thirty-four years after his *Heroes, hero worship and the heroic in history*, the first chapter of which deals with Norse mythology. The author of this article shares Carlyle's disappointment with *The early kings of Norway*, but proceeds to an account of the background to Thomas' interest, and to a more detailed and absorbing analysis of John's deeper interest, including his contacts with the Icelandic scholar Guðbrandur Vigfússon. The author concludes that John's acquaintance with Icelandic literature was that of a learned amateur; but this should not be interpreted pejoratively - Iceland has attracted a remarkable number of such devotees, and their activities, like John Carlyle's, are often illuminating.

764 William Morris, Eiríkur Magnússon and Iceland: a survey of correspondence.
Richard L. Harris. *Victorian Poetry*, vol. 13 (fall 1975), p. 119-30.

Eiríkur Magnússon, the Icelander who was sub-librarian at the University of Cambridge, was the man to whom William Morris owed much of his initial interest in and lasting enthusiasm for Iceland. Their collaboration bore fruit in two main fields, literature and social welfare. Between 1890 and 1895 they produced *The saga library* (q.v.), a series of translations of Icelandic sagas; and in 1882 they organised the Mansion House Relief Committee with the aim of averting the threatened famine in northern Iceland (see *The distress in Iceland* by Eiríkur Magnússon, q.v.). Correspondence relating to these and other literary and

Literature, Old Icelandic. History and criticism. Influence

welfare activities is quoted and discussed in this article, to illustrate Magnússon's influence on Morris. Also described is Morris' friendship with Jón Jónsson of Hlíðarendakot, the saddler who was Morris' guide during his visit to Iceland in 1873 (see Morris' *Journals of travels in Iceland*, q.v.).

Literature, Modern Icelandic

Historical aspects

765 Shakespeare in Iceland: an historical survey.
Stefán Einarsson. *English Literary History*, vol. 7, no. 4 (1940), p. 272-85.

If English writers were occasionally inspired by Icelandic literary tradition (see section: Old Icelandic, Influence on English literature), the reverse was hampered by restrictions imposed on Iceland by the Danish administration at the beginning of the 17th century. Designed to prohibit foreign trade, these also seem to have stymied cultural relations: certainly, Icelandic translations of English works are very scarce in the 17th century, and Shakespeare does not seem to have been translated at all. In this interesting article the writer traces the subsequent activity in translating Shakespeare into Icelandic, from the initial attempts via Danish translations in the early 18th century through the work of Steingrímur Þorsteinsson, Matthías Jochumsson and Eiríkur Magnússon in the 1860s, to the devoted attentions of Indriði Einarsson, who between 1922 and his death in 1939 translated no fewer than fourteen of Shakespeare's plays.

766 Alexander Pope and Icelandic literature.
Richard Beck. *Scandinavian Studies*, vol. 25, no. 2 (May 1953), p. 37-45.

After Shakespeare, Alexander Pope appears to have generated much interest among his Icelandic contemporaries. The author of this paper attributes this interest to Pope's spirit of the Enlightenment, a movement which had found many adherents in 18th-century Iceland; he proceeds to identify and discuss those Icelandic writers who translated some of Pope's work into their own language, particularly Benedikt Gröndal, Magnús Stephensen and Jón Þorláksson. Richard Beck offers further aspects of this theme in his paper 'Jón Þorláksson: Icelandic translator of Pope and Milton', which appeared in *Studia Islandica*, (Philosophical Faculty of the University of Iceland, 1957, vol. 16).

Literature, Modern Icelandic. Historical aspects

767 Literature and literary societies of Iceland.
John Bowring. *Foreign Quarterly Review* (UK), vol. 9 (Jan. 1832), p. 41-77.

An account of the activities of literary societies in Iceland, 1760-1830. These include the Invisible Society, founded in 1760; the Icelandic Literary Society, founded in Copenhagen in 1779 with Jón Eiríksson as President, which in 1827 established the oldest literary periodical in Scandinavia, *Skírnir* (still published annually to this day); the Royal Society for General Icelandic Instruction, founded jn 1780 by Magnús Stephensen; and the (later) Icelandic Literary Society (Islands bókmenntafélag), founded in Copenhagen in 1816 by the grammarian Rask. There are also brief notes on the Icelandic Bible Society and the Royal Arnamagnaean Commission.

768 Icelandic authors of today.
Halldór Hermannsson. Ithaca, New York: Cornell University Library, 1913. 69p. (Islandica, vol. VI).

For the literary historian this volume remains a useful biographical dictionary of the more important Icelandic writers active at the turn of the century. Brief account of their lives and careers are supplemented with lists of their writings and further references. An appendix lists a selection of works dealing with modern Icelandic literature. Series reprinted by Kraus.

769 Four Icelandic writers.
W. W. Worster. *Edinburgh Review*, vol. 238 (Oct. 1923), p. 302-19.

An early appraisal of the work of four major figures of modern Icelandic literature: Jónas Guðlaugsson, Jóhann Sigurjónsson, Guðmundur Kamban and Gunnar Gunnarsson. The critic here discusses their work as a contribution to Danish literature, a language in which Icelandic writers of the early 20th century were forced to express themselves artistically.

770 A history of Icelandic literature.
Stefán Einarsson. Baltimore, Maryland: Johns Hopkins Press for the American-Scandinavian Foundation, 1957. 409p. bibliog.

The value of this standard work is threefold: firstly, for the range of research behind its compilation; secondly, for the fact that it embraces within one volume the history of old, middle and modern Icelandic literature; thirdly, for the remarkably well ordered sequence of its presentation, whereby the author has neatly identified twenty-one major formal and chronological divisions of Icelandic literary history, thus making it easier for the reader to correlate the various strands. Further, for a work of considerable detail, it is by no means difficult to read. Particularly valuable are the substantial chapters on national romanticism (1830-74), realism to neo-romanticism (1874-1918), and tradition and revolt between the World Wars. There is also a useful chapter introducing the North American Icelandic writers. The work is completed by a well arranged bibliography and an excellent index. As a work of reference in the field this volume has yet to be surpassed, and thus remains in print a quarter of a century after its original publication.

Literature, Modern Icelandic. Poetry. Anthologies

771 **History of Icelandic prose writers, 1800-1940.**
Stefán Einarsson. Ithaca, New York: Cornell University Press, 1948. 269p. (Islandica, vol. XXXII-XXXIII).
An indispensible survey of Icelandic prose writing in the modern period. Prose is interpreted in the widest sense: novels, short stories, drama, essays, etc. The treatment is both thematic and individual, and though the volume includes a great amount of biographical detail this tends to illuminate the reasons for the development of the various strands and movements in Icelandic prose. The author assesses the rise of romanticism, the influence of Jón Sigurðsson, the folk-tale collections, realism and idealism, nationalism, the influence of socialism, the Danish-Icelandic writers, and the emigrant writers in North America. There is a final chapter on the remarkable writer of children's stories, Nonni (Jón Stefán Sveinsson) who emigrated to continental Europe in 1870.

772 **History of Icelandic poets, 1800-1940.**
Richard Beck. Ithaca, New York: Cornell University Press, 1950. 247p. (Islandica, vol. XXXIV).
Published as a companion volume to Stefán Einarsson's *History of Icelandic prose writers, 1800-1940* (q.v.) to form a survey of Icelandic literature of the 19th and early 20th centuries, this is a thorough and scholarly introduction to the modern Icelandic poetic tradition. The author divides his study into six major sections: the romantic poets, the unschooled poets, philosophical and religious poets, realist and neo-romantic poetry, currents of the 20th century, and the North American Icelandic poets. Within each section the poets (over 100 in all) are treated individually, so that the volume can be used as either a reference work on individual poets or as a history of modern Icelandic poetic development. Poets who are considered chiefly as prose writers are discussed in the companion volume above.

Poetry

Anthologies

773 **An anthology of Scandinavian literature from the Viking period to the twentieth century.**
Selected and edited by Hallberg Hallmundsson. New York: Collier; London: Collier MacMillan, 1965. 362p. bibliog.
The Icelandic section of this anthology appears on p. 183-260, and is largely devoted to poetry. An interesting mixture rather than a strict representation, translated by various hands. From the old period there is the Eddic *lay of Thrym* (*Þrymskviða*), and the later mediaeval ballad of Tristram; from the 17th century, two poems by Hallgrímur Pétursson; from the 19th century, poems by Jónas Hallgrímsson and Matthías Jochumsson; and from the turn of the century, poems by Einar Benediktsson and the Canadian-Icelandic poet Stephan G. Stephansson. The anthology also includes three short stories: Þórbergur Þórðarson's *The brindled monster*; Gunnar Gunnarsson's *Father and son*; and Halldór Laxness' leg-pulling piece *The defeat of the Italian airforce in Reykjavík*.

Literature, Modern Icelandic. Poetry. Anthologies

774 Oxford book of Scandinavian verse.
Chosen by Sir Edmund Gosse, William A. Craigie. Oxford, England: Clarendon Press, 1925. 432p.

The last hundred pages of this anthology are devoted to Iceland. The poems are introduced by William Craigie, and are taken from the work of twenty Icelandic poets born between 1620 and 1860, from Stefán Olafsson, through Jónas Hallgrímsson to Hannes Hafstein. The texts themselves are presented in Icelandic, and the anthology forms a useful reader for the student of the modern Icelandic literary language.

775 Modern Scandinavian poetry: the panorama of poetry, 1900-1975.
General editor Martin S. Allwood. New York: New Directions; Toronto: McLeod, 1982. 400p.

A fine anthology of Scandinavian (including, unusually, Greenlandic) poetry, published in collaboration with the Anglo-American center at Mullsjö in Sweden. The Icelandic section includes forty-six short poems by twenty-three Icelanders born between 1879 and 1949. The poems are translated by various hands, and have brief introductory notes. See the same editor's earlier anthology *20th century Scandinavian poetry: the development of poetry in Iceland... 1900-1950* (Stockholm: Kooperativa Forbundets Bokforlag, 1950, 396p.), in which eighteen Icelandic poets are represented in English translation.

776 The North American book of Icelandic verse.
Watson Kirkconnell. New York; Montreal: Carrier & Isles, 1930. 228p.

An important collection, not least for the fact that it is the only translated anthology of Icelandic poetry to acknowledge the full tradition from epic to modern. Thus the non-specialist reader is invited to appreciate a reasonably balanced presentation of translations from Eddic poetry, which has survived in 'complete anonymity', followed by the court poetry of the skalds, many of whose names and biographical details are known; the compiler is then a little too severe in his judgment of the poetry of the 13th to 16th centuries as 'blank and sterile', but does include some notable examples of the popular poetry of this period. The latter half of the collection is devoted to the modern period in all its remarkable variety. Nearly one hundred poets are represented, and the translations clearly reflect Kirkconnell's industry and imagination. This volume indeed fits the compiler's description as a tribute to the millenium of Iceland and its poetry.

777 Icelandic lyrics: originals and translations.
Selected and edited by Richard Beck. Reykjavík: Þórhallur Bjarnason, 1930. 263p.

An indispensible selection of the work of thirty Icelandic poets of the 19th century - the century of national awakening in Iceland. It is a finely produced volume with parallel Icelandic/English texts of the poems, and short biographies with drawings of the poets represented. Amongst these are the romantic Bjarni Thorarensen, the lyrical and much loved Jónas Hallgrímsson, the lyricist and translator Steingrímur Þorsteinsson, Jón Thoroddsen, Hjálmar Jónsson, Grímur Thomsen, Benedikt Gröndal, and the renowned Matthías Jochumsson, whose millennial hymn to Iceland, which became the national anthem set to the music of Sveinbjörn Sveinbjörnsson, is included here. Also represented are the poets of *Verðandi* (an Icelandic periodical devoted to realism in literature, founded in

Literature, Modern Icelandic. Poetry. Anthologies

1882 under the influence of the Danish critic Georg Brandes) who included Hannes Hafstein, Einar Kvaran and Gestur Pálsson. The collection is completed with examples of North American Icelandic poetry led by Stephan G. Stephansson.

778 **Icelandic poems and stories; translations from modern Icelandic literature.**
Edited by Richard Beck. Princeton, New Jersey: Princeton University Press for the American-Scandinavian Foundation; London: Oxford University Press, 1943. 315p. Reprinted Freeport, New York: Books for Libraries Press, 1968. (Granger Index Reprint Series).

Rather easier to obtain than the previous item, this volume includes many of the poets in *Icelandic lyrics: originals and translations* by the same author (q.v.), plus others, as well as examples of Icelandic prose from the 19th and early 20th centuries. Amongst the poets and story writers rarely translated elsewhere are Unnar Benediktsdóttir, one of the earliest women writers of Iceland, who under the pseudonym Hulda wrote both poems and short stories, and Þorgils Gjallandi (the pseudonym of Jón Stefánsson, a novelist and farmer from north-eastern Iceland). Each of the twenty-eight authors represented are introduced with a brief biography by the editor.

779 **Odes and echoes.**
Paul Bjarnason. Vancouver, Canada: Union Printers/People's Co-operative Bookstore, 1954. 186p.

A remarkable collection of translations from modern Icelandic poetry. The translator, a North American Icelandic poet of distinction, presents seventeen of his own poems in the section *Odes*, and in the section *Echoes* translations of seventy poems by some thirty Icelandic poets, including several by Einar P. Jónsson, Einar Benediktsson, and the émigré Stephan G. Stephansson. The translations are particularly notable for their preservation of the original metres (never easy for a translator, and yet, in this volume, never becoming stilted), and of the particularly Icelandic usage of alliteration, assonance and internal rhyming. A fine and intimate introduction to Icelandic poetry of the late 19th and 20th centuries.

780 **Northern lights.**
Jakobina Johnson. Reykjavík: Bókaútgáfa Menningarsjóðs, 1959. 91p.

Jakobina Johnson is another Canadian Icelander who, as a poet in her own right, also translated the modern poetry of her native land into English. Thirty Icelandic poets are represented in this book of translations, which are traditional, straightforward and sympathetic. The title of the book is taken from the first poem in the collection, Einar Benediktsson's *Northern Lights*. Publication sponsored by the Icelandic Cultural Fund.

Literature, Modern Icelandic. Poetry. Anthologies

781 **Anthology of modern Icelandic literature.**
Compiled and edited by Loftur Bjarnason. Berkeley, California: University Extension, University of California, 1961. 2 vols.

A mimeographed but convenient collection of translations from modern Icelandic writers (mainly poets), which draws extensively from a variety of previously published collections, but adds fresh material. The first volume covers the period from 1800 to 1914; the second extends to 1950. Apart from poetry, the volumes also include some drama and essays.

782 **An anthology of Icelandic poetry.**
Edited by Eiríkur Benedikz. Reykjavík: Ministry of Education, 1969. 148p.

A convenient selection of Icelandic poetry of the modern period, 1600-1930, representing thirty poets. Draws on existing translations. Brief notes on the poets.

783 **Poems of today.**
Selected and translated by Alan E. Boucher. Reykjavík: Iceland Review Library, 1971. 91p.

A selection of sixty-four poems by twenty-five Icelandic poets, all but two of whom were born in the 20th century. Chronologically arranged from Jóhannes úr Kötlum and Jón Helgason (1899) to Jóhannes Björn (1949). The range is extraordinary in the context of the small population, though it has to be remembered that poetry is the art form with the least broken traditions from the old period. The translation, a challenge in itself, retains the vitality of each of the poems. One might suggest that the five blank pages at the end of this attractive edition could have been filled with biographical notes on the poets - Icelandic poetry is so intensely personal that such details are of more than usual interest. In the same year Alan Boucher also presented translations of eight contemporary Icelandic poets in a feature entitled 'The poet's voice' which appeared in the magazine *Atlantica and Iceland Review*, vol. 9, no. 2 (1971), and includes three poems by Hannes Pétursson, with accompanying drawings by the figurative artist Einar Hákonarsson.

784 **Modern Icelandic poetry.**
Modern Poetry in Translation, no. 30 (spring 1977), p. 1-18.

A selection of poems introduced, translated, and with biographical notes by the Icelandic writer Sigurður A. Magnússon. The poets represented are Steinn Steinarr (including his brilliantly taut and evocative poem *Child*), Jón úr Vör, Stefán Hörður Grímsson, Jón Óskar, Hannes Sigfússon, Vilborg Dagbjartsdóttir, Matthías Jóhannesson, the particularly popular Hannes Pétursson, Þorsteinn frá Hamri, Nína Björk Árnadóttir, and Sigurður Magnússon himself. These eleven poets were all born in the 20th century, and their work as presented here reflects a remarkable variety of moods and influences within a 'modernist' approach, which seems to throw off the shackles from, though not the respect for, the traditions of Old Icelandic poetry.

Literature, Modern Icelandic. Poetry. Individual poets

785 **The post-war poetry of Iceland.**
Translated with an introduction by Sigurður A. Magnússon. Iowa City, Iowa: University of Iowa Press, 1982. 288p.

Published just prior to the submission of this bibliography (the compiler has not seen the volume) this is clearly an important and unique anthology. It contains translations of the work of twenty-eight Icelandic poets of the newer movements, most of the poems being translated here for the first time.

Individual poets

786 **Hymns of the Passion: meditations on the Passion of Christ.**
Hallgrímur Pétursson, translated by Arthur Charles Gook. Reykjavík: Hallgrím's Church, 1966. 214p.

Hallgrímur Pétursson (1614-74) lived through one of the hardest and most destitute periods of Icelandic history. His *Hymns of the Passion*, 50 in all, containing 817 verses, have from the time of their composition to the present day exerted a profound influence upon the Icelandic nation (as did the family sermons of Jón Vidalín written half a century later). His funeral hymn, also included, is sung to this day. These hymns rank as one of the pinnacles of Icelandic literature of any period. This welcome translation, by an Englishman devoted to the Icelandic church for most of his life, is especially fine in preserving the original metre, and was published by the recently constructed church in Reykjavík which bears Hallgrím's name. For a selected edition of these hymns see Charles Venn Pilcher's translation *Icelandic meditations on the Passion* (New York; London: Longman, 1923. 64p.).

787 **Bjarni Thorarensen: Iceland's pioneer romanticist.**
Richard Beck. *American-Scandinavian Review*, vol. 15, no. 3 (1938), p. 71-80.

Bjarni Thorarensen (1786-1841) was born at Brautarholt in southern Iceland, and from the age of three lived at Hlidarendi (home of Gunnar in *Njáls saga*). In public life he became a governor of northern Iceland and temporary governor of the whole country. But his fame lies in his poetry, particularly as the founder of the romantic movement in Iceland. A nationalist and a devotee of the ideals embodied in the traditions of the older literature, he was not a prolific writer, but his influence was immense. The author of this article draws attention to the way in which his devotion to his native classical literature was accompanied by a restraint in style and an admixture of realism 'whereby he and nearly all of his Icelandic successors were saved from the aberrations and excesses of Romanticism elsewhere'.

788 **Matthías Jochumsson: Icelandic poet and translator.**
Richard Beck. *Scandinavian Studies*, vol. 13, no. 8 (1935), p. 111-24.

Matthías Jochumsson (1835-1920) is both the product and the symbol of the development of Icelandic literature in the 19th century. The influence of the Romantic movement combined with the national awakening was responsible for a continuous flowering of Icelandic poetry. For half a century Matthías Jochumsson enjoyed a unique respect and popularity. Although he is most popularly identified

Literature, Modern Icelandic. Poetry. Individual poets

with the millennial hymn and national anthem of Iceland, his poetry is rich and varied. He was a man of letters in the full sense, being also dramatist, essayist, translator and literary editor. This article, by an eminent authority on Icelandic poetry who knew Matthías during his last years, is a tribute to his life and work to mark the centenary of his birth.

789 **Harp of the north: poems.**
Einar Benediktsson, selected and translated by Frederic T. Wood. Charlottesville, Virginia: University of Virginia Press, 1955. 91p.

Einar Benediktsson (1864-1940) was the outstanding Icelandic poet of his time. A journalist, lawyer and financier, he was also an ambitious traveller abroad, but, above all, he was a nationalist with great visions for his own country. He wrote five volumes of magnificent poetry between 1897 and 1930; fifty of his poems are included in this translation.

790 **Davíd Stefánsson.**
Stefán Einarsson. *American-Scandinavian Review*, vol. 55, no. 1 (March 1967), p. 34-40.

Davíd Stefánsson (1895-1964) was born in Eyjafjörður in northern Iceland, and although first and foremost a poet, indeed a national poet, he also wrote a major novel, collections of essays, and four plays (see *Fire and ice: three Icelandic plays*, q.v.). As a poet he was a traditionalist, and his mood is pervasively reflective, although a degree of moral, religious, social and political commitment characterises many of his poems. This portrait of his life and work (he was not the only Icelandic writer to be a librarian) is a tribute written shortly after his death, and includes translated passages from some of his poems.

791 **The poems of Tómas Guðmundsson.**
Richard N. Ringler. *American-Scandinavian Review*, vol. 63, no. 2 (1975), p. 27-39.

Although by no means a prolific poet (his work comprises four volumes of poetry) Tómas Guðmundsson, who was born in 1901, is held in the highest regard as a national poet. His themes are mainly urban and nostalgic, his tone both lyrical and ironic, and his diction flexible. This examination of his work is accompanied by translations of five of his poems, including the compelling *Autumn in the city*. Tómas Guðmundsson was the subject of a shorter article by Kristján Karlsson in the same periodical, vol. 60, no. 3 (1972), p. 249-52.

792 **Guðmundur Böðvarsson.**
Hallberg Hallmundsson. *American-Scandinavian Review*, vol. 53, no. 1 (March 1965), p. 44-49.

Guðmundur Böðvarsson (1904-74) was brought up in Borgarfjörður, western Iceland, amongst a traditional farming community. His poetry, considerable in quantity, contains a consistent quality engendered by the combination of the Icelandic character of its roots and spirit with the universality of its themes and moods. Not so much a modernist, as a poet striving for new expression within traditional forms. A translation of one of his shorter poems *Sound of weather* is appended to this sketch of his life and work.

Literature, Modern Icelandic. Poetry. Individual poets

793 **Time and the water.**
Steinn Steinarr, translated by Sigurður A. Magnússon. *Atlantica and Iceland Review*, vol. 16, no. 4 (1978), p. 9-13.

Icelandic poetry, because of its deep-rooted traditions, was comparatively late in attaining a 'modern' movement. A poet who led the way in this respect was Steinn Steinarr (pseudonym of Aðalsteinn Kristmundsson, 1908-58). He was a political, philosophical and essentially reflective poet, and his series of twenty-one short poems named *Time and the water* is a pessimistic yet particularly appealing reflection on loneliness. This translation is accompanied by the sympathetic drawings of Einar Hákonarson.

794 **The changing earth, and selected poems.**
Ólafur Jóhann Sigurðsson, translated from the Icelandic by Alan E. Boucher. Reykjavík: Iceland Review Library, 1979. 96p.

Ólafur Jóhann Sigurðsson was born in 1918, and in latter years has become a particularly respected figure in Icelandic literature. In 1976 he won the Nordic Council Literary Award for his poetry (four years later this was won by another Icelandic poet Snorri Hjartarson), selections from which are presented in this book of translations. He is also a novelist, and the choice of his short novel *Changing earth* (originally published in 1947) for inclusion in this volume was prompted by the fact that it is a recommended text in Icelandic schools. Although his essential quality is considered to be his sensitive use of the Icelandic language, the foreign reader will find much that is appealing in translation.

795 **J. F. K.**
Matthías Jóhannesson, translated from the Icelandic by Sigurður A. Magnússon. *American-Scandinavian Review*, vol. 52, no. 1 (March 1964), p. 37-38.

John F. Kennedy enjoyed no greater popularity outside his own country than he did in Scandinavia, and his assassination was felt with a particular keenness in Iceland. This poem, written by the editor of the Icelandic daily newspaper *Morgunblaðið*, is an eloquent expression of collective grief.

796 **Settlement poems I & II.**
Kristjána Gunnars. Winnipeg, Manitoba: Turnstone Press, 1980. 2 vols.

Kristjána Gunnars, born in Reykjavík in 1948, is a recent immigrant to Canada. This first collection of her poems is an evocation of episodes in the lives of earlier Icelandic immigrants, and her purpose is not to romanticise their experiences but to depict the harsher realities. Her second book of poems is entitled *One-eyed moon maps*.

General criticism

797 Tradition and innovation in twentieth century Icelandic poetry.
Peter Carleton. PhD thesis, University of California, Berkeley, 1967. 352p.
The first section of this thesis comprises a substantial review of the development of Icelandic verse up to 1900. The author proceeds to divide the character of Icelandic poetry of the present century into three categories, which he sees as determined by non-literary forces: the lyrist poetry which flourished, waned and reflourished; the realist poetry which arose in the 1930s and has held its position; and the modernist poetry typical of the post-war period.

798 The triumph of modernism in Icelandic poetry, 1945-1970.
Sveinn Skorri Höskuldsson. *Scandinavia*, vol. 12 (1973), suppl. p. 65-75.
Part of a special issue devoted to contemporary Scandinavian poetry, in which the author of this article starts by setting the scene of the profound social changes wrought in Iceland during the 1940s, before examining how they influenced the modernism of the poetry of this period and subsequently. Particular attention is paid to three collections of poetry which exerted a major influence: Snorri Hjartason's *Kvæði* (Poetry, 1944); Jón úr Vör's *Þorpið* (*The Village*, 1946); and Steinn Steinarr's *Tíminn og vatnið* (*Time and the water*, 1948 q.v.). He then discusses the so-called 'Atom Poets' of the 1950s and 1960s, especially Hannes Sigfússon, Einar Bragi, Jón Oskar, Sigfús Daðason and Stefán Hörður Grímsson, who reflect the cold war environment, and whose periodical mouthpiece *Birtingur* was founded in 1955. This article is an admirably balanced summary of post-war trends in Icelandic poetry for the reader seeking a general orientation.

History of Icelandic poets, 1800-1940.
See item no. 772.

Drama

799 Fire and ice: three Icelandic plays.
Jóhann Sigurjónsson, Davið Stefánsson, Agnar Þórðarson. Madison, Wisconsin: University of Wisconsin Press, 1967. 266p. (Nordic Translation Series).
The three plays presented here in translations sponsored by the Nordic Cultural Commission were among the first to be brought to the attention of an English-speaking audience. The collection comprises Jóhann Sigurjónsson's *The Wish* (*Galdra-Loftur*), a three-act play written in 1915, whose theme, an Icelandic version of the Faust legend, is man's stubborn quest for knowledge beyond his capacities; Davið Stefánsson's *The golden gate* (*Gullna hliðið*), written in 1941, a sharp comedy in four acts about a woman who tries to secure her undeserving husband's entry into heaven; and Agnar Þórðarson's *Atoms and Madams* (*Kjornorka og kvenhilli*), written in 1955, a satirical play in four acts concerning the contrast between the values of the older rural Iceland and the bourgeois attitudes

251

Literature, Modern Icelandic. Drama

of the modern post-war state. The first and last of these plays are here translated by Einar Haugen, who also contributes an introduction to the three plays and their authors, plus a useful bibliography; the second play is translated by G. M. Gathorne-Hardy. *Loftur* was also published separately in English translation by Jean Young and Eleanor Arkwright (University of Reading, 1939, 67p.). *The golden gate* also appears in the collection *Five modern Scandinavian plays* (New York: Twayne, 1971. Library of Scandinavian Literature, vol. 11).

800 **Sword and crozier: a drama in five acts.**
Indriði Einarsson, authorised translation by Lee M. Hollander. Boston, Massachusetts: Badger, 1912. 59p.

Originally published in 1899 as *Sverð og bagall* this is the only one of Indriði Einarsson's plays to have been translated into English, although it is not as well known as his first play *Nýársnóttin* (*New Year's Eve*). Indriði Einarsson (1851-1939) was a pioneer of Icelandic drama, in terms not just of his writing, but also of its application to the stage; he was the first producer with the Reykjavík Theatre Company in 1897, and the originator of the idea for the Icelandic National Theatre, which staged one of his plays at its eventual inauguration. His themes are usually drawn from folklore and history - *Sword and crozier* deals with the age of the Sturlungs.

801 **Eyvindur of the mountains (Fjalli Eyvindur): a play in four acts.**
Jóhann Sigurjónsson, translated from the Icelandic by Francis P. Magoun. Reykjavík: Helgafell, 1961. 120p.

Jóhann Sigurjónsson, one of the many Icelandic writers who worked in Copenhagen, died before the age of forty, but is nevertheless one of the revered names in Icelandic poetry and drama. *Eyvind of the Hills* was the third of his five plays and was written in 1912. It is a powerful, evocative and cathartic drama, fashioned on the life of Eyvindur Jónsson, an Icelandic outlaw of the 18th century. It was the play which established the author's reputation at home, and brought him respect in continental Europe, where the play received frequent productions. It has been made into a film in Sweden, and has enjoyed regular revivals on the Reykjavík stage. The sixth revival by the Reykjavík Theatre Company in 1967 provided the occasion for an analysis of the background theme to the play and the play itself, contributed by Sigurður A. Magnússon to the magazine *Iceland Review*, vol. 5, no. 1 (1968), p. 16-22, accompanied by photographs from the production. This play was also published along with another of Jóhann Sigurjónsson's plays *The Hraun farm* in an English translation by H. K. Schenke (New York: American-Scandinavian Foundation, 1916, 131p.). See *Fire and ice: three Icelandic plays* (q.v.).

802 **We murderers.**
Guðmundur Kamban, translated from the Danish by Einar Haugen. Madison, Wisconsin: University of Wisconsin Press, 1970. 74p.

Written in 1920, this is a strong and emotional play of personal tensions and conflicting expectations of love between wife and husband. There are definite echoes of Ibsen in the portrayal of the heroine. This worthy translation from the Danish obscures the fact that, unusually for Kamban, he wrote it originally in Icelandic. The translator's introduction is a helpful guide to this fine drama. A few years earlier Kamban had written another strong study of woman's character in his play *Hadda Padda*. This appeared in an English translation by Sadie L.

Literature, Modern Icelandic. Drama

Peller (New York: Knopf, 1917). This play, too has echoes of Ibsen, although not merely Ibsenesque.

803 Bishop Jón Arason.
Tryggvi Sveinbjörnsson, translated by Lee M. Hollander. In: *Modern Scandinavian plays*. New York: Liveright for the American-Scandinavian Foundation, 1954, p. 173-242.

A chronicle play in four acts, whose central theme is the last year in the life of Iceland's last Catholic bishop, Jón Arason (see Tryggvi J. Oleson's *Bishop Jón Arason* q.v.) who was executed along with two of his sons in 1550, and remains a national hero in a Lutheran country today, as much for his patriotism as his martyrdom. Set in Hólar, Sauðafell and Skálholt, this powerful historical drama was written by the diplomat Tryggvi Sveinbjörnsson (1891-1961) in 1950, and was performed at the National Theatre of Iceland in the same year to commemorate the 400th anniversary of the events which it dramatises.

804 Journey into winter: a play.
Kristján Albertsson, translated from the Icelandic by Muriel Jackson. Reykjavík: Helgafell, 1958. 107p.

A play in five acts, first performed at the National Theatre of Iceland in 1958. In its treatment of the theme of absolute power it displays a certain Nordic starkness; but behind this welcome translation, which is correct rather than theatrical, there is a drama of some force, relevance and suspense. Indeed, one feels that if it had been the work of a continental European playwright (which in a sense it could be, as, unusually with Icelandic writers, neither its theme nor its setting is Icelandic) it might well have entered the international repertoire.

805 Modern Nordic plays: Iceland.
Oslo: Universitetsforlaget; New York: Twayne, 1973. 427p. (Scandia books/Library of Scandinavian Literature).

In spite of its short tradition, Icelandic drama has not been slow to reflect avant-garde and other modernist movements in the post-war period. This volume is a particularly interesting collection of five plays translated into English by Alan Boucher (the first three) and Guðrún Tómasdóttir (the last two), with a useful introduction to post-war Icelandic theatre by Sigurður A. Magnússon. The plays are: Halldór Laxness' *The pigeon banquet* (*Dúfnaveizlan*), a widely satirical piece written in 1966 (production reviewed in *Iceland Review*, vol. 4, no. 3 (1966), p. 21-27); Jökull Jakobsson's *Seaway to Baghdad* (*Sjóleiði til Bagdad*, 1965) contrasting the old and the new Iceland; Erlingur E. Halldórsson's *Mink* (*Minkarnir*, 1965), a literary blast against the NATO base on Iceland, using the symbol of the mink; and two short pieces by Oddur Björnsson in the 'absurd' tradition, *Ten variations* (*Tíu tilbrigdi*, 1968) and *Yolklife* (*Jodlif*, 1965), a dialogue between two foetuses.

253

Literature, Modern Icelandic. The novel

The novel

806 Lad and lass: a story of life in Iceland.
Jón Þórðarson Thoroddsen, translated from the Icelandic by Arthur M. Reeves. London: Sampson Low, 1890, 209p.

Jón Thoroddsen (1818-68) is generally regarded as the father-figure of the Icelandic novel. *Piltur og stúlka* was written in 1849, and a second novel *Maður og kona* (*Man and wife*) was unfinished at the time of his death, but was edited and published posthumously. *Lad and lass* is a consistently appealing tale, echoes of which can be frequently found in the 20th-century novelists of Iceland.

807 Lost in the Arctic.
Nonni, translated from the German by M. M. Bodkin. New York: Kennedy; Dublin: Catholic Truth Society, 1927. 72p.

Nonni, or Jón Stefán Sveinsson, was born near Akureyri in 1857 and died at Cologne in 1944. He was brought up in Iceland, but as a youth left for the continent and became a Jesuit priest. At the age of 56 when he was in Germany he became a writer, and many of his books tell of his early life in Iceland. The 'Nonni' stories have been translated into several languages, yet strangely this story of Nonni and Manni, the adventures of two boys, is the only one to have been translated into English. He gained a considerable reputation on the continent, however, and his childhood home in northern Iceland is now a much visited memorial museum. Nonni's life is the subject of a brief illustrated sketch by Jónas Gíslason in the magazine *Atlantica and Iceland Review*, vol. 11, no. 3-4 (1973), p. 20-25.

808 Guest the one-eyed.
Gunnar Gunnarsson, translated by W. W. Worster. London: Gyldendal, 1920; New York: Knopf, 1922. 352p.

Gunnar Gunnarsson (1889-1975) was one of the generation of Icelandic writers forced by difficult conditions at home to emigrate to Denmark in search of a wider audience. His standing in Scandinavian literature as a whole can be seen as a vindication of his decision, and his debt to his native land was recognised when he returned to Iceland in 1939. The question of whether he should be considered a Danish or Icelandic writer thus became less relevant. This translation is an abridged version of the four-volume novel *The family at Borg*, which he wrote between 1912 and 1914. The title of this version is taken from the title of the third volume of the original work. It was Gunnar Gunnarsson's first full-length work (preceded by poems and short stories), and it was the one which established his reputation in Scandinavia. It takes the form of a family saga of life in rural Iceland of the 19th century, spanning several generations with its vivid characters.

809 The sworn brothers: a tale of the early days in Iceland.
Gunnar Gunnarsson, translated by C. Field, W. Emmé. London: Gyldendal, 1920; New York: Knopf, 1921. 315p.

A re-working of the story of Ingólfr Árnason, the first settler of Iceland, and his foster-brother Hjörleif. Gunnarsson's novel is more than just a tale retold,

Literature, Modern Icelandic. The novel

however, as he skilfully recreates the relationship between man and environment, and explores the psychological factors in the characters' relationship and their destinies. Written in 1918.

810 **Seven days darkness.**
Gunnar Gunnarsson, translated by Roberts Tapley. New York: MacMillan; London: Allen & Unwin, 1930. 294p.
Originally published in Danish in 1920, this novel reflects a period of pessimism in Gunnarsson's work, engendered by the events of the First World War. The background to this novel is the epidemic of Spanish flu in Reykjavík in 1918, and the theme, simple but universal, is the conflict of good and evil in the shape of the story's two main protagonists.

811 **Ships in the sky, The night and the dream.**
Gunnar Gunnarsson, translated by Evelyn Ramsden. Indianapolis, Indiana: Bobbs-Merrill; London: Jarrolds, 1938. 2 vols.
Generally considered to be Gunnar Gunnarsson's major work, this fictionalised autobiography 'compiled from Uggi Greipsson's notes' originally appeared in Danish in five volumes between 1923 and 1928 under the overall title *Kirken paa bjerget* (*The church on the hill*). In this translation *Ships in the sky* covers the first two volumes, which deal with the author's happy childhood in Fljótsdalur, and the family's unsettling removal to Vopnafjörður where his mother died. *The night and the dream* covers the last three volumes, which take the reader on from this environment to Denmark and the author's early years there in the quest to become a respected writer. This work exhibits a renewed optimism in Gunnarsson's outlook.

812 **The black cliffs.**
Gunnar Gunnarsson, translated from the Danish by Cecil Wood. Madison, Wisconsin: University of Wisconsin Press, 1967. 220p. (Nordic Translation Series).
Svartfugl was originally published in 1929, and was inspired by Gunnarsson's study of the events surrounding one of the most notorious murders in Icelandic history, which occurred on the north-western peninsula. This historical novel is a social and psychological study of the crime as he came to understand it and draw on it. The translation is accompanied by an excellent introduction, with full bibliography, by Richard N. Ringler.

813 **Advent.**
Gunnar Gunnarsson, translated by Evelyn Ramsden. London: Jarrolds, 1939. 80p.
This is the only one of the several novellas by Gunnar Gunnarsson to have been translated into English. It was also translated (by Kenneth C. Kaufman) and published under the title *The good shepherd* (Indianapolis, Indiana: Bobbs-Merrill, 1940), and proved very popular in North America, as it did in its German translations. *Advent*, as the title implies, is a form of Christmas story.

Literature, Modern Icelandic. The novel

814 Gunnar Gunnarsson: Iceland's first international novelist.
Sigurður A. Magnússon. *Atlantica and Iceland Review*, vol. 11, no. 1 (1973), p. 50-55.

An illustrated appreciation of the life and literary career of the writer who first brought modern Icelandic literature into the international arena. See the essay by Richard Beck in *Scandinavian studies: essays presented to Dr. Henry Goddard Leach on the occasion of his 85th birthday* (q.v.).

815 The virgin of Skálholt.
Guðmundur Kamban, translated from the Danish by Evelyn Ramsden. Boston, Massachusetts: Little, Brown, 1935. 400p. London: Nicholson & Watson, 1936. 463p.

This is only a partial translation of the great historical novel by Kamban (1888-1945) - two volumes out of the four in the original *Skálholt* which was published between 1930 and 1935. It is the story of the family tragedy which beset Bishop Brynjólfur Sveinsson, the renowned bishop of Skálholt (1605-75) and his daughter Ragnheiður, who, after taking an oath of innocence, conceives an illegitimate son by her tutor. Her death and its immediate effect on the family conclude this version, and the reader will be perplexed at the lack of English access to the further two volumes of the original. The hymn writer Hallgrímur Pétursson also figures in this epic novel of Iceland, which so clearly links the saga period with modern times. Another of Kamban's historical novels translated by the same hand is *I see a wondrous land* (New York: Putnam; London: Nicholson & Watson, 1938). The theme of this novel is the history of the Icelanders' discovery of North America.

816 Morning of life.
Kristmann Guðmundsson, translated from the Norwegian by Elizabeth Sprigge, Paul Napier. New York: Doubleday; London; Toronto: Heinemann, 1936. 318p.

Kristmann Guðmundsson was born in 1901 and emigrated to Norway in his twenties. His early novels were written in Norwegian, but after his return to Iceland (where he still lives) before the Second World War, he wrote in Icelandic. He is first and foremost a perceptive and compelling teller of love stories, and his mastery of structure and themes has earned for his novels a high number of translations into foreign languages. *Livets morgen* was originally published in 1929. Two other of Kristmann Guðmundsson's novels have been translated into English: *The bridal gown: a novel of Iceland*, translated by O. F. Theis (New York: Cosmopolitan Book Corporation, 1931); *Winged citadel*, translated by Barrows Mussey (New York: Holt, 1940).

817 Salka Valka.
Halldór Laxness, translated by F. H. Lyon. London: Allen & Unwin; New York: Houghton Mifflin, 1936. 429p.

This novel, the first of Laxness' four epic novels, was originally published in two parts in 1931 and 1932, under the titles *O, thou pure vine* and *The bird on the beach*. It was not until its second edition in 1951 that it generally acquired the overall title of *Salka Valka* after its chief character, the fishergirl from Óseyri, perhaps the most vivid character portrayal of a woman in all Laxness' works. To say that this novel is concerned with the stirrings of socialism in a small Icelandic community is to isolate only one of its many strands. The first part takes place

Literature, Modern Icelandic. The novel
during the period before the First World War, the second is set in the 1920s.
Translated into English from Icelandic via Danish.

818 **Independent people.**
Halldór Laxness, translated from the Icelandic by J. A.
Thompson. London: Allen & Unwin, 1945; New York:
Knopf, 1946. 470p. Reprinted Westport Connecticut:
Greenwood Press, 1976.
The second of Laxness' four epic novels. Originally published 1934-35 under the title *Sjálfstætt fólk*, it is pervaded by a starkness and beauty that is immensely powerful and lasting. The story of Guðbjartur Jónsson and of his struggle to maintain and run his own farm 'to be the king of his own small realm' is one with many messages for many societies today - its theme and its spirit are timeless. The translation is notably harmonious.

819 **World light.**
Halldór Laxness, translated from the Icelandic by Magnús
Magnússon. Madison, Wisconsin: University of Wisconsin
Press, 1969. 521p. (Nordic Translation Series).
World light (*Heimsljós*) was the overall title given to the second edition of this novel in four volumes, originally published between 1937 and 1940; for many, this, the third of Laxness' epic novels, represents the pinnacle of his literary development. It is the story of Ólafur Kárason, an outcast, rejected as a boy, who embarks upon the search for a transcending beauty against the background of his own feelings as poet, father, teacher and citizen, a beauty which, at his end, he knows that he is about to discover. The narrative is ever-changing in its rhythms, and the work is a kaleidoscope of images and moods; and yet the whole concept is magnificently structured. The setting and the character is Icelandic, the theme universal, and the execution a masterpiece.

820 **La cloche d'Islande: roman.** (Iceland's bell: a novel.)
Halldór Laxness, introduction and translation from the
Icelandic by Régis Boyer. Paris: Aubier Montagne, 1979.
512p. (UNESCO collection of representative works).
It is a matter of some surprise that this novel has so far not been translated into English (it is one of only two Laxness' major novels not to have been - the other being *The great weaver of Kashmir* which marked his breakthrough in 1927), and it has taken nearly forty years for a French translation to appear. *Iceland's bell* is the last of Laxness' epic novels, and comprises a trilogy written between 1943 and 1946, the title of one of the parts later being applied to the work as a whole *Íslandsklukkan*. Peter Hallberg, in his study of Laxness (q.v.), draws attention to the way in which several Scandinavian writers in the throes of the Second World War harked back to earlier periods of their nations' histories; thus it is with Laxness and *Iceland's bell*, which is set in the late 17th century. The situation and aspirations of Iceland in that period are presented through the relationships and destinies of the novel's three main characters: the peasant farmer, the almost ethereal daughter of a lawman, and a manuscript collector (a portrait of Árni Magnússon).

Literature, Modern Icelandic. The novel

821 **The atom station.**
Halldór Laxness, translated by Magnús Magnússon. London: Methuen; Toronto: Ryerson Press, 1961. 202p.

Originally published in 1948 as *Atómstöðin*, this is the most overtly satirical of Laxness' novels. Written some two years after the Icelandic parliament's decision to permit the peacetime establishment of the US military base on Icelandic soil - a decision which in previous speeches Laxness had opposed with total conviction and no little bitterness directed less at the United States than at what he saw as the treachery of decision-makers in his own country - this novel is basically his literary response to those events in a wider context. In his attack upon power and posturing, as seen through the eyes of a girl who has come from the north of Iceland to work in Reykjavík, virtually no group escapes Laxness' unswerving satire and vivacious humour.

822 **The happy warriors.**
Halldór Laxness, translated by Katherine John. London: Methuen, 1958. 257p.

Originally published in 1952 under the title *Gerpla*, this novel represents Laxness' inevitable, if for various reasons belated, examination of Iceland's ancient roots. The idea, and to some extent the characters, are based on one of the earliest of the sagas of Icelanders, *Fóstbræðra saga*. It is a novel of violence and non-violence (the contrast being poignantly drawn in the part describing Norsemen and Eskimos in Greenland) and a critical evaluation of the ideals of the heroic age. The translation is brave and commendable, although the novel's generally accepted prime quality - its skilful use of the style and idiom of the older period - is fully appreciated only by the native Icelander. 'This is as fine a testimony as any to the living power and continuity of the culture of Iceland, and to its hold on one who has grown up under its wing' (see Peter Hallberg's *Halldór Laxness* q.v.).

823 **The fish can sing.**
Halldór Laxness, translated by Magnús Magnússon. London: Methuen; New York: Crowell, 1966. 287p.

First published in 1957 under the title *Brekkukotsannáll*, this novel is a story of youth and changing attitudes in Reykjavík during the early 20th century, as seen through the eyes of one Alfgrím. The contrast between his relations with his grandparents who brought him up and with the mysterious singing star Garðar Hólm is beautifully and ironically drawn. The translation is especially sympathetic. This novel was also turned into a full-length feature film by a German enterprise, with an Icelandic cast including Jón Laxdal as Garðar Hólm.

824 **Paradise reclaimed.**
Halldór Laxness, translated by Magnús Magnússon. London: Methuen; New York: Crowell, 1962. 254p.

Paradísarheimt was first published in 1960. Its theme is that of an Icelandic farmer of the last century who is converted to Mormonism and settles in Utah. The reasons behind his rejection of the prosperity which he enjoys there, and for his final return to Iceland where he repairs stone walls, form the main strand of

Literature, Modern Icelandic. The novel

this anti-dogmatic novel. Turned into a film made on location, again starring Jón Laxdal.

825 Christianity at glacier.
Halldór Laxness, translated by Magnús Magnússon. Reykjavík: Helgafell, 1972. 268p.

The last of Laxness' novels to be translated into English, and one which he wrote after a period devoted to playwriting. Indeed, *Kristnihald undir Jökli* (written in 1968) was begun as a play, but the novelist in Laxness prevailed to produce what can perhaps best be described as a dramatic novel concerning a country parson on the Snæfellsness peninsula who, instead of concentrating on religious services, sees his work as the same as that of his parishioners in his aim of fostering a communal spirit.

826 Halldór Kiljan Laxness.
Kristján Karlsson. Reykjavík: Helgafell, 1962. 88p.

A volume of thirty-two photographs from the 1950s of Iceland's Nobel Prize winning author, taken on a variety of occasions. Short introductory text in English, plus useful bibliography of Laxness' works in translation, arranged by language.

827 Halldór Laxness.
Peter Hallberg, translated from the Swedish by Rory McTurk. New York: Twayne, 1971. 220p. (Twayne World Author Series, 89).

This work remains the only full-length study of Iceland's foremost literary figure. In his treatment of the life and work of Halldór Laxness (born in 1902 as Halldór Guðjónsson - he later changed to the name Laxness after the family farm where he spent his youth) Hallberg's approach is both chronological and thematic. He identifies three major phases of Laxness' development: the youthful, searching phase of his time spent in Europe and North America after the First World War; the socio-political phase of the 1930s and 1940s; the third phase, beginning with his Nobel award in 1955 has been described as a 'mellowing' - a more reflective period, during which Laxness, though continuing as novelist and short story writer, turned also to drama. This analytical biography and literary study brings out the essentially Icelandic spirit of Laxness' works, and is complemented by a useful chronology of his career, plus a substantial bibliography of his writings (in the original and in translation) and of critical appreciation. Hallberg's study covers Laxness' writings up to October 1967. As a literary biography of Laxness it is indispensable. (In the late 1970s Halldór Laxness embarked upon an autobiography - or so it seemed; but, perhaps typically, he shunned the straightforward, and has described it as laced with lies and fantasies. Besides, it ends when he is 20; 'It is always fun to write about one's life before twenty, but then realism intrudes, all kinds of nuisances appear... the result is just chaos and nonsense' - quoted from *Atlantica and Iceland Review*). See Hallberg's article 'Halldór Laxness and the Icelandic sagas', *Leeds Studies in English*, vol. 13 (1982), p. 1-22.

828 Special issue devoted to the work of Halldór Laxness.
Scandinavica, vol. 11 (1972), suppl. 116p.

A collection of eight articles published on the occasion of Halldór Laxness' seventieth birthday. Seven of the articles are on aspects of specific works: *Gerpla* - two

Literature, Modern Icelandic. The novel
articles by Régis Boyer and by R. W. McTurk; *Christianity under Glacier* - W. Friese; *Iceland's Bell* - Peter Hallberg; *Salka Valka* - T. L. Markey; *World Light* - Svetlana Nedelyaevna-Steponavichienie; and *Innansveitarkronika* (a local chronicle centring on the demolition of a church in Mosfellsveit) - Meulengrecht Sørensen. The eighth contribution is on Laxness' relationship with the Icelandic sagas, by Steingrímur Þorsteinsson. All but two of these articles are in English.

829 The writer in a small language community.
Halldór Laxness. *Times Literary Supplement* (UK), (25 Sept. 1969), p. 1,057-58.

A typically eloquent exposition on a theme which is of relevance to all nations whose language is barely known outside its own territorial limits. Laxness discusses a range of problems which face the writer, whether novelist, dramatist or poet, in Iceland, including subject matter, publication, finance, audience, etc. Throughout this piece there is a fierce strand of loyalty (Laxness travelled in his youth, but unlike some of his near contemporaries did not attempt to settle and write abroad). 'However limited it is, his home base will in the long run be a writer's mainstay. It is of paramount importance to build up one's production over the years in the place where you belong. The small community is just as much a part of the world as the large community. Make the place where you belong your stronghold; that would be my advice to small and large alike - at least until we know for sure what is large and what small in this world. You might have some success in faraway places where they make you king for a day. The only group that matters finally is the one, however small, which stands behind you through thick and thin in your own bastion'. In its issue of a fortnight earlier (11 Sept. 1969) the *TLS* carried an article (unsigned, as was the irritating custom of this periodical at the time) on Laxness' work, under the title *The Icelandic microcosm*, p. 1,001-02.

830 Writing in the shadow of the sagas.
Þor Vilhjálmsson. *Times Literary Supplement* (UK), (10 Sept. 1971), p. 1,093.

A cool and cogent assessment of the place of the writer in Icelandic society by the Icelandic novelist and short story writer (see *Faces reflected in a drop*, q.v.), in which he picks up some of the points raised by Laxness in *The writer in a small language community*, (q.v.). He defends the overriding necessity to write in Icelandic and to realise one's own artistic landscape; he sees his position as purely Icelandic rather than broadly Scandinavian. The overpowering tradition of the sagas is now less of an inhibition and more of a stimulant. His final paragraph hints at the problem of writing in the shadow of not so much the sagas as of Laxness. For an assessment of Þor Vilhjálmsson's writings, especially the novel *Quick, quick said the bird* (1968), see the article entitled 'The one who sees' by Peter Hallberg in *Books Abroad*, vol. 47 (1973), p. 54-59.

831 In search of my beloved.
Þórbergur Þórðarson, translated from the Icelandic by Kenneth G. Chapman. New York: Twayne for the American-Scandinavian Foundation, 1967. 119p. (Library of Scandinavian Literature, vol. 1).

Þórbergur Þórðarson (1899-1974) was from south-eastern Iceland. He acquired a reputation as a particularly versatile man of letters. In 1938 his autobiographical work *Íslenzkur aðall* (*An Icelandic aristocracy*) was published. *In search of my beloved* is a translation of the central episode of this work, and is described by

Literature, Modern Icelandic. The novel

the translator as a novella by itself, with the theme of the 'unattainable woman'. A welcome translation of this writer, socialist in ideology, self-deprecating in style.

832 The sword.
Agnar Þórðarson, translated from the Icelandic with introduction and notes by Paul Schach. New York: Twayne for the American-Scandinavian Foundation, 1970. 277p.

Agnar Þórðarson is both a playwright (see *Fire and ice: three Icelandic plays*, q.v.) and novelist. Originally published in 1953 under the title *Ef sverð þitt er stutt* (*If your sword is short*) this is a multi-faceted novel of honour and vengeance, in which the author mixes allegory, psychology and social criticism. A deep and difficult novel, but one which leaves an impression.

833 The golden future.
Þorsteinn Stefánsson, illustrated by V. G. Ambrus. London: Oxford University Press, 1974. 165p.

A distinctly appealing novel depicting youthful idealism: a boy brought up on an isolated coastal farm in Iceland desires more than anything to become a famous writer. The pressures of daily life in a harsh environment, and the competing demands from other members of his family, fail to dim his vision of the 'golden future'. This novel won the Hans Christian Andersen prize in Denmark, and has been translated into English by the author himself (the translation itself is rather quaint at times, although in a strange sense this adds to the story's distant appeal). Þorsteinn Stefánsson was born in 1912 in the eastern fjord, Löðmundarfjöður, and moved to Denmark in 1935.

834 The modern Icelandic novel: from isolation to political awareness.
Sigurður A. Magnússon. *Mosaic* (Canada), vol. 4, no. 2 (1970), p. 133-43.

A very helpful orientation into the development of the modern Icelandic novel. For a century or so, the Icelandic novel has always been interesting, sometimes outstanding, less frequently outward looking (not necessarily a criticism). But the author of this article draws attention to the nature of pre-war fiction in Iceland, firmly rooted both in its classical saga tradition and in its isolated physical environment - he calculates that up to as recently as 1960 more than 90 per cent of all Icelandic novels dealt with rural themes, even though 80 per cent of the urban population had been living in the urban environment for three decades. The other problem, although it was a problem of which to be proud, concerned the writer who rejuvenated Icelandic fiction, Halldór Laxness, but who achieved this in such a towering way that other avenues were, almost unconsciously, blocked. The author discusses the widening of view brought about by the Second World War and its effects upon the Icelandic nation and its writers, before concentrating on some of the novels which were written during the 1960s, and which marked the turning-point whereby the Icelandic novel finally broke with the epic tradition. The work of the following novelists is considered: Jóhannes Helgi, Ingimar Erlendur Sigurðsson, Njörður P. Njarðvík, Björn Bjarman, Indriði G. Þorsteinsson, Guðbergur Bergsson (whose novel *Tómas Jónsson Bestseller* symbolises the break sensationally), Þorsteinn frá Hamri, and two women writers - Jakobína Sigurðardóttir and Svava Jakobsdóttir.

Literature, Modern Icelandic. Short stories

Short stories

835 Seven Icelandic short stories.
Edited by Ásgeir Pétursson, Steingrímur J. Þorsteinsson. Reykjavík: Ministry of Education, 1960. 166p.

The short story has always been popular in Iceland, from saga times and the *þáttr*, to the present century when most novelists have also expressed themselves in the shorter form. This collection, translated by various hands, comprises one mediaeval story *Auðunn and the bear*, and six from the first quarter of this century, written by Einar H. Kvaran, Guðmundur Fridjónsson, Jón Trausti, Gunnar Gunnarsson, Guðmundur G. Hagalín and Halldór Laxness.

836 Short stories of today.
Translated by Alan E. Boucher. Reykjavík: Iceland Review Library, 1972. 95p.

A collection of short stories by twelve contemporary Icelandic authors: Halldór Stefánsson, Guðmundur Danielsson, Jón Dan, Olafur Jóhann Sigurðsson, Jakobína Sigurðardóttir, Jón Óskar, Geir Kristjánsson, Jóhannes Helgi, Indriði G. Þorsteinsson, Hannes Pétursson, Svava Jakobsdóttir and Jökull Jakobsson. The volume lacks an introduction and biographical notes, but forms a varied selection for the reader seeking an acquaintance with the flourishing art of the Icelandic short story. (At the time of writing Iceland Review were anticipating a new collection of twenty-five stories, entitled *A ray of sunshine*).

837 Icelandic short stories.
Selected edited and partially translated by Evelyn Scharabon Firchow. New York: Twayne for the American-Scandinavian Foundation, 1974. 214p. (Library of Scandinavian Literature, vol. 26).

A well chosen and varied selection of twenty-five short stories by modern Icelandic authors, displaying a full range of moods. Several of these translations had already appeared in the periodical *American-Scandinavian Review*. There is a useful introduction by Sigurður A. Magnússon, after which the stories are left to speak for themselves.

838 A quire of seven.
Halldór Laxness, translated by Alan E. Boucher. Reykjavík: Iceland Review, 1974. 96p.

Newcomers to the work of Laxness might be recommended to start with his short stories as appetisers for his novels. Those who have read his novels here have the opportunity to see how he has also mastered the short story form. This collection was originally published in 1964 under the title *Sjöstafakverið*. Sympathetically translated, and issued in the attractive and convenient format of the Iceland Review Library. One of Laxness' 'long' short stories appeared separately in English translation under the title *The honour of the house* (Reykjavík: Helgafell, 1959), twenty-five years after its original publication.

Literature, Modern Icelandic. Short stories

839 Faces reflected in a drop.
Þór Vilhjálmsson, translated by Kenneth G. Chapman. Reykjavík: Helgafell, 1966. 154p.

Originally published in 1957 under the title *An dlit í spegli dropans* this collection of short stories offers the English reader the only chance of becoming acquainted with the writing of the first of the avant-garde writers in Iceland. Þor Vilhjálmsson was born in 1925, and as both novelist and short story writer has exerted considerable influence upon the recent generation of Icelandic writers. This collection shows him as simultaneously compelling and elusive; the reader is somehow forced to dwell on the images without being certain what they reveal. One critic, Sigurður A. Magnússon, has aptly described them as 'still life'; another, Peter Hallberg, as a succession of states of mind. Perhaps the reader should not worry, but accept them purely for the magnetic effect which they create.

840 Lighten our darkness: a short story.
Guðmundur Friðjónsson, translated from the Icelandic by Peter Crabb. *American-Scandinavian Review*, vol. 51, no 1 (March 1963), p. 61-71.

Guðmundur Friðjónsson (1869-1944) was a farmer from northern Iceland. He is still held in high regard as poet, essayist, novelist and, above all, a writer of short stories, of which he produced a dozen collections. Many of his stories are concerned, as is this story, with propagating the traditional, particularly the religious, values of the Icelander.

841 When I was on the frigate: a story.
Jón Trausti, translated from the Icelandic by Bertha Thompson. *American-Scandinavian Review*, vol. 20, no. 10-11 (Oct.-Nov. 1932), p. 501-10.

Jón Trausti (or Guðmundur Magnússon, 1873-1918) was a printer by trade, and a historical novelist renowned for his depiction of life in 18th and 19th century Iceland. Sadly, none of his novels have been translated into English, and English readers have little more to introduce them to Jón Trausti than some of his short stories. This story is an exquisite composition about old Hrólf, an Icelandic fisherman in a world of his own.

842 Two big shots.
Guðmundur Hagalín, translated by Mekkin S. Perkins. *American-Scandinavian Review*, vol. 43, no. 3 (Sept. 1955), p. 281-86.

Guðmundur Hagalín was born at the turn of the 20th century and wrote several novels as well as short stories, many of which are set in the western fjords. This example is about an obstreperous member of the local community meeting his match in the shape of an equally obstreperous goat.

Literature, Modern Icelandic. Short stories

843 **The big fish: a short story.**
Gudmundur Danielsson, translated from the Icelandic by Hallberg Hallmundsson. *Atlantica and Iceland Review*, vol. 6, no. 3 (1968), p. 41-44.

An angling story by a historical novelist (b.1910) with a wide reputation in Iceland; also a poet and professional journalist. Yet another Icelandic novelist available to English readers mainly through short stories. For further short stories of Guđmundur Danielsson see *American-Scandinavia Review* as follows: *Bottomless pit* in vol. 46, no. 2 (Jan. 1958), p. 173-76; *Initiation story* in vol. 50, no. 4 (Dec. 1962), p. 423-28; and *Lost battle* in vol. 53, no. 3 (Sept. 1965), p. 288- . The first two are translated by M. S. Perkins, the third by P. Kidson.

844 **In times of peace: a short story.**
Indriđi G. Þorsteinsson, translated by Hallberg Hallmundsson. *Iceland Review*, vol. 4, no. 4 (1966), p. 21-23.

Indriđi G. Þorsteinsson was born in 1926. He is a writer concerned with the theme of rural-urban migration, but this taut story is in a different vein, taking the form of a conversation between two steelmen, one from Iceland, one from Luxembourg; the conversation turns on an aircrash over an Icelandic glacier... The story is accompanied by two drawings by the well known Spanish-Icelandic artist Baltasar. Other short stories by this writer translated in periodicals include *Sedgegrass*, translated by E. S. Firchow, *Atlantica and Iceland Review*, vol. 20, no. 1 (summer 1982), p. 89-93; *An old story*, translated by D. E. Askey, *American-Scandinavian Review*, vol. 57, no. 1 (March 1969), p. 62-64.

845 **The Icelandic short story: Svava Jakobsdóttir.**
Sigurđur A. Magnússon, Dennis Auburn Hill. *Scandinavian Studies*, vol. 49, no. 2 (spring 1977), p. 208-16.

This article traces the emergence of a new generation of Icelandic writers, and proceeds to a discussion of the work of Svava Jakobsdóttir, who was born in 1930, and has become one of the most respected feminist writers in Iceland. She has written plays, novels and collections of short stories including *Tólfkonur* (*Twelve women*, 1965) which traces the stages of a woman's life and her emotional disintegration under the demands of modern society. One of the stories from this collection *Slys* (*Accident*) is here presented in English translation; the emotional power generated in a short space is striking, and owes much to the economy of style and depiction of detail. This article appears in an issue specially devoted to the Scandinavian short story. For other stories by Svava Jakobsdóttir in English-language periodicals, see *The stone-wall party*, translated by P. Karlsson, *Sixty-five Degrees*, vol. 2, no. 4 (summer 1968), p. 21-24; *The children's mother*, translated by Hallberg Hallmundsson, *Atlantica and Iceland Review*, vol. 7, no. 4 (1969), p. 50-54.

Foreign Literature on Icelandic Themes

Medieval settings

846 **Thiodolf the Icelander.**
F. de la Motte Fouqué.   London: Burns; New York: Wiley, Putnam, 1845. 2 vols. in 1. 364p.
Þjóðolf Árnason was court poet to King Harald Sigurðsson. Fouqué, the German aristocrat, as prolific in literary output as in his appellation (Friedrich Heinrich Karl de la Motte Fouqué, Baron), considered this work to be his most successful, and the translation from the German was apparently urged by Sir Walter Scott. It is a romance of imagination based on the Norse Varangian adventures in Byzantium in the 11th century, and is made to revolve around Þjóðolf the Icelander. The original German edition was published in 1814.

847 **An old captivity.**
Nevil Shute.   London: Heinemann, 1940. Reprinted London: Pan, 1965. 286p.
An historical novel from the pen of the popular novelist, in which an Oxford professor and his daughter on a trip to Greenland come under a haunting spell which transports them back to the time of the Icelandic settlement of Greenland nearly a millennium earlier. An abridged version for the younger reader is published by Heinemann in their New Windmill Series, and for the poorly sighted reader there is an edition published by Ulverscroft Large Print Books.

Foreign Literature on Icelandic Themes. Medieval settings

848 I Tell of Greenland: an edited translation of the Saudarkrokur manuscripts.
Francis Berry. London: Routledge & Kegan Paul, 1971. 205p.

The supposed autobiography of one Ingólf Brandsson who joined the exodus from Iceland to Greenland and Vinland in the 11th century. The Professor of English at Royal Holloway College has produced an historical novel which stands in its own right, but which he introduces in a cloak of academic spoofery. For the student familiar with scholarly descriptions of textual history in introductions to editions of the sagas, the author's account of the discovery of and research into the phantom Sauðárkrókur manuscripts and their interrelations will raise smiles. The story itself, with its familiar characters such as Leif, Gudrid, Freydis and Thorvald, affords an entertaining diversion.

849 Two ravens.
Cecilia Holland. London: Gollancz; New York: Knopf, 1977. 192p.

A good novel by any standards, set in Iceland either side of the year 1000, the time of the conversion to Christianity. It is a story of families and feuding, with a reasonably researched background, and requires little or no knowledge of the early history of Iceland to carry the reader through. Paperback edition published by Sphere Books, 1979. The raven is also the titular symbol used by the respected writer for children and adults, Naomi Mitchison, in her story *The land the ravens found* (London: Collins, 1955, 152p). This illustrated story is woven around the settlement of Iceland by Vikings from Scotland and the Northern Isles.

850 Four plays.
F. L. Lucas. Cambridge, England: Cambridge University Press, 1935. 338p.

The lovers of Guðrún (p. 161-256), an unheralded item, hiding away without explanation in a collection of plays by a writer whose reputation lay in Hellenic rather than Nordic studies. It is a play in five acts, somewhat dated in style, but not without feeling for the historical spirit of Iceland, and is a re-working of the story of Guðrún (heroine of *Laxdæla saga*) in verse form. This play may well have been inspired by William Morris' saga poem *The lovers of Guðrún*, which is one of the re-told stories in his monumental work *The earthly paradise*.

851 Heimskringla, or, The stoned angels.
Paul Foster. London: Calder & Boyars, 1970. 92p.

A play in two acts by one of the leading playwrights of the 'off-off Broadway' movement. It is a vibrant and provocative re-creation of the Norse discovery of the North American continent by Leif Eiríksson. This re-creation is, naturally, imaginative rather than documentary, and its spirit is compelling. First performed by the influential La Mama Troupe in 1969.

Modern settings

852 Olaf Thorlacksen: a story of Iceland.
Wilhelm Oertel. London: Society for Promoting Christian Knowledge, 1868. 128p.

Something of a curio, and not without appeal. A translation from the German of the story about a Danish boy who survives a shipwreck, is fostered in Iceland, and eventually, in manhood, recovers his roots. Published as a spiritual narrative also by the Lutheran Board in Philadelphia.

853 Three sketches of life in Iceland.
Carl Andersen, translated by Myfanwy Fenton. London: Washbourne, 1877. 122p.

Three attractive short stories by the Danish writer on Icelandic folklore. The stories are: *The cairn of Grim's height*, *The raven*, and *The settler* (a story of the millenium of Iceland).

854 Journey to the centre of the earth.
Jules Verne, edited and translated by I. O. Evans. New York; London: Arno Publications, 1965. 224p.

Although this story by Jules Verne (1828-1905) is generally regarded as one of the first examples of science fiction (it was originally published in French in 1864), and though its basic theory has since been shown to be fallacious, no geologist with any sense of the development of his own discipline will read it without considerable respect - it was based on what at the time was a credible scientific theory - and, indeed, excitement. The non-geologist with an interest in Iceland will share the excitement, and may be tempted to swallow the 'hollow earth' theory pursued by Professor Lindenbrock and his nephew accompanied by the rather well-drawn character of their imperturbable Icelandic guide, as they enter and descend the crater of Snæfellsjökull (or Sneffels, as Verne calls it) in western Iceland, which they hope will lead them to the centre of the earth, and justify the runic clues which had first stimulated their adventure. This book has been presented in numerous editions. One particularly noteworthy translation is that by Robert Baldick (Penguin, 1965. Reprinted nine times). Baldick also translated the edition in Dent's Children's Illustrated Classics series, 1970 - one of several abridged versions for the younger reader.

855 Iceland fisherman.
Pierre Loti, translated by W. P. Baines. London: Dent, 1935. 242p. (Everyman's Library).

Loti, a French novelist of standing, wrote *Pêcheur d'Islande* in 1886. His own background in the French navy shows through powerfully and sympathetically in his novel of Breton family life, in which the seas around Iceland, the destination of the Breton fishermen, are never far from the thoughts or actions of the characters.

Foreign Literature on Icelandic Themes. Modern settings

856 **The wild horses of Iceland.**
Svend Fleuron, translated from the Danish by E. Gee Nash. London: Eyre & Spottiswoode; New York: Holt, 1933. 236p. illus.

Originally published in 1926 with the title *Sigurd Torleifsson's heste* this story is one of many which Svend Fleuron wrote about animals, and which became very popular in German translations. This story, set in southern Iceland, is about the life of the Icelandic ponies and the people who tended them, though it is the ponies who are the central characters. Illustrated with drawings, the story will appeal also to the younger reader.

857 **Black eggs.**
Nicolette Devas. London: Collins, 1970. 190p.

Nicolette Devas is best known for her acclaimed autobiography *Two flamboyant fathers* which revolved around the artistic life of the inter-war years. Her skill in drawing the characters of real life is here applied to fictional characters in the shape of a party of fifteen naturalists on a trip to Iceland. This novel has no great pretensions to acute observation of Icelandic scenery or life, but the ornithologist visiting Iceland will find it worth taking as recreational reading - a good book to have in the tent.

858 **A free man.**
Laurence Lerner. London: Chatto & Windus, 1968. 213p.

Written by a professor of English at the University of Sussex, this novel has Iceland as its setting, presumably for its occasional reputation for enabling people to get away from it all and 'find themselves', if only temporarily, which, as the title implies, is the theme of this novel. An English travel agent decides to settle in Iceland as a tour leader. The environment, however, proves incapable of either protecting him from externally imposed relationships and events, or, in consequence, of freeing him from himself. A decent story, with its climax on an Icelandic fellside.

859 **Running blind.**
Desmond Bagley. London: Collins, 1970; New York: Doubleday, 1971. 256p.

Set in Iceland throughout, this is a fast moving spy story of the best kind, by one of its most popular exponents. The Icelandic background has been well researched, and the descriptions are generally authentic and keenly observed. In 1979 this novel was successfully serialised on British television, shot partly on location, and starring the Icelandic actress Ragnheiður Steindórsdóttir. Also issued in paperback format by Fontana in 1972, this is a good piece of escapist reading to take when travelling around Iceland.

860 **The chill factor.**
Richard Falkirk. London: Joseph; New York: Doubleday, 1971. 224p.

Another spy thriller set in Iceland, with the usual British agent running the gauntlet of American and Russian espionage, and inevitably involving an Icelandic air hostess and an Icelandic chief of police. Rather more stereotyped than the previous item, but again a fast moving story.

Foreign Literature on Icelandic Themes. Modern settings

861 Men at Axlir.
Dominic Cooper. London: Chatto & Windus, 1978. 286p.

Most foreign novels concerning Iceland use the country as a backcloth for stories which display observation rather than insight into the country - one or two could quite easily have been set elsewhere. What makes Dominic Cooper's third acclaimed novel the most interesting foreign novel concerning Iceland is the fact that it deals with a specifically Icelandic theme, seriously researched, in addition to being unusually well written. The author describes it as a novel based upon historical fact, rather than as an historical novel. Set in 18th-century Iceland, it makes use of the well-known and variously transmitted case of Sunnefa Jónsdóttir, and a crime whose repercussions extended into the following century. The story is presented using the successive viewpoints of those involved in the case, and the author (an Englishman who has lived in Iceland) has enveloped it in a vivid atmosphere which conveys the natural, social, political and economic environment of Iceland at the time of the events.

862 Island on fire.
Joseph Hayes. New York: Grosset & Dunlop; London: Deutsch, 1979. 374p. Reprinted (paperback) London: Sphere 1981.

A novel full of bestselling ingredients, by one practised in the field, in which the author uses the volcanic eruption on Heimaey (Westmann Islands) in 1973 as a factual backdrop for fictional characters and relationships arising from the event. Written perhaps a little too soon after the catastrophe for one to feel entirely comfortable about the novel's motivation and presentation, and stylistic clichés abound, but the author has re-created an atmosphere and tension in the story.

863 Icelandic solitaries.
Alan Gould. St. Lucia, Australia: University of Queensland Press, 1978. 57p.

Alan Gould is a young Australian poet, whose father is British and mother Icelandic. The core of this collection of short poems consists of two challenging and evocative sets on Icelandic themes: *Skald mosaic*, which is a personal view of themes from skaldic poetry; and *Six Icelandic interiors*, which include reflections on Akureyri, Mývatn, Dyrhólaey and Heimaey - the last of these at the time of the volcanic eruption in 1973 - 'The wharf is now for nightgowns / as ash invades the kitchens / drowning like a sea / the heirloom spoons / the clocks / great grandfathers had sworn by.'.

Letters from Iceland.
See item no. 114.

Children's Presentations

Ancient themes

864 Scandinavian legends and folk-tales.
Re-told by Gwyn Jones, illustrated by Joan Kiddell-Monroe. Oxford, England: Oxford University Press, 1956. 222p. (Oxford Myths and Legends).
Several reprintings testify to the popularity of this selection which is dedicated 'til allra barna' (to all children). Eight tales from Iceland are presented along with others from Denmark, Norway and Sweden. Both the style of the story-telling and the illustrations are in tune with the younger reader.

865 The saga of Asgard.
Re-told from the Old Norse poems and tales by Roger Lancelyn Green, illustrated by Brian Wildsmith. Harmondsworth, England: Penguin, 1960. 255p.
An entertaining presentation, in which the Norse myths from the beginning to the end of the world are presented in simple translation, accompanied by the imaginative drawings of a well-known illustrator of books for children. Other presentations of this theme for the younger reader include *Asgard and the Norse heroes*, re-told by Katherine F. Boult (London: Dent, 1914, 268p. Everyman's Library); also *Of gods and giants: Norse mythology* by Harald Hveberg (Oslo: Tanum, 1962. 72p.).

Children's Presentations. Ancient themes

866 **Icelandic stories, as told on Jackanory by Magnús Magnússon.**
Magnús Magnússon, illustrated by Paul Birbeck. London: BBC, 1969. 80p.

Five Old Icelandic stories chosen for re-telling on the long running programme for children presented by BBC television. Told here under the titles *Freyfaxi* (from *Hrafnkels saga*), *Prince Sigurd and his dog*, *The polar bear* (*Auðunn and the bear*), *Thór and his hammer*, and *Greyman*.

867 **Vinland the good.**
Henry Treece. London: Bodley Head; New York: Phillips, 1964. 144p. Harmondsworth, England: Penguin (Puffin), 1971.

One of several stories about the Viking world, as recorded in the old Icelandic sources, which have flowed from the pen of this popular writer of books for children. This story, along with *The last of the Vikings*, *Swords of the north*, etc., are full blooded tales best appreciated by children of middle school years. Henry Treece's main interest was in the strife within Europe during the first thousand years A.D., and he maintained that the violence in his stories is there to be distrusted rather than glorified; more than one critic, however, has drawn attention to the precariousness of this approach when applied to literature for younger readers. Treece also re-told *Njáls saga* is his *The burning of Njál* (London: Bodley Head, 1964).

868 **The lands of fire and ice: how Christianity came to Hawaii and Iceland.**
Dorothy O van Woerkom, illustrated by J. Cummings. Saint Louis, Missouri: Concordia, 1979. 32p.

A book for the younger child, in which the story of how Christianity was accepted on two volcanic islands is told, with some licence, in a simple and lively way, with strong illustrations.

Iceland: new world outpost.
See item no. 21.

Everyday life in the Viking age.
See item no. 286.

An old captivity.
See item no. 847.

Two ravens.
See item no. 849.

The land and people of Iceland.
See item no. 870.

271

Modern themes

869 Volcanoes and glaciers: the challenge of Iceland.
Sturges F. Cary. New York: Coward McCann, 1959. 96p. illus.

An illustrated guide to Iceland for the younger reader, with the emphasis upon the country's natural features.

870 The land and people of Iceland.
Erick Berry, i.e. Allena Best . Philadelphia, Pennsylvania: Lippincott, 1972. rev. ed. 158p. (Portraits of the Nations Series).

Erick Berry is a well-known writer of books for children, and this enthusiastic account of Iceland can be particularly recommended, as it introduces all the major features of the country and its people in a balanced and lively manner. Erick Berry also wrote a book on the early period, entitled *Leif the Lucky, discoverer of America* (Champaign, Illinois: Garrard, 1961; London: Watts, 1972, 80p. Discovery Series).

871 Let's visit Iceland.
I. O. Evans. London; Ajax, Ontario, Canada: Burke, 1976. 96p. map. illus.

A very suitable book for the young traveller to Iceland. Short chapters on the landscape, history, population, towns, occupations, customs, etc. Well presented, with illustrations, map and index. Worth taking on a visit if there are nine to fourteen year olds in the party. Also to be recommended in this context is the section on Iceland in Geoffrey Williamson's book *Young traveller in the far north* (London: Phoenix House, 1958, 123p.), which is in the educationally respected Young Traveller Series.

872 Smoky bay: the story of a small boy in Iceland.
Steingrímur Arason, illustrated by Gertrude Howe. New York: MacMillan, 1942. 190p.

An appealing portrait of rural Iceland in the early part of this century, presented in the form of a story about children and their activities in the family and on the farm through the four seasons, with thoughts of America in the background.

873 The Hornstranders.
Alan E. Boucher. London: Constable Young Books; Don Mills, Ontario, Canada: Longman, 1966. 144p.

Another good story for children in the nine to fourteen age group, written by an Englishman turned Icelander well known for his re-telling of Icelandic stories. It tells of the adventures of Gísli, a boy aged twelve, in Hornstrandir, the extreme peninsula of north-western Iceland.

Children's Presentations. Modern themes

874 Asgeir of Iceland.
Howard Liss. New York: Messner, 1970. 64p. maps. photos.

From the pen of a prolific author of books on children's sport, this book is a description of the home, family, friends, school and other activities of a boy aged fourteen living on a farm in northern Iceland. Includes photographs and map. A similarly motivated book, this time for pre-teenagers is *Sigurđur in Iceland* by Alida V. Shinn (New York: MacKay, 1942, 39p.). Photographs and text about an American boy of Icelandic descent returning to visit his parent's native country and learning of the traditional way of life there.

Iceland and the Icelanders.
See item no. 16.

When I was a girl in Iceland.
See item no. 18.

Iceland in pictures.
See item no. 39.

Climbing higher: an Iceland adventure.
See item no. 116.

Iceland and Greenland.
See item no. 160.

Lost in the Arctic.
See item no. 807.

Journey to the centre of the earth.
See item no. 854.

The wild horses of Iceland.
See item no. 856.

Made in Iceland.
See item no. 877.

Fine Art

875 **Icelandic art.**
Kristján Eldjárn. Munich: Reich, 1957; London: Thames & Hudson; New York: Abrams, 1961. 84p. illus.
An excellent starting point for the visual study of the history of Icelandic art in all forms from the beginnings to the 19th century. A clear and helpful introductory text is followed by seventy photographs (mostly by Hans Reich) of the most significant examples of Iceland's artistic heritage. See the article by Björn Þ. Björnsson 'Icelandic art of the Middle Ages', *American-Scandinavian Review*, vol. 55, no. 4 (Dec. 1967), p. 345-59.

876 **Peasant art in Sweden, Lapland and Iceland.**
Edited by Charles Hume. London: The Studio, 1910. 48p. plates.
A special issue of *Studio* art magazine. The essay by Jarno Jessen on the history of folk art in Iceland is disappointingly sketchy, although some points of interest are made. It is followed by plates showing examples of traditional Icelandic wood and horn carving, metal work and jewellery. The chief interest of the volume is the comparison between traditional objects of art from three parts of the northern world.

877 **Made in Iceland.**
Grace Blaisdell Golden. New York: Knopf, 1958. 165p. illus.
Intended as a book for the young reader, but must also be commended to the adult reader as the only substantial account in English of the traditional arts and crafts of Iceland. The author, Director of the Children's Museum in Indianapolis, describes in particular the arts of woodcarving, metalworking, weaving and embroidery. It is a sympathetically presented book, full of interest, and one which emphasises that the Icelandic expression of folk art is national rather than regional. Includes illustrations.

Fine Art

878 Íslenzk myndlist: 20 listmálarar. (Art in Iceland: 20 artists.)
Reykjavík: Kristján Friðriksson, 1943. 160p.

A fine, though rather rare, volume presenting the development of modern Icelandic art up to 1940. An introductory text by Emil Thoroddsen on Icelandic painters (texts in English and Icelandic) is followed by a hundred colour/black-and-white plates of examples of the work of twenty Icelandic artists, with photographs of the artists and biographical details in English. Artists include: Sigurður Guðmundsson, Þórarinn Þorláksson, Ásgrímur Jónsson, Jón Stefánsson, Jóhannes Kjarval, Kristín Jónsdóttir, Júliana Sveinsdóttir, Guðmundur Þorsteinsson, Finnur Jónsson, Gunnlaugur Blöndal, Guðmundur Einarsson, Sveinn Þórarinsson, Snorri Arinbjarnar, Karen Þórarinsson, Gunnlaugur Scheving, Þorvaldur Skúlason, Jóhann Briem, Jón Engilberts, Nína Tryggvadóttir and Gunnar Gunnarsson (son of the novelist).

879 Landscape painting: an almost religious art.
Aðalsteinn Ingólfsson. *Atlantica and Iceland Review*, vol. 19, no. 3 (1981), p. 52-57.

Given the varied and evocative nature of the Icelandic landscape, it is scarcely surprising that this form of painting should be the one to display the most coherent tradition in Icelandic artistic history. This article is a brief, illustrated introduction to landscape painting in Iceland and to some of its major exponents in the late 19th and 20th centuries.

880 Kjarval: a painter of Iceland.
Aðalsteinn Ingólfsson, Matthías Jóhannesson, translated by Haukur Böðvarsson. Reykjavík: Iceland Review, 1981. 96p.

A welcome publication devoted to the paintings of Jóhannes S. Kjarval (1885-1972), one of the great pioneers of Icelandic painting. This finely printed volume contains about ninety reproductions of his landscapes, drawings, etc. There is an authoritative introduction by a respected art critic and historian who examines the career, influences and complex personality of Kjarval, plus texts of conversations with, and photographs of, the artist. Kjarval's work is as varied in mood as it is prolific, and no other painter has come quite so close to the natural environment of Iceland. See the article 'Jóhannes Kjarval; Icelandic painter laureate' by Hallberg Hallmundsson, *American-Scandinavian Review*, vol. 53, no. 4 (Dec. 1965), p. 353-61.

881 Ásgrímur Jónsson.
Tómas Guðmundsson. Reykjavík: Helgafell, 1962. 139p. illus.

A volume in tribute to Ásgrímur Jónsson (1874-1958), the first of the great painters of Iceland, and the first who can be called a full-time painter. He had already established a reputation in his own country before being supported by the nation in a long trip to study in Italy when in his late twenties, but his influences were applied almost solely to Icelandic themes, whether landscapes, or the later and more subjective themes related to folklore and the Icelandic spirit. Since the time of his death, his home and his studio in Reykjavík have been open to the public. This volume contains one hundred reproductions of his works, many in colour, and is accompanied by a text in English and Icelandic.

Fine Art

882 Gunnlaugur Blöndal.
Introduced by Eggert Stefánsson. Reykjavík: Helgafell, 1963. 107p. illus.

A volume of reproductions, many in colour, of over a hundred paintings by Gunnlaugur Blöndal (1893-1962), a highly-trained artist, schooled in France and Italy, and particularly renowned for his portraitures. English text accompanying.

883 Naivist painter Ísleifur Konráðsson.
Björn Þ. Björnsson. *Atlantica and Iceland Review*, vol. 9, no. 2 (1971), p. 44-49.

Naive art has enjoyed a considerable re-awakening of interest during the last two decades in many countries. This was reflected in the emergence, late in life, of a painter born on the north-western peninsula of Iceland in 1889, Ísleifur Konráðsson. He retired at the age of 72 after a lifetime of manual work in Copenhagen and in Reykjavík, and without any family; he then started to paint, motivated by the memories of his roots and of Icelandic folk life and folklore. Several exhibitions of his work have been mounted in Reykjavík. This article, with examples of his work, captures the unaffected spirit of his life and the genuine naivism of his art.

884 A white horse and a rough sea: the art of Gunnlaugur Scheving.
Bragi Asgeirsson. *Atlantica and Iceland Review*, vol. 7, no. 1 (1969), p. 27-35.

Gunnlaugur Scheving (1904-72) was an Icelandic painter with a Scandinavian reputation. He is surprisingly unusual amongst Icelandic painters in that his paintings are predominantly on the theme of man in his daily traditional environment, particularly the fisherman and the farmer. His work possesses a notable strength, and is highly reflective. The same critic contributed illustrated assessments of two other Icelandic painters in later issues of the same magazine: the abstract painter Þorvaldur Skúlason (b. 1906), vol. 8, no. 4 (1970), p. 42-46; and the versatile Kristján Davíðsson (b. 1917), vol. 8, no. 1 (1970), p. 35-39. Bragi Asgeirsson is a well-known art critic and teacher at the Reykjavík School of Arts and Crafts, and a respected artist in his own right, who was himself the subject of a critical appreciation by Oddur Björnsson in the same magazine, vol. 9, no. 1 (1971), p. 42-47.

885 Sverrir Haraldsson.
Oddur Björnsson. *Atlantica and Iceland Review*, vol. 6, no. 1 (1968), p. 30-35.

Sverrir Haraldsson (born on the Westmann Islands in 1930) is regarded as an original talent in Icelandic painting. His development has ranged from abstract art to a fluid form of landscape painting, and his career involved an unsettling period in Berlin. Two striking examples of his landscapes are reproduced in this brief survey of his life and work.

Fine Art

886 Erró: an Icelandic artist.
Matthías Jóhannesson, with an introduction by Bragi
Ásgeirsson. Reykjavík: Iceland Review, 1978. 80p.

Erró (and prior to that Ferro) is the artistic pseudonym of the painter Guðmundur Guðmundsson, who was born in 1932. He grew up in Iceland, but latterly worked abroad, especially in Paris. An uncompromising modernist, he has experimented with several styles, but is at his most striking with his surrealist, sometimes macabre, representations of the relationships between mankind and the new technology. Some seventy-five of his paintings are reproduced in colour in this volume, which offers an excellent introduction to the work of Iceland's most provocative and least typical painter.

887 Coming to terms with the present: Einar Hákonarson.
Aðalsteinn Ingólfsson. *Atlantica and Iceland Review*, vol. 14, no. 2 (1976), p. 38-43.

Einar Hákonarson (b. 1945) is a young painter whose talents flowered with the emergence of pop art in the 1960s - he was particularly influenced by the Irish figurative artist Francis Bacon. His work, however, is full of new ideas, both in his paintings and his graphic art, which he also teaches. For a profile, by the same critic, of another young Icelandic painter influenced by Bacon, Gunnar Örn Gunnarsson (b. 1947), see the same magazine, vol. 15, no. 2 (1977), p. 33-36; Gunnar Örn is one of several Icelandic artists who have worked at the collective art studio in the converted farm at Korpulfsstaðir some five miles from Reykjavík.

888 Nína Tryggvadóttir.
Þór Vilhjálmsson. *American-Scandinavian Review*, vol. 61, no. 3 (Sept. 1973), p. 213-25. illus.

A warm and sympathetic portrait of the celebrated and versatile Icelandic artist Nína Tryggvadóttir (1913-68). She spent many years in the United States and Europe and acquired an international reputation as a painter (particularly in oils), and also for her stained glass and mosaic creations. In spite of her time abroad, her work is pervaded by an Icelandic spirit, and the unifying element lies in her use of colour. This article is accompanied by seven plates illustrating her work, including her particularly fine composition of the Parliament at Þingvellir. At the time of completion of this bibliography, a major exhibition of Nína Tryggvadóttir's work was about to be held in Reykjavík, in connection with which a new book was announced under the title *N. Tryggvadóttir: serenity and power* by the art historian Hrafnhildur Schram, translated by May and Hallberg Hallmundsson (Reykjavík: Iceland Review, late 1982). Contains fifty-eight colour reproductions and drawings.

889 Leifur Breiðfjörd: artist in stained glass.
Aðalsteinn Ingólfsson. *Atlantica and Iceland Review*, vol. 13, no. 1-2 (1975), p. 21-27.

Although there is no historical tradition of stained glass work in Iceland to match that of continental Europe, the development of the art in modern Iceland has been striking, and the visitor will soon come across many impressive examples. Two female artists were responsible for the rise of Icelandic stained glass work: Gerða Helgadóttir and Nína Tryggvadóttir (q.v.). Their mantle has more recently been taken on by Leifur Breiðfjörd, whose background and approach to this form are described in this illustrated article, with aparticular reference to his windows at Iceland's National Theatre restaurant, the National Bank's branch at Húsavík, and

Fine Art

at individual apartments; his work, therefore, is to be regarded as a part of the daily scene, rather than as purely monumental.

890 **Sculptor Ásmundur Sveinsson: an Edda in shapes and symbols.**
Matthías Jóhannesson. Reykjavík: Iceland Review, 1974. 96p.

A volume in tribute to the art of Ásmundur Sveinsson (b. 1893), whose name, along with that of Einar Jónsson (b. 1873) is synonymous with Icelandic sculpture. This remarkable man has, during the course of his long career, spanned all the major forms and materials of the sculptor's art and craft. The visitor to Reykjavík will be hard put to miss many of his public sculptures, and his famous semi-circular workshop-cum-gallery radiates enjoyment. Ásmundur is particularly loved by his countrymen because so much of his work has drawn on Icelandic folklore and the old culture. He died recently at the age of 89. An earlier tribute to the grand old sculptor was the volume *Ásmundur Sveinsson*, with introduction by Halldór Laxness, text in three languages (including English), and over 150 plates. (Reykjavík: Helgafell, 1961, 67p.).

891 **Individuality and imagination: Sigurjón Ólafsson.**
Sigurður A. Magnússon. *Atlantica and Iceland Review*, vol. 6, no. 3 (1968), p. 25-35.

A near contemporary of Ásmundur Sveinsson, Sigurjón Ólafsson (b. 1908) established his reputation in Denmark but returned to Iceland after the war. His work is in a variety of materials and styles. His portraits are particularly sensitive, but his most striking work is the abstract relief which adorns the wall of the Búrfell hydroelectric power plant.

892 **Pottery reflects nature.**
Aðalsteinn Ingólfsson. *Atlantica and Iceland Review*, vol. 13, no. 4 (1975), p. 12-15.

Pottery is another of the arts which have come to the fore in Iceland only in the last few decades. This brief, illustrated article introduces the work of Steinunn Marteinsdóttir, who makes her pottery reflect aspects of the natural environment of her country. For features by the same critic on other Icelandic potters, see those on the husband and wife team of Robin Lökker from Denmark and Tove Kjarval (granddaughter of the renowned painter Jóhannes Kjarval) in the same magazine, vol. 14, no. 4 (1976), p. 30-35; and on Gestur Þorgrímsson and Sigrún (Grúna) Guðjónsdóttir, vol. 19, no. 1 (1981), p. 33-37.

893 **Secrets in silver.**
Ole Villumsen Krog. *Scandinavian Review*, vol. 68, no. 2 (June 1980), p. 49-53.

An illustrated sketch of the history of Icelandic silver. The lack of war and plunder on Icelandic soil has resulted in more than two-thirds of the silver in Iceland having been registered before 1800. Particular mention is made of the Icelandic silversmith of the mid-18th century, Sigurður Þorsteinsson. In the late 1970s an Icelandic-Danish team of experts conducted an inventory of all important silver objects in Iceland, with illuminating results. The writer describes this project also in *Atlantica and Iceland Review*, vol. 17, no. 2 (1979), p. 11-15. Two modern Icelandic silversmiths, Ísleifur Kaldal and Jóhannes Jóhannesson, are portrayed in a feature in *Iceland Review*, vol. 3, no. 1 (1965), p. 14-18.

Fine Art

894 Icelandic embroidery.
Elsa E. Guðjónsson. Reykjavík: National Museum of Iceland, 1970. 10p.

The National Museum of Iceland houses an interesting collection of domestic embroideries. In this illustrated pamphlet, the author, Curator at the Museum, who has contributed several publications on this topic in Icelandic, describes some of the pre-Reformation church embroideries such as pattern books and altar frontals, as well as later ecclesiastical and secular needlework, particularly coverlets in white work and floral embroidery. See the same author's article in the *Bulletin of the Needle and Bobbin Club* (US), vol. 47 (1963), p. 4-31, in which she concentrates on the stitching techniques employed in Icelandic embroidery. In another article, *Textile History* (UK), vol. 10 (1973), p. 207-10, she writes briefly about the National Museum's collection of tog woolcombs.

895 Icelandic design.
Franzisca Gunnarsson. *Atlantica and Iceland Review*, vol. 20, no. 1 (summer 1982), p. 97-104.

An introduction to modern Icelandic design in a variety of forms. It presents brief, illustrated features on the following designers and their work: Hulda Jósefsdóttir (woollens), Sigrún Ólöf Einarsdóttir (glassware), Elísabet Haraldsdóttir (pottery), Jens Guðjónsson (gold and silver work), Pétur B. Lúthersson (furniture), and Stefán Snæbjörnsson (lighting).

Music

896 Grove's dictionary of music and musicians.
Þorkell Sigurbjörnsson, Hreinn Steingrímsson. London: MacMillan, 1981. rev. ed. vol. 9.

This seven-column entry under Iceland in the standard encyclopaedia of music is virtually the only general account of Icelandic music in the English language. As such, it is useful, but editorially short, being confined to a summary of the development of classical and traditional folk-music (instruments and songs), and a musical description of the *rímur*.

897 The music of old Iceland.
Margaret S. Selden. *American-Scandinavian Review*, vol. 45, no. 4 (Dec. 1957), p. 369-76.

It was only as recently as last century that Icelandic music became exposed to the influences of continental European traditions. The author of this paper examines some of the reasons for the conservatism and continuity of Icelandic folk-music from mediaeval times up to the last century, such as national pride, geographical isolation, linguistic stability, links with the church, and a vocal rather than instrumental tradition (instrumental music of any description was virtually unknown until the middle of the 19th century). She then assesses the materials available to the researcher into Icelandic musical history, before describing two of its long-standing forms: the *tvísöngur*, or two-part songs, based on parallel fifths; and the *rímur*, or ballads.

898 Ashkenazy moves to Iceland.
Matthías Jóhannesson. *Atlantica and Iceland Review*, vol. 8, no. 2 (1970), p. 18-26.

An interview by the editor of *Morgunblaðið* with the Russian-born concert pianist Vladimir Ashkenazy, who married an Icelander and came with his family to live in Iceland in 1967, where he himself adopted Icelandic nationality. He has since contributed much to the musical life of Iceland, and was a prime mover in the now firmly-established International Arts (particularly music) Festival held biennially in Reykjavík.

Music

899 **Unified curriculum construction: the Icelandic-American comprehensive musicianship project.**
David G. Woods. *Bulletin of the Council for Research in Music Education* (US), vol. 57 (winter 1978), p. 23-27.

A project shared by schools in Ames, Iowa, and in Reykjavík, supported by the Ford Foundation, and designed to improve musical literacy through the curriculum over two periods of four years (1973-81). It resulted from a study tour of the United States by Stefán Edelstein (Director of the Children's Music School in Reykjavík). The Director of the project here describes the emerging programme built on a wide range of musical concepts experienced and reinforced at all levels.

Facts about Iceland.
See item no. 32.

Theatre and Cinema

900 **Theatre in a minute nation.**
Rodney M. Bennett. *Drama*, no. 120 (spring 1976), p. 28-33.

A foreign critic's brief view of the state and achievements of Icelandic theatre. The correspondent sketches the facilities and activities of the Reykjavík Theatre Company and the Icelandic National Theatre, with an assessment of their range of repertoire. See two earlier articles on these theatres: 'The theatre on Hope Street' by Hallberg Hallmundsson in the magazine *Theatre Arts* (US), Oct. 1961, p. 62-65; and 'On stage, back stage' by Róbert Arnfinnsson, actor at the National, and Sveinn Einarsson, manager of the Reykjavík Theatre, in the Icelandic magazine *Sixty-five Degrees*, no. 7 (Aug. 1969), p. 28-31.

901 **The Reykjavík Theatre Company.**
Sveinn Einarsson. Reykjavík: Leikfélag Reykjavíkur, 1972. 20p. illus.

This brief and informative booklet on the history and organisation of the remarkable Reykjavík Theatre Company (Leikfélag Reykjavíkur) was produced to commemorate the 75th anniversary of the founding of the theatre. It includes photographs from some of its productions of both Icelandic and foreign drama. This municipal theatre, which until recently had as its managing director Vigdís Finnbogadóttir (now President of Iceland) was the first regular theatre in Iceland. To replace the present IÐNÓ building with its 200 seats, a new theatre has been planned for the late 1980s with an auditorium for 500, plus an experimental theatre.

902 **Actor turns successful playwright.**
Magdalena Schram. *Atlantica and Iceland Review*, vol. 20, no. 2 (winter 1982), p. 52-59. illus.

A fascinating interview with Kjartan Ragnarsson, an actor with the Reykjavík Theatre Company since 1965, but who turned to playwriting in 1975, since when he has become recognised as Iceland's most versatile and popular playwright. The article is illustrated with photographs from productions of four of his plays.

Theatre and Cinema

903 **International film guide: Iceland.**
Árni Þórarinsson, Björn Vignir Sigurpálsson. London: Tantivy Press; San Diego, California: Barnes, 1981, p. 173-77.

The Icelandic film industry became fully established in 1979. In that same year four major films were produced. This article is a brief sketch of the new organisation of Icelandic cinema, and a description of the films recently screened, the first of which was the widely acclaimed *Land og Synir* (*Land and Sons*) from the novel by Indriði G. Þorsteinsson, directed by Agust Guðmundsson. The International Film Guide is published annually - updated information can therefore be obtained from the Icelandic section.

904 **The outlaw: a saga becomes a screen success.**
Árni Þórarinsson. *Atlantica and Iceland Review*, vol. 20, no. 1 (summer 1982), p. 12-23.

An all-Icelandic feature film based on a classical saga - the fulfillment of Icelandic cinematic ambition. *Útlaginn* (The Outlaw) is a film of the 13th-century *Gísli's saga*, directed by Agust Guðmundsson and starring Arnar Jónsson and Ragnheiður Steindórsdóttir. A production of the Isfilm enterprise, it was produced on what, in international terms, was a shoestring budget (about £350,000), but in Icelandic terms a huge outlay for a film which required an audience of 150,000 in a nation of perhaps 100,000 cinema-goers. This feature article presents the background to the film, and a review accompanied by colour stills. For a feature review of Agust Guðmundsson's earlier film *Land and Sons*, see the same magazine vol. 18, no. 2 (1980), p. 26-31.

Television

905 Pattern of radio listening and television viewing in Iceland.
Ulf Berg. Stockholm: Sveriges Radio, 1971. 24p.
A piece of mini-research involving a sample of 839 Icelanders aged between 14 and 79. The findings are hardly startling: consumption relates to daily work and habits; radio satisfies the middle-aged and the elderly, television the young; radio is more popular in rural areas, etc. However, the statistical appendices contain several interesting indications of Icelandic listening and viewing patterns, by time of day, sex, age, residence and receiver ownership.

906 Children and television in Iceland: a study of ten to fourteen year old children in three communities.
Þorbjörn Broddason. Lund, Sweden: University of Lund, Department of Sociology, 1970. 113p.
A valuable research study, sponsored by UNESCO, into television viewing habits of adolescents in Reykjavík, Akureyri, and the Westmann Islands, and of its effect upon their values, attitudes and general knowledge. At the time of this survey in 1968 many parts of Iceland were still without a television service, and it was therefore possible to compare results for regular viewers with those for children without regular access to television. Data collected include viewing intensity, the United States versus the Icelandic service, favourite programmes, comparisons with other media, educational factors, influences on career expectation, and the effects of television on homework and sleeping patterns. For further data on this topic, with especial reference to children's behaviour, see the article 'Television and the adjustment of Icelandic children to family and peers', by Thomas P. Dunn, Bragi Jósepsson (educational commissioner for Iceland) and J. Gipson Wells, in *Journal of Comparative Family Studies* (Canada), vol. 7, no. 1 (spring 1976), p. 87-95.

907 Cultural diffusion: the role of US TV in Iceland.
David E. Payne, Christy A. Peake. *Journalism Quarterly*, vol. 46 (autumn 1967), p. 523-31.
An American television station was established on the NATO base at Keflavík in 1956. Five years later, a licence to increase its wattage resulted in its transmissions becoming capable of reception in the south-western district of Iceland,

Television

which includes the capital. In 1966 (thirty-six years after the introduction of state radio) an Icelandic State Television service was established, gradually increasing its range and transmission hours in subsequent years (by 1980 to four hours of adult viewing each evening except on Thursdays and during July) and being viewed alongside US TV. This paper is a summary of research into the effects of an alien broadcasting system upon a national culture; the broad conclusion is that there is no significant support for the hypothesis of 'cultural imperialism' in the context of foreign television exposure amongst Icelanders. It has to be said that this conclusion would not pass unchallenged by many Icelanders.

908 Television as we like it?
Pétur Guðfinnsson, Warren J. Papin. *Sixty-five Degrees*, no. 7 (Aug. 1969), p. 9-14.

A comparative feature comprising two interviews: one with the Director of Television in Iceland concerning the Icelandic State Television service; the other with the Public Affairs Officer at the Keflavík base on US TV in Iceland. The contrasts in purpose and organisation are illuminating. For a report ten years on, by which time 99 per cent of Icelanders could receive television, with one TV set for every three inhabitants, see the article 'TV watching' by Markús Örn Antonsson in *Atlantica and Iceland Review*, vol. 17, no. 2 (1979), p. 17-21, on the past, present and future of Icelandic television.

909 Focus on tele-communications in Iceland.
Haraldur J. Hamar. *Atlantica and Iceland Review*, vol. 16, no. 3 (1978), p. 29-32.

A brief survey of Iceland's international telecommunication facilities, including the submarine cables SCOTICE with Scotland and ICECAN with Canada, and the satellite potential of INTELSAT - in the specific context of the media, however, this article is of interest for its indication of the proposals for and reactions to the longer term and more controversial NORDSAT, as a Nordic television relay system.

Periodicals

Newspapers and magazines

910 A nation of newspaper addicts / The Reykjavík daily press.
Haraldur J. Hamar, Anders Hansen. *Atlantica and Iceland Review*, vol. 19, no. 3 (1981), p. 46-49.

A feature on the newspaper reading habits of the Icelanders, with a summary of the characteristics of the six (now five) daily papers published in the capital. An interesting aspect of the Icelandic dailies is that they are all sold at the same price.

911 Alþýðublaðið. (The people's paper.)
Reykjavík: Alþýðublaðið, 1916- . daily.

Alþýðublaðið is the daily organ of the Social Democratic Party (Alþýðuflokkurinn). Its circulation of around 5,000 reflects the relatively low-key state of the Party's electoral fortunes at present. However, its weekend edition *Helgarpósturinn* (*Weekend post*) enjoys a circulation several times this figure. The Party also publishes weekly papers in Akureyri (*Alþýðumaðurinn*) and in Ísafjörður (*Skutull*).

912 Morgunblaðið. (Morning paper.)
Reykjavík: Morgunblaðið, 1913- . daily.

Morgunblaðið is the daily paper with by far the largest circulation (around 43,000 or more than one in five of the total population of Iceland); its share of the morning paper sales is almost two-thirds, and it attracts the lion's share of advertising. It represents the interests of the largest political party, the Independence Party (Sjálfstæðisflokkur), although not directly affiliated to it, and sets the tone of the Icelandic press in general with both quantity and vigour of its political coverage of domestic and international affairs. There is a Sunday magazine supplement *Lesbók*. Former editors have included Bjarni Benediktsson who became Prime Minister of Iceland, and the present editor is Matthías Jóhannesson, active also in cultural affairs. The paper's cartoonist Sigmund enjoys wide popularity. *Morgunblaðið's* office building is a landmark in central Reykjavík.

Periodicals. Newspapers and magazines

913 Tíminn. (The Times.)
Reykjavík: Tíminn, 1917- . daily.

Tíminn is the newspaper of the Progressive Party (Framsóknarflokkur) and offers a good coverage of affairs outside the capital. With a circulation of around 17,000 it is the second most widely read of the morning dailies, and is sold mainly by subscription. The Progressive Party also publishes a twice-weekly paper in Akureyri (*Dagur*), and a weekly in Vestmannaeyjar *Framsóknarblaðið*).

914 Þjóðviljinn. (The people's will.)
Reykjavík: Þjóðviljinn, 1936- . daily.

Þjóðviljinn, 'organ of socialism, the labour movement and national independence', is the daily paper of the People's Alliance Party (Alþýðubandalagið), and represents the viewpoints of the Icelandic communist movement. Editors Arni Bergmann, Einar Karl Haraldsson. Circulation 12,000 copies.

915 Dagblaðið / Vísir. (Daily paper / Pointer.)
Reykjavík: Dagblaðið/Vísir, 1981- . daily.

Until 1981, when an abrupt and controversial merger occurred, there had been two afternoon dailies in Reykjavík. *Vísir*, established in 1910, had long been a popular paper in Iceland, and the noontime cries of 'Vísir' from the small boys who sold it on the street corners was a distinguishing feature of the capital's bustle. In 1975, however, a group of journalists left *Vísir* to found a rival paper *Dagblaðið*, which for the next six years ensured a cut-throat competition between the two papers. At the time of the merger *Dagblaðið*'s circulation had overtaken that of *Vísir*, although both papers were claiming around 25,000 copies. They differed from the morning press in much the same way as morning and local afternoon dailies differ in Britain, with the emphasis on home news, entertainment, sport and classified advertisements. Both papers were noted for political opinion polls, with *Dagblaðið* having an uncannily accurate record. Both were politically independent, although both editors (Jónas Kristjánsson of *Dagblaðið* and Ellert B. Schram of *Vísir* (now joint editors of the newly-merged paper) have strong links with the Independence Party.

916 Vikan. (The week.)
Reykjavík: Hilmir, 1938- . weekly.

An illustrated weekly magazine for the general reader, with a circulation of around 12,500. The same publishers also issue a popular monthly *Úrval* (Digest). Another weekly paper of general interest is *Mánudagsblaðið* (Monday paper).

917 News from Iceland.
Reykjavík: Iceland Review, 1975- . monthly.

An extremely enterprising and useful publication in small newspaper format, designed to bring to the English-speaking reader abroad news and editorial comment on the social, political, economic and cultural affairs of Iceland. Material is taken from the full range of the Icelandic press, from official news releases and other sources. This publication grew out of the former supplement on commercial affairs which had appeared as part of the following item, and has expanded into a separate monthly publication of sixteen to thirty-two pages. Particular attention is paid to the coverage of governmental measures, the fishing industry (a quarterly supplement on Atlantic fishing has been included since 1981), energy resource projects, and tourism. Regular features include exchange rates of the Icelandic króna, practical information for visitors, a column on postage stamp issues, and a monthly recipe from Icelandic cuisine. Readily available on a reasonably priced

Periodicals. Newspapers and magazines

subscription, this publication is a convenient means for those abroad to keep abreast of current affairs in Iceland.

918 **Atlantica and Iceland Review.**
Reykjavík: Iceland Review, 1963- . quarterly.

It is a tribute to the editor of this independent magazine (Haraldur J. Hamar has held this position from the beginning to date) that it not only got off the ground, but has stayed on course and expanded over a period of twenty years, in spite of inflationary pressures. Basically it is a high-quality prestige publication designed to promote the cultural, social, and economic progress of Iceland to an English-speaking readership by means of feature articles on a wide range of topics. The articles themselves are introductory rather than analytical, but they are invariably accompanied by photography of the highest artistic and reproductive quality. The presentation of the magazine has attracted considerable attention from Icelandic and foreign advertisers. Until 1968 its title was simply *Iceland Review*. Its international circulation figure is around 28,000, and any one with an interest in and affection for Iceland will find a subscription rewarding. The time is ripe, after 20 years, for a cumulated index of subjects; in the meantime, a selection of the more interesting and unusual articles has been included in the appropriate sections of this bibliography.

919 **65°: the reader's quarterly on contemporary Icelandic life and thought.**
Reykjavík: Sixty-five Degrees, 1967-70. quarterly.

It was with considerable regret that many subscribers learnt of the cessation of this excellent magazine with its tenth issue after three years of brave enterprise. Despite a continuously rising circulation, it folded for economic reasons perhaps associated with the question of whether the market could support two English-language magazines devoted to Iceland and the foreign reader. Edited and published by Amalia Líndal (see her book *Ripples from Iceland* q.v.) it appeared to this reader to complement rather than to rival its longer-established counterpart, *Atlantica and Iceland Review* (q.v.). Promoting the Icelandic cause in a lower key, with the emphasis on text rather than illustration, it offered a wide variety of unusual contributions which collectively seemed to get beneath the skin of Icelandic society.

920 **Icelandic writing today.**
Edited by Sigurður A. Magnússon. Reykjavík: Sigurður A. Magnússon, Sept. 1982- .

The first issue of a projected regular literary magazine, which would fill a long felt gap for the foreign student of contemporary Icelandic literature. Supported by the Ministry of Education and distributed by Iceland Review, this attractively produced issue comprises an introductory essay on the post-war literature of Iceland by the editor Sigurður A. Magnússon, followed by translations of prose and poetry by thirty-three living Icelandic writers. Also included are texts of interviews with the writers, plus biographical notes and, helpfully, their photographs. The work of five graphic artists is also included. A particularly interesting feature to emerge is the range of professions from which Icelandic writers are drawn. This first issue contains sixty-eight pages, and on its own can be highly recommended as an excellent orientation into the contemporary Icelandic literary scene.

Periodicals. Newspapers and magazines

921 Lögberg-Heimskringla.
Winnipeg, Manitoba: Lögberg-Heimskringla Publ. Co., 1886- . weekly.

A general literary and political review for Canadians of Icelandic descent. Its publishing history extends back to within a few years of the first emigration from Iceland to Canada. The text is in both English and Icelandic, and it has a circulation of over 4,000 copies. Also published for the Icelandic community in Canada is the quarterly general magazine *Icelandic Canadian*, issued in English by the Icelandic Canadian Club in Winnipeg, with a circulation of 2,500. For the much smaller Icelandic community in the United States a new general magazine *Gustur* (Breeze) was launched by the Icelandic American Association in Los Angeles, issued quarterly in English.

922 Scandinavian Review.
New York: American-Scandinavian Foundation, 1913- . quarterly.

A long-established and informative magazine devoted to the cultural and social affairs of the Scandinavian countries. Icelandic topics have been regularly represented over the years in good proportion. Its publisher is a non-profitmaking educational institution with a considerable history of promoting exchange between North America and Scandinavia, and has initiated many important books in the field. Until 1975 this periodical was entitled *American-Scandinavian Review*. Each issue is substantial (over 100 pages) and contains many regular features such as book reviews.

Subject magazines in Iceland

923 Eimreiðin. (Progress.)
Reykjavík: Hilmir, 1895- . quarterly.

A literary and political magazine, long respected and latterly international in outlook. Title literally means 'Locomotive'. Two other well established literary magazines are *Helgafell*, quarterly since 1942, and *Tímarit Máls og menningar*, founded in 1937.

924 Heima er bezt. (Home is best.)
Akureyri, Iceland: Bókaforlag Odds Björnssonar, 1951- . monthly.

A cultural magazine, thoroughly Icelandic in character, and one of the few nationwide magazines to be published outside the capital. Edited by Steindór Steindórsson frá Hlöðum.

925 Líf. (Life.)
Reykjavík: Frjálst framtak, 1977- . 6 per annum.

A fashion magazine also covering women's wider interests and representing the women's movement. Has quickly established itself with a wide circulation. Edited by Katrín Pálsdóttir.

Periodicals. Specialist periodicals. Science

926 **Íþróttablaðið.** (Sports news.)
Reykjavík: Frjálst framtak, 1935- . monthly.
The main magazine for sport in Iceland.

927 **Samvinnan.** (Co-operation.)
Reykjavík: Samband íslenzkra samvinnufélaga, 1907- . monthly.
A magazine published by the Federation of Icelandic Co-operative Societies, representing the interests of the co-operative movement.

928 **Sjávarfréttir.** (Sea news.)
Reykjavík: Frjálst framtak, 1973- . monthly.
A magazine covering all aspects of the Icelandic fishing industry. Compare the longstanding periodical *Aegir* (Sea), founded in 1905 and published fortnightly by the Fisheries Association of Iceland (Fiskifélag Íslands).

929 **Freyr.**
Reykjavík: Búnaðarfélag Íslands/Stettarsamband Íslands, 1904- . fortnightly.
A farming magazine, attractively produced by the Icelandic Agricultural Society and the Farmers' Union.

930 **Iðnaðarblaðið.** (Business news.)
Reykjavík: Frjálst framtak, 1976- . monthly.
A lively magazine for the business community. A regular complement to the semi-annual *Tímarit iðnaðarmanna* (Businessman's journal) published by Landssamband Iðnaðarmanna since 1927.

931 **Frjálsverzlun.** (Free trade.)
Reykjavík: Frjálst framtak, 1939- . fortnightly.
An important magazine dealing with all aspects of Iceland's domestic and foreign trade.

Specialist periodicals

Science

932 **Ísland: bulletin of the Iceland unit.**
London: Young Explorers' Trust, 1972- . biannual.
The Iceland Unit of the Young Explorers' Trust (the Association of British Youth Exploring Societies) is responsible for this enterprising publication in mimeograph form. Its aim is to provide data on recent expeditions, practical information for fieldworkers, and feature articles. Certain issues include a recur-

Periodicals. Specialist periodicals. Science

rent and valuable list of recent books, articles, research reports and theses (in Icelandic or English) on relevant topics, compiled by Paul Sowan; the emphasis of the publication is on geology, natural history and related fields. Each issue runs to over twenty pages, and an index is available covering the first twelve issues (1972-76). The Unit also publishes continually-revised broadsheets on aspects such as accommodation for explorers, maps, routes, transportation, radio contact, recorded movements, birdwatching, etc. The Young Explorers' Trust is located at the headquarters of the Royal Geographical Society.

933 Acta Naturalia Islandica.
Reykjavík: Icelandic Museum of Natural History, 1946- . irregular.
Each issue of this serial publication comprises a monograph on a geological, botanical or zoological topic, contributed by an Icelandic or foreign specialist. Volume one contained ten issues (1946-55); volume two a further ten (1955-71); since 1971 a straight numerical sequence is used from twenty-one onwards. Almost all the papers are in English. Also of importance in this context is the series of publications issued by the Scientific Society of Iceland (Vísindafélag Íslendinga). This commenced in the 1920s and has now run to over forty volumes, the majority of which cover glaciology, seismology and botany - particularly regional studies of vegetation. The Society also published two volumes of a journal entitled *Science in Iceland* in 1968 and 1970.

934 Acta Botanica Islandica: a journal of Icelandic botany.
Akureyri, Iceland: Náttúrugripasafnið, 1972- . annual.
A research periodical devoted to the botany of Iceland. Most of the articles are written in English, a few in French, German or Icelandic with English summaries. Each issue also contains a list of recent references to Icelandic botanical studies in other sources. The precursor of this periodical was called *Flóra* and appeared in six annual issues, 1963-68. *Acta Botanica* is published by the Museum of Natural History in Akureyri, with the emphasis on 'floristics, plant sociology, taxonomy and ecology'.

935 Jökull. (Glacier.)
Reykjavík: Jöklarannsóknafélag Íslands, 1951- . annual.
This journal is the yearbook of the Glaciological Society of Iceland. Each issue contains several substantial articles, mostly in English, reflecting recent research in all aspects of Icelandic glaciology. Contributors include Icelandic and foreign specialists - joint projects have been a feature in this field. The bibliographic production of this publication is of high standard; photographs, maps and tabular material are well presented. It should be a first point of reference for any serious student of glaciers in Iceland.

936 Læknablaðið: the Icelandic Medical Journal.
Reykjavík: Læknafélag Íslands / Læknafélag Reykjavíkur, 1915- . quarterly - bimonthly.
The journal of the Icelandic Medical Association and the Medical Association of Reykjavík. Professional news, comment, and research articles with summaries in English. Annual index also in English.

Surtsey research progress reports.
See item no. 190.

Periodicals. Specialist periodicals. Humanities

Humanities

937 Islandica: an annual relating to Iceland and the Fiske Icelandic Collection.
Ithaca, New York; Cornell University Library, 1908-32; Cornell University Press, 1933- . irregular.

An astonishing enterprise by virtually one man, Halldór Hermannsson (see P. M. Mitchell's biography, q.v.), who between 1908 and 1945 himself wrote, compiled or edited all 31 of the volumes. This series has exerted a great influence on the study of mediaeval and modern Icelandic culture, and a full list of the individual titles can be consulted in the most recent volumes. The first 37 volumes have been reprinted by Kraus. The latest volume, XLII, is entitled 'Old Norse Court poetry: the dróttkvætt saga', edited by Roberta Frank, 1978, 223p. Several of the earlier volumes have been separately described in the relevant subject sections of this bibliography.

938 Mediaeval Scandinavia.
Odense, Denmark: Odense University Press, 1968- . annual.

'A journal devoted to the study of mediaeval Scandinavia and Iceland'. The subject coverage includes archaeology, history, language, literature, religion, etc. The distinguishing feature of this journal is the series of collective contributions in which several scholars pool their resources to consider a major topic and present articles on different aspects of it; often these scholars are from different subject areas and thus collectively convey an interdisciplinary approach to each topic. The majority of the articles are in English. Volume seven (1974) is wholly devoted to a symposium on early Icelandic literature. Volume ten (1977) contains a complete index to the first ten volumes.

939 Saga-book.
London: University College, Viking Society for Northern Research, 1895- . irregular.

A long-established, highly-respected journal, which for nearly a century has attracted papers from all the important names in Icelandic and northern scholarship from Britain, and occasionally from further afield. The Viking Club, as it was originally called, was founded in 1892, and this journal has been the medium for communicating its members' researches and comments in Old Norse/Icelandic culture. The first eighteen volumes, 1895-1973 have been reprinted by AMS Press, New York. There is a cumulative index to volumes one-sixteen (1965). The Viking Society for Northern Research has more recently been an instigator of the International Saga Conferences, the first of which was held at Edinburgh in 1971; subsequent conferences were held at Reykjavík in 1973, Oslo in 1976, Munich in 1979, and Toulon in 1982. The collections of papers presented at these conferences are available in mimeograph form.

940 Scandinavian studies.
Lawrence, Kansas: Allen Press, 1911- . quarterly.

The journal of the Society for the Advancement of Scandinavian Study. It has acquired an academic reputation in the language, literature, history and society of the northern countries. Icelandic studies have been well represented in both the articles and the book reviews carried in this established journal, which has also featured regular bibliographies of Scandinavian studies.

Periodicals. Specialist periodicals. Humanities

941 Skírnir.
Reykjavík: Hið íslenzka bókmenntafélag, 1827- . annual.
The oldest periodical in Scandinavia, published in Copenhagen until the end of the 19th century, and founded by the Icelandic Literary Society. It remains an influential and prestigious journal. Each annual issue contains well over 200 pages. Another important literary journal founded in the 19th century and still appearing annually is *Andvari* (Breeze), published by the Cultural Fund and the Icelandic Patriotic Society; it first appeared in 1874, continuing from *Ný félagsrit* (1841-1873), the periodical founded by Jón Sigurðsson (q.v.). *Andvari* like *Skírnir* carries articles only in Icelandic.

Directories

942 **Viðskiptaskráin.** (Commercial and industrial directory for Iceland.)
Reykjavík: Steindórsprent, annual. c. 700p. map.

This directory has been established for over forty years, and is designed for both domestic and foreign use. It is arranged in eight sections: 1) a guide to parliament, the ministries and the embassies; 2-3) municipal institutions in Reykjavík and the rest of the country; 4) trades register of firms arranged by product or service, with subject index of terms in English; 5) agencies; 6) a very useful and up-to-date geographical, political and economic survey of Iceland (text in English and available separately as an offprint); 7) Faroese section; and 8) international section. Many extras, including map showing territorial waters and location of lighthouses.

943 **Íslensk fyrirtæki.** (Icelandic firms.)
Edited by Hákon Hákonarson. Reykjavík: Frjálst framtak, annual c. 650p.

A comprehensive directory of enterprises, associations and institutions in Iceland, arranged three ways: by brand name, by type of product or service (sub-headings in English), and by locality. It includes importing-exporting enterprises, and the register of Icelandic shipping. An introductory chapter in English presents general information on travel and business in Iceland. Another useful directory along the same lines and of similar size is *Viðskipti og þjónusta* (*Business directory of Iceland*) published annually in Reykjavík by Arblik, comprising a geographical arrangement of firms and institutions, with annotations in English.

944 **Directory of Iceland.**
Reykjavík: Icelandic Yearbook, annual. (publication suspended).

Although this directory ceased publication in the 1970s, it is still worth mentioning for the fact that it was presented entirely in the English language. It has been publishing official and commercial information since 1907 and had changed hands three times in its history. In latter years its arrangement comprised a section on the organisation of the country, a conventional directory of enterprises, and an important supplement on import regulations. An early revival would be very

Directories

welcome. Another directory of historical interest is *Iceland today: the land and the nation, the economy and culture,* edited by Guðmundur Jakobsson, (Reykjavík: Landkynning, 1961, 489p.). Sectoral surveys by specialists are followed by descriptions of Icelandic firms, with photographs of personalities.

945 Símaskrá. (Telephone directory.)
Reykjavík: Post and Telecommunications Office. annual. c. 480p.

The telephone directory of the whole of Iceland in one volume, arranged, according to custom, by first name followed by patronymic. The directory has two main sections, the first for Reykjavík and its environs, the second for the rest of the country alphabetically by town. Other useful information includes charging bands and rates (a controversial issue at the time of writing), and a street map of the Reykjavík area showing locations of post offices. The Telex directory of Iceland *Telexskrá* also appears annually, c. 24p.

946 Íslenzkir samtíðarmenn. (Icelandic contemporaries.)
Jón Guðnason, Pétur Haraldsson. Reykjavík: Bókaútgáfan Samtíðarmenn, 1965-67. 2 vols.

A 'who's who' of some 5,000 contemporary Icelanders, giving details of family, career, etc. Arranged by first name. Icelandic text. Jón Guðnason also contributed the last volume of the Icelandic equivalent of the British *Dictionary of National Biography.* Páll Eggert Ólason's *Íslenzkar æviskrár* presents biographical details of more than 10,000 eminent Icelanders from the time of the settlement through to 1940. The last volume extends the work to 1965. Six volumes in all, published in Reykjavík by the Icelandic Literary Society, 1948-76.

947 Who's who in Scandinavia.
Munich: Who's Who Verlag, 1981-82. 2 vols.

In the absence of an English language biographical dictionary specifically devoted to Iceland this expensive but substantial work of reference (one of a proven series) can be recommended. It contains biographical details of around 10,000 Danish, Finnish, Icelandic, Norwegian and Swedish personalities from all walks of life. Iceland is reasonably well represented. There is a useful appendix of societies, associations and institutions. Cheaper, though very unsatisfactory because of its low 'hit-rate' for Icelanders is *Dictionary of Scandinavian biography,* edited by E. Kay (London: Melrose Press, 1976, 2nd ed. 497p.) which contains 4,000 entries, and the English text of the Nordic countries' Treaty of Co-operation.

948 Handbók Útanríkisráðuneytisins. (Manual of the Ministry for Foreign Affairs of Iceland.)
Reykjavík: Ministry for Foreign Affairs, 1979. 125p.

A reference book of official information concerning Iceland's presence overseas. The major portion of the directory is a guide to Icelandic embassies, consular offices and delegations in the countries and organisations of the world. There are also details of the internal establishment of the Foreign Ministry. A glossary of terms enables this handbook to be easily used by the English-speaking reader.

Kennsluskrá. (Háskóli Íslands.)
See item no. 430.

Museum and Library Services

949 **National Museum of Iceland: summary guide to the exhibition rooms.**
Þorkell Grímsson. Reykjavík: National Museum, 1976. 5th ed. 42p.

The origins of the National Museum of Iceland were in the 1860s. In connection with Icelandic republican independence in 1944 a purpose-designed building was commissioned and was ready for the housing of exhibits in 1950. A full tour of the museum is not a fatiguing exercise - this is not to criticise the relative quantity of the exhibits, but rather to commend the compactness and relevance of the displays. This printed guide, in convenient format, is well presented, and enables the visitor to proceed smoothly from room to room and from case to case.

950 **Árbær Museum.**
Nanna Hermannsson. *Atlantica and Iceland Review*, vol. 14, no. 2 (1976), p. 24-29.

A brief photographic feature on the Árbær folk museum where, on a site in the suburbs of Reykjavík, a collection of old homes and other buildings from various parts of Iceland have been re-sited, with their interiors reconstructed, to provide an unusual insight into past living conditions. Árbær is part of the Reykjavík Municipal Museum.

951 **Norræna húsið.** (Nordic House.)
Reykjavík: Nordic House. 8p.

A brochure, available in several languages, briefly describing the facilities of the Nordic House in Reykjavík, designed by the Finnish architect Alvar Aalto and inaugurated in 1968 as a cultural and social centre, with library and other facilities, for forging links between Iceland and the other Nordic countries, whose gift to Iceland it was.

Museum and Library Services

952 **Libraries in Iceland.**
C. F. Scott. *Library Association Record*, vol. 67, no. 12 (Dec. 1965), p. 423-33.
A useful survey of the state of Icelandic libraries by the mid-1960s. The writer describes the establishment and stock of all the main libraries, with the emphasis on the system of public libraries, created by the Public Library Act of 1958. He reports from all quarters of Iceland, and also outlines the organisation and training of library staff. Dr Scott returned to Iceland six years later and recorded his updated impressions in *Focus on International and Comparative Librarianship*, vol. 2, no. 2 (Aug. 1971), p. 29-39. See the brief sketch 'North Iceland's new library at Akureyri' by Indriði Hallgrimsen, *Library World* (UK), vol. 2, no. 2 (July 1969), p. 4-7.

953 **Library services to the sick and handicapped in Iceland.**
Kristin H. Pétursdóttir. *Book Trolley*, vol. 3, no. 3 (Sept. 1971), p. 9-12.
A brief outline of hospital library services in Iceland, with reference to government subsidy, the Red Cross, and facilities for the blind. The reporter is not optimistic about future development.

954 **Library education in Iceland.**
Susan Bury. *International Library Review* (UK), vol. 9, no. 3 (July 1977), p. 303-18.
An account of the way in which librarians are trained at the University of Iceland under a system started in 1956 within the Philosophical Faculty with courses run by the University Librarian, and of the prospects for a proper Department of Librarianship (approved by the University in the mid-1970s) within the Faculty of Social Sciences.

Catalogues and Bibliographies

955 Íslensk bókaskrá. (Icelandic national bibliography.)
Reykjavík: Landsbókasafn Íslands, 1974- . annual.
The Icelandic national bibliography, produced by the National Library of Iceland, is the prime source of bibliographical information on Icelandic publications in a given year. It is a continuation of *Íslenzk rit*, which appeared as part of the yearbook of the National Library, and of the annual list issued by the Booksellers' Association. The arrangement is alphabetical by author's given name or other main heading, with a classified subject section, and a list of maps. It also includes a statistical summary of the year's publishing activities. Quinquennial cumulations are planned. Introductory remarks in English. A preliminary edition appears each year entitled *Íslensk bókatíðindi*.

956 Islandica: books on Iceland.
Reykjavík: Snæbjörn Jónsson (the English Bookshop) h.f., 1972. 48p.
The sales list of the long-established and well-known 'English Bookshop' of Snæbjörn Jónsson on Hafnarstræti in central Reykjavík. This subject arranged list reflects the wide range of general and specialised books, series and maps available in English and Icelandic for the student of Icelandic culture, society and landscape. Produced mainly for the purpose of international mail order, it contains both recent and older material, and has been updated with typed supplements.

957 Checklist of principal books in English on Iceland and Faroe.
Compiled by Dick Phillips. Alston, Cumbria: Dick Phillips, 1980. rev. ed. 28p.
A very useful list, prepared originally for the compiler's personal purposes (see *On foot in Iceland 1983* q.v.) but now more generally available. It contains over 300 items, with occasional annotations. The emphasis of the selection is on natural history and travel in Iceland, and, within these limits, no item of importance appears to have been missed. The compiler has drawn on the Fiske catalogue (see *Catalogue of the Icelandic collection bequeathed by Willard Fiske*, q.v.) and has

Catalogues and Bibliographies

asterisked all those items which are to be found in the library at his youth hostel at Fljótsdalur in south-west Iceland.

958 Scandinavia in social science literature: an English language bibliography.
Sven Groennings. Bloomington, Indiana: Indiana University Press for the International Affairs Center, 1970. 284p.

'This bibliography lists English-language literature, including unpublished theses, on Denmark (and Greenland), Finland, Iceland, Norway and Sweden, in the fields of economics, education, geography, history, international relations, law, political science, and sociology... the listing is almost exclusively of twentieth-century sources, and within this timespan is based on a systematic and thorough search for all the years through 1963'. The list also includes items encountered at random from 1964 to 1967. It benefits from a detailed arrangement by subject, with an index of authors appended. The best part of 10,000 entries are included (Iceland is well represented) and, although these are not annotated, each major subject section is introduced by a helpful essay on its literature. Both the stated purpose and the arrangement of this bibliography is to promote comparative analysis and teaching about Scandinavia, which, in this reviewer's experience with students, it manifestly achieves. An updated edition would serve to increase its usefulness.

959 A bibliography for ethnographic research on Iceland.
Frederick E. Bredahl-Petersen. *Behavior Science Research* (US), vol. 14, no. 1 (1979), p. 1-35.

A list of references relevant to the ethnography of Iceland in English and other western languages. Selective rather than systematic (it contains some 200 items) it is nonetheless useful, especially for its introductory essay evaluating the printed sources available to the researcher in this field.

960 Index Nordicus: a cumulative index to English language periodicals in Scandinavian studies.
Janet Kvamme, Edwin Brownrigg. Boston, Massachusetts: G. K. Hall for the American-Scandinavian Foundation; Eastbourne, England: Holt-Saunders, 1981. 770p.

Nearly 5,000 articles and 3,500 book reviews published between 1911 and 1976 are indexed in this enterprising, computer-based work of reference. Six major journals are covered: *Co-operation and Conflict* (Nordic journal of international relations), *Scandinavian Economic History Review, Scandinavian Political Studies, Scandinavian Review, Scandinavian Studies* and *Scandinavica*. One alphabetical sequence of index entries allows approach by author or subject term. Although not free from errors, this is a unique and useful aid for those engaged in the humanities or social sciences of the Nordic world, and, specifically, Iceland. It is to be hoped that supplements have been planned.

961 Bibliography of Old Norse-Icelandic studies.
Edited by Hans Bekker-Nielsen. Copenhagen: Royal Library, 1963- . annual.

This important annual bibliography has proved a valuable source of reference for students of Old Icelandic language, literature and history. It covers books, monographs and serials (e.g. in volume 16, for 1978, almost 100 journals were

Catalogues and Bibliographies

scanned) and contains around 500 entries annually. Publication is three to four years in arrears of the year covered. Each annual volume of BONIS also contains an introductory essay by a scholar on some aspect of Old Norse studies, e.g. 'Rímur and lausavísur' by Sigurður Nordal (1966); 'Old Norse bibliography' by J. A. B. Townsend (1967); 'Skaldic poetry' by G. Turville-Petre (1969); 'Teaching of Old Norse-Icelandic in the United States' by G. G. Gage (1970); 'Translating the sagas into English' by G. Johnston (1972); 'Death in autumn: the tragic element in early Icelandic fiction' by Hermann Pálsson (1973). Hans Bekker-Nielsen also compiled a useful volume which acts as a selective precursor to BONIS. *Old Norse-Icelandic studies: a select bibliography* (Toronto: University of Toronto Press, 1967, 94p.), covers language, literature and background material, with an index of authors.

962 Motif index of early Icelandic literature.
Inge M. Boberg. Copenhagen: Munskgaard, 1966. 268p.
(Bibliotheca Arnamagnaeana, vol. XXXVII).

A unique and compendious work of reference for the comparative study of Old Icelandic literature. It comprises a detailed index of motifs and themes to be found in over 300 texts - sagas, Eddic and skaldic poetry, etc. The initial arrangement is by broad category: mythological motifs, animals, tabu, magic, the dead, marvels, ogres, tests, wisdom and folly, deceptions, reversals of fortune, ordaining the future (vows, bargains, prophecies, curses, etc.), chance and fate, social structure, rewards and punishments, captives and fugitives, cruelty, sex, religion... There are numerous subdivisions within each category, accompanied by detailed citations. This work had not been quite completed at the time of the author's death, which may explain the only major gap, the theme of humour, which, grim or otherwise, is an arresting feature of several saga passages. The student of early Icelandic literature hardly needs to be reminded of the echoes and wealth of parallels throughout the corpus of surviving texts - this admirable volume, the product of a labour of love, demonstrates that no Icelandic text can be seriously studied in isolation, and offers the means for comparative study of the recurrent motifs.

963 A bibliography of skaldic studies.
Lee M. Hollander. Copenhagen: Munskgaard, 1958. 117p.

A valuable aid to the advancement of the study of skaldic poetry, this bibliography covers collections of skaldic verse in both original and translated form, general critical commentaries, and writings on the individual poets.

964 Norse sagas translated into English: a bibliography.
Donald K. Fry. New York: AMS Press, 1980. 139p.

A really useful bibliography, current to 1978, in which the aim is to list all those Icelandic sagas and the Þaettir (shorter stories) so far translated into English. The arrangement is alphabetical by Icelandic title, with cross references from variant titles, and under the heading for each saga the translations are listed alphabetically by translator. Over 150 sagas are included, from all categories. The compiler appends an index of editors and translators, and a list of sagas suggested for translation at a future date.

Catalogues and Bibliographies

965 Bibliography of modern Icelandic literature in translation.
Compiled by P. M. Mitchell, Kenneth H. Ober. Ithaca, New York: Cornell University Press, 1975. 324p. (Islandica, vol. XL).

An exhaustive enterprise in the spirit of Halldór Hermannsson (in whose *Islandica* series it appears). It lists those works of modern Icelandic literature translated into any major language, whether in book form or in parts of periodicals. It covers anthologies, individual authors (the largest section), and anonymous writings. Each author is subdivided by the language of the translation. Also includes index of translators.

966 Willard Fiske and Icelandic bibliography.
Halldór Hermannsson. *Papers of the Bibliographical Society of America*, vol. 12, no. 3-4 (1918), p. 97-106.

A short biography of the American scholar and bibliophile Willard Fiske (1831-1904), whose collection of Icelandic materials was bequeathed to Cornell University Library. It is written by his successor at Cornell (see *Halldór Hermannsson* and *Catalogue of the Icelandic collection bequeathed by Willard Fiske*, q.v.).

967 Halldór Hermannsson.
P. M. Mitchell. Ithaca, New York: Cornell University Press, 1978. 167p. bibliog. (Islandica, vol. XLI).

Halldór Hermannsson's contribution to Icelandic scholarship and the promotion of that scholarship abroad was immense. This volume commemorates the centenary of his birth in 1878, and is a review of his life as scholar and bibliographer, followed by a bibliography of his own writings, which shows the wealth of his activity. The cornerstone of his career and reputation is his exploitation of the Willard Fiske Icelandic Collection at Cornell University Library. His association with Fiske, Professor and Librarian at Cornell, had begun in 1899 and led to his taking over the mantle. Icelandic literature, palaeography, cartography and bibliography were all encompassed by his studies, and as the author of this volume states 'the Icelandic collection, its catalogues, and the series *Islandica* (q.v.) constitute his monument'. He died in 1958 and, notwithstanding his career in America, retained his Icelandic citizenship to the end.

968 Catalogue of the Icelandic collection bequeathed by Willard Fiske.
Compiled by Halldór Hermannsson. Ithaca, New York: Cornell University Library, 1914. 755p. Reprinted, including supplements, Cornell University Press, 1960.

The first major list of research sources for Icelandic studies of all periods, compiled from the Fiske Collection at Cornell. The original catalogue, arranged by author with an index of subjects, contains over 10,000 items. A similar number is listed in the two supplementary volumes of additions to the collection, 1913-26 (published 1927), 284p., and 1927-42 (1943), 295p. The later reprinting of the full set is testimony to its continuing value.

Catalogues and Bibliographies

969 **Catalogue of the books published in Iceland from A.D. 1578 to 1880 in the Library of the British Museum.**
Compiled by Thomas W. Lidderdale. London: Clowes, 1885. 55p.

This catalogue of the first 300 years of printing in Iceland is arranged chronologically and by location of the printing presses, notably those at the episcopal seats of Hólar and Skálholt, the islands of Viðey and Hrappsey (the latter island in Breiðafjörður having housed the largest press in Iceland in the 18th century), and the main townships of Reykjavík and Akureyri. Includes index of titles of works, and a list of printers in Iceland during this period with their locations and dates.

970 **Bókaskrá Gunnars Hall.** (Catalogue of the library of Gunnar Hall.)
Gunnar Hall. Akureyri, Iceland; Björn Jónsson; Copenhagen: Munskgaard, 1956. 520p.

The catalogue of a remarkable private library in Akureyri, north Iceland, listing over 10,000 items relating mainly to early and in some degree modern Icelandic studies, and covering Eddic, skaldic and balladic poetry, sagas, folk-tales, commemorative pieces, etc. Gunnar Hall was himself an author, chiefly on the subject of Icelandic nationhood.

971 **A catalogue of the Icelandic Collection.**
Leeds, England: University of Leeds Library, 1978. 166p.

One of the major British collections of old and modern Icelandic materials is to be found in a separate and well-organised room in the library of the University of Leeds. The basic collection is that of the Icelandic historian Bogi Þorarensen Melsted, which was acquired in 1929, and consists of over 5,000 volumes - it has been regularly supplemented to support the teaching and research in Old and modern Icelandic studies at the University. The publication of this catalogue is a very welcome and valuable enterprise. The catalogue is arranged alphabetically by author, otherwise by title, and is provided with an index of broad subjects. The layout is commendably clear, and the volume is a pleasure to use.

Index

The index is a single alphabetical sequence of authors/editors (personal and corporate), titles of publications (excluding articles in periodicals), subjects and places. Index entries refer both to the main items and to other works mentioned in the notes to each item. As the index contains many non-Icelandic personal authors, Icelandic personal names have been entered (contrary to Icelandic practice) under patronymic, etc., followed by given name, except in the case of personalities of the early period known almost exclusively by their given name (e.g. Ari, Snorri). The Icelandic letters Þ and ð have been filed as TH and d respectively. Also æ and ö have been filed according to English rather than Icelandic alphabetical order. Diacritical marks are ignored in the filing. Title entries are in italics. Numeration refers to items as numbered.

A

Á Njálsbúð 744
Aalto, Alvar 951
Abbreviations
  modern Icelandic 636
ABECOR country reports 553
Abstract art 884—885, 888, 891
Absurd, Theatre of 805
Accidents 408, 416
Achen, Sven Tito 281
Ackroyd, P. 6
Across Iceland 108
Across Iceland: the land of frost and fire 110
Across the Vatnajökull: or, scenes in Iceland 97
Act of Union 1918 333
Acta Botanica Islandica: a journal of Icelandic botany 934
Acta Naturalia Islandica 933
Aðalkort yfir Ísland 144
Aðalskipulag Reykjavíkur 1983 571
Aðalsteinsson, Jón Hnefill 360
Aðalsteinsson, Stefán 526
Adam of Bremen 282
Advanced geography of northern and western Europe 159
Advent 813

Advertising executives 389
Æðey 226
Aegir 928
Aesir 352
Age of the Sturlungs: Icelandic civilisation in the 13th century 310
Age of the Vikings 289
Agricultural policy in Iceland 511
Agricultural Research Institute
  maps 146
Agriculture 158, 168, 406, 511, 513—526, 929
  Rural life 19
  statistics 439, 512
Ahlmann, Hans Wilhelmsson 207
Air sports 586
Airlines 34, 559—561
Airports 341
Akranes
  family life 382
Akureyri 150
Akureyri
  description 48—49, 102, 113
  diet 415
  family organisation 381
  libraries 952, 970
  newspapers 911, 913

303

Akureyri *contd.*
 television viewing 906
 town plans 150
Akureyri and the picturesque north 49
Álafoss 526
Alaska
 Icelandic immigrants 52, 331
Albertsson, Kristján 804
Alcoholism 29, 416
Alehood (see Ölkofra þáttr)
Alexander, Lewis M. 157
Alexander, M. J. 166
Álftafjörður 197
Algerian pirates 220, 319
Allen, R. B. 666
Allen, Richard F. 745
Allwood, Martin S. 775
Almanacs (see Calendars)
Alþing 43, 302, 389, 447—450
Althing: Iceland's thousand years old parliament 448
Alþingistíðindi 450
Alþýðflokkurinn (see Social Democratic Party)
Alþýðubandalagið (see People's Alliance)
Alþýðublaðið 911
Alþýðumadurinn 911
Aluminium smelting 546
Ambáles saga 687
Ambrus, V. G. 833
America
 Norse discovery 58—60, 125, 156, 270, 287, 299, 663, 815
America not discovered by Columbus: a historical sketch of the discovery of America by the Norsemen in the tenth century 59
America to Iceland 92
American-Icelandic writers 770—772
American in Iceland: an account of its scenery, people and history 93
American-Scandinavian Foundation 660, 922
American-Scandinavian Review 922
American soldier in Reykjavík 346
Ampleforth College 172
Ancestry (see Genealogy)
Andersen, Carl 853
Anderson, J. R. L. 125
Anderson, John 219
Anderson, Rasmus B. 59, 349
Anderson, S. A. 495
Andersson, Theodore M. 699, 717, 726
Andreæ, Guðmundur 605

Andvari 941
Angevin Britain and Scandinavia 691
Angling 130, 588—589
Animal communities (see Zoology)
Animal populations in relation to their food resources 252
Annandale, Nelson 220
Áns saga bogsveigis 728
Anthology of Icelandic poetry 782
Anthology of modern Icelandic literature 781
Anthology of Scandinavian literature from the Viking period to the twentieth century 773
Anthropological approach to the Icelandic saga 721
Anthropology (see Physical anthropology, Social anthropology)
Antonsson, Markús Örn 908
Arason, Guðmund 679
Arason, Jón 362, 803
Arason, Steingrímur 872
Árbær folk museum 950
Arbman, Holger 266
Árbók Hagstofa Íslands 436
Árbók Reykjavíkurborgar 440
Archaeology 264—277, 284, 300, 315, 517, 938
Architects 388
Architecture
 design 572
Arctic fox 256
Arctic living: the story of Grímsey 50
Arctic pilot. Volume II, Iceland, Jan Mayen, Bjørnøya, Svalbard and the east coast of Greenland, together with adjacent areas 129
Arent, A. Margaret 671, 692
Ari Þorgilsson 278, 306, 675, 698
Arinbjarnar kviða 733
Arinbjarnar, Snorri 878
Arkwright, Eleanor 799
Armstrong, Neil 201
Árnadóttir, Hólmfriður 18
Árnadóttir, Nína Björk 784
Arnamagnaean manuscripts 321, 767
Arnason, David 54
Árnason, Gunnar 367
Árnason, Ingólfr (see Ingólfr Árnason)
Árnason, Jóhann P. 462
Árnason, Jón 688—689, 755—757
Árnason, Kristján 623
Árnason, Örnólfur 572
Árnavatnsheiði 167

Arne Magnússon: the manuscript collector 321
Arnfinnsson, Róbert 900
Arnold, Matthew 762
Around the year in Iceland 116
Arrow-Odd: a medieval novel 685
Art 875—877
 design 895
 embroidery 894
 mosaics 888
 painting 122, 241, 878—888
 pottery 892
 Ringerike 272
 sculpture 890—891
 silversmithing 893
 stained glass 888—889
Art and ethics in Hrafnkel's saga 738
Art galleries 881
Art in Iceland: 20 artists 878
Art of Icelandic poetry 709
Art studios 887, 890
Ásbyrgi 179
Ásgarð 652, 865
 (see Mythology)
Asgard and the Norse heroes 865
Ásgeir of Iceland 874
Ásgeirsson, Ásgeir 465
Ásgeirsson, Bragi 884, 886
Ásgrímsson, Eystein 651
Ásgrímur Jónsson 881
Ashkenazy, Vladimir 898
Ashwell, I. Y. 170, 213, 513, 519, 521
Áskelsson, Jóhannes 179
Askey, D. E. 844
Askja 97, 101, 109, 199—201
Askja: Iceland's largest volcano 199
Askja on fire 200
Ásmundur Sveinsson 890
Astraudo, A. 17
Athletics 582
Atlakviða 644, 693
Atlamál 644
Atlantic ridge 174—175
Atlantic Salmon Trust 235
Atlantica and Iceland Review 918
Atlas blöðin 145
Atlases and maps 144—148, 152—153, 161
 18th century 67
 19th century 70
 cave system 194
 geology 178
 history 154—155
 map lists 956
 Reykjavík 440

road maps 138—140, 142—143
soil maps 520
Þingvellir 442
town plans 149—150
Vinland map 156
wall map 151
Atom poets 798
Atom station 821
Atoms and madams 799
Auden, W. H. 64, 114, 645
Audio language courses
 modern Icelandic 619
Auðunn and the bear 676
Auðunn and the bear 662, 670, 675, 835, 866
Auk (see Great auk)
Axarfjörður 167

B

Babcock, Melinda 755
Bacon, Francis, painter 887
Bægisárdalur 165
Bagley, Desmond 859
Baine, John 68
Baines, W. P. 855
Balance of payments 506, 532, 556
Balchin, Nigel 743
Baldick, R. 854
Baldr 352, 355, 357
Baltasar 12
Bandamanna saga 101, 658, 660—661, 695
Banking 506
Banking history 493
Banks, Joseph 63—67, 325
Banks, William M. 99
Baptism 369
Barclays Bank Group 553
Bárðarson, Hjálmar R. 42, 530
Baring-Gould, Sabine 83, 667
Barlau, S. B. 381
Barmby, Beatrice H. 666
Barrow, John 72
Barston, R. P. 484
Barth, Tom F. W. 182
Bayerschmidt, Carl F. 672, 691
Bealby, J. T. 178
Beck, Richard 691, 766, 772, 777—778, 787—788
Beckett, J. Angus 206
Beenhakker, A. J. 276

305

Beidelman, T. O. 721
Bekker-Nielsen, Hans 321, 693, 961
Belgium
 fishing agreements 485
Bellamy, David 222
Bellamy's Europe 222
Bellows, Henry A. 643
Bemmelen, R. W. van 198
Benedict, G. 17
Benediktsdóttir, Unnar 778
Benediktsson, Bjarni 449, 464, 486
Benediktsson, Einar 773, 779−780, 789
Benediktsson, Hreinn 594−595, 627
Benediktsson, Jakob 308, 316
Benedikz, Benedikt S. 317, 647, 689, 757
Benedikz, Eiríkur 782
Benners, Isaac 68
Bennett, R. M. 900
Benson, A. B. 19
Beowulf 752
Berg, Ulf 905
Berger, A. 443
Bergman, M. 75
Bergmann, Árni 914
Bergsson, Guðbergur 834
Berry, Erick 870
Berry, Francis 848
Bessason, Haraldur 304
Bessastaðir 219, 466, 632
Best, Allena (see Berry, Erick)
Bible 363, 767
Bibliographies 932, 937, 955−963, 965−971
 Language 591
 sagas 964
 travellers' accounts 89
Bibliography of modern Icelandic literature in translation 965
Bibliography of Old Norse-Icelandic studies 961
Bibliography of Scandinavian languages and linguistics, 1900-1970 591
Bibliography of skaldic studies 963
Biering, Gunnar 409
Big fish: a short story 843
Binns, Alan L. 266, 751
Biographical dictionaries 946−947
Birbeck, Paul 866
Bird life in Iceland 243
Bird painting 241
Bird photography 242
Birds (see Ornithology)

Birth of a nation 305
Birth rates 407, 438
Birtingur 798
Bishops 304, 316, 361−363
Bishops' sagas 678−679
Bisiker, W. 108
Bittner, Donald F. 338
Bjarkamál 648
Bjarman, Björn 834
Bjarnar, Vilhjálmur 323
Bjarnarson, Hörður 570
Bjarnason, Björn 341
Bjarnason, Björn, politician 476
Bjarnason, Hákon 522
Bjarnason, Loftur 729, 781
Bjarnason, Margrét R. 541
Bjarnason, Ólafur 261, 410, 412
Bjarnason, Paul 779
Bjarnason, Stefán 280
Bjarnfredsson, Magnús 453, 516, 525
Björkman, Staffan 567
Björn, Jóhannes 783
Björnsson, Anrljótur 454
Björnsson, Árni 373
Björnsson, Axel 176, 202
Björnsson, Björn 382
Björnsson, Björn Þ. 36, 44, 875, 883
Björnsson, Guðmundur 420
Björnsson, Hafsteinn 379
Björnsson, Oddur 805, 884−885
Björnsson, Ólafur 496
Björnsson, Sigurjón 404, 418
Björnsson, Sveinbjörn 174, 548
Björnsson, Sveinn 335
Björonöya 129
Black cliffs 812
Black eggs 857
Blackburn, Mrs Hugh 98
Blackwell, I. A. 283
Bláfjall 198
Blake, C. C. 543
Blake, D. H. 197
Blake, N. F. 657
Blöndal, Gísli 497
Blöndal, Gunnlaugur 878, 882
Blöndal, Sigfús 61, 703
Bloodgroups 259, 261
Boberg, Inge M. 962
Bodkin, M. M. 807
Böðvarsson, Ágúst 149
Böðvarsson, Árni 188, 608, 629
Böðvarsson, G. 179
Böðvarsson, Guðmundur 792
Böðvarsson, Haukur 880
Bogadus, E. S. 401

Bogason, Sigurður Örn 609
Bókaskrá Gunnars Hall 970
Boland, Charles M. 160
Bolton, W. F. 739
Bolungarvík 168, 570
BONIS (see Bibliography of Old Norse-Icelandic Studies)
Book of the Icelanders 306
Book of Settlements (see Landnámabók)
Book ownership 425
Book reviews 922, 940, 960
Booksellers' Association 955
Borg 664
Borgarfjörður 69, 668
Bósa saga 683
Botany 108, 115, 169, 219, 222, 225, 227−230
Botany of Iceland 225
Boucher, Alan 3, 12, 326, 390, 408, 669, 674−675, 690, 726, 783, 794, 805, 836, 838, 873
Boult, Katherine, F. 865
Bouman, A. C. 727
Bow Group 480
Bowering, J. 494
Bowring, John 767
Boyer, Régis 820, 828
Brady, P. 531
Bragi, Einar 798
Bragi, god 652
Bragi, skald 707
Brandes, Georg 777
Branston, Brian 351
Bratby, Michael 239, 344
Brathay Exploration Group 211, 244
Brattahlíð 315
Bray, Olive 644
Breakdown and restoration of ecosystems 522
Bredahl-Petersen, Frederick E. 405, 959
Bredsdorff, Peter 571
Breiðamerkurjökull 170
Breiðfjörd, Leifur 889
Brekkukotsannáll 823
Brendan voyage 125
Brennu-Njáls saga (see Njáls saga)
Brevis commentarius de Islandia.. 316
Bridal gown: a novel of Iceland 816
Brief survey of the Icelandic farming industry today 512
Briem, E. 546
Briem, Helgi P. 16, 327
Briem, Jóhannes 878

Bright, Richard 70
'Brindled monster' 773
British Admiralty Naval Intelligence 161
British aggression in Icelandic waters 488
British Museum 291, 969
British occupation of Iceland, 1940-1942 338
British Overseas Trade Board 554
British Schools Exploring Society 213
British Schools Exploring Society report 1975-1976: 1975 central Iceland expedition 170
Britton, W. 126
Broadcasting 905−909
Broddason, Þorbjörn 403, 906
Brodeur, Arthur G. 652
Brokarjökull 211
Brøndsted, Johannes 266
Brown, E. D. 481
Brown, Ursula 677
   (see also Dronke, Ursula)
Browne, E. C. 458
Browne, John Ross 64, 85
Brownrigg, Edwin 960
Brunanburh 733
Bruun, Daniel 131
Bryans, Robin 119
Bryce, James 64, 88, 441
Brynjólfsdóttir, Ragnheiður 815
Bryson, Alexander 79
Buckhurst, H. M. 598
Bukdahl, J. 30
Búnaðarskýrslur 439
Bunsen, Robert W. 76
Búrfell power plant 546, 891
Burials (see Graves)
Burks, J. B. 39
Burning of Njál 867
Burton, Richard 64, 89, 96
Bury, Susan 954
Bus timetables 141
Buses 561
Business directory of Iceland 943
By fell and fjord: or, summer scenes in Iceland 95
By the roadside: descriptive notes on the route Reykjavík-Akureyri 139

C

Cabinet 458
Cable communication 909

307

Calendars 373
Calvert, W. E. 315
Campbell, J. G. (see
 Graham-Campbell)
Camping 91, 120
Canada
 Icelandic immigrants 53—54, 921
Canadian-Icelandic writers 770—772,
 779, 796
Cancer 408, 410
Capitalism 462
Careers (see Professions)
Carleton, Peter 797
Carlyle, John 763
Carlyle, Thomas 762—763
Carnegie Endowment for International
 Peace 493
Caröe, E. A. G. 562
Cars (see Motor vehicles)
Cartography
 history 154—155, 178
Cartography of Iceland 154
Cartoons 912
Cary, Sturges F. 869
Cassidy, V. H. de P. 691
Castberg, F. 449
*Catalogue of the books published in
 Iceland from A.D. 1578 to 1880
 in the Library of the British
 Museum* 969
*Catalogue of the Icelandic
 Collection* 971
*Catalogue of the Icelandic collection
 bequeathed by Willard Fiske* 968
Catalogue of Icelandic stamps 565
*Catalogue of the Library of Gunnar
 Hall* 970
Cathay, James E. 600
Catholic church 361—362
Cattle 253
Cattle, Sauđadalur 524
Caves 194
Cawley, Frank S. 670
Celtic motifs 761
Celts 260, 265
Censuses 392—393, 395, 400
Central Bank of Iceland 31, 437
*Central Bank of Iceland: annual
 report* 506
Central Intelligence Agency
 maps 152
Cereals 9
Cerely, Stanley 247
Chadwick, Henry M. 356
Chamberlin, William C. 492

Chambers, Robert 79
*Changes in Icelandic social structure
 since the end of the eighteenth
 century* 400
*Changing earth, and selected
 poems* 794
Chanter, Ll. 325
Chapman, Kenneth G. 592, 601, 619,
 831, 839
Chapman, Olive M. 110
Character of races 258
Charms 369, 371
Chater, A. G. 56
*Checklist of principal books in
 English on Iceland and Faroe* 957
Chelsea College 165
Chess 51, 578—579
*Chess in Iceland and in Icelandic
 literature, with historical notes on
 other table games* 578
Chieftan priests (see Gođar)
Child care 428
Child psychiatry 418
Children 390, 404, 872, 874, 906
 legal rights 391
*Children and television in Iceland: a
 study of ten to fourteen year old
 children in three communities* 906
Chill factor 860
Choran, L. M. 346
Christian conversion 289, 299, 302,
 304, 359—360, 669, 698, 724,
 727, 868
Christian poetry 650—651
Christianity (see Religion, Christian)
Christianity at glacier 825
Christmas 373
Christmas stories 813
Church and state 366, 447
Church history 361—367, 678—679
Churchill, A. J. 62
Ciklamini, Marlene 701
Cinema (see Films)
Citizenship (see Naturalised
 Icelanders)
Civil liberty 447
Clapperton, C. M. 192
Clark, Austin H. 160
Clark, D. 4
Clarke, D. E. M. (see Martin-Clarke)
Clarke, G. 181
Class (see Social classes)
*Classification of educational systems:
 Iceland..* 434
Clausing, S. 603

Cleasby, Richard 605
Clergy 400
Cliff, A. D. 413
Clifford, Charles C. 84
Clifford, K. C. 343
Climate 5, 9, 34, 129, 162, 166, 170, 212−217, 221, 224, 231, 258, 518−519
  fogs 90
Climate and weather of Iceland 217
Climatic data 436
Climbing higher: an Iceland adventure 116
Clinton, G. 443
La cloche d'Islande: roman 820
Co-operative movement 23, 401, 503, 509−510, 515, 526, 927
Coalitions 458
Coastguard 538
Coastline 128−129, 212
Coats of arms 281
Cod wars and how to lose them 486
Codex Regius 645
Coinage 501, 567
Cole, G. D. H. 1
Cole, G. R. F. 330
Coles, John 101
Collection of agreements concluded by the European Communities 551
Collection of voyages and travels 62
Collier, R. V. 244
Collingwood, W. G. 106, 644
Columbus, Christopher 55
The Comic in the Icelandic family saga 731
Commercial and industrial directory for Iceland 942
Commonwealth (see History, Commonwealth)
Communications (see Transport, Posts etc)
Communism 461
Compensation systems 454
Concise dictionary of Old Icelandic 607
Concise history of Iceland 296
Condren, E. I. 740
Confederates (see also Bandamanna saga)
Confederates, and Hen Thórir: two Icelandic sagas 661
Conflict and consensus in Icelandic politics, 1916-1944 459
Conservation 574−577
  fish stocks 527−529, 531, 534

Conservation in Iceland 574
Constitution of the republic of Iceland 447
Constitutional history 441, 445−446, 449
Constitutions
  1944 25, 447
Consulates 948
Continental shelf (see Law of the sea)
Contributions to the physiography of Iceland, with particular reference to the highlands west of Vatnajökull 177
Conversion of Iceland: a survey 359
Convict king: being the life and adventures of Jorgen Jorgensson 327
Conybeare, Charles A. V. 302
Cook on a cool cat 124
Cook, R. S. 736
Cookery (see Recipes)
Cooper, Dominic 861
Cornell University Library 937, 966−968
Corporation tax 498
Corpus poeticum boreale: the poetry of the old northern tongue from the earliest times to the thirteenth century 642
Costume
  National dress 19, 374
Cottle, A. S. 643
Coull, J. R. 534
Course in modern Icelandic 621
Court poetry (see Skaldic poetry)
Court reporting 451
Courts 451
Cowan, E. J. 763
Crabb, Peter 840
Crafts 277, 876−877, 892−895
Craigie, William A. 3, 15, 350, 605, 709, 711, 774
Crime 452−453
  sagas 743
Crimes, historical 812, 861
Crossley-Holland, Kevin 641
Cult of Othin: an essay in the ancient religion of the north 356
Cultural co-operation 468
Cultural identity 13
Culture 14−15, 23, 30, 37, 39
Cummings, J. 868
Currency 506, 567
Currency reform 501

309

Curriculum 427
Customs 368−371, 373−379

D

Daðason, Sigfús 798
Dagbjartsdóttir, Vilborg 784
Dagblaðið 915
Dagblaðið / Vísir 915
Dagur 913
Dairy farming 515−516
Dakota (see North Dakota)
Dalvík 515
Dan, Jón 836
Dances 370
Daníelsson, Guðmundur 836, 843
Danish-Icelandic writers 771
Danish language 632
Danske Selskab 456
Dasent, George Webbe 89, 596, 605, 652, 666, 672
Dating the Icelandic sagas: an essay in method 718
Daughter of fire: a portrait of Iceland 27
Davidson, H. R. Ellis 352, 760
Davíðsson, Ingólfur 227
Davíðsson, Kristján 884
Davis, M. 479
de Fonblanque (see Fonblanque)
de Groote (see Groote)
de Lange, J. (see Lange, Joost de)
de la Martinière (see Martinière)
de la Peyrère (see Peyrère)
de Vries, Jan 358
Death 378
Death rates 407
'Defeat of the Italian airforce in Reykjavík' 773
Defense (see also Security)
Deforestation 521
Democracy 456
Demography (see Population)
Denmark
 history 282
Denmark and Sweden with Iceland and Finland 295
Dennis, A. 442
Dentists 388
Deserts 181
Design 895
 housing 572
Destination Iceland 135
Devaluation 496, 501

Devas, Nicolette 857
Dexter, C. 533
Diabetes 415
Dialects
 modern Icelandic 627
Diatomite 544
Dictionaries
 modern Icelandic 603, 605−607, 609−613
 Old Icelandic 602, 604−605, 607
Dictionary of Scandinavian biography 947
Diego, Sonja 422, 429, 466, 585
Diet 23, 375, 415
Dillon, Arthur 73
Dioceses (see Skálholt, Hólar)
Directories 945
 biographical 946−947
 commercial 942−944
 Educational 430
 Ministry for Foreign Affairs 948
Directory of Iceland 944
Disability in Iceland 408
Disabled (see Handicapped)
Discovery 20
Discovery and exploration 55−60, 125, 156, 170, 172, 205−208, 287
 (see also Travellers' accounts)
Diseases 70
 cancer 408, 410
 diabetes 415
 elephantiasis 67
 glaucoma 420
 inherited 260
 leprosy 322
 measles 413
 multiple sclerosis 411
 smallpox 412
 Spanish flu 810
 Tuberculosis 414
Distress of Iceland 332
Diver (see Loon)
Divorce 417
 statistics 438
Djúivogur 89
Djúpalaek, Kristján fra (see Kristján frá Djúpalaek)
Doctors 388, 400, 407, 422, 936
Dogs (see Iceland dog)
Donegani, J. A. 261
Drama 781, 799−805, 902
 set in Iceland 850−851

Drangajökull 215
Dreamers of the day: an Arctic adventure 124
Dreams 758
 sagas 727
Dreams in Old Norse literature and their affinities in folklore 758
Drechsel, Edwin 566
Drift ice 9, 216−217
Dronke, Ursula 644, 677, 693, 706
 (see also Brown, Ursula)
Droplaugarsona saga 660
Drost, Kurt 36
Dróttkvætt 707−708
Ducks
 eider 250
Dufferin, Frederick 64, 78
Dumézil, Georges 354
Dungal, N. 261, 410
Dunn, C. F. 342
Dunn, T. P. 906
Durham University Vestfirðir project: fieldwork report and research notes 166
Dust storms 213
Dwarfs 759
Dye, Frank 127
Dye, Margaret 127
Dyngjufjöll 198
Dyrfjöll 124

E

Eagle Air 560
Eagles 372
Early Icelandic manuscripts in facsimile 595
Early Icelandic script 595
Early kings of Norway 763
Early Norse reader 597
Earthly paradise 850
Earthquakes 105
East Yorkshire in the sagas 751
Ecology 167, 190, 223−224, 233−235, 252, 522
Ecology of eutrophic, subarctic Lake Mývatn and the river Laxá 224
Economic Development Institute (see Framkvaemdastofnun Ríkisins)
Economic development of Iceland through World War II 492
Economic geography 159, 162, 471, 495

Economic geography of the Scandinavian states and Finland 159
Economic history 313−314, 320, 492−497
Economic indicators 504−508
Economic Intelligence Unit 504
Economic statistics 437
Economic surveys: Iceland 505
Economics 498−503
Economy 30, 38
 20th century 11, 15, 20, 31
Ecuador 483
Edda
 Poetic Edda 271, 638−647, 680, 692, 698−700, 704−706, 730
 Prose Edda 283, 638, 641, 652, 702
Edda and saga 700
Edda: its derivation and meaning 694
Edda: prologue and Gylfaginning 652
Eddison, E. R. 664
Edelstein, Stefán 899
Edelstein, W. 404
Education 23, 400, 423−434
 history 89
Education College of Iceland 428
Education in Iceland: its rise and growth with respect to social, political and economic determinants 424
Educational attainment 404
Educational history 423−424
Edvaldsson, Jóhannes 583
Edwards, Paul 307, 664−665, 683−685, 753
EEC (see European Economic Community)
EFTA (see European Free Trade Association)
Eggert Ólafsson: a biographical sketch 218
Eggertsson, Þráinn 471
Egil Skallagrímsson 707
Egils saga 664
Egils saga 691, 693, 727, 732−733
Egypt and Iceland in the year 1874 92
Eider ducks 250
Eighteenth century Iceland 65
Eimreiðin 923
Einarsdóttir, Sigrún Ólöf 895
Einarsson, Erlendur 510
Einarsson, Guðmundur 878
Einarsson, Guðmundur frá Miðdal 187
Einarsson, Indriði 765, 800
Einarsson, Ólafur R. 460

311

Einarsson, Páll 202
Einarsson, Sigurbjörn 361, 364, 367
Einarsson, Stefán 615, 619, 691, 710,
 732, 765, 770−771, 790
Einarsson, Sveinn 900−901
Einarsson, Þorleifur 189, 191
Einarsson, Þorsteinn 581
Einarsson, Trausti 179, 184, 187
Eirík the Red 57, 315
Eirík the Red, and other Icelandic sagas 662
Eiríks saga rauða 58, 662−663
Eiríksjökull 167, 213
Eiríksson, Jón 563, 767
Eiríksson, Leif (see Leif Eiríksson)
Elder Edda (see Edda, Poetic Edda)
Elder Edda and ancient Scandinavian drama 705
Elder or Poetic Edda 644
Eldey 245, 251
Eldjárn, Kristján 36, 38, 264, 268−269, 272, 466, 875
Elections 458−459, 462−463
 statistics 435
Electricity supply 546, 548
Elementary grammar of Old Icelandic 598
Elephantiasis 67
Elíasson, Bjarki 452
Elísson, Gunnar 467
Élitism 457
Elkington, J. 568
Ellwood, T. 307
Elton, Olivier 282, 679
Embassies 486, 948
Embleton, C. 5
Embroidery 877, 894
Emigration 23, 398
 to Alaska 331
 to Canada 53−54, 397, 796
 to the United States 52, 397
Emmé, W. 809
Employment 502
 working hours 455, 507
Encyclopaedia Britannica 301
Endurminningar 335
Energy, Geothermal 5, 47, 175, 179, 183, 202−203, 547−550, 568
Energy resources 503, 546−550
Engagement 382−383
Engilberts, Jón 878

English and mediaeval studies presented to J. R. R. Tolkien 706
English Bookshop 956
English-Icelandic dictionary
 Bogason 609
 Zoëga 607
English-Icelandic, Icelandic-English pocket dictionary 611
English-Icelandic vocabulary 606
English language 593
English literature
 influence of Norse
  literature 762−764
 influence on Norse
  literature 765−766
 saga parallels 727−728
Enlightenment 299, 324, 766
Ensk-Íslenzk orðabók 609
Environment 557, 568−577
Epic and romance: essays on mediaeval literature 695
Epidemiology (see Diseases)
Epidemiology of mental disorders in Iceland 417
Equal Rights Commission 389
Ericke, K. A. 550
Erlendsdóttir, Guðrún 389
Erlingsson, Þorsteinn 270
Erró: an Icelandic artist 886
Eruption of Hekla, 1947-1948 187
Eruption on Heimaey 191
Eruptions of Hekla in historical times: a tephrochronological study 187
Escritt, E. A. 203, 210, 214
'Esja' steamship 118
Eskimo 315
Espólín, Jón 324
Ethics and morals in Icelandic saga literature 725
Etymology 604
European Coal and Steel
 Community 551
European Economic Community 475, 485, 551
European Free Trade Association 552
European integration 471
Evans, I. O. 854, 871
Evans-Pritchard, E. E. 721
Everyday life in the Viking age 286

Exchange of notes between the Government of the United Kingdom of Great Britain and Northern Ireland and the Government of the Republic of Iceland concerning fishing in the Icelandic fisheries zone, Oslo, 1 June 1976 490
Exchange rates 437, 506, 917
Expeditions
  Cambridge 205—206, 209, 238
  Danish-Icelandic 177
  Polish 208
  Swedish-Icelandic 207
Experimental farms 516
Explorations in social inequality stratification dynamics in social and individual development in Iceland 404
Explorers 55—57, 61, 172
Exports 527, 553
  (see also Trade, overseas)
Eyjafjallasveit 517
Eyjafjörður 165, 169, 515
Eylands, Árni G. 512
Eyrarbakki 453
Eyrbyggja saga 665
Eyrbyggja saga 658
Eysteinn the monk (see Ásgrímsson, Eysteinn)
Eysteinsson, Sölvi 42
Eyþórsson, Jón 204, 215, 217
Eyvindur of the mountains: a play in four acts 801

F

Faber book of northern legends 641
Fabian Society 480
Faces reflected in a drop 839
Facts about Iceland 32
Faeroe (see Faroe)
Fairy-tales 688—690, 756
Falcon (see Gyr falcon)
Falcon, Order of (see Order of the Icelandic Falcon)
Falkirk, Richard 860
Family organisation 380—387, 390—391, 405—406, 500
Family organisation in rural Iceland 405
Family sagas (see Sagas of Icelanders)
Famine 323, 332, 396, 412, 764

Farm abandonment in Eyjafjallasveit, southern Iceland 517
Farm sites 269, 272—275, 517
Farming (see Agriculture)
Farming in Iceland 512
Faroe Islands 46, 68, 74, 79, 98—99, 104, 128, 220, 228, 230, 240, 342, 398, 491, 514, 942, 957
Faroes and Iceland: studies in island life 220
Fascism (see Nazism)
Fashion 925
Fáskrúðsfjörður 196
Fatal fascination: a choice of crime 743
'Father and son' 773
Fauna 86, 231—233, 254
Fawkes, Anthony 652
Feasts (see Festivals)
Federation of Icelandic Co-operative Societies (see Samband Íslenzkra Samvinnufélaga)
Fell, Christine 292, 664
Feminism (see Women's rights)
Fenton, Myfanwy 853
Ferðafélag Íslands 143
Ferðamál á Íslandi 555
Ferðaskrifstofa ríkisins 557
Ferro (see Erró)
Fertility myths 692, 705—706
Festivals 18, 373
Feudalism 302
Field, C. 809
Field key to the flowering plants of Iceland 229
Fieldtrips 91, 135, 165—172, 211, 213—214, 244, 932
Fietz, Helga 36, 255
Films 823—824, 903—904
Finch, R. G. 680
Finding of Wineland the Good: the history of the Icelandic discovery of America 58
Finnbogadóttir, Vigdís 140, 467
Finnbogason, Guðmundur 8
Finsen, Hannes 324
Firchow, Evelyn S. 837, 844
Fire and ice: three Icelandic plays 799
Fire and iron: critical approaches to Njáls saga 745

313

Firms 942—944
First grammatical treatise: the earliest Germanic phonology; an edition, translation and commentary by Einar Haugen 594
Fish
 species 234—235
Fish and ships 480
Fish can sing 823
Fish catch 437, 527—529
Fish processing 527—528, 531—534
Fish stocks
 conservation 527—529, 531, 534
Fisher, C. 448
Fisher, James 221, 249
Fisheries 168, 505, 527—536, 539—540, 917, 928
Fisheries Association (see Fiskifélag Íslands)
Fisheries dispute between the United Kingdom and Iceland, 14th July 1971-19th May 1973 489
Fisheries jurisdiction in Iceland 488
Fishermen 535—536
Fishing (see also Angling)
 salmon 235
 trawlers 123
Fishing agreements
 with Belgium 485
Fishing and the stocks of fish at Iceland 529
Fishing disputes 482
Fishing fleet 527—528, 530, 534, 536
Fishing gear 488
Fishing limits 25, 157, 471, 476, 479—481, 483—491, 534
Fishing limits of Iceland: 200 nautical miles 488
Fishing - safety measures (see Trawlers, Safety)
Fishwick, A. B. 211
Fiske, Willard 578, 937, 966—968
Fiskifélag Íslands 928
Five modern Scandinavian plays 799
Five northern countries pull together 469
Five weeks in Iceland 100
Fjalldal, Magnús 334
Fjölnir 632
Fjord formation 180, 196
Fjórðungsblöðin 146
Flags 281
Flatatunga 272
Flateyri 168
Fleuron, Svend 856

Fljótsdalur 811
Fljótshlíð 168
Flora 34, 86, 108, 115, 169, 219, 222, 225—230, 934
Flora of Iceland and the Faroes 228
Flosaskarð 213
Flugfélag Íslands (see Icelandair)
Flugleiðir 560
Fluoridation 545
Fogs 90
Folk arts 876—877, 883
Folk-dance 19
 horse-dance 370
Folk medicine 371
Folk museums 950
Folk music 896—897
Folk-tales 104, 688—690, 755, 757, 771, 864
Folklore 220, 370—374, 377, 756, 758—760, 881, 890, 962
 magicians 689, 757
 spells 761
Fonblanque, C. A. de 100
Food (see Recipes, Diet)
Football 50, 583
Foote, Peter G. 288, 359, 442, 654, 661, 666—668, 671, 693, 724
Forbes, Charles S. 80
Foreign exchange rate (see Exchange rates)
Foreign language teaching 427
Foreign policies of northern Europe 470
Foreign policy 458, 470—472, 474—477, 481—483, 487
Foreign relations 23, 445, 468, 948
 with Great Britain 325—326, 336—338, 340—341, 479—480, 484—490
 with the United States 20, 339—340, 343, 472—473, 478
 with the USSR 473
Foreign trade (see Trade, overseas)
Forestry 521—522
Forman, Werner 290
Fornaldarsögur (see Sagas of ancient times)
Fossil resources 544
Fóstbræðra saga 660, 729, 822
Foster, C. Le N. 96
Foster, Paul 851
Fósturskóli 428
Fouqué, F. de la Motte 846
Four Icelandic sagas 659
Four plays 850

Fox, Denton 667, 746
Foxes 256
Framkvæmdastofnun Ríkisins 507
Framsóknarbladid 913
Framsóknarflokkurinn (see Progressive Party)
Frazer, James George 357
Frederick, Prince of Denmark 72
Free man 858
Free movement of workers 469
Freedom and welfare: social patterns in the northern countries of Europe 399
Freemasonry 376
Freezing plants 532
French, A. 667
Freudenberg, K. 76
Frey and Freyja 300, 352, 670, 706
Freyr 929
Fridjófs saga 658
Fridjónsdóttir, Katrín 29
Fridjónsson, Gudmundur 835, 840
Fridjónsson, Jón 621
Fridriksson, Gudjón 467
Fridriksson, Kristján 878
Fridriksson, Sturla 223, 523
Friedman, D. 444
Friends in conflict: the Anglo-Icelandic cod wars and the law of the sea 487
Friese, W. 828
Friis, E. J. 691
Frímerkjasalan 565
Frjálsverzlun 931
From England to Iceland: a summer trip to the Arctic Circle 102
From Viking ship to super-jet 560
Fry, Donald K. 964
Funeral customs 368
Furniture design 895
Fylgja 377

G

Gaelic language 593
Gage, G. G. 961
Gaimard, Paul 62, 64, 86
Galdra-Loftur 799
Galon, Rajmund 208
Gannets 238, 251
Gardarsson, Arnþór 251−252
Gardens 230
Garefowl (see Great auk)
Garmes, Sarah 623

Garmonsway, G. N. 597
Garrison in Iceland 342
Gathorne-Hardy, G. M. 58, 799
Gathorne-Hardy, Robert 115
Gautreks saga, and other medieval tales 683
Gayet-Tancrède, Paul (see Samivel)
Gazetteers 153
Geese 239
  pink-footed goose 249
Geipel, John 593
Gelsinger, Bruce E. 313
Genealogy 278−280, 300, 304, 721−722
Genetics 260−261
Geodynamics of Iceland and the north Atlantic area: proceedings of the NATO Advanced Study Institute Symposium held in Reykjavík, Iceland, 1-7 July 1974 175
Geodynamics Project 176
Geographical Field Group 168
Geography 157−158, 160−162, 164−172
Geography, Economic 159, 162, 471, 495
Geography, Historical 162−163
Geography of Norden 158
Geography, Political 162
Geology 5, 23, 38, 107, 179−192, 195, 197−214, 218−219, 932−933, 935
  fjords 196
  lava tunnels 194
  maps 144, 178
  pillow lava 193
  Reykjavík 148
Geomorphology 173, 176−177, 179, 231
  ocean ridge-rift system 174−175, 202
Geoscience Society of Iceland 174
Geothermal brine 548−549
Geothermal energy 5, 47, 175, 179, 183, 202−203, 547−550, 568
Germany 335, 337
Gerpla 822
Gesta Danorum. The first nine books of the Danish history of Saxo Grammaticus 282
Gestsson, Gísli 274
Geysers 80, 89, 91, 97−98, 182, 184
  (see also under specific names e.g. Geysir)

315

Geysir 72, 77, 89, 91, 97−99, 105, 182−184
Geysir Committee 184
Ghost stories 688, 690
Gibbons, Stanley 566
Gibson, I. L. 196
Gibson, O. D. R. (see MacRae-Gibson)
Gilberg, T. 461
Gilbert, R. 172
Gilchrist, Andrew 486
Gill, Ann Pinson (see Pinson, Ann)
Ginnunga-gap 691
Girl's ride in Iceland 103
Gísla saga 666, 728, 734, 904
Gíslason, Gylfi Þ. 10−11, 38, 456
Gíslason, Jónas 363
Gíslason, Konráð 605
Gizursson, Ísleif (see Ísleif Gizursson)
Gjallandi, Þorgils 778
Gjáskógar 269
Gjerset, Knut 297
Glacial outwash (see Sandar)
Glacier: adventure on Vatnajökull, Europe's largest ice-cap 204
Glacier burst (see Jökulhlaup)
Glaciers 5, 80, 166, 171, 193, 204−210, 214, 519, 590, 869, 935 (see also under specific names e.g. Vatnajökull)
 climatic effect 213, 215
 ice margins 211, 215
Glaciological Society of Iceland 935
Glacken, B. 637
Glámr 667
Glassware 895
 (see Stained glass)
Glaucoma 420
Glavnoe Upravlenie Geodesii i Kartografii
 maps 152
Glen, D. 532
Glendening, P. J. T. 617
Gliding 586
Glíma 580−581
Goðar 302, 311, 402
Gods (see Religion, pre-Christian)
Gods and heroes from Viking mythology 351
Gods and myths of northern Europe 352
Gods of the ancient Norsemen 354
Gods of the north 351

Godwin, W. H. 561
Godwinson, Harold (see Harold Godwinson)
Golden bough 357
Golden future 833
Golden gate 799
Golden, Grace B. 877
Golden Iceland 37
Goldsmiths 895
Golf 584
Gollancz, Israel 687
 Memorial lectures 733
Göngu-Hrolfs saga: a study in Old Norse philology 684
Göngu-Hrolfs saga: a Viking romance 684
Good shepherd 813
Goodell, Jane 117
Gook, Arthur C. 786
Gordon, E. V. 599, 682, 737
Gordon, Seton 240
Gosse, G. 271
Götumál
 modern Icelandic 628
Gould, Alan 863
Gould, Ruth R. (see Richter-Gould)
Gould, S. B. (see Baring-Gould)
Government coalitions in western democracies 458
Graded readings and exercises in Old Icelandic 601
Grænlendinga saga 58, 663
Grágás 268, 369, 442
Graham-Cambell, James 291
Grammar
 modern Icelandic 603, 614−615, 617, 619−621
 Old Icelandic 594, 596−601
Grammar of the Icelandic or Old Norse tongue 596
Grant, K. 122
Graphic art 887, 920
Grassland 513, 523
Gravels 520
Graves 269−270
Gray, E. F. 58
Gray, Thomas 762
Great auk 245−246
Great auk, or gare-fowl: its history, archaeology and remains 246
Great Britain
 Board of Trade 494, 537
 foreign relations 325−326, 336, 479−480, 484−487, 489−490

316

occupation 337—338, 340—341, 344—345, 347, 492
trade 554
Great Geysir and the hot-spring area of Haukadalur, Iceland 184
Great Skua (see Skua)
Great weaver of Kashmir 820
Green, Roger L. 865
Green, W. C. 638, 664
Greenhouse cultivation 514
Greenland 56—58, 74, 125, 127, 160, 315, 542, 847
Greenlandic poetry 775
Greenpeace 541
Gregersen, Aage 446
Grettir's saga 667
Grettis saga 667, 692, 728, 735
Gribbin, J. 173
Grieve, Symington 246
Griffiths, J. C. 25
Grimm brothers 688
Grimsby 539
Grímsey 50—51, 578
 birdlife 238
Grímsson, Magnús 688
Grímsson, Ólafur Ragnar 432, 457—458, 463
Grímsson, Stefán Hörður 784, 798
Grímsson, Þorkell 949
Grímsvötn 209
Grindavík 548
Grjótaþorp 574
Gróðurkort 146
Groemping, Franz A. 455
Groennings, Sven 958
Gröf 269
Gröndal, Benedikt 474
Gröndal, Benedikt, poet 766, 777
Gröndal, Benedikt, politician 465
Grönke, Ulrich 625, 628
Gröntved, Johannes 225, 228
Groot, D. G. 210
Groote, Eugène de 62
Grossman, K. 178
Grove, N. 192
Grove's dictionary of music and musicians 896
Growth of vocabulary in modern Icelandic 626
Gruisen, N. L. van 100
Guðfinnsson, Pétur 908
Guðjohnsen Einar 138
Guðjónsdóttir, Sigrún 892
Guðjónsson, Elsa E. 374, 894
Guðjónsson, Jens 895

Guðjónsson, Pétur 385
Guðjónsson, Þór 235
Guðlaugsson, Jónas 769
Guðmundar saga Arasonar 679
Guðmundsson, Ágúst 903—904
Guðmundsson, Albert 583
Guðmundsson, Ásgeir 334
Guðmundsson, Barði 300
Guðmundsson, Bjarni 14
Guðmundsson, Finnur 243
Guðmundsson, Guðmundur (see Erró)
Guðmundsson, Gunnar 411
Guðmundsson, Ívar 550
Guðmundsson, Kjartan R. 411
Guðmundsson, Kristmann 816
Guðmundsson, Sigurður 878
Guðmundsson, Tómas 791, 881
Guðnadóttir, Margrét 388
Guðnason, Jón 946
Guðnason, Stefán 408
Guðrún Ósvífsdóttir 671, 850
Guðrúnarhvöt 644
Guest the one-eyed 808
Guide to birdwatching in Europe 240
Guide to Iceland: a useful handbook for travellers and sportsmen 130
Guidebooks 128, 130—138, 140—141
Gulland, J. A. 529
Gunnars hólm 105
Gunnars, Kristjána 796
Gunnars saga Þiðrandabana 674
Gunnarsdóttir, Kristjana 317
Gunnarsholt 516
Gunnarsson, Árni 191
Gunnarsson, Franzisca 895
Gunnarsson, Gísli 462
Gunnarsson, Gunnar 691, 769, 773, 808—814, 835
Gunnarsson, Gunnar Örn 887
Gunnarsson, Gunnar, painter 878
Gunnarsson, Gunnar, security commissioner 477
Gunnarsson, Ólafur 18
Gunnlaugs saga Ormstungu 668
Gunnlaugs saga Ormstungu 658, 660, 662, 736
Gunnlaugur Blöndal 882
Gustur 921
Gylfaginning 652
Gyr falcon 247, 314
Gyr falcon adventure 247

317

H

Hachisuka, Masa U. 237
Hadda Padda 802
Hænsna Þóris saga 658, 661−662
Hafliðason, Einar 679
Hafnafjörður
 town plans 149
Hafstein, Hannes 774, 777
Hagalín, Guðmundur G. 835, 842
Hagfræðideild Reykjavíkurborgar 440
Hagstofa Íslands (see Statistical Bureau of Iceland)
Hagtíðindi 437
Hakluyt, Richard 316
Hakluyt Society 61
Hákonarson, Einar 783, 793, 887
Hákonarson, Hákon 943
Hale, C. S. 634
Hálfdánarson, Örlygur 138
Hall, Gunnar 970
Hall, Wendy 159
Hallberg, Peter 704, 716, 739, 827−828, 830
Halldór Hermannsson 967
Halldór Kiljan Laxness 826
Halldór Laxness 827
Halldórs þáttr 670
Halldórsson, Erlingur E. 805
Halldórsson, Halldór 616, 632
Halldórsson, Hreinn 582
Halldórsson, Óskar 674
Halleux, P. 631, 739
Hallfreðar saga 359
Hallfreðar saga vandræða 669
Hallgerðr
 Njála 727
Hallgrimsen, Indriði 952
Hallgrímsson, Geir 476
Hallgrímsson, Hallgrímur 425
Hallgrímsson, Jónas 105, 773−774, 777
Hallgrímur Pétursson (see Pétursson, Hallgrímur)
Hallmundsson, Hallberg 191, 204, 373, 773, 792, 843−845, 880, 900
Hallmundsson, May 191, 204, 373
Hallormsstaðir 521
Hamar, Haraldur J. 40, 201, 373, 378, 390, 526, 538, 909−910, 918
Hamarinn 170
Hamðismál 644
Hamlet 282
Hamlet in Iceland 687

Hammer of the north: myths and heroes of the Viking age 290
Hamri, Þorsteinn frá (see Þorsteinn frá Hamri)
Handball 583
Handbók Útanríkisráðuneytisins 948
Handbook of the birds of Iceland 237
Handicapped 408, 953
Handy facts on Iceland 33
Hannell, F. G. 213
Hannesson, Guðmundur 262, 420, 570
Hannesson, Gunnar 11, 44, 204
Hannesson, Hjalmar W. 484
Hannesson, Jóhann 188
Hannesson, Jóhann S. 310
Hannesson, Pálmi 35
Hannibalsson, J. B. 502
Hanseatic League 314, 318
Hansen, Anders 910
Hansen, H. M. 225
Hanson, George 424
Hansson, Ólafur 32
Happy warriors 822
Haralds saga harðráða 655, 751
Haraldsdóttir, Elísabet 895
Haraldsson, Einar Karl 914
Haraldsson, Erlendur 378−379
Haraldsson, Pétur 946
Haraldsson, Sverrir 885
Haralz, Jónas H. 499
Harbours 128−129
Harðar saga 728
Harðarson, Sólrún B. Jensdóttir 340, 425
Hardy, G. M. G. (see Gathorne-Hardy, G. M)
Hardy, R. G. (see Gathorne-Hardy, R)
Harley, Ethel B. 103
Harold Godwinsson 655
Harp of the north: poems 789
Harris, R. L. 332, 764
Harshberger, J. W. 230
Hartmann, Jakob W. 684
Háskóli Íslands 429, 432, 954
Hastrup, K. 312
Háttatal 652
Haugen, Einar 354, 591, 594, 625, 633, 663, 692, 799, 802
Hauk Valdísarson 674
Haukadalur 184
Hávamál 645−646
Hávamál, with selections from other poems of the Edda, illustrating the wisdom of the north in heathen times 646

318

Hávarðar saga 658
Hayes, Joseph 862
Head, Edmund 673
Headley, Phineas C. 294
Health 407−422, 936
Health in Iceland 407
Heating systems 547−548
Heðins saga ok Högna 658
Heiðarvíga saga 729
Heiðreks saga (see Hervarar saga)
Heima er bezt 924
Heimaey (see Vestmannaeyjar)
Heimdall 352
Heimskringla 654
Heimskringla 655, 658, 701−702, 749
Heimskringla, or, The stoned angels 851
Heineman, F. J. 739
Hekla 69, 76−77, 89, 97, 104, 107, 116, 187−188, 273, 590
Hekla eruption of 1970 188
Hekla: a notorious volcano 188
Hekla on fire 188
Helgadóttir, Gerða 889
Helgadóttir, Guðrún P. 693
Helgafell 923
Helgarpósturinn 911
Helgason, Jón 595, 783
Helgason, Lárus 417
Helgason, Þórir 415
Helgason, Tómas 417
Helgi, Jóhannes 834, 836
Hen Thorir (see Haensna Þoris saga)
Henderson, Ebenezer 64, 71
Henderson, Kenneth A. 590
Henry VIII 318
Heraldry 281
Herdsmen and hermits: Celtic seafarers in the northern seas 265
Herðubreið 198, 590
Hereward the Wake 728
Herjólfsnes garments 315
Hermannsson, Halldór 154, 218, 306, 325, 624, 663, 677, 768, 937, 966−968
Hermannsson, Nanna 950
Hermannsson, Steingrímur 190
Heroes, hero worship and the heroic in history 763
Heroic age of Scandinavia 284
Heroic ideal
 sagas 726−727
Herring 531, 540
Hersteinsson, Páll 256
Heruli 300

Hervarar saga ok Heiðreks 681
Hesteyri 120, 540
Hewlett, Maurice 666
Higgs, W. J. 169
Hight, George A. 667
Hill, A. W. 108
Hill, D. A. 845
Hinckley, T. C. 331
Hints to exporters: Iceland 554
Historical and descriptive account of Iceland, Greenland and the Faroe Islands, with illustrations of their natural history 74
Historical element in the Icelandic family sagas 720
Historical geography 162−163
Historical works of Jón Espólín and his contemporaries: aspects of Icelandic historiography 324
Historiography 324
History 14−15, 23, 28, 30, 37−39, 293−299
 Commonwealth 300−315, 441−442, 444
 Danish rule 316−333, 446
 Denmark 282
 Independence 333−335
 maps 154−155, 178
 Norway 297
 Republic 340, 348
 Reykjavík 44, 72
 Scandinavian 282−292
 Viking 268−269, 283−292, 368, 593
 Vinland map 125, 156
 World War II 336−347
History of education in Iceland 423
History of Iceland 297
History of Icelandic literature 770
History of Icelandic poets, 1800-1940 772
History of Icelandic prose writers, 1800-1940 771
History of the Norwegian people 297
History of the Old Icelandic Commonwealth; Íslendinga saga 304
History of the Vikings
 Jones 287
 Kendrick 285
Hitzler, Egon 524
Hjálmar's death song 648, 681
Hjaltalín, Jón Andrésson 102, 301, 386, 606
Hjartason, Snorri 794, 798

Hjul, P. 531
Hliðarendi 787
Hlíðdal, Guðmundur 563
Hnefatafl 578
Hoare, Dorothy M. 762
Höfðingar 311
Hofsjökull 249
Hogan, James F. 327
Hogg, John 293
Hólar 316−317, 362−363, 365, 679
Hólarhreppur 406
Holdgate, M. W. 522
Holiday in Iceland 100
Holidays 373
Holland, Cecilia 849
Holland, E. T. 82
Holland, Henry 70
Holland, K. C. (see Crossley-Holland, K)
Holland-Martin, Derek 537
Hollander, Lee M. 300, 643, 648−649, 654, 657, 660, 665, 672−673, 692, 800, 803, 963
Holmes, P. F. 238
Home is a tent 120
Home of the Eddas 96
Home ownership 500, 572−573
Honour of the house 838
Hood, John C. F. 365
Hooker, William Jackson 64, 69
Horn 129
Horncarving 876
Hornstranders 873
Hornstrandir 120, 577, 873
Horrebow, Niels 219
Horse-dance 370
Horses 34, 220, 255, 856
Horsford, Cornelia 270
Höskuldsson, Svein Skorri 798
Hospital libraries 953
Hospitals 407, 417, 419, 421
Hot springs 182, 184, 232−233
 radioactivity 183
Hot springs of Iceland 183
Hot springs of Iceland: their animal communities and their zoogeographical significance 232
Hough, Frank O. 343
Housing 500, 570, 572−574
 heating systems 547−548
 statistics 436, 439
Hovgaard, William 59
How the 'Mastiffs' went to Iceland 98
How to say it in Icelandic 613
Howard the Halt (see Hávarðar saga)

Howe, Gertrude 872
Howell, Frederick W. W. 104
Howes, Helen C. 548
Hrafnkel's saga, and other stories 670
Hrafnkels saga Freysgoða 101, 659, 662, 732, 737−740
Hrafnkels saga Freysgoða: a study by Sigurður Nordal 737
Hrappsey 317, 969
Hraun farm 801
Hreiðar the fool 670
Hreppar 320
Hróa þáttr heimska 658
Hrolf Gautreksson: a Viking romance 683
Hrolf the Tramper 684
Hrólfs saga kraka 662, 682, 752
Hrútafjörður 106, 248
Hughes, S. F. D. 710
Hulda (see Benediktsdóttir, Unnar)
Humbolt, W. 262
Hume, C. 876
Hume, Kathryn 722, 735, 759
Humour
 sagas 716, 731
Hungarian uprising 472
Húngrvaka 678
Hunt, John J. 339
Hunter, Leslie S. 364
Huntington, Ellsworth 258
Húsavík 547, 570
Huseby, Gunnar 582
Húsnæðisskýrslur 439
Hutchinson, Isobel W. 111
Huxley, Julian 221
Hvalfjörður 541
Hvammsfjörður 106, 671
Hvannadalshnúkur 185
Hveberg, Harald 865
Hveravellir 167, 183
Hydroelectric power 546
Hydrography 231
Hymns of the Passion: meditations on the Passion of Christ 786

I

I see a wondrous land 815
Ice age
 fauna 232
 flora 226
Ice and fire: contrasts of Icelandic nature 42
Ice-caps (see Glaciers)

320

Ice with everything 127
Icecan cable 909
Iceland.. 34, 36, 38, 41, 152, 161
Iceland
 Drost 36
 Leith 105
 Linden 38
 Roberts 161
Iceland 1918-1968 10
Iceland 1946 31
Iceland 1966 31
Iceland 874-1974 31
Iceland: a nation of ancient culture, a country of contrasts 14
Iceland: a traveller's guide 134
Iceland adventure: the double traverse of the Vatnajökull by the Cambridge expedition 206
Iceland and Greenland
 Boland 160
 Clark 160
 Peck 160
Iceland and the Icelanders 16
Iceland and the mediaeval world: studies in honour of Ian Maxwell 693
Iceland and mid-ocean ridges: report of a symposium 174
Iceland and the war 493
Iceland and the war 336
Iceland as we know it 3
Iceland: bastion of the north 21
Iceland: the Co-operative island 509
Iceland: country and people 33
Iceland: daughter of fire 27
Iceland dog 220, 257
Iceland: economic report 553
Iceland: evolution, active tectonics, and structure 176
Iceland extends its fisheries limits: a political analysis 479
Iceland: the first American republic 20
Iceland: the first new society 29
Iceland first seen 1
Iceland fisheries yearbook 527
Iceland fisherman 855
Iceland from neutrality to NATO membership 474
Iceland: a handbook 132
Iceland: horseback tours in saga land 109
Iceland: impressions of a heroic landscape 38
Iceland in a nutshell 134

Iceland in pictures 39
Iceland in the Second World War, 1939-1946 337
Iceland: the island in the limelight 17
Iceland: its scenes and sagas 83
Iceland: its volcanoes, geysers and glaciers 80
Iceland: land in creation 36
Iceland: land of challenge 135
Iceland: a land of contrasts 19
Iceland: a multi-level coalition system 458
Iceland: nature and nation in photographs 35
Iceland: new world outpost 21
Iceland: official standard names approved by the United States Board on Geographic Names 153
Iceland, old-new republic: a study of its history, life and physical aspects 23
Iceland: or, the journal of a residence in that island during the years 1814 and 1815 71
Iceland papers. Volume 1, Scientific results of Cambridge expeditions to Iceland, 1932-1938 238
Iceland past and present 15
Iceland presents 344
Iceland: reluctant ally 472
Iceland Review 918
Iceland road guide 138
Iceland roundabout 21
Iceland: routes over the highlands.. 131
Iceland: some impressions 3
Iceland summer: adventures of a bird painter 241
Iceland: the surprising island of the Atlantic 40
Iceland today: the land the nation, the economy and culture 944
Iceland Tourist Bureau (see Ferðaskrifstofa ríkisins)
Iceland: the unspoiled land 40
Iceland yesterday and today 22
Icelandair 34, 560
Icelanders 8
Icelanders
 Arnason 54
 Finnbogason 8
Icelanders and their island 26
Icelanders in Canada 53
Icelanders in Canada 53, 921
Icelanders in United States 52, 921

321

Icelandic art 875
Icelandic authors of today 768
Icelandic Bible Society 767
Icelandic birds 239
Icelandic Canadian 921
Icelandic Christian classics 650
Icelandic church saga 365
Icelandic coins 1836, 1922-1963 567
Icelandic conversations 619
Icelandic economy: developments, 1980-1981 508
Icelandic economy: riches under risk 508
Icelandic embroidery 894
Icelandic-English dictionary 605, 607
Icelandic-English dictionary
  Cleasby 605
  Sigurðsson 610
  Zoëga 607
Icelandic enterprise: commerce and economy in the Middle Ages 313
Icelandic expedition 1965: report 165
Icelandic family saga: an analytic reading 717
Icelandic feasts and holidays: celebrations past and present 373
Icelandic firms 943
Icelandic fishery limits 488
Icelandic folktales 690
Icelandic folktales and legends 689
Icelandic grammar, texts, glossary 615
Icelandic in easy stages 620
Icelandic jaunt: a study of the expeditions made by Morris to Iceland in 1871 and 1873 87
Icelandic journals 87
Icelandic legends 688
Icelandic Literary Society 767, 941, 946
Icelandic lyrics: originals and translations 777
Icelandic medical journal 936
Icelandic meditations on the pattern 786
Icelandic-Norwegian linguistic relationships 592
Icelandic people in Manitoba: a Manitoba saga 54
Icelandic phonetics and pronunciation 618
Icelandic phrasebook 612
Icelandic pictures drawn with pen and pencil 104

Icelandic poems and stories; translations from modern Icelandic literature 778
Icelandic posts 1776-1919 under Danish administration 562
Icelandic primer 598
Icelandic prose reader 597
Icelandic saga 716
Icelandic sagas 711
Icelandic sagas and manuscripts 703
Icelandic short stories 837
Icelandic Society for the Learned Arts 632
Icelandic solitaries 863
Icelandic spring 118
Icelandic stories, as told on Jackanory by Magnús Magnússon 866
Icelandic studies
  teaching 603, 961
Icelandic Survey (see Landmaelingar Íslands)
Icelandic wrestling 580
Icelandic writing today 920
Icelandic yearbook 132, 944
Iceland's bell 820
Iceland's great inheritance 298
'Iceland's thousand years' (see Millennial hymn)
Iceland's thousand years: a series of popular lectures on the history and literature of Iceland 299
Iceland's unique history and culture 14
Iðnaðarblaðið 930
Iðnaðarskýrslur 439
Ikin, E. W. 261
Illegitimacy 382−385
Imports 553
  (see also Trade, overseas)
In the morning of time: the story of the Norse god Balder 357
In northern mists: Arctic exploration in early times 56
In search of the gyr falcon 247
In search of my beloved 831
In search of northern birds 240
Income tax 498
Incomes (see Wages)
Independence of Iceland: a parallel for Ireland 333
Independence Party 459, 464, 912
Independent people 818
Index Nordicus: a cumulative index to English language periodicals in Scandinavian studies 960

Indriðason, Ottar 577
Industrial archaeology 276—277
Industrialisation 400
Industry 31, 158, 552, 930
  directories 942
  production 506
  statistics 439
Inflation 496, 499—503
Influence of Old Norse literature on English literature 762
Ingólfr Árnason 305, 809
Ingólfshöfði 129, 212
Ingólfson, Guðmundur 255
Ingólfsson, Aðalsteinn 879—880, 887, 889, 892
Ingólfsson, Ásgeir 588
Ingstad, Helge 57
Innansveitarkronika 828
Insects 220
Insurance 454—455, 498
INTELSAT 909
Interest groups (see Pressure groups)
Internal migration 164
International compilation of sports historical documents 580
International Conference on the Environmental Future 568
International Court of Justice 481—482
International film guide: Iceland 903
International Geographical Congress, 19th 179
International relations (see Foreign relations)
International saga conference 939
International Whaling Commission 541
Interpreters 554
Introduction to Old Norse 599
Investment 504, 506
Invisible Society 767
Ireland 333
Irish literature 761
Ísafjörður 82, 168
  birdlife 247
  newspapers 911
  planning 570
  vegetation 226
Ísaksson, Andrí 427
Ísfilm 904
Ísland 143
Ísland 42
Ísland: bulletin of the Iceland unit 932
Ísland: landlagskort 151

Island of fire: or, a thousand years of the old Northmen's home, 874-1874 294
Island on fire 862
Islande: son statut à travers les âges 446
Islandica 967
Islandica: an annual relating to Iceland and the Fiske Icelandic Collection 937
Islandica: books on Iceland 956
Isländisches etymologisches Wörterbuch 604
Islands 180
  (see also Individual names e.g. Grímsey)
Íslandsklukkan 820
Ísleif Gizursson 361, 678
Íslendinga saga 304, 309
Íslendingabók 306
Íslendingabók 58, 675
Íslendingadrápa 674
Íslensk bókaskrá 955
Íslensk fyrirtæki 943
Íslensk bókatíðindi 955
Íslenzk-ensk orðabók 610
Íslenzk fornrit 732
Íslenzk frímerki 1980 565
Íslenzk myndlist: 20 listmálarar 878
Íslenzk orðabók handa skólum í almenningi; ritstjóri 608
Íslenzk rit 955
Íslenzka bókmenntafélag (see Icelandic Literary Society)
Íslenzkar æviskrár 946
Íslenzkar þjóðsögur og Æfintyri 688
Íslenzkir samtíðarmenn 946
Íslenzkur aðall 831
Íþróttablaðið 926
Ívars þáttr 670
Ives, J. D. 518

J

Jack, Robert 50
Jackson, E. L. 396
Jackson, Muriel 804
Jackson, Thorstina (see Walters, Thorstina)
Jacoby, W. 176
Jakobsdóttir, Svava 834, 836, 845
Jakobsson, Asgeir 541
Jakobsson, Guðmundur 944
Jakobsson, Jökull 44, 805, 836

323

Jan Mayen Island 78, 129
Jarðfræðikort 144
Jarðfræðikort af Reykjavík og nágrenni 148
Jenkins, H. D. 128
Jensdóttir, Sólrún B. 340, 425
Jensen, Amy E. 23
Jensen, O. K. (see Klindt-Jensen, Ole)
Jessen, Jarno 876
Jewellery 876—877, 895
Jochumsson, Matthías 32, 92, 650, 666, 765, 773, 777, 788
Jóhannes úr Kotlum 783
Jóhannesson, Alexander 429, 604
Jóhannesson, Björn 520
Jóhannesson, Broddi 242, 255
Jóhannesson, Jóhannes 893
Jóhannesson, Jón 304, 308
Jóhannesson, Matthías 784, 795, 880, 886, 890, 898, 912
Jóhannesson, Ólafur 464
Jóhannsson, Ingi V. 500
Jóhannsson, Freysteinn 579
John, B. 540
John, B. S. 166
John, Katherine 822
Johns Mannville Corporation 544
Johnsen, Árni 251
Johnson, Brian 480
Johnson, Jakobina 780
Johnson, Skúli 299
Johnson, Sveinbjörn 303
Johnston, George 666, 961
Johnston-Lavis, H. J. 107
Jöklarannsóknafélag Íslands (see Glaciological Society of Iceland)
Jökulhlaup 185, 209—210, 518
Jökull 935
Jökulsá canyon 179
Jómsvíkinga saga 657, 751
Jón Jónsson of Vogar: his life, 1829-1866 330
Jón úr Vör 784, 798
Jonason, J. C. 423
Jónasson, Magnús R. 415
Jónasson, Pétur M. 224
Jones, Gwyn 58, 287, 659, 662, 664, 691, 733, 742, 750, 752, 864
Jones, J. G. 193
Jones, O. F. 628, 633, 635
Jónsdóttir, Hólmfríður 375
Jónsdóttir, Kristin 878
Jónsdóttir, Kristín E. 388
Jónsdóttir, Sunnefa 861
Jónsson, Agust 587

Jónsson, Arnar 904
Jónsson, Arngrímur 316, 632
Jónsson, Ásgrímur 878, 881
Jónsson, Björn 335
Jónsson, Einar 890
Jónsson, Einar P. 779
Jónsson, Eyvindur 801
Jónsson, Finnur, painter 878
Jónsson, Finnur, scholar 718
Jónsson, Hannes 14, 487
Jónsson, Hjálmar 777
Jónsson, Ingimar 580
Jónsson, J. H. 631
Jónsson, Jakob 391
Jónsson, Jón Aðalsteinn 564
Jónsson, Jón, of Hlíðarendakot 764
Jónsson, Jón, of Vogar 330
Jónsson, Karl Ó. 547
Jónsson, Ólaf 61
Jónsson, Sigfús 534
Jónsson, Snæbjörn 132, 335—336, 614
Jónsson, Snæbjörn, bookshop 956
Jónsson, Þórhallur 545
Jónsson, Vilmundur 407
Jónsvatn 167
Jörgensen, Jörgen 69—70, 326—327
Jósefsdóttir, Hulda 895
Jósefsson, Jóhannes 580
Jósepsson, Bragi S. 424, 906
Jósepsson, Þorsteinn 14, 43
Journal of a tour in Iceland in the summer of 1809 69
Journalists 389
Journals of the Stanley expedition to the Faroe Islands and Iceland in 1789. Volume 1: Introduction and diary of James Wright 68
Journals of travels in Iceland 87
Journey into winter: a play 804
Journey to the centre of the earth 854
Journey to Iceland and travels in Sweden and Norway 75
Judiciary 447, 451
Júlíusson, Steinar 582

K

Kaldal, Ísleifur 893
Kalfafellsdalur, south-east Iceland: a study of landform and depositional assemblages associated with the wastage of a valley glacier 211

Kamban, Guðmundur 2, 769, 802, 815
Kamenskii, M. I. S. (see
 Steblin-Kamensky)
Kampp, Aa. H. 398
Karlsson, Gunnar 311, 328
Karlsson, Kristján 791, 826
Karlsson, Pétur (see Kidson, Peter)
Kastner, P. W. (see Wilson-Kastner)
Katz, S. R. 482
Kaufman, K. C. 813
Kay, Ernest 947
Keflavík military base 475, 478
Keith, D. B. 238
Keith, W. A. 36
Kelchner, Georgia D. 758
Kelly, Joseph 618
Kelpies 372
Kendrick, T. D. 285
Kennedy, John F. 795
Kennings 707—708
Kennsluskrá 430
Ker, William Paton 309, 695—696
 Memorial Lectures 709, 720, 750
Kerlingarfjöll 183, 590
Kew Gardens
 lava blocks 66
Keyser, Rudolph 368
Kiddell-Monroe, Joan 864
Kidson, Peter 11, 36, 134, 138—139,
 188, 242, 564, 576, 843, 845
Kindred and clan 700
King, Cuchlaine A. M. 212
King, Cynthia 357
*King Harald's saga, from Snorri
 Sturluson's Heimskringla* 655
Kingdom of Vatnajökull 9
Kings and Vikings A.D. 700-1000 289
Kings, beasts and heroes 752
King's College, London 165
Kings' sagas 654—657, 749—751
Kingsley, Charles 762
Kinship 278, 380—381, 403, 457, 721
 (see also Genealogy)
Kinsman, D. J. J. 196
Kirkconnell, Watson 776
Kirken paa bjerget 811
Kistufell 97
Kjalnesinga saga 659
Kjaran, Birgir 254, 576
Kjartansson, Guðmundur 144, 179,
 187
Kjartansson, Helgi Skúli 397
Kjarval, Jóhannes S. 878, 880
Kjarval: a painter of Iceland 880
Kjarval, Tove 892

Kjölur 108, 131
Kleppur hospital 419
Klindt-Jensen, Ole 288
Kneeland, Samuel 64, 93
Knirk, James E. 749
Knowles, Elizabeth 605
Koht, H. 712
Kolderup-Rosenvinge, J. L. A. 225
König, Fritz H. 731
Konráðsson, Ísleifur 883
Kópavogur
 town plans 149
Korean war 472
Kormáks saga 660
*Körpermasse und Körperproportionen
 der Isländer: ein Beitrag zur
 Anthropologie Islands* 262
Korpulfsstaðir 887
Kortasaga Íslands 155
Krafla 109, 202—203
Krappner, K. 404
Kratz, L. A. 258
Kress, Helga 618
Kristinsson, Gunnar H. 547
Kristinsson, Hörður 230
Kristinsson, Valdimar 31, 394
Kristján frá Djúpalæk 49
Kristjánsdóttir, Elín 375
Kristjánsdóttir, Þuríður J. 428
Kristjanson, W. 54
Kristjánsson, Geir 836
Kristjánsson, Jónas 703, 915
Kristjánsson, L. 175
Kristjánsson, Svanur 459
Kristmundsson, Aðalsteinn (see
 Steinarr, Steinn)
Krísuvík 77, 109, 543
Krog, Ole V. 893
Króna 496, 501
Kuhn, H. 644
Kvamme, Janet 960
Kvaran, Ævar 379
Kvaran, Einar H. 777, 835
Kydd, Dafydd 291

L

Labor law and practice in Iceland 455
Labour 469
Labour force 507
Labour law 455
Labour movement 460
Lack, D. 238

325

Lad and lass: a story of life in Iceland 806
Læknablaðið: the Icelandic Medical Journal 936
Laing, Samuel 654
Lakes 224, 589
  (see also Individual names e.g. Mývatn)
Laki 69, 107, 186, 323, 396, 412
Land and people of Iceland 870
Land of ice and fire 207
Land of the loon 248
Land of Thor 85
'Land og synir' 903
Land the ravens found 849
Land reclamation 514, 516, 522—523
Land registers 320
Land under the pole star: a voyage to the Norse settlements of Greenland, and the saga of the people that vanished 57
Landmælingar Íslands 138, 143—147, 149—151
Landmannalaugar 577
Landnámabók 307
Landnámabók 58, 308
Landnámabók: some remarks upon its value as a historical source 308
Lands of fire and ice: how Christianity came to Hawaii and Iceland 868
Landsbanki Íslands 506
Landsbókasafn (see National Library of Iceland)
Landscape 1, 5, 9, 28, 35—42
  painting 122, 879—881, 885
Landscapes of Iceland: types and regions 180
Landspítalinn 421
Landsvirkjun 546
Langanes 124
Lange, Joost de 728
Langjökull 171, 213
Language
  Danish 632
  purity 13, 592, 625, 628, 630—632
Language, English 593
Language, Gaelic 593
Language, modern Icelandic 19, 29, 592, 616, 624—625, 637
  abbreviations 636
  dialects 627
  dictionaries 603, 605—613
  götumál 628
  grammar 603, 614—615, 617, 619
  language courses 619—621

  linguistic theory 622—623
  loanwords 626, 628—632
  names 634
  neologisms 631
  orthography 632
  phonetics 618
  phonology 623
  phrasebooks 612—613
  placenames 635
  pronouns 633
  pronunciation 615, 617—618
  proverbs 617
  slang 628
  sletta 628
Language, Norwegian 592
Language, Old Icelandic 591—592
  dictionaries 602, 604—605, 607
  grammar 596—601
  loanwords 593
  palaeography 595
  phonology 623
  vowels 594
Language teaching 427
Lapland 73, 876
Larsen, Henning 371
Larsen, Stein U. 334
Lárusdóttir, Karolína 690
Lárusson, Björn 320
Lárusson, Magnús Már 364
Lárusson, Ólaf 268
Last of the Vikings 867
Laugarvatn 193
Laurentius saga 679
Lausavísur 961
Lava flow
  heat tapping 548
Lava tunnels 194
Lavis, H. J. J. (see Johnston-Lavis)
Law
  environmental 575
  planning 570
  tourism 557
Law, ancient 268, 302—303, 369, 441—446
Law, the courts and the citizen 451
Law, educational 424
Law, modern 391, 444—447, 449—455
Law of the sea 480
Law of the sea 481—482, 487, 491
Law on the organisation of tourism 557
Laws of early Iceland: Grágás 442
Lawspeakers 304, 360
Lawyers 400

Laxá 224, 589
Laxdæla saga 671
Laxdæla saga 727, 729
Laxdal, Jon 823—824
Laxness, Halldór 38, 41, 714, 773, 805, 817—829, 834—835, 838, 890
Lay of the Sun (see Sólarljóð)
Lays 648
Leach, Henry Goddard 521, 639, 691
Leaf, H. 22
Lebrec, Georges 555
Leeds University (see University of Leeds)
Legal essays: a tribute to Frede Castberg 449
Legendary history of Óláf Tryggvason 750
Legendary sagas (see Sagas of ancient times)
Legends 688—690, 864
(see also Mythology, folk-tales)
Legends of Icelandic magicians 689
Lehmann, W. P. 692
Leiðabók: áætlanir sérleyfisbifreiða 141
Leif Eiríksson 60
Leif Ericksen: discoverer of America A.D. 1003 58
Leif the Lucky, discover of America 870
Leikfélag Reykjavíkur (see Reykjavík Theatre Company)
Leirárgarður 317
Leisure (see Recreation)
Leith, Mary C. J. 105, 678
Leith, Mrs Disney (see Leith, Mary C. J)
Leprosy 322
Lerner, Laurence 858
Lesbók 912
Lethbridge, T. C. 265
Let's visit Iceland 871
Letters from high latitudes... 1856 78
Letters from Iceland 114
Letters on Iceland. 67
Lettres sur l'Islande 62
Lewis, David 124
Lewis, Ernest 247
Lewis, W. V. 212
Lexicography 602—603, 605
Libraries 951—954
Library education 954
Lidderdale, Thomas W. 969
Liestøl, Knut 715

Líf 925
Life and customs 2—4, 6—8, 10, 16—18, 21, 24, 26—28, 45—46
Life of Guðmund the Good, Bishop of Hólar 679
Life of the Icelander Jón Ólafsson, traveller to India 61
Life of Laurence, Bishop of Hólar 679
Lighten our darkness: a short story 840
Lighthouses 942
Lighting design 895
Lilja 650
Lilja: an Icelandic religious poem of the fourteenth century 651
Líndal, Amalia 24, 919
Líndal, Sigurður 456
Lindal, W. J. 53
Linden, Franz-Karl von 38
Lindgrenson, Sonja 704
Lindow, J. 708
Lindroth, Hjalmar 19, 64
Linguaphone Icelandic course 619
Linguistic theory
  modern Icelandic 622—623
Linguistics (see Language)
Linklater, Eric 342
Linton, W. J. 104
Liss, Howard 874
Literacy 425
Literary societies 767
Literature, English
  influence of Norse literature 762—764
  influence on Norse literature 765—766
Literature, modern
  Icelandic 765—818, 820—827, 829—843, 845, 920, 937, 941
  bibliographies 965, 971
Literature, Old Icelandic 638—717, 719—764, 819, 844, 937—939, 941
  bibliographies 961—964, 970—971
Litla Hraun 453
Livestock (see Cattle, Horses, Sheep etc)
Living costs 437
Living standards 394
Lloyds Bank Group 553
Loanwords 593
  modern Icelandic 626, 628—632
Local government taxation 498
Lock, Alfred G. 543
Lock, Charles G. W. 96

Lock, W. G. 130, 199
Lockley, R. M. 46
Loftleiðir 559—560
Loftsson, Einar 376
Loftur 799
Lög um náttúrvernd no. 47/1971 575
Lögberg-Heimskringla 921
Loki 352, 357—358
London School of Economics 165
Longfellow, Henry 762
Lönnroth, Lars 713, 746
Loon 248
Lost in the Arctic 807
Loti, Pierre 855
Lovers of Guðrún 850
Lowe, P. 602, 636
Lucas, F. L. 850
Lúðvíksson, Steinar J. 583
Lund, Mats Wibe 12, 273
Lung cancer 410
Lutheran church 50, 361, 364—367, 382
Lutheran doctrine of marriage in Icelandic society 382
Lúthersson, Pétur B. 895
Lygisögur 754
Lyon, F. H. 817

M

McClean, R. J. 626
McCormick, William T. 103
McCreesh, Bernadine 724
McCririck, M. 26
McCurdy, John Chang 41
McGill, Alexander 333
McGovern, P. D. 571
McGrew, Julia H. 309
McHaffie, I. 428
McKay, D. 326
McKeever, P. 473
Mackenzie, George Steuart 64, 70
McKinnell, J. 647
MacLennan, L. 426
Macnaghten, Angus 345
McNeice, Louis 64, 114
MacRae-Gibson, O. D. 741
McTurk, R. W. 827—828
McWilliams, J. P. 521
Made in Iceland 877
Madeley, J. 463
Maður og kona 806
Magazines (see Periodicals)

Magerøy, Hallvard 661
Magic 300
Magicians
 folklore 689, 757
Magnússon, Árni 321, 820
Magnússon, Árni, Arnamagnaean manuscripts 703
Magnússon, Eiríkur 332, 651, 658, 667—668, 680, 688, 694, 764—765
Magnússon, Guðmundur 552
 (see also Trausti, Jón)
Magnússon, Leifur 586
Magnússon, Magnús 7, 37—38, 41, 140, 267, 290, 655, 663, 671—672, 819, 821, 823—825, 866
Magnússon, Páll 47
Magnússon, Sigurður A. 28, 33, 255, 321, 464, 466—467, 478, 559—560, 784—785, 793, 795, 801, 805, 814, 834, 845, 891, 920
Magoun, F. P. 801
Malacca straits 483
Mallet, Paul Henri 283
Malmström, Vincent H. 162—163, 519
Manitoba
 Icelandic immigrants 54
Mannfjöldaskýrslur árin 1961-70 438
Manntál á Íslandi 392
Manpower (see Labour force)
Mansion House Relief Fund 332, 764
Manual of the birds of Iceland 236
Mánudagsblaðið 916
Manuscripts 321, 594—595, 703
Maps and atlases 144—148, 152—153, 161
 18th century 67
 19th century 70
 cave system 194
 geology 178
 history 154—155
 map list 956
 Reykjavík 440
 road maps 138—140, 142—143
 soil maps 520
 Þingvellir 442
 town plans 149—150
 Vinland map 156
 wall map 151
Marcus, G. J. 314
Marines 343
Marketing in Iceland 554

Markey, T. L. 596, 828
Marmier, Xavier 62
Marriage 382—386, 400, 417
  statistics 438
Marshall, F. H. A. 220
Marteinsdóttir, Steinunn 892
Martha's Vineyard 125
Martin-Clarke, D. E. 646
Martin, D. H. (see Holland-Martin)
Martin, John Stanley 355, 693
Martinière, Martin de la 62
Masonic lodges 376
Mass media (see Media)
Mattila, R. W. 321
Maxwell, Gavin 250
Maxwell, Ian 693
Mead Moondaughter and other Icelandic folktales 690
Mead, W. R. 159, 495
Meaning of Snorri's categories 652
Measles 413
Media 905—909
  (see also Newspapers)
Mediaeval Scandinavia 938
Medical districts 407
Medical geography 413
  (see Diseases)
Medical lore 371
Medicine (see Health, Doctors)
Medieval leper and his northern heirs 322
Mediums 379
Melsted, Bogi Þ. 296, 971
Members of Parliament (see Alþing)
Memories of travel 88
Men at Axlir 861
Mennell, G. 66
Mental health 404, 408, 417—419
Merrill, R. T. 380
Merton, T. E. 156
Metalworking 876—877, 895
Metcalfe, Frederick 64, 81
Meteorological investigations 213, 217, 219
Midnight Sun: Icelandic series 347
Migration
  statistics 438
Migration, external (see Emigration)
Migration, internal 164, 398, 417
Miles, Pliny 64, 77
Millennial celebrations 92—93
Millennial hymn 777
  (see also National anthem)
Miller, K. 209
Mills, D. 235

Mills, Stella M. 682
Milton, John 766
Mímir Language School 620
Mineralogy 70, 74
Ministry for Foreign Affairs 488, 948
Mink 805
Missionaries 71, 678
Mitchell, Bruce 485
Mitchell, John 3
Mitchell, P. M. 965, 967
Mitchison, Naomi 849
Mitchison, Rosalind 328
Mjöllnir 760
Móberg formation 179
Modern Iceland 25
Modern Icelandic: an essay 624
Modern Icelandic poetry 784
Modern Icelandic reader for foreign students 616
Modern Nordic plays: Iceland 805
Modern sagas: the story of the Icelanders in North America 52
Modern Scandinavian plays 803
Modern Scandinavian poetry: the panorama of poetry, 1900-1975 775
Möðrufell 272
Möller, D. 176
Möller, J. G. P. 67
Monsen, Erling 654
Monsters 759
Moon mission
  training programme 201
Morality
  sagas 725—726, 738
More than a drop in the ocean 173
Morgan, E. D. 101
Morgunblaðið 912
Morning of life 816
Morphology
  linguistic 594
Morris, James 87
Morris, May 87
Morris, William 1, 64, 87, 332, 658, 667—668, 671, 680, 762, 764, 850
Morrison, A. 238
Mortality 407, 409, 412, 414, 416, 438
Mosaics 888
Moss, Robert 252
Mosses 233
Motif index of early Icelandic literature 962
Motor racing 585
Motor vehicle registrations 437

329

Motz, Lottie 759
Mountaineering 590
Mountains 172
 (see also Glaciers)
Mourant, A. E. 261
Mrs President 467
Multiple sclerosis 411
Munro, D. A. 250
Muscroft, F. 342
Museum of Natural History 933
Museum of Natural History,
 Akureyri 934
Museums 949—950
Music 23, 896—899
 national anthem 32
Musical education 899
Musicians 389
Mussey, B. 816
Myntir Íslands, 1836, 1922-1963 567
Mýrdalsjökull 97, 107, 172
Myth and religion of the north: the religion of ancient Scandinavia 353
Mythology 292, 349—358, 641, 652, 691—692, 865
 (see also Edda)
 fertility myths 692, 705—706
Mývatn 89, 97, 101, 179, 182—183, 198, 224, 330, 543
 birdlife 240
 maps 147

N

N. Tryggvadóttir: serenity and power 888
Nagel's encyclopaedia guide: Iceland 133
Nairac, Rosemonde 267
Naive painting 883
Námaskarð 91
Names 279—280, 380, 593, 630, 634
Nansen, Fridtjof 56
Napier, Paul 816
Narrative of the voyage of the Argonauts in 1880 99
Nash, E. G. 856
National anthem 32
National Bank (see Landsbanki Íslands)
National bibliographies 955
National character 7—8, 10, 13, 21, 35, 39, 74, 93, 258, 402
National consciousness 478

National costume of women in Iceland 374
National dress (see Costume)
National Economic Institute 508
National income 497
National Library of Iceland 955
National Museum of Iceland 277, 374, 894, 949
National Museum of Iceland: summary guide to the exhibition rooms 949
National parks 147, 576—577
National parks of Iceland 576
National Register 392, 416
National Research Council (see Rannsóknarráðríkisins)
National socialists 334
National Theatre 900
National Tourist Board of Iceland 557
Nationalism 328—329, 472, 755, 771, 787—789
NATO (see also North Atlantic Treaty Organisation)
NATO Advanced Study Institute 175
Náttúrugripasafn Íslands (see Museum of Natural History)
Natural history 27, 69, 77, 83, 160, 162, 165, 218—257, 932—934
Natural history of Iceland 219
Natural parks 244
Natural resources 542—550
Naturalised Icelanders 12, 438
Nature Conservation Act 575
Nature protection 575—577
Navigation 128—129
Nawrath, Alfred 38
Naydler, Merton 124
Nazism 334
Neckel, G. 644
Nedelyaevna-Steponavichienie, Svetlana 828
Needlework 894
Nelson, G. R. 399
Neologisms
 modern Icelandic 631
Nerman, Birger 271
New bottles for new wine 221
Newcastle University (see University of Newcastle)
Newfoundland 57
News from Iceland 917
Newspapers 910—917
Newton, Alfred 83, 245
Nicknames 369
 modern Icelandic 634

Nicol, James 74
Nielsen, Hans B. (see Bekker-Nielsen)
Nielsen, Niels 177
Nigeria 531
Night and the dream 811
Nine Norse studies 758
Njáls saga 87, 94, 105, 443, 672,
 720—721, 726—727, 729,
 742—747
 for children 867
Njáls saga: a critical introduction 746
Njáls saga: a literary masterpiece 744
Njarðvík, Njörður P. 305, 702, 834
No depression in Iceland 344
Nobel Prize
 literature 827
Nonni (see Sveinsson, Jón Stefán)
Nordal, Jóhannes 31, 400
Nordal, Sigurður 335, 647, 652, 720, 732, 737, 961
Nordby, Conrad H. 762
Norðfjörður 570
Nordic co-operation 456, 468—469
Nordic Council 468—469
Nordic democracy.. 456
Nordic House 951
Nordic integration 470
Nordic languages and modern linguistics 628
Nordic security 470, 476
Nordic Statistical Secretariat 435
NORDSAT 909
Norðurfari: or, rambles in Iceland 77
Nørlund, Poul 315
Norræna húsið 951
Norris, F. T. 270
Norse (see Language, Old Icelandic)
Norse Atlantic saga: being the Norse voyages of discovery and settlement to Iceland, Greenland and America 58
Norse discoveries of America: the Wineland Sagas 58
Norse mythology; or, the religion of our forefathers, containing all the myths of the Eddas 349
Norse myths 641
Norse poems 645
Norse sagas translated into English: a bibliography 964
North American book of Icelandic verse 776

North Atlantic Treaty
 Organisation 474—478, 485
North Cape 123
North Dakota
 Icelandic immigrants 52
North Iceland Glacier Inventory: manual for field survey parties 214
North-west peninsula of Iceland: being the journal of a tour in Iceland in the spring and summer of 1862 82
Northern antiquities. 283
Northern garrisons 342
Northern lights 780
Northern sphinx: Iceland and the Icelanders from the settlement to the present 28
Northern world: the history and heritage of northern Europe 292
Northmen talk: a choice of tales from Iceland 640
Norway
 history 297, 654
Norwegian language
 dialects 592
Notes of a trip to Iceland in 1862 79
Novak, W. S. W. 544
Novels 794, 806—827, 829—834
 set in Iceland 846—849, 852—853, 855—862
Nuechterlein, Donald E. 472
Numismatics 567
Núpsstaður 97, 274
Nursing 421
Ný Félagsrit 329, 941
Nýársnóttin 800
Nye, J. F. 209

O

Ober, Kenneth H. 723, 965
Occupation
 Great Britain 337—338, 340—341, 344—345, 492
 United States 117, 337, 339—340, 343, 346—347, 472, 492
Ocean-crossing Wayfarer: to Iceland and Norway in an open boat 127
Ódáðahraun 198—199
Odes and echoes 779
Odhe, Thorsten 509
Odin 352, 356, 358

331

OECD (see Organisation for Economic Co-operation and Development)
Oertel, Wilhelm 852
Oesper, R. E. 76
Of gods and giants: Norse mythology 865
Off to the geysers: or, the young yachters in Iceland 91
Official gazette 450
Offshore geography of northwestern Europe: the political and economic problems of delimitation and control 157
Ögmundar þáttr 673
Olaf sagas 654
Olaf Thorlacksen: a story of Iceland 852
Ólaf Tryggvason 359, 669, 750
Ólafsson, Eggert 218
Ólafsson, Friðrik 579
Ólafsson, Jón, colonist 331
Ólafsson, Jón, scholar 632
Ólafsson, Jón, traveller 61
Ólafsson, Páll Eggert 946
Ólafsson, Pétur 341
Ólafsson, Ragnar 510
Ólafsson, Sigurjón 891
Ólafsson, Stefán 774
Old captivity 847
Old Icelandic: an introductory course 600
Old Icelandic land registers 320
Old Icelandic medical miscellany 371
Old Icelandic poetry: Eddic lay and Skaldic verse 704
Old Norse (see Language, Old Icelandic)
Old Norse literature and mythology: a symposium 692
Old Norse poems: the most important non-Skaldic verse not included in the Poetic Edda 648
Old Norse sagas 712
Oleson, Tryggvi J. 362
Ölkofra þáttr 670
Olmsted, Mary S. 461
Olszewska, E. S. 679
Ommanney, F. D. 123
On the age and immigration of Icelandic flora 226
On complementation in Icelandic 622
On foot in Iceland 1983 136
On the geology and geophysics of Iceland 179

On thermal activity in Iceland and geyser action 183
One-eyed moon maps 796
One hundred years of Icelandic stamps, 1873-1973 564
Onomastics (see Names, Placenames)
Önund Treefoot 667
Opinion polls 915
Or de l'Islande 37
Öræfajökull 82
Öræfi 244, 518
Oral tradition 697, 699, 715, 756
Oratory in the Kings' sagas 749
Orðasafn íslenzkt og enzkt 606
Order of the Icelandic Falcon, Knights 267, 287, 692−693
Orfield, L. B. 445
Organisation for Economic Co-operation and Development 433−434, 505, 511, 555
Origin and development of the Icelandic nation 298
Origin of the Icelanders 300
Origin of the Icelandic family sagas 715
Origines Islandicae.. 653
Origins of Icelandic literature 698
Ornithology 34, 38, 77, 82−83, 167, 220−221, 236−252, 589, 857
Ortelius 155
Orthography
  modern Icelandic 632
Örvar-Odds saga 685
Óskar, Jón 784, 798, 836
Óskarsson, Skúli 582
Ostenfeld, C. H. 228
Oswald, Elizabeth J. 95
Otito, Michael 54
Outlaw 666
'Outlaw', film 904
Outlawry 690, 728
  (see also Gísla saga, Grettis saga)
Oxford book of Scandinavian verse 774
Oxonian in Iceland 81

P

Pagan Scandinavia 352
Page, R. I. 354
Pageant of old Scandinavia 639

Painter, G. D. 156
Painting 122, 878—888
 birds 241
Pajkull, Carl W. 86
Palaeography 595
Palmeson, Jón G. 296
Pálsdottir, Katrín 925
Pálsson, Bjarni 218
Pálsson, E. 620
Pálsson, Gestur 777
Pálsson, Gísli 535—536
Pálsson, Halldór 512
Pálsson, Hermann 307, 655, 661, 663—665, 667, 670—672, 683—685, 738, 753, 961
Pálsson, Jens 263
Pálsson, Kjartan L. 584
Pálsson, Ólaf 104
Papin, W. J. 908
Paquebot marks of Norway, Denmark, Finland, Iceland and Sweden 566
Paradise reclaimed 824
Parapsychology 378—379
Parks, National 576—577
Parliament (see Alþing)
Parliamentary debates 450
Passion hymns 650, 786
Patronymics 279—280
Pattern of radio listening and television viewing in Iceland 905
Patterns in Old English and Old Icelandic literature 727
Payne, D. E. 907
Peake, C. A. 907
Peaks, passes and glaciers 82
Peasant art in Sweden, Lapland and Iceland 876
Peats 520
Pêcheur d'Islande 855
Peck, Helen 160
Peller, Sadie L. 802
Pen and pencil sketches of Faroe and Iceland 104
Pension funds 454, 506
People's Alliance 461, 914
Percy, Bishop Thomas 283
Perinatal mortality 409
Periodicals 910—919, 921—931
 humanities 920, 937—941
 science 932—936
Perkins, H. A. 590
Perkins, Mekkin S. 319, 375, 377, 387, 842—843
Perkins, R. 442

Personal names 279—280, 593, 630, 634
Perspective analysis of the Icelandic fishing industry: a status report and forecast to 1980 528
Petersen, F. E. B. (see Bredahl-Petersen)
Petre, E. O. G. (see Turville-Petre, E. O. Gabriel)
Petre, Joan T. (see Turville-Petre, Joan)
Pétursdóttir, Kristin H. 953
Pétursdóttir, María 421
Pétursson, Ásgeir 835
Pétursson, Esra 419
Pétursson, Hallgrímur 299, 322, 365, 638, 650, 773, 786
Pétursson, Hannes 783—784, 836
Pétursson, Pétur, footballer 583
Pétursson, Pétur, language teacher 619
Peyrère, Isaac de la 62
Pfeiffer, Ida 64, 75
Phalaropes 239
Phelps, Samuel 326
Phenylketonuria 260
Philately 562, 564—566
Phillips, Dick 7, 136, 957
Phillips, Mrs Una McGrigor (see Ratcliffe, Dorothy U)
Phillpotts, Bertha S. 61, 700, 705
Phonetics
 modern Icelandic 618
Phonology 594, 623
Photography
 birds 242
Phrasebooks
 modern Icelandic 612—613
Physical anthropology 258—263, 268
Physical geography (see Geomorphology)
Pierce, Benjamin M. 542
Pigeon banquet 805
Pigmentation 259, 263
Pilcher, Charles V. 650, 786
Pilgrimage to the saga steads of Iceland 106
Pillow lava 193
Pink-footed goose 249
Pinson, Ann 381, 406
Pioneers of freedom: an account of the Icelanders and the Icelandic free state, 874-1262 303
Piracy 220, 319
Place of Iceland in the history of European institutions 302

333

Placenames 153, 593, 630, 635
Plays (see Drama, Theatre)
Poems of today 783
Poems of the Vikings 643
Poetic Edda 643
Poetic Edda (see Edda, Poetic Edda)
  Bellows 643
  Hollander 643
Poetic Edda in the light of archaeology 271
Poetic Edda. Volume I: heroic poems 644
Poetry 92
  Eddic 271, 638−647, 652, 680, 692, 698−700, 702, 704, 706, 730
  Greenlandic 775
  Icelandic themes 863
  lays 648
  modern Icelandic 772−798
  religious 650−651, 772, 786
  skaldic 300, 639, 642, 649, 652, 692, 699, 704, 707−710, 733, 961, 963
Poetry, Old Icelandic (see Edda, Skaldic poetry, Lays, Religious Poetry, Rímur)
Polar bears 372
Police 452
Political geography 162
Political parties 456, 458−459, 479
Political power in Iceland prior to the period of class politics 457
Political science 432
Politics 22, 30, 457−467, 479
  (see also Foreign policy)
  20th century 11, 15
Pollenghi, A. de P. (see Pollitzer-Pollenghi)
Pollitzer-Pollenghi, Andrea de 590
Pollution 569
Polomé, E. C. 692
Ponies (see Horses)
Ponzi, F. 65
Pop art 887
Pope, Alexander 766
Pope, S. 376
Population 9, 161, 392−398, 401, 438
Population and vital statistics 438
Population censuses 392
Population movement 164
Portrait painting 882
Portrayal of women in the Icelandic family sagas 730
Ports (see Harbonrs)
Post-war poetry of Iceland 785
Postage stamps 562, 564−566, 917

Postal history 562−566
Postal service in Iceland, 1776 - 13th May 1951 563
Pottery 892, 895
Poultry farming 515
Powell, F. York 282, 301, 642, 653
Powell, George E. J. 597, 688
Power stations 203, 546, 548−549
Presidency 447, 465−467
Press (see Newspapers)
Press, Muriel 671
Pressure groups 479
Preusser, Hubertus 180
Prices 506
Prime ministers 464
Primer of modern Icelandic 614
Principall navigations 316
Printing presses 317, 969
Prisons 453
Pritchard, E. E. Evans (see Evans-Pritchard)
Private life of the old Northmen 368
Problem of being an Icelander: past, present and future 11
Problem of Loki 358
Problems of Icelandic saga origins 717
Professions 388−389, 400, 403, 421−422
Progressive Party 464−465, 510, 913
Pronouns of address
  modern Icelandic 633
Pronunciation
  modern Icelandic 615, 617−618
Propaganda 485
Prose Edda 652
Prose Edda (see Edda, Prose Edda)
Prose Edda of Snorri Sturluson: tales from Norse mythology 652
Proverbs 617
Psychiatric Register 416
Psychiatry 417−419
Psychic experiences 378−379
Ptarmigan 252
Public expenditure 497
Public Health (see Health)
Public libraries 952
Public opinion 479
Public opinion polls 915
Publishing statistics 955
Puffins 251
Pulvercroft, C. 66
Purkis, John 87
Pytheas 55

Q

Quantity in historical phonology: Iceland and related cases 623
Quantity in Icelandic 623
Quarterly economic review: Denmark, Iceland 504
Quest in the northland 116
Quick, quick said the bird 830
Quire of seven 838
Quirk, Randolph 668

R

Racial and geographical factors in tumour incidence 410
Radio 905
Radioactivity 183
Ragnarök 349, 355
Ragnarök: an investigation into Old Norse concepts of the fate of the gods 355
Ragnars saga loðbrókar 680, 751
Ragnarsson, Kjartan 902
Railway projects 558
Rally driving 585
Ramsden, D. M. 112
Ramsden, Evelyn 811, 813, 815
Rannsóknarráðríkisins 528
Rask, Rasmus K. 596, 767
Ratcliffe, Dorothy U. 118
Rauschenberg, R. A. 66
Raven seek thy brother 250
Ravens 372
Ray of sunshine 836
Reading habits 425, 910
Recipes 375, 917
Recollections of an Icelandic statesman: being a chapter in the autobiography of Sveinn Björnsson 335
Recreation 19, 578—590
Recreational areas 575—577
Red Cross 117, 953
Reed, Lawrence 480
Reeves, Arthur M. 58, 663, 806
Reforestation 521
Reformation 320, 362, 365—366
Regional geography of Iceland 162
Reich, Hans 875
Reich, J. R. 194
Reichart, K. 692
Reindeer 254

Relation and development of English and Icelandic outlaw traditions 728
Religion 23
Christian 359—367, 382
pre-Christian 267, 289, 304, 349—360, 368
Religion of ancient Scandinavia 350
Religion of the northmen 368
Religious instruction 366
Religious poetry 650—651, 772, 786
Report of the expedition to Iceland, 1973 167
Report on economic and commercial conditions in Iceland 494
Report on the resources of Iceland and Greenland 542
Research 431—432
Research and development 433
Research on the Iceland dog 257
Residential mobility, life cycle stages, housing and the changing social patterns in Reykjavík 573
Rettedal, Alan 47—48
Review of fisheries in OECD member countries 505
Review of ornithological studies in south-east Iceland, 1973-75 244
Reviews of national science policy: Iceland 433
Reykholt 108—109, 116
Reykir 183, 547
Reykjahlíð 543
Reykjanes 107
Reykjavík 149
Reykjavík 77
airport 341
art festivals 898
conservation 574
Family attitudes 385
geology 148
golf courses 584
heating systems 547—548
historical geography 163
history 44, 72
housing 500, 572—573
libraries 952
Living costs 437
maps 148, 440, 945
mental health 418
newspapers 910—916
perinatal mortality 409
planning 570—571
statistics 440
street names 635

335

Reykjavík contd.
 television viewing 906
 town plans 149
 travel guides 140
*Reykjavík: a panorama in four
 seasons* 44
Reykjavík: the capital of Iceland 44
Reykjavík City Council 571
Reykjavík Theatre Company 901
Reykjavík Theatre
 Company 800−801, 900, 902
*Reykjavík within your reach: the city
 past and present: a walking
 guide* 140
Reynarsson, Bjarni 573
Reynolds, J. H. 88
Rich, G. W. 381, 383
Richards, Peter 322
Richter-Gould, Ruth 752
Riddarasögur 686, 754
Riddles 708
*Ride across Iceland in the summer of
 1891* 103
Rímur 687, 704, 709−710, 896−897, 961
Ringerike style 272
Ringler, R. N. 791, 812
Ripples from Iceland 24
Rivers 224, 588−589
 (see also Individual names e.g. Laxá)
Rivers of Iceland 589
Road maps 138−140, 142−143
Road racing 585
Road to Hel 352
Road transport 561
Roberts, Brian B. 161, 205−206, 238
Robin Hood 728
Rochdale weavers 510
Rodwell, B. H. 165
Roesdahl, Else 292
Rollo (see Hrolf the Tramper)
Roman coins 264
Romance in Iceland 754
Romances 683−686, 695, 753−754
Romanticism 756, 770−772, 787−788
*Roots of nationalism: studies in
 northern Europe* 328
Rosenvinge (see Kolderup-Rosenvinge)
Rothery, A. M. 21
Rottray, W. H. W. (see Wolf-Rottray)
Roussell, A. 273
Royal Society for General Icelandic
 Instruction 767

*Ruins of the saga time: being an
 account of travels and
 explorations in Iceland in the
 summer of 1895* 270
Runes 284
Running blind 859
Rural life 19
Rural sociology 405−406
Russell, Waterman S. C. 109
Rutherford, Adam 298, 558
Rutten, M. G. 198

S

Saemund (see Edda, Poetic Edda)
Sæmundsdóttir, Sigurlaug 388
Sæmundsson, Bjarni 234
Sæmundsson, Kristján 202
Saga-book 939
Saga library 658
Saga mind 723
Saga of Asgard 865
Saga of Gísli 666
Saga of Grettir the Strong 667
*Saga of Hallfred the troublesome
 Scald* 669
Saga of the Heath-slayings (see
 Heiđarvíga saga)
Saga of Hrolf Kraki 682
Saga of the Jómvíkings 657
Saga of King Heiđrek the Wise 681
Saga of Tristram and Ísönd 686
Saga of the Volsungs 680
Saga translating 961
Sagas 638−640, 653−687, 695, 700, 711−715, 717−724, 727−728, 732−737, 739−742, 744−754, 762, 764
 (see also Individual titles)
 audiences 693
 bibliographies 964
 crime 743
 dating 718
 endings 722
 humour 716, 731
 morality 725−726, 738
 translations 692
 women 729−730
Sagas of ancient times 680−685, 728, 752−754
Sagas of Icelanders 443, 658−676, 697−699, 715−747
Sagasteads 81, 83, 87, 95, 106, 741
Sailing 124, 126−128

Sailing directions for the fjords, ports and anchorages of Iceland 128
St. Kilda 98
Sales tax 498
Salisbury, W. F. 320
Salka valka 817
Salmon 235
Salmon and trout in Iceland 235
Salmon fishing 34, 235, 588—589
Salmon in Iceland 235
Salvason, Gunnar 586
Samband Íslenzkra Samvinnufélaga 509—510, 927
Samivel 37
Samper, Baltasar (see Baltasar)
Samvinnan 927
Samvinnan 510
Sandar 179—180
Saskatchewan Icelanders: a strand of the Canadian fabric 53
Satellite transmission 550, 909
Satire 661, 799, 821
Saugstad, L. F. 260
Sawyer, P. H. 289
Saxo Grammaticus 282
Scaldic (see Skaldic)
Scaldic poetry 707
Scandinavia 159
Scandinavia in social science literature: an English language bibliography 958
Scandinavia past and present 30
Scandinavian churches: a picture of the development and life of the churches of Denmark, Finland, Iceland, Norway and Sweden 364
Scandinavian languages 591
Scandinavian legends and folk-tales 864
Scandinavian mythology 352
Scandinavian Review 922
Scandinavian studies 940
Scandinavian studies: essays presented to Dr. Henry Goddard Leach on the occasion of his 85th birthday 691
Scargill, M. H. 660
Schach, Paul 665, 686, 691—692, 704, 716, 744, 832
Scharm, Hrafnhildur 888
Schell, I. I. 216
Schenke, H. K. 801
Scheps, W. 747
Scherman, K. 27
Scheving, Gunnlaugur 878, 884

Schlauch, Margaret 660, 680, 729, 754
Schlenker, Hermann 242
School achievement (see Educational attainment)
Schools 426—427
Schram, Ellert B. 915
Schram, Magdalena 902
Schramm, Gunnar G. 569
Science in Iceland 933
Scientific policy 433
Scientific Society of Iceland (see Vísindafélag Íslendinga)
Scotice cable 909
Scott, C. F. 952
Scott, Douglas H. 130
Scott, Peter 249
Scott, Walter 283, 762, 846
Sculptor Ásmundur Sveinsson: an Edda in shapes and symbols 890
Sculpture 890—891
Seaway to Bagdad 805
Secret of culture: nine community studies 402
Security 470—477
Seðlabanki Íslands 506 (see Central Bank of Iceland)
Seismicity 175—176
Sel: Untersuchungen zur Geschichte des isländischen Sennwesens seit der Landnahmezeit 524
Selby, Alice 113
Selden, Margaret S. 897
Senkovskii, O. I. 723
Sephton, John 656
Sérkort af.. 147
Setberg 195
Settlement 307—308 (see also History, Commonwealth)
Settlement poems I & II 796
Seven days darkness 810
Seven Icelandic short stories 835
Severin, Tim 125
Severn Wildfowl Trust 249
Seyðisfjörður 109, 124, 570
Shakespeare, William 765
Sheep farming 256, 515, 525—526
Sheepdogs 257
Shepherd, C. W. 82
Shepstone, J. G. 613
Sherriffs, W. R. 233
Shetland cattle 253
Shielings 524
Shinn, Alida V. 874
Shipping registers 943

337

Ships in the sky, The night and the dream 811
Shirebrook School Icelandic expedition 171
Shivas, A. A. 410
Short stories 773, 778, 781, 835—845 (see þaettir)
Short stories of today 836
Shotputting 582
Shute, Nevil 847
Sigfússon, Hannes 784, 798
Sigmund, cartoonist 912
Sigtryggson, Hlynur 217
Sigurbjörnsson, Þorkell 896
Sigurðardóttir, Anna 388
Sigurðardóttir, Jakobína 834, 836
Sigurðardóttir, Valborg 428
Sigurðsson, Arngrímur 610
Sigurðsson, Birgir H. 574
Sigurðsson, Gísli 275, 572
Sigurðsson, Haraldur (see Haralds saga harðráða)
Sigurðsson, Haraldur 155, 195
Sigurðsson, Ingi 324
Sigurðsson, Ingimar Erlendur 834
Sigurðsson, Jón 771
Sigurðsson, Jón, economist 508
Sigurðsson, Jón, statesman 329
Sigurðsson, Ólafur Jóhann 794, 836
Sigurðsson, Páll 105
Sigurðsson, Sigurður 414
Sigurgeirsson, Gísli 48
Sigurgeirsson, Vigfús 16
Sigurjónsson, Jóhann 769, 799, 801
Sigurpálsson, Björn Vignir 903
Sigurvinsson, Ásgeir 583
Silts 520
Silver 877, 893, 895
Sim, George C. 102
Símaskrá 945
Simmons, M. 503
Simpson, Colin 121
Simpson, Jacqueline 286, 640, 654, 689, 760
Simpson, Myrtle 120
Sir Joseph Banks and Iceland 325
Siruður in Iceland 874
Six weeks in the saddle: a painter's journal in Iceland 94
Sixty-five Degrees 919
Sjálfstaeðisflokkur (see Independence Party)
Sjávarfréttir 928
Skaftafell 207, 244, 576—577
   maps 147

Skaftártunga 226
Skagafjörður 113, 406
Skaldic poetry 300, 639, 642, 649, 652, 692, 699, 733, 863, 961, 963
   kennings 707—708
   riddles 708
Skalds: a selection of their poems 649
Skáldskaparmál 652
Skálholt 105, 316, 361, 365, 678, 815, 969
Skálholtsstaður 361
Skeið 405
Skeiðará 518
Skeiðarárjökull 208
Skelton, R. A. 156
Skiing 34
Skilding stamps 564
Skírnir 767, 941
Skírnismál 705—706
Skraeling (see Eskimo)
Skua 244
Skúladóttir, Sigriður 421
Skúlason, Þorlákur 316
Skúlason, Þorvaldur 878, 884
Skutull 911
Skyr 375
Slang
   modern Icelandic 628
Slater, Anne S. 739
Slater, Henry H. 236
Slavery 312
Sletta
   modern Icelandic 628
Sletten, Vegard 469
Smallpox 412
Smith, F. K. T. 514
Smith, R. Angus 90
Smith, S. R. 603
Smoky bay: the story of a small boy in Iceland 872
Snæbjörn Jónsson bookshop 956
Snæbjörnsson, Stefán 895
Snædal, Gunnlaugur 409
Snæfellsjökull 590, 854
Snæfellsness 108, 195, 665, 825
Snioland: or, Iceland, its jokulls and fjalls 70
Snorri Sturluson 701
Snorri Sturluson 278, 299, 652, 654—655, 664, 701—702, 712, 732
   (see also Edda, Prose Edda)

338

Soccer (see Football)
Social anthropology 89, 258, 402, 535−536, 721, 959
Social change 392−395, 397−406
Social classes 304, 312, 403−404, 457, 459
Social Democratic Party 460, 474, 911
Social equality 389, 402−404
Social Scandinavia in the Viking age 368
Social security 408, 454, 498
Social structure 29, 400, 404
Social welfare 25, 399
Socialism 462
Socialism and literature 771
Society 22, 30
 20th century 11, 20
Society for the Advancement of Scandinavian Study 940
Sociology 431
Soil erosion 9, 177, 179, 181, 519, 521−523
Soil maps 520
Soils of Iceland 520
Sólarljóð 648, 650
Sólheimajökull 166
Some Icelandic recipes 375
Sømme, Axel 158
Sonatorrek 664, 693, 727
Song of the Sybil (see Völuspá)
Songs 370, 897
Sørensen, M. 828
Soviet Union
 foreign relations 473
 military flights 476
 naval strategy 477
 trade 532
Sowan, P. 932
Spanish flu 810
Sparring, A. 475
Spatial diffusion: an historical geography of epidemics in an island community 413
Speculum norroenum 693
Spelling
 modern Icelandic 632
Spells 761
Spiders 233
Spitsbergen 78, 120, 129
Spooner, Jane 549
Sport 19, 23, 47, 580−587, 926
 football 50, 583

Sportmen's and tourists' handbook to Iceland 130
Spread of printing: western hemisphere; Iceland 317
Sprengisandur 96, 101, 131
Sprigge, Elizabeth 816
Stained glass 888−889
Stallion of the north 255
Stamps (see Postage stamps)
Standard of living (see Living standards)
Stanley Gibbons stamp catalogue. Part II, Scandinavia 566
Stanley, John Thomas 65, 68
Statistical abstract of Iceland 436
Statistical Bulletin 437
Statistical Bureau of Iceland 392, 436−439
Statistics 392, 435−440, 507
Steblin-Kamensky, M. I. 723, 756
Stefánsson, Davíd 790, 799
Stefánsson, Eggert 882
Stefansson, Evelyn 51
Stefánsson, Halldór 836
Stefánsson, Jón 270
Stefánsson, Jón, historian 106, 295
Stefánsson, Jón, painter 878
Stefánsson, Jón, poet (see Gjallandi, Þorgils)
Stefánsson, Ólafur E. 512
Stefánsson, Stefán 132
Stefánsson, Þorsteinn 833
Stefansson, Vilhjalmur 20, 50, 55, 60, 372
Steffensen, Jón 259, 268, 369, 412
Steinarr, Steinn 784, 793, 798
Steindorsdóttir, Ragnheiður 859, 904
Steindórsson, Steindór 218, 225−226
Steindórsson, Steindór, frá Hlödum 138, 924
Steingrímsson, Hreinn 896
Steingrímsson, Jón 186
Steingrímsson, Páll 45
Stephansson, Stephan G. 773, 777, 779
Stephens, C. A. 91
Stephens, J. 693
Stephensen, Magnús 324, 766−767
Sterry, D. R. 556
Stevenson, I. 379
Stewart, R. N. 589
Stjórntídindi 450
Stockfish industry 277, 314
Stone, K. H. 164
Stöng 269, 273

339

Stories of the bishops of Iceland 678
Story of Burnt Njal 672
Story of the Volsungs and Niblungs, with certain songs from the elder Edda 680
Stott, M. 244
Strabo 55
Straumsvík 546
Street maps (see Town plans)
Street names 635
Strömbäck, Dag 359, 370
Structuralism 354
Studies for Einar Haugen 625
Studies in history and jurisprudence 441
Study on teachers, training, recruitment and utilisation of teachers 434
Stúfs saga 675
Sturla the historian 309
Sturla Þórðarson 307, 309, 748
Sturlubók 307
Sturlung Age 309−310, 650, 748, 800
Sturlunga saga 309
Sturlunga saga 299, 677, 699, 748, 758
Sturluson, Snorri (see Snorri Sturluson)
Stykkishólmur 89
Súðavík 168
Suðureyri 168
Suðurnes heating project 548
Sugar, J. A. 126
Suicides 416
Sulphur 89, 543
Sulphur in Iceland 543
Summer in Iceland 86
Summer saga: a journey in Iceland 119
Summer travelling in Iceland 101
Sundelius, Bengt 470
Superstition 377−378
Surrealist painting 886
Surtsey 38, 189−190, 223
  maps 147
Surtsey eruption in words and pictures 189
Surtsey: evolution of life on a volcanic island 223
Surtsey: the new island in the north Atlantic 189
Surtsey research progress reports 190
Surtsey Research Society 190
Surtshellir 104, 108, 194

Sutton, George Miksch 241
Sutton Hoo 760
Svalbard (see Spitzbergen)
Svarfaðardalur 515
Svartsengi 548−549
Sveinbjarnardóttir, Guðrún 517
Sveinbjörnsson, Sveinbjörn 32
Sveinbjörnsson, Tryggvi 803
Sveinsdóttir, Júliana 878
Sveinsson, Ásmundur 890
Sveinsson, Brynjólfur 316, 815
Sveinsson, Einar Ól. 268, 310, 718−719, 742, 744, 761
Sveinsson, Jón R. 500
Sveinsson, Jón Stefán 771, 807
Sverris saga 749
Sverrissaga, the saga of Sverrir of Norway 656
Sweden, Norway, Denmark and Iceland in the World War 493
Sweet, Henry 598
Swimming 587
Sword 832
Sword and crozier: a drama in five acts 800
Sworn brothers (see Fóstbræðra saga)
Sworn brothers: a tale of the early days in Iceland 809
Sylgjujökull 170
Symington, Andrew J. 104
Synopsis of the fishes of Iceland 234
Syntax
  modern Icelandic 622
Sýslur 320

T

Table mountains of northern Iceland 198
Tale of Icelanders 675
Tales from the Eastfirths. 674
Tapley, R. 810
Taxation 498
  history 89
Taylor, Arnold R. 599, 611, 676
Taylor, Bayard 64, 92
Taylor, Denis 7
Taylor, Paul B. 645
Taylor, R. 539
Teach yourself Icelandic 617
Teacher training 428, 434
Teaching hospitals 421
Telecommunications 909
Telephone directories 945

Television 478, 905−909
Television producers 389
Telexskrá 945
Tell I of Greenland: an edited translation of the Saudarkrokur manuscripts 848
Temple, R. 61
Temples 273, 304
Ten variations 805
Tephrochronology 187, 269
Territorial waters 157, 476, 479−485, 487−491
Terry, Patricia 643
Þættir 675
Theatre 900−902
 (see also Drama)
Theis, O. F. 816
They sent me to Iceland 117
Þiðranda þáttr 662
Þingeyrar 750
Þingeyri 168
Þingvallavatn 224
 birdlife 240, 248
Þingvellir 43, 77, 98−99, 268, 576−577
 maps 147, 442
Thingvellir: birthplace of a nation 43
Thiodolf the Icelander 846
Third World 470
Þjoðleikhusið (see National Theatre)
Þjóðminjasafn (see National Museum of Iceland)
Þjóðviljinn 914
Þjórsá 546
Þjórsárdalur 177, 179, 269, 273
Þjórsárver 249
Thomas, R. George 309, 732, 737, 748
Thompson, Bertha 841
Thompson, E. A. 261
Thompson, J. A. 818
Thompson, Laura M. 402
Thomsen, Grímur 777
Thór 352, 760, 866
Thorarensen, Bjarni 777, 787
Þórarinsson, Alma A. 416
Þórarinsson, Árni 12, 903−904
Þórarinsson, Karen 878
Þórarinsson, Sigurður 9, 36, 158, 179, 185−189, 200, 204, 207, 215, 268, 393, 577
Þórarinsson, Stefán 501
Þórarinsson, Sveinn 878
Þórarinsson, Þórarinn 361
Þorbjörnsson, Sigurbjörn 498
Þorbjörnsson, Sverrir 399

Þorðar saga hreða 101
Þórðarson, Agnar 799, 832
Þórðarson, Björn 15
Þórðarson, Jón (see Throddsen, Jón Þórðarson)
Þórðarson, Matthías 60, 448
Þórðarson, Sturla (see Sturla Þórðarson)
Þórðarson, Teitur 583
Þórðarson, Þórbergur 773, 831
Þoresteinsson, Steingrímur 765
Þorfinn Karlsefni 60
Þorgeir 360
Þorgils saga ok Hafliða 677
Þorgilsson, Ari (see Ari Þorgilsson)
Þorgríms saga 658
Þorgrímsson, Gestur 892
Þorkelsson, Þorkel 183
Thorlacius, Henrik 612
Þorláks saga biskups 678
Thorlakson, Edward J. 329
Þorláksson, Guðbrandur 154−155, 363
Þorláksson, Jón 766
Þorláksson, Þórarinn 878
Þorláksson, Þórður 154
Þórlindsson, Þórólfur 431
Þoroddsen, Gunnar 463
Thoroddsen, Jón 777
Thoroddsen, Jón Þórðarson 806
Þoroddsen, Magnús 451
Þoroddsen, Þorvaldur 178, 225
Thorpe, Benjamin 643
Þorsteinn frá Hamri 784, 834
Þorsteinn Mansionmight 683
Þorsteinn Staffstruck 658, 662, 670, 674
Þorsteinn the White 659, 674
Þorsteinsson, Björn 43, 139, 318
Þorsteinsson, Guðmundur 878
Þorsteinsson, Indriði G. 834, 836, 844, 903
Þorsteinsson, Leifur 44
Þorsteinsson, Sigurður 565, 893
Þorsteinsson, Steingrímur J. 756, 777, 828, 835
Þorsteinsson, Þorsteinn 31, 493
Þorvald the Farfarer 678
Þorvaldsdalur 169
Thousand geese 249
Thousand years struggle against ice and fire 9
Þráinsson, Höskuldur 622
Thraldom in ancient Iceland 312
Three acres and a mill 115

341

Three Icelandic sagas 660
Three northern love stories 658, 668
Three sketches of life in Iceland 853
Three visits to Iceland 105
Þriðji Víkingafundur 268
Þrymskviða 773
Thule 55, 89
Thurgood, M. 657
Tides 129
Tilman, H. W. 127
Tímarit iðnaðarmanna 930
Tímarit Máls og menningar 923
Timber 521
Timber housing 570
'Time and the water' 793, 798
Timetables 141
Tíminn 913
Tissot, L. 62
Tjörn 515
To Iceland in a yacht 90
Tölfræðihandbók 436
Tolkien, Christopher 681
Tolkien, J. R. R. 706
Tómasdóttir, Guðrún 805
Tomasson, Richard F. 29, 64, 279, 384, 395, 425
Toorn, M. C. van den 725
Tort liability 454
Tour to Iceland in the summer of 1861 82
Tourism 503, 555—557, 917
  statistics 437
Tourism policy and international tourism in OECD member countries 555
Tourist Association of Iceland (see Ferðafélag Íslands)
Tourist Association of Reykjavík 555
Tourist guides (see Travel guides)
Tours
  horseback 103, 109—111
Town planning 23, 570—571, 574
Town Planning Act
  1931 570
  1964 571
Town plans 138, 140, 149, 440
Townsend, J. A. B. 961
Tracing of Iceland and the Faroe Islands 79
Trade
  directories 942—944
  EEC 551
  Great Britain 554
  overseas 313—314, 318, 504, 552—553, 931

statistics 437, 439
United States 532, 554
USSR 532
Trades unions 460, 479
Tradition and innovation in twentieth century Icelandic poetry 797
Tramping through Iceland 112
Transformational grammar
  modern Icelandic 622
Transhumance and ecology: a study of changing patterns of economic activity and continuities in social organisation in a rural Icelandic township 406
Translation of culture: essays to E. E. Evans-Pritchard 721
Translations from the Icelandic 638
Translators 554
Transport 158, 401, 561
  statistics 435
Transport history 558—560, 562
Transport in Iceland 558
Trausti, Jón 835, 841
Travel agencies 557
Travel guides 128—141
Travellers' accounts 61—62
  18th century 64—68, 218
  19th century 63—64, 69—107, 270
  20th century 108—123
Travels by 'Umbra' 84
Travels in Iceland 218
Travels in the island of Iceland during the summer of the year MDCCCX 70
Trawler safety: interim report of the Committee of Inquiry into trawler safety 537
Trawlermen 123
Trawlers 490, 530, 533
  safety 527, 537—538
  skippers 535—536
Treaty of co-operation between Denmark, Finland, Iceland, Norway and Sweden 468
Treece, Henry 867
Trial, George T. 423
Tristram's ballad 773
Tristrams saga 686, 691—692
Troil, Uno von 64, 67
Tröllaskagi 172, 214
Trollope, Anthony 64, 98
Trolls 688, 690
Trout 235, 589
Tryggvadóttir, Erla 619
Tryggvadóttir, Guðrún 388

342

Tryggvadóttir, Nína 878, 888
Tryggvason, Björn 341
Tryggvason, Eysteinn 202
Tryggvason, Ólaf (see Ólaf Tryggvason)
Tuberculosis 414
Tuberculosis in Iceland: epidemiological studies 414
Tucker, D. G. 276−277
Tungnaá 177
Turf farms 274−275, 570
Turner, V. W. 721
Turville-Petre, E. O. Gabriel 284, 353, 672−673, 679, 681, 692−693, 697−698, 707, 758, 961
Turville-Petre, J. 278
Tuxen, S. L. 232
Tweedie, Mrs A. (see Harley Ethel B)
Twelve women 845
Twentieth century Scandinavian poetry 775
Twickenham Travel 135
Two ravens 849
Two treatises on Iceland from the 17th century 316

U

Ultima Thule 55, 89
Ultima Thule: further mysteries of the Arctic 55
Ultima Thule: or, a summer in Iceland 89
Umbra (see Clifford, C. C)
Under the cloak: the acceptance of Christianity in Iceland, with particular reference to the religious attitudes prevailing at the time 360
United States
  foreign relations 472−473
  Icelandic immigrants 52, 921
United States Marines in Iceland, 1941-1942 343
United States occupation of Iceland, 1941-1946 339
University College of Wales 169
University of Iceland (see Háskóli Íslands)
University of Leeds Library 971
University of Newcastle upon Tyne 167
Unwin, Stanley 3

Uppruni Íslendinga 300
Urban history 44
  19th century 72
Urbanisation 400
Úrval 916
US Board on Geographic Names 153
US Department of Commerce 554
US occupation 117, 337, 339−340, 343, 346−347, 472, 492
US television station 478, 906−908
US trade 532
USSR (see Soviet Union)

V

Valfells, Sigrid 600
Valley of Thorvaldsdalur: report of the 1977 U.C.W. expedition 169
Valtýsson, Helgi 254
van den Toorn (see Toorn, M. C. van den)
van Gruisen (see Gruisen)
van Woerkom (see Woerkom)
Vanir 352
Vápnfirðinga saga (see Vopnfirðinga saga)
Vatnajökull 9, 93, 97, 170, 204−209, 211, 518, 590
Vatnsdæla saga 659
Vatnsdalur 109
Väyrynen, R. 483
Veblen, Thorsten 671
Vegakort Ísland 142
Vegetation (see Flora)
  maps 146
Vehicle registrations 437
Veiðivötn 577
Verðandi 777
Verne, Jules 854
Verzlunarskýrslur 439
Vesey, Ernest (see Lewis, E)
Vestfirðir 166, 168, 540
Vestfirðir studies: Farming, fishing and settlement in Iceland 168
Vestmannaeyjar 45
Vestmannaeyjar
  birdlife 220, 251
  description 45−46, 102
  energy 47
  fisheries 47
  folklore 220
  heating systems 548
  history 319
  maps 147

343

Vestmannaeyjar *contd.*
 newspapers 913
 sport 47
 television viewing 906
 volcanic eruptions 191−192
 volcanic eruptions: literary
  settings 862−863
 water supply 545
Vidalín, Jón 365, 786
Viðey 22, 317, 969
Viðskiptaskráin 942
Viðskipti og Þjónusta 943
Viewdials 138
Víga-Glúms saga 673
Vigfússon, Guðbrandur 309, 332, 597, 605, 642, 653, 688, 694, 763
Vigil in Iceland: a fragment of autobiography, 1940-1942 345
Víglundar saga 658
Vigur 276
Vík 18
Vikan 916
Viking achievement: the society and culture of early mediaeval Scandinavia 288
Viking archaeology 266−268
Viking archaeology in Iceland 269
Viking art 288
Viking Century in East Yorkshire 751
Viking Circle 121
Viking Congress, Fourth 269
Viking Congress, Second 272, 370
Viking Congress, Third 268
Viking expansion westwards 267
Viking: hammer of the north 290
Viking history 268, 283−292, 368, 593
Viking legacy: the Scandinavian influence on the English and Gaelic languages 593
Viking settlers in Greenland and their descendants during five hundred years 315
Viking Society for Northern Research 270−271, 939
Viking world 286
Víkingavatn 167
Vikings 266, 291
Vikings
 Arbman 266
 Brøndsted 266
 Graham-Campbell 291
 Magnússon 267

Vikings and their origins: Scandinavia in the first millenium 288
Vikivaki 370
Vilhjálmsson, Þór 830, 839, 888
Vinland 57−58, 60, 125, 270, 692
Vinland the good 867
Vinland map 156
Vinland map and the Tartar relation 156
Vinland sagas
 Hermannsson 663
Vinland sagas: the Norse discovery of America 663
Vinland voyage 125
Vinland voyages 60
Vinnumarkaðurinn 1980 507
Virgin of Skálholt 815
Vísindafélag Íslendinga 183, 187, 933
Vísir 915
Visit to Iceland and the Scandinavian north 75
Visit to Iceland, by way of Tronyem in the 'Flower of Yarrow' yacht in the summer of 1834 72
Vital statistics 392, 438
Vogar 330
Volcanic geology, hotsprings and geysers of Iceland 182
Volcano: ordeal by fire in Iceland's Westmann Islands 191
Volcanoes 69, 76, 80, 89, 93, 97, 107, 177, 179, 182, 185−193, 195, 197−203, 209, 223, 323, 396, 590, 869
 (see also under specific names e.g. Hekla)
Volcanoes and glaciers: the challenge of Iceland 869
Völsunga saga 680
Völuspá 647
Völuspá 75, 647, 692
von Bemmelen (see Bemmelen)
von Linden (see Linden)
von Troil (see Troil)
Vopnafirðinga saga 674
Vopnafjörður 811
Vopnfirðinga saga 659, 662
Vör, Jón (see Jón úr Vör)
Voters
 middle class 459
 women 459
Voting age 447
Vowels 594
Voyage en Islande 62
Voyages des pays septentrionaux 62

Voyages of the Norsemen to America 59
Voyages to Vinland 663
Vries, Jan de 358

W

Waag, Árni 240
Waders 239
Wages 455, 506−507
Wahlgren, E. 692
'Waking of Angantýr,' 681
Walford N. 57
Walker, G. P. L. 196
Waller, S. E. 94
Walters, Thorstina 52, 60, 387
Warming, J. E. B. 225
Water heating 547−548
Water supply 545
Waterfalls 5
  (see also under specific names e.g. Dettifoss)
Watermills 276
Watkins, Ernest 344
Watson, A. 252
Watson, Mark 257
Watson, Marshall 253
Watts, William L. 97
Wawn, A. 68
We murderers 802
Weather (see Climate)
Weaving 877, 894
Weber, G. W. 693
Wegener, Alfred 177
Wells, J. G. 906
Wergild ring 442
West, J. F. 68
Western fjords (see Vestfirðir)
Westmann Islands (see Vestmannaeyjar)
Westward to Vinland 57
Whaling 527, 541
Wheeler, P. T. 168
When I was a girl in Iceland 18
Where the sun shines at midnight 132
Whipple, F. 173
White, B. 63
White falcon 347
Whitehead, Thor 337
Whittaker, J. 348
Who were the fascists? Social roots of European fascism 334
Who's who in Scandinavia 947
Widding, Ole 321

Wild horses of Iceland 856
Wildsmith, Brian 865
Wilhelmsson, Hans Ahlmann 207
Willey, C. K. 546
William Morris: stories in prose, stories in verse, shorter poems... 1
Williams, Alan Moray 51
Williams, Carl O. 312
Williams, Mary W. 368
Williamson, Geoffrey 871
Wilson, David M. 288, 292
Wilson-Kastner, Patricia 366
Windmills 276
Wings over Iceland 242
Winnipeg
  Icelandic immigrants 54
Winter in Iceland and Lapland 73
Wish 799
Witchcraft 690
Within the Circle: portrait of the Arctic 51
Woerkom, Dorothy O van 868
Wolf-Rottray, W. H. 630
Wolley, John 245
Wolseley, Pat 229
Women
  employment 388−389
  saga literature 386, 729−730
Women's costume 374
Women's magazines 925
Women's rights 300, 386−389, 925
Wood, C. 515
Wood, Cecil 812
Wood, F. T. 789
Woodcarving 876−877
  Ringerike style 272
Woodman, M. J. 522
Woods, D. G. 899
Wool 314, 525−526
  designs 895
Woolcombs 894
Works of Morris and Yeats in relation to early saga literature 762
World light 819
World War I 493
World War II 117, 335−347, 472, 492
Worster, W. W. 769, 808
Wrestling 580−581
Wright, James 68

345

Y

Yates, Elizabeth 116
Yearbook of Nordic statistics 435
Yeates, G. K. 248
Yeats, W. B. 762
Yeh, Shang-Lan Sophia 730
Yggdrasill 694
Yolklife 805
Yorkshire
  sagas 733, 751
Yorkshire Regiment 342
Young, Elizabeth 480
Young explorers 172
Young Explorers' Trust 214, 932

Young, Jean I. 652, 799
Young traveller in the far north 871
Youth 390
Youth hosteller's guide to Denmark and Iceland 137
Youth hostels 136—137

Z

Zimmerman, J. L. 340
Zoëga, Geir T. 85, 607
Zoology 206, 217—220, 231—257
Zoology of Iceland 231

Map of Iceland

The map refers to many of the places (both natural features and settlements) mentioned in the bibliography, plus several other locations of significance. Iceland has many rivers — for reasons of space only three of the most important are included, although most of the main fjords

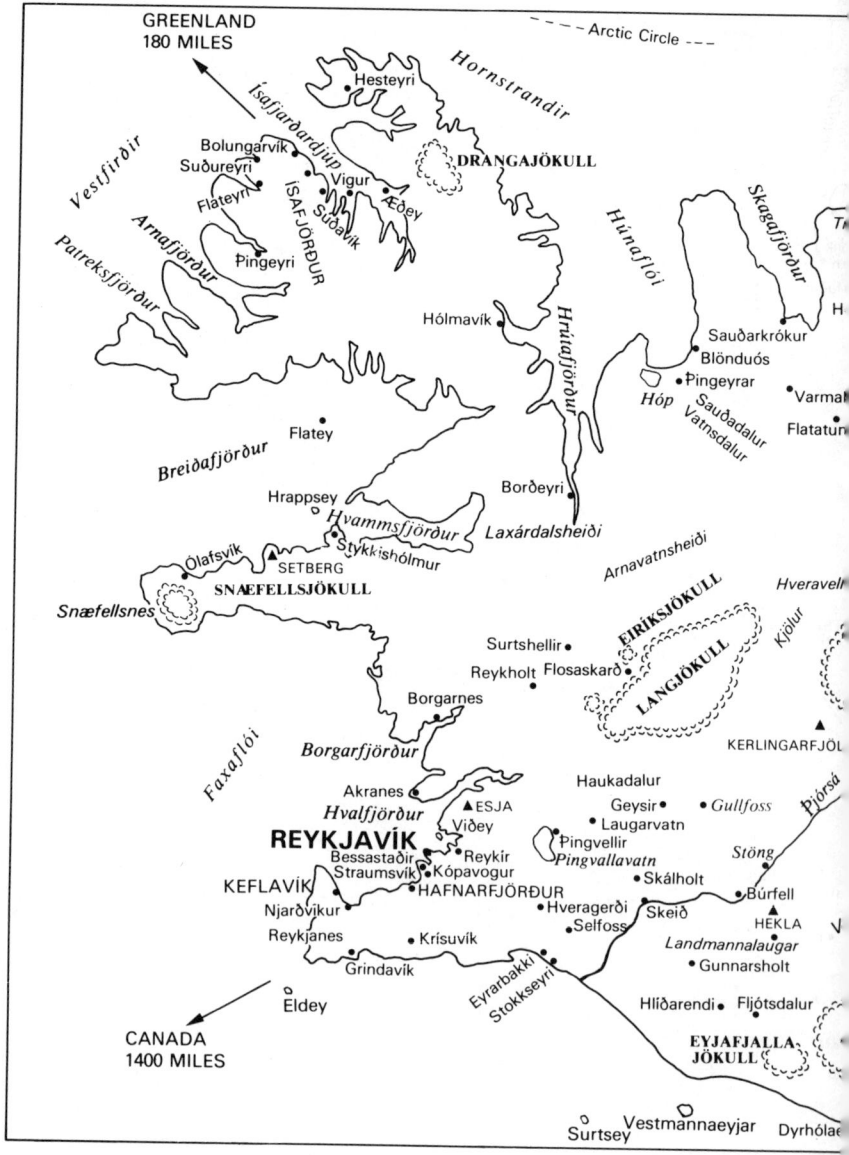

are shown. Roads are not shown, but in recent years it has become possible to travel by road right round the circumference of the country. The traveller should be cautious in identification of certain place-names which are often repeated in different parts of Iceland.

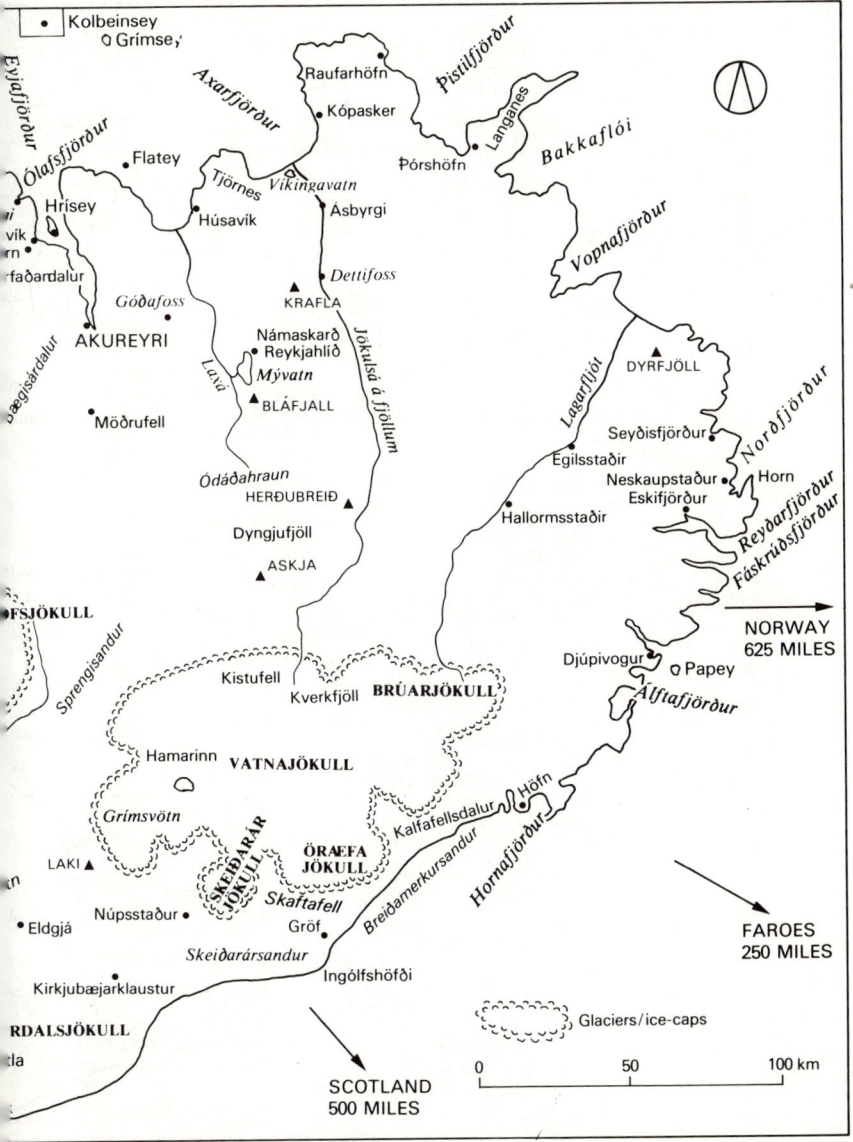